DESIGN AND TECHNOLOGY IN YOUR SCHOOL

This book addresses the practicalities of establishing design & technology as a worthwhile subject in the secondary school. Written by two leading experts in the field, it explores the way in which design & technology may be taught so that it makes a unique contribution to the learning of young people. It provides design & technology departments with practical information and guidance around key issues such as planning and assessing the subject, justifications for teaching it, as well as ways in which schools can manage and sustain teaching design & technology long term.

In dealing with the breadth and depth of design & technology this book:

- Provides rationales for design & technology which go far beyond the usual limited economic utility argument.
- Considers the underpinning philosophies of technology and design and the essential place of values, clarifying the substantive and disciplinary knowledge.
- Discusses five important issues: decolonising the subject, gender, disruption, global warming, pollution and waste.
- Describes how a design & technology curriculum may be planned, taking into account content, resources, and learning activities to achieve breadth, balance, and progression.
- Defines how the subject may be taught through a range of complimentary methods.
- Considers a wide range of assessment practices that meet the varied learning embedded within the subject.
- Discusses how support for the subject can be achieved by collaboration with a wide range of interested parties.

This book is a valuable resource for heads of departments, trainee and practicing teachers, those engaged in further professional development, and all who want to make the learning of design & technology an interesting, motivating, and exciting experience for young people.

HildaRuth Beaumont (formerly David Barlex) is an acknowledged leader in design & technology education, curriculum design, and developing curriculum materials. A former schoolteacher, Senior Lecturer in Education at Brunel University, and now an Honorary

Senior Research Associate at the Institute of Education, UCL, Hilda's curriculum development activities stem from her conviction that classroom practice should be informed by academic research.

Torben Steeg has been variously (and in some cases remains) a secondary school teacher, curriculum developer, teacher trainer, local authority curriculum leader, provider of CPD to schools and teachers, maker, and education researcher.

DESIGN AND TECHNOLOGY IN YOUR SCHOOL

Principles for Curriculum, Pedagogy and Assessment

HildaRuth Beaumont with Torben Steeg

Routledge
Taylor & Francis Group

LONDON AND NEW YORK

Designed cover image: © Getty Images

First published 2024
by Routledge
4 Park Square, Milton Park, Abingdon, Oxon OX14 4RN

and by Routledge
605 Third Avenue, New York, NY 10158

Routledge is an imprint of the Taylor & Francis Group, an informa business

British Library Cataloguing-in-Publication Data
A catalogue record for this book is available from the British Library

Library of Congress Cataloging-in-Publication Data
Names: Beaumont, HildaRuth, author. | Steeg, Torben, author.
Title: Design and technology in your school : principles for curriculum, pedagogy and assessment / HildaRuth Beaumont with Torben Steeg.
Description: Abingdon, Oxon ; New York, NY : Routledge, 2024. | Includes bibliographical references.
Identifiers: LCCN 2023037763 (print) | LCCN 2023037764 (ebook) |
ISBN 9780367441586 (hardback) | ISBN 9780367441593 (paperback) |
ISBN 9781003008026 (ebook)
Subjects: LCSH: Design--Study and teaching (Secondary) | Technology--Study and teaching (Secondary)
Classification: LCC NK1170 .B43 2024 (print) | LCC NK1170 (ebook) | DDC 744--dc23/eng/20231206
LC record available at https://lccn.loc.gov/2023037763
LC ebook record available at https://lccn.loc.gov/2023037764

ISBN: 978-0-367-44158-6 (hbk)
ISBN: 978-0-367-44159-3 (pbk)
ISBN: 978-1-003-00802-6 (ebk)

DOI: 10.4324/9781003008026

Typeset in Interstate
by MPS Limited, Dehradun

CONTENTS

ABOUT THE AUTHORS

Dr HildaRuth Beaumont

HildaRuth has worked in education for some 50 years and for most of that time was known as David Barlex, becoming an acknowledged leader in design & technology education, curriculum design, and curriculum materials development. A former schoolteacher, head of faculty, and Senior Lecturer in Education at Brunel University, HildaRuth draws her professional activities from her conviction that there should be a dynamic relationship between curriculum development and academic research. She continues to carry out research and academic writing and is working with schools on curriculum development. She is currently an Honorary Senior Research Associate in the Department of Curriculum, Pedagogy & Assessment at the Institute of Education, University College, London.

Torben Steeg

Torben is an Educational Consultant with a background in secondary teaching of design & technology, science, and computing. He works in teacher education, CPD, and curriculum development, and is particularly interested in new technologies and the Maker Movement. He is a Fellow of the Royal Society of Arts (FRSA), a consultant member of the D&T Association, a member of the editorial board for the D&T Association's *Design and Technology Education: An International Journal,* and an owner and editor of the online journal *ECT Education.* He is the course lead for the D&T PGCE at Manchester Metropolitan University and a visiting lecturer on the ITE programme at Birmingham City University. Current projects include working with a UK/US collaborative developing educational hardware, software, and courseware focussed on developing systems thinking with young children; and working with a company in India to develop practical resources to support secondary Engineering and Technology education.

FOREWORD

Every so often you come across a piece of work which leaves you in awe of its scope, its fresh insights, and its deep humanity. It is no exaggeration to say that *Design and Technology in Your School* had this impact on my thinking. It is truly impressive in its scope, in its attention to detail, and in its call to arms for a truly thoughtful, intentional, and ambitious design & technology curriculum for every pupil.

Jerome Bruner argued that 'if a curriculum cannot change, move, perturb, inform teachers, it will have no effect on those whom they teach. It must be first and foremost a curriculum for teachers'. And it strikes me that this brilliant book by HildaRuth Beaumont and Torben Steeg provides exactly the kind of intellectual nourishment for Bruner's ambition to be realised.

Design and Technology in Your School makes a significant contribution to the curriculum canon in general and to design & technology in particular. In its scope, structure, and depth of the subject's philosophy, purpose, and connection to other disciplines, it sets a high bar for other subjects. This is a truly impressive synthesis of design & technology's aims, structures, controversies, and contribution to the human development of individuals and to society. For those involved in planning and teaching design & technology in schools, it is an absolute gift.

This book is ambitious in its scope and intellectually satisfying in the detail, and stands as a model of how to interrogate the purpose and justify the inclusion of any subject within a school's curriculum. Furthermore, it is grounded in the tough practicalities of planning the subject, delivering it to pupils and students, and capturing the myriad ways in which it might be assessed.

The scope of design & technology ranges across how technology works to technology capability. Folded within these dual perspectives are a range of complex, beautiful ways of interacting with and shaping the constructs with which we navigate and enjoy and sometimes spoil our environments. What Beaumont and Steeg have managed to do is provide us with one of the most elegant, enjoyable, and truly thought-provoking insights into the beauty, the potential, and the dilemmas within the subject. It is structured in such a way that the reader is invited to become involved in the conversation.

The structure for each chapter takes the reader on an intellectually satisfying journey of insights, provocations, and a 'pause for thought' with a stimulus for conversations with professionals and students: an invitation to enter into a scholarly conversation about the significance of the subject. These are balanced with scenarios and examples from the classroom. And then thought pieces within most chapters, standing in conversation with the substance of the main text. An ingenious way of both including a range of thought leaders in the field and of holding a space for respectful alternative views.

Design and Technology in Your School manages to be both a panegyric, appreciated by a general audience on the one hand, and a practical guide for a specialist audience on the other. So, who needs to read this? I hope I've made the case that it's for anyone with an interest in the curriculum in general, and for those concerned with the design and delivery of the Design & Technology curriculum in particular.

Mary Myatt
24 July 2023

Mary Myatt is an education adviser, writer, and speaker. She trained as an RE teacher and is a former local authority adviser and inspector. She engages with pupils, teachers, and leaders about learning, leadership, and the curriculum.

Mary has written extensively about leadership, school improvement and the curriculum. Her current work focuses on the Huh Curriculum series for primary, secondary, and SEND alongside the Huh Academy with John Tomsett. She has established Myatt & Co, an online platform with films for ongoing professional development, including the popular Primary Subject Networks and Secondary Subject Networks.

Mary is a patron of CAPE, and is a member of the Cultural Education Plan Expert Advisory Panel. She has been a governor in three schools, and a trustee for a Multi Academy Trust. She maintains that there are no quick fixes, and that great outcomes for pupils are not achieved through tick boxes.

PREFACE

Hilda and Torben have been working together in design & technology education, on and off, for over 25 years. Both took science degrees, Hilda in chemistry and Torben in physics and computer science before qualifying to teach in secondary schools via the PGCE route. Both taught science and design & technology related subjects in secondary schools for over 15 years before becoming involved in curriculum development and teacher education. Given our similar backgrounds and interests, it is not surprising that we have collaborated on a number of initiatives, notably the Nuffield Design & Technology Project and more recently in developing the idea of technological perspective as a necessary complement to technological capability within design & technology education. Most recently we have been involved in developing our joint website on which we blog about all matters concerned with design & technology education and publish working papers on topics we consider of particular relevance to design & technology education.

Hence it was almost inevitable that we should collaborate in writing a book for design & technology teachers which distilled our expertise and experience into what we see as a definitive statement about teaching, learning, and assessing design & technology. We are under no illusions as to the difficulties that have been faced, and continue to be faced, by design & technology in maintaining and extending its place in the secondary school curriculum. However, we are convinced that when taught well it provides essential learning not available through any other school subject. We must make it plain from the outset that we have not considered the place of food as part of design & technology within this book. Hilda has written separately about the teaching and learning food technology in *Food Futures in Education and Society* published by Springer in 2023. Working together we have been able to critically support each other drawing to a large extent on previous collaborations. Hilda has undertaken the lion's share of developing the final manuscript but throughout has been supported by conversations with and critique from Torben. We hope that all those taking part in design & technology education, whether as teachers, teacher educators or researchers as well as other with an interest, will find our writing timely and useful.

HildaRuth Beaumont
Torben Steeg
June 2023

ACKNOWLEDGEMENTS

We relied on several members of the design & technology community of practice to comment on our writing as we developed the book. They responded with generosity and insight and the result is significantly better because of their comments. Hence, we are grateful to the following critical friends:

Nick Givens: Senior Lecturer, College of Social Sciences and International Studies University of Exeter (retired) Associate at University of Exeter

Jonas Hallström: Professor of Technology Education, Technology and Science Education Research Linköping University

Mary Myatt: Education adviser, writer, and speaker

Dr Mike Martin: School of Education, Liverpool John Moores University

Kay Stables: Professor of Design Education Goldsmiths, University of London

We have deliberately written a short book and are conscious that this is a mixed blessing. On the one hand, the shortness required us to write in a disciplined and focussed way, making key ideas easier to access, but on the other hand there is the possibility that we had not given sufficient consideration to some of the key ideas. To mitigate this, we asked other authors, who are experts in particular aspects of design & technology education, to write Thought Pieces in which they make further comment on a key idea. In this way we hoped that the expertise of the wider design & technology education community would inform the book. We were not disappointed. The following gave unstintingly of their time, experience, and thoughtfulness in contributing Thought Pieces that make significant additions.

Louise Attwood: Head of Curriculum, Design & Technology for the Awarding Organisation AQA

Ed Charlwood: National Lead Practitioner for design & technology at the Oasis Learning Trust, Co-founder of Badgeable.org

Dr Alison Hardy: Associate Professor, writer, researcher, and podcaster at Nottingham Trent University

Philip Holton: Senior Strategy Manager for Pearson UK Schools

Dr Dawne Irving Bell: Professor of Learning and Teaching, BPP University

Richard Kimbell: Emeritus Professor, Goldsmiths University of London

Dr Paul Mburu: Head of Design & Technology Department, Harlington School
Dr Matt McLain: School of Education, Liverpool John Moores University
Andy Mitchell: Ex Deputy CEO, The Design and Technology Association
Dominic Nolan: Corporate Social Responsibility Leader, Kyndryl UK & Ireland
James Pitt: Honorary Professor of Education, Amur State University of Humanities and Pedagogy, Russia
Ulrika Sultan: Educator and researcher, Örebro University
Dr Malcolm Welch: Professor Emeritus, Queen's University, Kingston, Ontario

We are particularly grateful to Annamarie Kino at Routledge for her invaluable comments on our writing and to Molly Selby and Lauren Redhead and their colleagues for the unfailing support through the production process.

1 Justifying design & technology

This chapter consists of four parts:

- Design & technology's role in the curriculum
- Four possible justifications
- Revisiting the role of design & technology in the curriculum
- The educational intentions of our subject in a nutshell.

Throughout there are "Pause for thought" blocks and a Thought Piece from Alison Hardy to help reflection. Finally, there are References and Recommended reading. Some comments about design & technology from a parents' evening are shown in Panel 1 on page 2.

Design & technology's role in the curriculum

Any subject taught at school must justify its place in the curriculum from a variety of perspectives. Should it be taught because it will be useful in helping learners find employment on leaving school and enable them to contribute to the economy? Should it be taught because it provides learners with knowledge and skills useful in everyday life? Should it be taught because it will help the learner become an active citizen able to develop well thought out views on the decisions needed for a just and fair society? Or should it be taught because it is part of a cultural inheritance that should be available to all learners? It is likely that any subject can be justified by a mix of these reasons with the significance of the reasons within the mix varying according to the age and aspirations of the learner. Hence, we think that it is important for design & technology not to rely on a single justification but to maintain a broad appeal through co-existing diverse justifications. In the following sections, we deal with four different justifications for design & technology as a subject to be taught in school: economic, personal, social, and cultural; but with the health warning that all are important, and none should be ignored.

> Pause for thought
>
> *All subjects should have a justified place in the curriculum, and other subjects will also appeal to economic, personal, social, and cultural purposes.*

DOI: 10.4324/9781003008026-1

> As you read the following sections, describing possible justifications for design & technology, think about what it is that makes the subject unique in the curriculum. That is, in what ways would a young person's education be impoverished if they didn't experience design & technology as a subject? We will reflect on this question in the following sections. For now, think about the implications if we can't provide an answer to this question with clarity.

Panel 1 Comments and thoughts at a parents' evening

What they said	What I thought
And then the deputy said to the parents Of course, D&T is really useful for being able to do DIY, putting up shelves and the like.	
And then the Head of Careers said, Of course, if you want to be a plumber or an electrician then D&T is great for teaching you relevant practical skills.	Well, that's bound to appeal to all those kids doing triple science!
And then the Head said to the parents The thing I find about D&T is that it's not just practical, which of course it is, but it's so interesting and really makes your children think especially about the sort of world they want to live in.	Blimey, she actually gets it!

Four possible justifications

Preparation for work

This is an economic argument and starts from the position that a steady supply of people who have studied design & technology is essential to maintain and develop the kind of society we value and that teaching the subject is central to the innovation on which our future economic success as a nation depends. For those young people who achieve a design & technology qualification at school, the experience may well predispose some of them to consider a design-based or technical career.

However, this economic argument is difficult to justify as a rationale for teaching design & technology to all young people, as the total of professional engineers, technologists, and designers is only a few per cent of the whole population of an industrialised country. Employers might argue, however, that unless a high percentage of the school population is exposed to design & technology, then not all of those who might be inclined to take up careers in this area will be reached. Nevertheless, the foremost goal of a general design & technology education cannot be to train the minority who will actually "do" designing or technology as a career.

Personal empowerment

This argument starts from the position that the learning achieved through studying design & technology at school is useful in everyday situations, as it enables young people to deploy design skills and technical problem solving to address and solve practical problems at both the personal and community levels. The argument can be extended to a consideration of the personal qualities developed by being able to deploy design & technical problem-solving skills. For example, the creative activities of designing and making, which are a major part of design & technology courses, not only give immense personal satisfaction but, importantly, develop a sense of self-efficacy which provides young people with a positive self-image about their ability to be successful. We have no doubt that these are important elements of a rounded education, and ones that design & technology is well placed to provide. Yet we don't believe they are sufficient, on their own, to justify the subject's place in the curriculum. The expert panel for the 2011 Curriculum Review took a similar view arguing that design & technology did not have "sufficient disciplinary coherence to be stated as (a) discrete and separate National Curriculum 'subject'" (Department for Education, 2011, p. 24). Fortunately, other views prevailed, and design & technology was retained as a National Curriculum subject at that time. We cannot be optimistic that any future curriculum review would have the same outcome, unless the design & technology community can provide a unified and clear vision for the subject that encompasses the breadth of purpose outlined here.

Cultural transmission

This argument starts from the position that technologies and the design thinking behind them are major achievements of our culture. Everyone should be helped to appreciate these, in much the same way that we teach young people to appreciate literature, art, and music. This argument leads us to ask, "What are the grand narratives of design & technology?" There have been moments in time when the outcomes of design & technological doing and thinking have had a profound effect on human history. For example, early in this historical narrative, the development of cooking, the invention and development of simple tools from flint and bone, the ability to refine ores to produce metal, the ability to grow and farm crops and livestock, the production of shelters, and the development of clothing made huge differences to the quality of human life. Basic needs could be met more easily, leaving time and energy available to develop cultural identity through a wide range of creative and commercial activities. Subsequently there has been a succession of technological "revolutions" – the industrial revolution, the electrical revolution, and the information revolution being among the most recent. Many argue that we are at the start of a fourth, 'cyber-physical' revolution (see for example WEF, 2016).

These have all been enabled by humanity's ability to envisage what might be and take action to realise these as yet unreached visions. So, any grand narratives of design & technology must consider imagination and intervention. Such imagining must of course be grounded in the realities of the physical universe; more and more the scientific understanding of the phenomena that constitute the physical universe underpin the interventions that result from the imagination. The variety and impact of these interventions are key components of the grand narratives. The interventions stemming from an imagined but not yet realised future reality might take many forms, with different degrees of success. And, inevitably, any intervention will have unintended consequences beyond its intended benefit. The story of humanity's interventions, their variety and consequences, both intentional and accidental, provide the grand narratives of design & technology. These narratives can be explored through the history of specific technologies; through the lives of individual designers, engineers, architects; through the development of different civilisations; through investigating products, as well as through the designing and making that learners engage in.

Preparation for citizenship

This argument starts from the position that in their communities, their workplaces, and through the media, people encounter questions and disputes that have matters of design and/or technology at their core. Often these matters are contentious. Significant understanding of design and of technology are needed to reach an informed view on such matters and engage in discussion and debate. The role of education to produce informed citizens able to take an active role at various 'levels' in their community and able to engage in informed and rationale debate lies at the heart of this justification for the subject. There seems little doubt that the pace of technological development is accelerating. Some, such as Ray Kurzweil (2005), argue that it is doing so at an exponential rate. While new technologies have always created a degree of concern in certain elements of society, it is noteworthy that some of the worries being expressed about imminently widespread new technologies are coming from within the technology community itself (e.g., Achenbach, 2016). Even if one takes a reasonably sanguine view, many of these new and emerging technologies are likely to have significant impact on society, almost certainly being disruptive to many current practices in people's personal, social, and working lives. There is clearly a need for an informed public discourse about the development and deployment of such technologies. This is the nub of the social argument: Enabling individuals to contribute significantly and intelligently to such discourse.

Pause for thought

Reflecting on the previous four sections (the economic, personal, cultural, and social justifications for teaching design & technology), how well does the design & technology curriculum in your school reflect these justifications?

- *Are there opportunities for learners to find out about the kinds of occupations through which artefacts and systems are created? Do they learn about innovation and the various ways that new ideas can be shared and protected?*
- *Does your curriculum enable young people to deploy their design & technical problem-solving skills to address and solve practical problems at both the personal and community levels? Does it provide the opportunity for learners to design what they are going to make, and to make what they have designed, with ample opportunity for reflection on how both their designing and making could be improved?*
- *Are there opportunities to explore some of the grand narratives of design & technology? To examine the contributions of particular individuals to the designed and made world? To investigate the products of the human-made world?*
- *How does your curriculum make space for learners to explore new developments in technology, looking at the potentials for both positive and negative outcomes?*

Revisiting the role of design & technology in the curriculum

We believe that each of these four arguments (the economic, personal, social, and cultural) should inform a school design & technology curriculum. While an individual school's circumstances may vary the relative profile of the arguments, to produce a curriculum that did not respond in part to each of them would be a curriculum that was lacking an important dimension. It seems to be the case, however, that too often the current justification for design & technology rests on the economic and personal arguments. As the above discussion makes clear, we take a strong view that these are not sufficient and, indeed, that relying on these two only puts the future of the subject at risk. By the same token, the cultural and social justifications often seem underdeveloped in the rationales one sees presented for the subject. We believe that this collection of reasons for design & technology, allied to the particular way in which the subject is experienced (e.g., through practical and intellectual engagement with designing, making, and critique), makes its contribution to the curriculum both highly valuable and unique – that is, if it was missing, the curriculum hole could not be filled through other subjects and young peoples' education would be impoverished.

Alison Hardy has done significant research into the views of stakeholders on the worth of design & technology and it is to her thought piece we now turn.

Justifying to whom? – *A Thought Piece by Alison Hardy*

Alison Hardy is an Associate Professor, writer, researcher, and podcaster at Nottingham Trent University.

My first thought is: who are we justifying the place of design & technology to? We will emphasise different arguments to different people: to government we may focus more on the economic and citizenship arguments, to pupils and their parents the economic and personal empowerment ones. From this position, we also realise that not everyone will agree, so these arguments can help with understanding and empathising different perspectives. What this empathy gives us is a way to come alongside those who disagree with us (like the deputy who thinks it's about DIY), acknowledge their perspective whilst holding true to our own. It also gives us language to understand what might, on first hearing, be a different perspective. The deputy's DIY argument fits within the personal empowerment, so we can try to move their thinking on to discuss with them how the subject empowers pupils now and in the future. I've argued elsewhere that understanding different perspectives helps build more positive relationships rather than antagonistic ones (Hardy, 2020).

When we think about justifying the subject, we often focus on trying to influence those higher up the power chain, those who can make or break design & technology's curriculum time and budget (school senior leaders) or the subject's significance in the education system (like government and the Department for Education). However, I think we need to have the same conversations with pupils. In chapter 14 of Learning to Teach Design & Technology, I cite Priniski, Hecht, and Harackiewicz (2018) whose study proposes asking pupils to explain the personal meaningfulness of a task or activity. They argue that the outcome of this will be pupils who are more engaged because they have identified their own intrinsic motivation for participating in the activity.

My second thought is about what I see implied in Hilda and Torben's four arguments: the prevailing political ideology of individualism (argument 1 and 2), being a good citizen (argument 4), and that curriculum is about knowledge (argument 3). Now, I'm not denying the importance of economic success for the individual or the subsequent contribution to the country's economy, or why we need to be good citizens, but I'm left wondering where community and society is within these four arguments. How do others, our community, benefit from D&T being taught in schools? How does D&T help others to flourish (Reiss & White, 2013), except economically? I don't have the space to explore this thought in depth here, but I encourage you to reflect on what you see as the aim of education and how, or whether, your aims are fully incorporated into Hilda and Torben's four arguments.

So I urge you to think about:

* *Who are you justifying D&T to?*
* *Ask key people who have an influence on the status of D&T what they see as the justification for D&T? Map these views onto Hilda and Torben's four arguments, and use this to help you empathise with and expand these people's views.*
* *Use the four arguments as a framework for discussing with pupils how they value different activities or tasks in your lessons.*

As we would expect, there is much food for thought in Alison's Thought Piece. We very much like the idea of "who are you justifying D&T to?" and think that as well as Government, parents and pupils SLT, Governors, MAT leaders, and industrial partners are all key audiences. We like the idea of empathising with different arguments as a way of enabling stakeholders to appreciate and perhaps even adopt other arguments. Widening the stakeholder group to include pupils is very welcome. Whilst the cultural transmission justification is dependent on knowing about design & technology, we believe that this knowledge and understanding can lead to an appreciation of the nature of technology and its impact on our lives. As for who benefits from design & technology, we believe an in-spection of the justifications will reveal that for each justification community and society do benefit.

The educational intentions of our subject in a nutshell

We believe the educational intentions of our subject can be captured as two main thrusts. These are technological perspective and technological capability. We define these as follows. Technological perspective provides insight into 'how technology works' which informs a constructively critical view of technology, avoids alienation from our technologically- based society, and enables consideration of how technology might be used to provide products and systems that help create the sort of society in which young people wish to live. Technological capability is designer-maker capability, capturing the essence of technological activity as intervention in the made and natural worlds. We think it is important to keep these intentions at the forefront of our thinking whenever we are trying to justify the subject or developing ways in which it might be taught, learned, or assessed.

References

Achenbach, J. (2016) Pondering 'what it means to be human' on the frontier of gene editing, Washington Post, 3 May 2016, https://www.washingtonpost.com/national/health-science/pondering-what-it-means-to-be-human-on-the-frontier-of-gene-editing/2016/05/03/a639b3ae-0bbb-11e6-bfa1-4efa856caf2a_story.html.

Department for Education (2011) *The Framework for the National Curriculum: A Report by the Expert Panel for the National Curriculum Review*, https://assets.publishing.service.gov.uk/government/uploads/system/uploads/attachment_data/file/175439/NCR-Expert_Panel_Report.pdf

Hardy, A. (2020) (ed.) *Learning to Teach Design and Technology in the Secondary School: A Companion to School Experience, 4th Edition*, Oxon: Routledge.

Kurzweil, R. (2005) *The Singularity Is Near: When Humans Transcend Biology*, London: Duckworth Overlook.

Priniski, S., Hecht, C., & Harackiewicz, J. (2017) Making Learning Personally Meaningful: A New Framework for Relevance Research, *The Journal of Experimental Education*, 86 (1):1-19.

Reiss, M., & White, J. (2013) *An Aims-based Curriculum: The Significance of Human Flourishing for Schools*, London: Bedford Way Papers.

World Economic Forum, Annual Report for 2015-2016, https://www3.weforum.org/docs/WEF_Annual_Report_2015-2016.pdf.

Recommended reading

Hardy, A. (2020) (ed.) *Learning to Teach Design and Technology in the Secondary School: A Companion to School Experience, 4th Edition*, Oxon: Routledge.

Myatt, M., & Tomsett, J. (2021) *Huh Curriculum Conversations between Subject and Senior Leaders*, Woodbridge, John Catt.

2 Understanding design & technology

This chapter is in seven parts. The first part discusses the philosophy of technology, the second part considers the philosophy of design, and the third part reflects on the place of values in design & technology. The fourth part discusses the nature of substantive and disciplinary knowledge and how these ideas might be applied to design & technology. The fifth part considers how substantive knowledge, disciplinary knowledge, and values interact in interventions in the made world that are the hallmark of design & technology activity. The sixth part considers the relationships between design & technology and other subjects in the school curriculum with particular emphasis on maintaining subject identity. Within each part there are *Pauses for thought* to help reflection and a short piece identifying relevant curriculum considerations. Finally, there is a short summary followed by references and recommended reading.

Philosophy of technology

Technology has been considered from a philosophical viewpoint since the time of the Ancient Greeks. Interestingly Socrates was suspicious of technical abilities and their use to produce wealth and affluence beyond what is necessary, leaving people soft and predisposed to the easy life because the pursuit of perfection of anything, including human nature, is the opposite of soft and easy. He worried that such abilities seek out defects or discomforts and are concerned to remedy them as opposed to seeking out what is already good and strive towards this. Those who strive toward this transcendence are seen to have spiritual wisdom as opposed to the wisdom of one with technical or low-grade handicraft skills. Perhaps this contempt for the technical has lingered on in the view of those who do not value design & technology in the school curriculum. The author who has done most to clarify philosophical views of technology recently is Carl Mitcham (1994), Professor Emeritus of Humanities, Arts, and Social Sciences at the Colorado School of Mines and Visiting International Professor of Philosophy of Technology at Renmin University of China.

Carl identified four different ways of thinking about technology as follows:

- Technology as artefacts
- Technology as activities

DOI: 10.4324/9781003008026-2

- Technology as knowledge
- Technology as volition.

Each will be considered in turn.

Technology as artefacts

This is perhaps the most common view today among the population at large. It is easy to see why. We live our lives embedded in a technological world that manifests itself through the artefacts we use every day. The houses we live in, the clothes we wear, the roads we travel on, the cars, buses and bicycles we ride, the communication devices and computers we use are all obvious. And although not so obvious but still integral to this technological world are energy supplies, transport networks, health services, water supply, and sewage disposal. Using all these different artefacts, both knowingly and un-knowingly changes the way we are in the world and our understanding of the world around us. If we designate any technology that we use as 'instrument', then this relationship can be represented as follows.

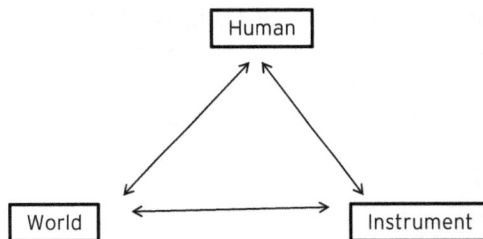

Figure 2.1 The relationship between humans, technological artefacts, and the world

This dynamic interaction between us, the instruments we use, and the world we live in gives order to our lives and influences the way we see ourselves. The technologies we use do not just spring into existence. They are produced by technological activity. Hence it is to this that we turn next.

Technology as activities

Carl identifies the following broad range of activities considered to be technological:

- Crafting
- Inventing
- Designing
- Manufacturing
- Working
- Operating
- Maintaining.

He divides these into two broad themes: production and use. He categorises 'production' as an initiating action and places crafting, inventing, and designing in this category. The others he sees as 'processes' that are dependent on the initiating actions. Once an instrument has been crafted, invented, or designed then it may be manufactured, worked, operated, or maintained. In terms of considering the consequences of technology as activity, it is the processes that give rise to consequences, both intended and unintended. However, without the initiating production of crafting, inventing, and designing there would be no grist for the process mill. Hence one might argue that those who craft, invent, and design have the primary responsibility for the consequences of technology as activity.

Technology as knowledge

It is important to distinguish technological knowledge from scientific knowledge. The difference between these is related to the differing overall purposes of technology and science. Science is concerned with observing and explaining natural phenomenon with the intention of establishing scientific knowledge, which is seen as 'true' but open to review in the light of further observations and explanations. Technology on the other hand is not concerned with 'truth' but in taking action. Hence technological knowledge should be seen as the knowledge necessary to take action. Carl identifies four distinct forms of technological knowledge which play out with different significance in any technological endeavour depending on the nature of that endeavour:

Sensorimotor skills – the knowing 'how' as opposed to knowing 'that'
Technical maxims – rules of thumb that are known to work in certain situations and applied accordingly
Technological rules which are to some extent like scientific laws but do not as yet have a clearly identified theory underpinning them
Technological theories which can be seen as involving the specific application of science; for example, the theories of aerodynamics apply fluid dynamics.

It is worth noting that scientific knowledge will of necessity be called upon in taking action. The nature of phenomena as revealed by science cannot be ignored as they set the ground rules for what is possible but in calling on such knowledge it often has to be re-conceptualised to be useful for taking action. The life cycles of parasites provide an interesting example. For the scientist, understanding the life cycles is sufficient. For the doctor who wants to prevent the spread of diseases caused by parasites, life cycle information needs to be reconfigured to identify how and where the parasites are transmitted to humans so that action may be devised and taken that prevents this transmission. Marc de Vries (2005) also makes the interesting point that scientific knowledge is declarative, but when it is used for technology purposes it becomes normative in that the technologist has to make a judgement as to its usefulness in the particular situation in which she is trying to take action. So, while the material scientist can produce a list of the properties of materials, which material is a 'good one' to choose in a particular situation will depend on more than just these properties although they will of course be important. But so will working properties, availability, cost, environmental impact, working conditions of those who produce the materials, and these may all have to be taken into account in making the judgment of which is the material to use – the so called 'good one'.

Technology as volition

The dictionary definition of volition is "the power or ability to decide something by yourself and to take action to get what you want". In using this term Carl puts human nature at the centre of being technological in that as humans we have the will to survive, take control of our situation, and make our lives more efficient and through technology we can do this and overcome our inherent physical weaknesses. In this pursuit *of* control over the way we can live our lives through technology, there is concern as to who or what is *in* control. We will return to this later when discussing the views of two other philosophers of technology: Jacques Ellul and Kevin Kelly.

Carl developed the following diagram to describe his four ways of thinking about technology.

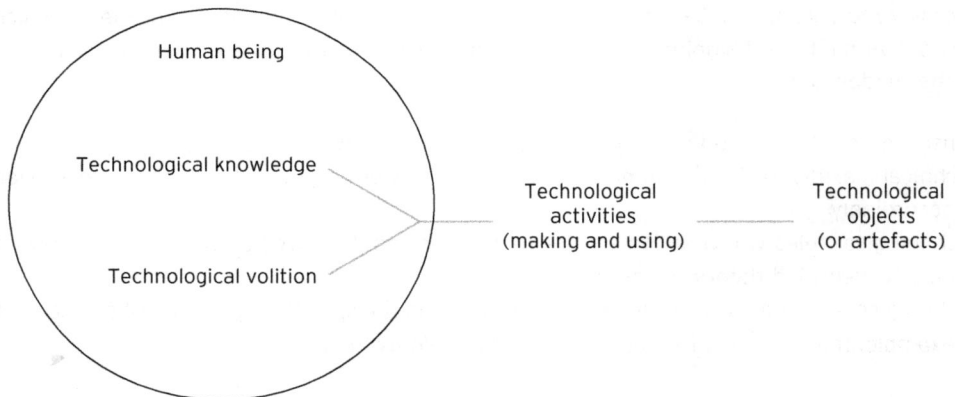

Figure 2.2 Carl Mitcham's diagram of the four ways to think about technology

This diagram elegantly captures that technology is a human activity and shows that by pursuing purpose (volition) informed by knowledge technological activity leads to the multifarious artefacts that now comprise our made world.

Being with technology

Carl also identified three ways of being with technology (we might call these attitudes towards technology) that have arisen since ancient times and which, to some extent, are still prevalent today.

Ancient scepticism

In ancient times philosophers were wary of technology from the viewpoint that it is 'bad but necessary' or 'necessary but dangerous'. From this point of view, being-with technology is an uneasy being-alongside-of and working-to-keep-at arms-length. To some extent this view was underpinned by the idea that the natural world was superior to the made world. This attitude can be seen today in the way that various technologies are used but sometimes reluctantly or with reservations. Some peoples' attitudes towards vaccination programmes and genetically modified crops are examples.

Enlightenment valorisation

With the advent of the Enlightenment in Western Europe in the 17th century, the stage became set for a very different view. The rise of science as a way of explaining both the natural world and made world using the same set of ideas for both displaced the 'superiority of the natural' so the criticism that somehow technology was inferior became invalid, and the obvious benefits of technology could be enjoyed without fear of bad consequences or guilt that one was somehow going against the will of God. From this point of view, being-with technology is something to be embraced at all levels of society – individually, collectively, informing government policy and business practice, and becoming fully integrated into everyday life. This may perhaps be summed up by the attitude that whatever befalls us 'technology will save us'. The proposal and adoption of 'technological fixes' in response to various issues in today's society mirrors this attitude in, for example, advocating the use of Big Data and AI to control crime and catch criminals without any effort to understand the reasons for the criminal activity and alleviate the situations that cause it.

Romantic ambivalence

The experiences of working people during the Industrial Revolution in England provided a stark reality check of Enlightenment enthusiasm. Critics, ranging from William Blake with his condemnation of 'dark satanic mills' in the poem *Jerusalem* to Charles Dickens in his novel *Hard Times*, identified the dehumanising consequences of factory labour and overcrowded slum living conditions with very poor public sanitation as being directly caused by technology. Yet at the same time in response to this we see the successful development of the London Sewer system, widely regarded as a triumph of Victorian engineering. Hence, we see an almost bipolar response to technology – attracted and repulsed in almost equal measure, with technology creating more and more of itself though enterprise and innovation yet overstepping its rightful bounds, creating great wealth for the few, leaving many in poverty and undermining social cohesion. And alongside this internal conflict, thinkers of the Romantic movement in the 18th and 19th century found themselves beguiled by beauty and excellence of technological artefacts. From this point of view, being-with technology is a constant battle between two opposing positions. And in today's society this view plays out in the question, 'We can, but should we?' with regard to technology and the way it is being developed across a variety of fields. There is the realisation that there will be unintended consequences beyond intended benefits whenever a new technology is deployed and starts to be widely adopted. For example, the humble origins of Facebook belie what it would become, and recent events have shown that there are more than a few downsides to its ubiquity.

Pause for thought

In the light of the above, it is worth considering your own relationship with technology. Where do you sit? Are you wary and see technology as necessary but dangerous, or are you trusting seeing technology as benign enhancing our lives and solving our problems? Or do you waver between these two positions? Or does your position vary according to the particular technology you are considering?

Who or what is in control?

Finally, it is worth considering the extent to which technology might be within our control or in control of us. Kevin Kelly (2010) argues that there are three drivers affecting the way technology plays out in the world. The first and most significant is the intrinsic nature of technology, the way it works, interacting within itself in ways that are self-organising. The second is the influence of technological history in that all technologies build on previous ones. The third is society's collective free will in responding to the way technology is playing out either aligning with developments or opposing them. He argues that the least significant of these by far is society's free will and that opposing technology will only have a very limited effect. He is a technological optimist and views new and emerging technologies as providing ever-increasing opportunities for humans to 'self-realise' in ways not available to those in previous generations acknowledging that in reality humans actually have little control of technology. The thinking of Jacques Ellul (1964) is in direct contrast to that of Kelly in that he is most definitely a technological pessimist. He views the intrinsic nature of technology with its emphasis on efficiency and standardisation as inimitable to the human spirit and the wide-ranging influence that technology is having, and continuing to have, on society as both dehumanising and outside human control.

Thomas Hughes (1994) offers an intermediate path between Ellul's pessimism and Kelly's optimism. He has developed the idea of technological momentum, particularly with regard to the large technological systems that underpin much of modern life. He argues that as such systems come into being it is relatively easy for society to have an influence on their development but once they become established this is much more difficult requiring significant disruption and at that stage in their development these technologies become autonomous and outside human control. Hence in considering Kelly's view that humanity can exert an influence on technology, albeit limited, by aligning itself with particular trajectories in order to achieve good, Hughes' idea of technological momentum suggests that to be effective this alignment needs to be at the beginning of the trajectory. Once the technology is established it will not be possible for any alignment to give rise to change. Human involvement will become acquiescence. Jonas Hallström (2022) challenges this 'humans will have no alternative but to go with the flow' in response to the way new and emerging technologies influence society by arguing that it is the responsibility of technology education to teach learners that 'all technologies will be the result of designerly acts, and a multitude of choices made by engineers and designers, be it the design of stools, electronic circuits, or autonomous systems' (p. 29).

Curriculum considerations: Four key questions derived from the thinking of Carl Mitcham

If we see it as important that young people develop a clear view of the sort of future they want and that design & technology education should enable them to articulate this, then it might be important to engage them with the following questions related to ways of thinking about technology articulated by Carl Mitcham:

* What sort of artefacts should be designed and made?
* What sort of knowledge should be discovered?
* What sort of activities should be pursued?
* To what extent should the volition be tempered?

Philosophy of design

Philosophy of design is different in nature to philosophy of technology. Technology is best seen as a socio-cultural phenomenon which can be thought about from different perspectives as in Carl Mitcham's artefacts, activity, knowledge, and volition. The word design when a noun, according to the Cambridge Dictionary, means "a drawing or set of drawings showing how a building or product is to be made and how it will work and look" as in "Have you seen the designs for the new shopping centre?" As a verb the Cambridge Dictionary defines it as "to make or draw plans for something, for example clothes or buildings". This definition hides the complexity of the activity; sometimes in the very beginning of an act of designing the nature of the intended outcome is not clear. Gunther Ropohl (1997, p. 69) has described this activity as requiring:

> [The development and design of] a novel technical system, anticipat[ing] the object to be realised through mental imagination. [The designer] has to conceive of a concrete object which does not yet exist, and he [sic] has to determine spatial and temporal details which cannot yet be observed but will have to be created by the designing and manufacturing process.

Brian Lawson (2004, p. 20) makes an intriguing analogy with playing chess:

> Designing then, in terms of chess, is rather like playing with a board that has no divisions into cells, has pieces that can be invented and redefined as the game proceeds and rules that change their effects as moves are made. Even the object of the game is not defined at the outset and may change as the game wears on. Put like this it seems a ridiculous enterprise to contemplate the design process at all!

Hence, we can see designing is an activity within technology through which artefacts, environments, and systems are conceived and ultimately made manifest. The following vignettes of daily life in cities across world give testament to the breadth and diversity of the outputs from designerly activity and identify designs that are successful in that they have been conceived, realised, and are widely used.

Family at breakfast in the kitchen at home before going to work/school

The mother, dressed smartly in a business suit, is asking a personal assistant what appointments she has today. The father is dressed much more casually as he works from home and is making hot drinks. As the children, both in school uniform, approach the breakfast table the boy is carrying cutlery and crockery and the girl is carrying a tablecloth. They move their mobile phones off the table so the girl can cover it with the cloth. The clacking noise of the mother's shoes on the hard kitchen floor disappears as she walks into the carpeted hall and out of the front door. In summary we have people wearing and using textiles, using utensils and communication devices, enclosed in a structure, a flat within a larger building which is serviced by a range of utilities - water, gas, electricity, and the Internet.

Commuters travelling to work by various means

A young woman is on a scooter, another is about to get on a tram. A young man is cycling, and an older woman is about to board a bus. An older man has parked his electric car and is connecting it to a charging point before he goes into the office block where he works. An autonomous taxi drops a passenger at a hotel which services travellers from the local airport, and in the distance one can just see people exiting a railway station. In summary we have lots of people using a wide range of different transportation devices, all of which are utilising mainly electricity and moving across transport infrastructure - roads, rails, and pavement. Embedded within this complex transport system are communication devices reliant on computer hardware and software and the Internet.

Customers shopping in a large supermarket

They are walking along the aisles between shelving units, some of which are simply display shelves whilst others are chilled cabinets and some are freezers. They select items and put them in their baskets or trolleys and use a reader to indicate the purchase and the total of their spending. When they have finished shopping, they put their cash cards into the reader and the amount they have spent is debited from their bank account. They are then free to leave with their shopping having paid the bill. The supermarket is a nexus of a very large number of supply chains, and this operates through transport utilities, utilising communication devices reliant on computer hardware and software and the Internet. Maintaining stock on the shelves at the moment requires large amounts of human labour but this may change in the future through automation using sophisticated AI.

Pause for thought

Writing descriptions of daily life identifying the designed items that are being used is an exercise that encourages reflection about the lives we lead and their dependency on technology and design. It is worth asking learners at school to do this, but it is important for the teacher to have tried it for themselves to experience and appreciate the demands this makes. So with this in mind write descriptions of the following identifying the designed items that are being used.

- Workers in an office
- Family at leisure at home
- Workers in a factory.

In the light of the above it becomes clear that the sentence, 'Everything in the made world has been designed,' is not designer arrogance. However, the breadth, diversity, and scale of designerly activity makes it unlikely that we can identify an all-embracing philosophy of design. But can we identify common, desirable features of the designed items described in the vignettes? Here are six possibilities:

1   *Technically sound*
    They work well.
2   *Aesthetically stimulating*
    Arousing a response from our senses and intellect, sometimes to the point of being 'arresting'; they look so good that people want them even before they know what they do, so called visceral appeal. Or even shocking, making people recoil initially before becoming attracted.
3   *Materially appropriate*
    They incorporate materials that are fit for purpose.
4   *User friendly*
    Using them is often intuitive and fluency in their use is easy to acquire.
5   *Commercially successful*
    They are utilised widely and generate significant profit for the designers and producers.
6   *Environmentally sound*
    In their production, use, and retirement they leave a minimal carbon footprint.

This is perhaps an overly simplistic list and there will be other, different lists covering the same ground, but it is sufficient for our purposes. Designers of all shades will undoubtedly try to meet these features although some will do this more successfully than others. As the activity is highly personal, particular designers develop their own personal philosophies, so one way to engage with philosophy of design is to identify those designers who have been so successful in achieving some, if not all, of these features that their designs are regarded as iconic and to find statements they have made that reveal their personal philosophy. So here is an eclectic selection of quotes from designers of renown from across the spectrum of design activity going back over 100 years. Are there common threads? Or does each one have a particularly idiosyncratic approach that somehow defines their work?

Charles was an architect, and Ray was an artist. Together, the American husband and wife team created some of the most iconic mid-century designs, including the ubiquitous Eames plastic armchair, Eames lounge chair and ottoman, and "Hang it all" coat rack.

- *What works good is better than what looks good, because what works good lasts.*
- *The details are not the details, the details make the product.*

Milton Glaser was an American graphic designer. His designs include the I Love New York logo, the psychedelic Bob Dylan poster, and the logo for DC Comics.

- *There are three responses to a piece of design – yes, no, and WOW! Wow is the one to aim for.*

Margaret is widely considered to be the mother of modern-day information design and made a major contribution to the redesign of the UK's entire road sign system, which replaced the chaotic mishmash of different typefaces and symbols commissioned by various bodies that existed previously.

- *It required completely radical thinking. The information wasn't there in terms of reading distance, clarity and letter spaces. We had to make up the signs and then test them. It was instinctive.*

Dame Zaha Mohammad Hadid DBE RA was a British Iraqi architect. She was the first woman to receive the Pritzker Architecture Prize, in 2004. She received the UK's most prestigious architectural award, the Stirling Prize, in 2010 and 2011.

- *Architecture is like writing. You have to edit it over and over, so it looks effortless.*
- *If you think about making a city that is much more porous, many accessible spaces, that is a political position, because you don't fortify, you open it up so that many people can use it.*

Sir Jonathan Paul 'Jony' Ive KBE Hon FREng RDI is an English industrial, product, and architectural designer. Ive was Chief Design Officer of Apple Inc., and is now the serving Chancellor of the Royal College of Art.

- *Simplicity is not the absence of clutter, that's a consequence of simplicity. Simplicity is somehow essentially describing the purpose and place of an object and product.*
- *We try to develop products that seem somehow inevitable, that leave you with the sense that that's the only possible solution that makes sense.*

It is worth noting that there has been criticism from various quarters on the grounds that designers in general, whether famous or obscure, are designing for a small minority yet this is resulting in consuming the Earth's resources at an unsustainable rate and causing irretrievable damage to the world's ecosystems. Here are some examples.

Paul Polak (2007) of International Development Enterprises is blunt with a call to re-envision design as activism to achieve social justice:

> *The majority of the world's designers focus all their efforts on developing products and services exclusively for the richest 10% of the world's customers. Nothing less than a revolution in design is needed to reach the other 90%.*

From Allan Chochinov:

> *Perhaps the wholesale poisonings of every natural system through industrialisation are 'unintended' consequences but there is a cruel irony in designers running around, busily creating more and more garbage for our great grandchildren to dig up, breathe, and ingest, all the while calling themselves 'problem solvers'.*

Annie Leonard (2010), the author of *The Story of Stuff*, echoing Chochinov, argues that the monetary price we pay for the goods we buy in no way reflects the true cost, asking:

> *How do you adjust the price of a laptop to reflect the cancer and neurological damage in workers, the loss of habitat for gorillas in the Congo's coltan reserves, and the contamination of soil and groundwater after the computer gets trashed? Prices go way up, that's for sure.*

Mike Berners-Lee, the author of *There is no planet B* (2019), suggests that:

> *We humans need urgently to develop our thinking skills and habits in at least eight respects. These include big picture thinking, joined up thinking, future thinking, critical thinking, dedication to truth, self-awareness, global empathy, and a better appreciation of the small things in this beautiful world we live in.*

Interestingly the Ellen McArthur Foundation has responded to this critique by advocating the development of a circular economy in direct contrast to the current linear economy and this is gaining significant traction within the business community.

Curriculum considerations

Feasibility

To what extent is it feasible to ask learners to design and make artefacts that meet all or some of the six, common, desirable features identified above?

Designing for the majority

And in selecting a context for design and make activity is it appropriate to consider the situations of people in the 90%? Asking learners to devise better ways for some of those in the 90% to tackle their situation is almost certainly inadvisable. Although struggling in their endeavour, these people bring generations of knowledge, understanding and skill to bear on the problem and it would be arrogant for young people in more favourable circumstances to tell them how to do such demanding tasks. Some of the needs and wants of both the 10% and the 90% are identical yet these are often met in quite different ways so comparisons might be informative and reveal the sophistication of 90% design activity and inform the design of items to be used in 10% situations. A particularly useful reference here is *Design with the other 90%: Cities* (Smith, 2011), which examines the complex issues arising from unprecedented urban growth mostly in informal settlements of emerging and developing economies. A key feature of many of the examples is the involvement of local communities in the design activity moving away from the idea of 'designer as hero' to the position where everyone can be a designer and use design to influence their situation for the better.

Confronting the linear economy

And where will designing for a circular economy fit into your curriculum?

The place of values in design & technology

A consideration of values should always be present in design & technology. Whether learners are making, designing, designing and making, or considering the consequences of technology, a deliberation about values is necessary. When, for example, learners are tackling design and make tasks it is important they appreciate the values which might inform the nature of the need or opportunity underpinning the task and to find ways to take them into account. Learners should consider their own values and move towards a recognition and understanding of the values of others. They need to think about situations where there are value conflicts and move from simple, two-sided arguments to understanding complex conflicts involving many-sided arguments. Arguments where qualitative values, for example aesthetic considerations, conflict with quantitative values, for example economic considerations, are probably the most difficult to resolve. The Nuffield Design & Technology Project identified the following headings under which different values might be described:

*   technical
*   moral

- social
- aesthetic
- economic
- environmental.

They do not represent mutually exclusive sets and there will often be overlap between the categories. In order to engage learners with this set of values and encourage classroom discussion, the Project articulated what these values might mean in particular designing and making tasks. Table 2.1 provides an example of the values embedded in designing and making of a toddler's hat.

Table 2.1 Values embedded in a design and make task

	To design and make a toddler's hat for either winter or summer wear, suitable for production as a ready-to-sew kit.
Technical Value	Learners should consider the implications of changing their designs to simplify the construction.
Social Value	Learners should consider the role of self-assembly items in the way people dress themselves and members of their families.
Economic Value	Learners should use the idea of value for money to think about the influence of price on marketability. They should consider how they might ensure that their design is appropriately priced.
Moral Value	Learners should consider the way textile items are manufactured in both developing and developed countries.
Environmental Value	Learners should consider the source of the materials used, their disposal after the garment or accessory has completed its useful life, and the effect of the manufacturing processes.
Aesthetic Value	Learners should consider the relationship between the appearance of their designed items and the style they are trying to achieve.

Whether equal priority should be given to each of the identified categories is a matter of debate. In developing a values sensitive curriculum in design & technology it will be important for teachers to identify relevant values for each element of the scheme of work they teach. This has implications for the learning activities that teachers devise. For example, an activity that teaches a wide and useful range of knowledge and skills, through the production of a relatively trivial item, such as a desk tidy or a steady hand game perhaps, will need revising so that the item produced has more intrinsic worth which can be considered through the values embedded within it.

In a designing and making task there is a constant iteration between reflection and action. At the beginning of the task there is reflection on the problem being addressed and what might constitute a reasonable and realistic response. Further into the task the reflection concerns what to do next: sketch, 3D model, find out about materials, make some parts; and this reflection leads to action – sketching, modelling, collecting materials, making certain parts. These actions interact and inform one another and are oft times repeated, the 3D model needing a sketch before it is developed, the choice of material leading to difficulties in making and needing to be reconsidered. These interactions are informed by reflection. Eventually this reflection-action 'dance' leads to the realisation of a finished prototype in physical form and the opportunity for more reflection in an evaluation. Learners will not necessarily engage with the values identified by the teacher so it will be important to develop teaching strategies that provoke them to consider the values embedded within the activity and respond in ways that are sensitive to the issues involved. In addition, it is possible for learners to have a skewed active-reflective balance such that their actions may be on the one hand too hasty and poorly thought through or on the other hand over considered so that the actions are insufficiently definitive. Questioning of the learner by the teacher is a powerful way to both provoke a consideration of values and addressing any skew in active reflective balance. The exact nature of the question a teacher might use will depend on the learner being questioned and the extent to which they are already sensitive to values issues.

This on-going experience of engaging with values will be particularly important when learners are faced with identifying a problem to resolve as they are required to do in the GCSE contextual challenge. It is here that their sensitivity to values issues developed over their previous design & technology experience will pay big dividends. Allan Chichinov's challenge to move from good design to design for good is important here regarding both the problem identified and the approach to its resolution. His view that "the design conversation moves from form, function, beauty and ergonomics to accessibility, affordability, sustainability and social worth" (Pilloton, 2009) might well come into play.

Pause for thought

For the teacher the question is how to achieve a reflective classroom in which a consideration of values is central without causing the whole enterprise to slow down so much that the designing and making task does not get finished. Using a design and make task with which you are very familiar identify the opportunities in the way learners might tackle the task where you might use questions to engage learners in values. These questions might be to the whole class or to small groups or individual learners.

Curriculum considerations

A vocabulary for values thinking

If learners are to identify their own value positions, recognise the value positions of others, and discuss how values affect design & technology activity, they will need an appropriate vocabulary. They will not acquire this by accident, and a starting point might be for a class to discuss and develop agreed meanings for the value headings developed by the Nuffield Project and a consideration of the difference between 'good design' and 'design for good'.

Progression in values thinking

As learners move through a design & technology curriculum, it will be important that their thinking about values and the way they use this becomes more sophisticated and that they appreciate different people will hold different views according to the values they hold. This is discussed further in chapter 4 (in the section on 'Considering the consequences of technology') and in chapter 5 (in the section 'Teaching critique').

The politics of values thinking

As learners become older, they become aware of the way politicians adopt particular value positions in the way they promote their beliefs and policies. For example, in public debates about providing people with employment and unemployment caused by automation, different political parties may have different views based on their values. It will be important for you, as a teacher, to be aware of this and help learners unpick the way such values inform policies.

Substantive and disciplinary knowledge in design & technology

Introduction

We can define substantive knowledge as what a field of study believes to be true at a particular moment in time. Within any field there may be competing claims for what might be true and also speculative statements of truth awaiting validation. In most fields of study, the aim is to provide justifiable explanations leading to the acceptance of a substantive body of knowledge. Disciplinary knowledge is an understanding of and ability to deploy the ways and means by which substantive knowledge is revealed and validated. Most school subjects can be defined in terms of what is known and accepted as true and an appreciation of the methods and tests of truth that are used to validate what is currently accepted.

In physics, for example, the phenomenon of gravity is well understood, and there is a large body of evidence to support this understanding. Substantive knowledge about gravity developed by Isaac Newton in the 17th century was as follows: gravity is a force causing any two bodies to be attracted toward each other, with the magnitude of the attraction being proportional to the product of their masses and inversely proportional to the square of the distance between them. This is still useful for most everyday applications, although it has since been superseded by the work of Albert Einstein in the early 20th century. Wynne Harlen and colleagues (2010) provided a useful classification for science in terms of Big Ideas *of* science, the discoveries made by scientists (substantive knowledge) and Big Ideas *about* science, the way science works in order for scientists to make discoveries (disciplinary knowledge).

However, things are a little different for design & technology. Although knowledge and understanding are important in our subject, developing such knowledge and understanding is not the main purpose of design & technology. Whereas the scientific endeavour is concerned with exploring and explaining the natural and made worlds, design & technology is concerned with intervening in the made and natural worlds with the intention of improving a situation in which there are problems. David Layton wrote about this compellingly in his book *Technology's Challenge to Science Education* (Layton, 1993). So in addition to being a field of study in the sense that it is a school subject that is taught, design & technology provides an arena in which learners are required to use their knowledge, skills, understanding, and values to decide upon deliberate action which they can take themselves in response to a particular problem or issue. This fundamental difference makes the identification and clarification of substantive and disciplinary knowledge in design & technology more difficult than for other school subjects. Nonetheless it is worth trying as it provides insight into both what we teach and how we might teach it in design & technology.

'Rightness' trumps truth

When a designer, engineer, architect, or technologist intervenes to solve a problem or engage with an issue, there will be a myriad of possible outcomes, some of which will be better than others. Even for those that are deemed as equally good, there is a wide range of possibilities. Hence the outcomes of interventions do not have to be true in the sense that a scientific explanation or mathematical proof has to be true; they have to be 'right'.

What does it mean for an intervention to have been right? Here is a preliminary list of criteria. It should:

- be an appropriate response to the brief
- meet the requirements of the specification
- be able to be sold to/bought by/leased by those for whom it is intended
- be acceptable to the society in which it is to be used
- meet a range of stakeholder requirements
- not compromise social justice or stewardship.

To what extent will we be able to ask learners whether their interventions, that is, what they have designed or designed and made are 'right'?

Whilst in theory someone wishing to intervene, for example, an architect, designer, engineer, technologist, might call upon any potentially useful knowledge, this doesn't help with defining substantive knowledge in the current schools' context, where subjects are expected to teach an identifiable body of knowledge and skills. Also, and perhaps more importantly, if a young person needs to learn more about a particular field because it is relevant to an intervention they are pursuing, it is much easier to learn more about it if they already know a little about it. So, one of the tasks of defining substantial knowledge that should be taught in design & technology is to identify areas of knowledge that are likely to be useful in a range of interventions.

The authors have, using the work of Wynne Harlen as a model, developed a listing of Big Ideas *about* design & technology and Big Ideas *of* design & technology (Barlex & Steeg, 2017). These are discussed in more detail in chapter 4. Suffice it to say here that we can use these to tease out the nature of substantive and disciplinary knowledge for design & technology.

Important ideas *about* design & technology that capture its intrinsic nature are summarised In Table 2.2.

Some important ideas *of* design & technology can be grouped under the three headings Materials, Manufacture, and Function (Table 2.3).

Table 2.2 Features about design & technology that define its intrinsic nature

Ideas about *design & technology*
Through design & technology people develop technologies and products to intervene in the natural and made worlds.
The worth of such interventions is a matter of judgment.
Design & technology uses knowledge, skill, and understanding from a wide range of sources.
There are always many possible and valid interventions some of which will be more efficacious than others.
Technologies and products always have unintended consequences beyond their intended benefits which cannot be anticipated.

Table 2.3 Three important features of substantive knowledge in design & technology

Materials	*Manufacture*	*Functionality*
Sources	By subtraction	Through powering
Properties	By addition	Through structuring
Footprint	By forming	Through controlling
Longevity	By assembly	
	With finishing	

Some knowledge may come from outside design & technology and inform a learner's understanding of these Big Ideas. For example, early scientists established the idea of properties and chemists, physicists and materials scientists have since established the chemical, physical, and mechanical properties of individual materials. This information is very useful in deciding which material to use in a particular intervention. Such a decision, however, is always a trade-off between a range of considerations including intrinsic properties, working properties, availability, cost, and environmental impact. This is where disciplinary knowledge comes in. In design & technology it is not used to establish that which has already been established by other disciplines but uses this in conjunction with other considerations to make the decisions necessary to define the detail of the item needed for intervention. So, in design & technology there is interplay between substantive and disciplinary knowledge. We use the disciplinary knowledge to figure out how to deploy the substantive knowledge.

Two further important ideas *of* design & technology that can be taught are (a) critique and (b) design, and these ideas come from within design & technology. To some extent these ideas can be seen as sitting in a blurred region lying between substantive and disciplinary knowledge in that they are most usefully seen as verbs rather than nouns (that is, critiquing and designing), but a learner does have to know about the nature of design and critique (Table 2.4).

Teachers must also ask about the nature of the interventions they can legitimately require of learners. There is little point in constructing a conceptual edifice of substantive and disciplinary knowledge for design & technology if it turns out to be irrelevant to the sorts of intervention that are possible in school. We must embed our thinking in the awareness that

Table 2.4 Two important features of design & technology knowledge lying at the boundary between substantive and disciplinary knowledge

Critique(ing)	Design(ing)
For justice	Identifying peoples' needs and wants
For stewardship	Identifying market opportunities
	Generating, developing, and communicating design ideas
	Evaluating design ideas

most if not all learners in secondary school are fledgling interveners often with little previous experience of intervention. This is where the four ways of teaching design & technology, discussed in detail in chapter 4, are important in that they can be used to develop and deploy both substantive knowledge and disciplinary knowledge. These four ways of teaching are:

- Making without designing (or mainly making)
- Designing without making (sometimes called mainly designing or design fiction)
- Designing and making
- Considering the consequences of technology.

Here we will note the interplay between substantive and disciplinary knowledge within each way of teaching.

Making without designing (or mainly making)

Consider making a simple spinning top to a prescribed design (Figure 2.3).

There are several areas of substantive knowledge involved: names of tools and equipment, names and properties of materials, names of assembly techniques. Learning this knowledge needs to be accompanied by learning the skills of using the tools and equipment to handle the necessary materials to achieve a sound assembly. Might we consider this skill

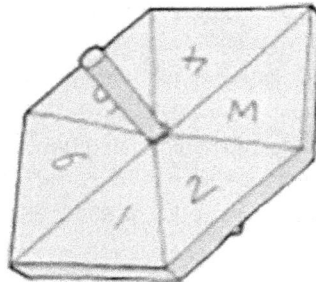

Figure 2.3 A simple hexagonal spinning top that can be used as a dice, made from sheet plywood and dowel

acquisition as disciplinary knowledge? If so, then we have an interesting relationship at a high level of generality between substantive and disciplinary knowledge for the following features of design & technology: knowledge of tools, equipment and materials (substantive knowledge), and skill in using these for making (disciplinary knowledge).

Designing without making (or mainly designing or design fiction)

Consider designing, but not making, an application for shape memory alloys. A learner would need to know about the nature of such alloys (an alloy that can be deformed when cold but returns to its pre-deformed shape when heated) and within this there is knowing about the nature of deformation (changing form or shape), and sources of heat that give rise to an increase in temperature. This is substantive knowledge and unless the learner has this, the task is impossible. In devising a possible use for a shape memory alloy, the learner needs to use the disciplinary knowledge of designing, which will include generating and developing design ideas with possible user needs and wants in mind.

Designing and making

In designing and making any artefact the learner will need to make decisions about the various features of the proposed design. Such decisions are considered in detail in chapter 5. Here we can say that they will inevitably include (a) technical decisions (how the proposed design might work), (b) aesthetic decisions (what the design might look like), and (c) constructional decisions (how the various parts of the design can be made and assembled). Even for a relatively simple artefact this represents a significant amount of substantive knowledge, and without this the learner is unlikely to be successful in the task. And the disciplinary knowledge of designing is required to deploy this substantive knowledge in conceiving and realising that which the learner envisages.

Considering the consequences of technology

In considering the consequences of a potentially disruptive technology such as, for example, the use of robots in the workplace, it is important that the learner has (a) knowledge about current workplace robots, (b) the extent to which they are in use, and (c) possible developments both in terms of increasing use of existing types of robots and the development of new types of robots. This information is relatively easily available, but unless the learners have access to this and some sense of what it means then they are unlikely to be able to carry out any critique. Knowledge and understanding of this information can be seen as substantive knowledge. Whether the learner has to learn this for themselves through independent research or by attending a lesson given by a teacher is a matter of judgement for the teacher. But once they have acquired this knowledge and understanding they are in a position to critique with regard to social justice and ask questions about who wins and who loses and to explore possible unintended consequences for particular groups or individuals. And this critique has to be carried out in the contexts of current development and future possibilities.

Curriculum considerations

In the teaching methods described above there was always the need for learners to acquire and use both substantive knowledge and disciplinary knowledge. It is worth looking at the balance of these features in your programme of study with a view to finding out if learner's achievements might be enhanced through adjusting the balance.

Pause for thought

Ask yourself and discuss with colleagues what might be the consequences of either of the following learners' experience of design & technology:

- An over-emphasis on teaching substantive knowledge at the expense of disciplinary knowledge
- An over-emphasis on teaching disciplinary knowledge at the expense of substantive knowledge.

What about misconceptions?

The work of Rosalind Driver in science education indicated clearly that may learners have misconceptions with regard to their understanding of important scientific ideas. These ideas have developed in the learners' minds through making sense of their everyday experiences. Something we do from the moment we are born. A difficulty with science ideas is that many are counterintuitive and are difficult to reach through a 'common sense' interpretation of everyday experience. Driver's research found that once formed, these ideas became deeply held and were very resistant to change. Elegant explanations provided by teachers were often to little avail. The only person who could supplant the misconceptions from learners' minds are the learners themselves. The learners had, quite literally, to change their minds. This raises the question as to whether learners have misconceptions concerning the Big Ideas which we are using as the basis for substantive knowledge. We don't know the answer as we have found little research on misconceptions in design & technology. We will return to this issue in chapter 7.

The place of skills, knowledge, understanding, and values in intervening

For any intervention in the made world to take place, the intervener (designer, engineer, technologist, architect, or whoever) must deploy disciplinary knowledge and substantive knowledge in developing a response to the identified needs or wants and the way this knowledge is deployed will depend to some considerable degree on the values held by the intervener. If she is concerned that the response should be environmentally sound, she will use her disciplinary and substantive knowledge to ensure that in its production, use, and retirement the response will leave a minimal carbon footprint. She may go further and develop a response that embeds itself within a circular economy. If, however she is concerned to keep the cost of materials used in the response to a minimum, she may well choose to use readily available, inexpensive, oil-based materials and develop a response that might be discarded as opposed to entering a recycling system. This, admittedly over simplified and general, description indicates that the values held by the intervener will to a large extent govern the nature of the intervention. How will this play out in the designing and making undertaken by learners in the secondary school? One way to engage learners with values is to begin with a very open starting point for a designing and making task (Figure 2.4).

The overall theme of the task is Playtime and through a series of questions learners can explore aspects of playing as they work towards producing a design brief to which they can respond through designing and making. Such an exploration might lead a learner to produce a brief along these lines: design and make a board game that can be played on by two or more elderly people in community centre with a playing session lasting no more than an hour.

In developing such a game, the learner will need to use substantive knowledge to identify which materials to use, how to manufacture the necessary parts, and how to achieve the necessary functionality (in terms of structure obviously but perhaps also in terms of power and control if the game incorporates light and sound effects). The choices made here through the disciplinary knowledge of designing will be informed by the values of the learner. Ideally the game would be technically sound, aesthetically stimulating, materially appro-priate, user friendly, and environmentally sound (desirable features of the designed items as indicated on page 17). In addition, the requirements of playing the game in terms of the balance between using intellect, body skills, and chance will be informed by the sensitivity of

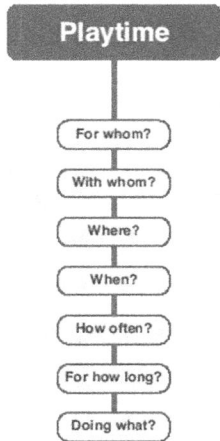

Figure 2.4 Using Playtime as an open starting point

Source: The Design and Technology Association, www.designtechnology.org.uk

the learner to the likely capabilities of elderly people, and this reveals something of the learner's social and moral values.

Pause for thought

As you encourage learners to take values into account in their design decisions, it is possible that they might reveal values which are different from your own or not in line with the school ethos. How will you and your colleagues respond in this situation?

Andy Michell was for a long time the deputy CEO at the D&T Association, so he has ample experience and expertise in matters concerning the design & technology curriculum. In the following Thought Piece, he considers how different starting points might enable learners to integrate their knowledge, understanding, skill, and values in the way they make design decisions.

Starting points in D&T - *A Thought Piece Andy Mitchell*

Andy Mitchell is Ex-Deputy CEO, The Design and Technology Association.

Starting points for design & technology have always presented a challenge. So too the finishing point, i.e., what represents a worthy outcome must be considered. Sometimes we want student design activity to result in an artefact that is functional in all respects and for instance, illustrates values to do with craft and quality of finish. But at other times, freeing the student from the requirement to manufacture all aspects in a finished form is beneficial. It liberates the ability to be creative and allows them to address a much wider range of challenges if the resulting prototype or concept is not restricted to outcomes that can be made in the comparatively limited school environment.

Engaging with the processes of designing provides students with the opportunity to confront their own and other people's values. Teaching and learning design should require students to consider the validity of the perceived need and question if the use of consumable resources to manufacture an artefact is ethically sound, justifiable, or even really necessary. But it also leads to considering the concept of product life cycle analysis, the young designer being required to consider any proposals made from a 'cradle to grave' perspective. Prioritising environmental impact at the outset as part of the specification they draw up will have significant ramifications on what is ultimately proposed and help ensure the outcomes validity.

Creativity in Crisis (2002) illustrated the inputs required for creative activity: stimulus, context, reflection, knowledge, and skill as inputs into a four input AND gate. But it pointed out, this output will not lead to creative activity unless it takes place in a situation in which 'risky' activity is possible and this risk is managed. Hence these three conditions become inputs into a triple AND gate, which gives an output of creative activity providing all three inputs take place simultaneously.

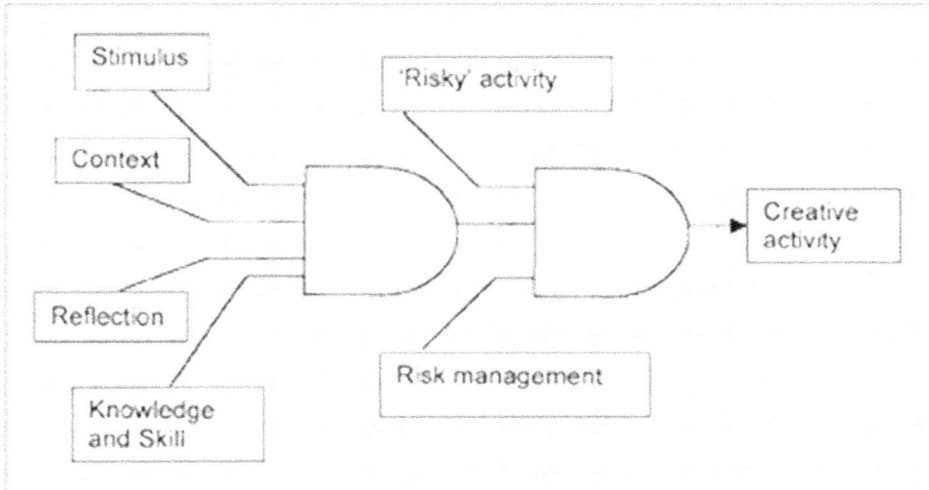

Figure 2.5 Inputs required for creative activity

Let's explore two scenarios where the teacher can manage open tasks in ways that encourage risk taking, values thinking, and creativity, allowing learners to retain ownership of the task but at the same time be protected from failure.

The first example of the board game referred to in the main text, illustrates how the teacher, starting with a theme encourages students to either work to a design brief they develop together as a class or their own individual variations.

The substantive knowledge the teacher has identified, includes simple use of computer aided design/manufacture (CAD/CAM), together with the use of both laser cutter and fused deposition modelling (FDM) 3D printing. In addition, they want to introduce the concept of material properties, and a range of related environmental factors associated with their proposal in terms of product lifecycle. Students will also be required to consider alternatives, some of which might utilise low tech and natural resources.

Having provided sufficient stimulus, a wide range of design ideas will be generated (either individually or in groups), giving rise to valuable discussion. Decisions over construction materials, means of production, cost, and feasibility within the time constraints will have been made. But importantly, the resource needs, type and levels of teacher intervention needed to support learning can be largely anticipated and planned for. Ultimately, a range of working prototypes including boards and 3D printed pieces will result that can then be tested and evaluated by both intended users and students.

But in order to a develop a wide range of substantive and disciplinary knowledge, it is not always necessary to have such a functional prototype as the outcome. Removal of the need to manufacture does not remove the need to consider materials and manufacturing methods (if indeed a physical product is the outcome). But it does eliminate some of the logistical challenges for both students and teacher. It also liberates time for experiencing design decisions making, resulting in a proof-of-concept presentation. Engaging with more open design challenges where the teacher is able to retain control over much of the learning focus, is a way of achieving this. So, what might that look like in practice?

In this second scenario, the teacher wishes to engage students in design thinking. Design thinking is a non-linear, iterative process that teams use to understand users, challenge assumptions, redefine problems, and create innovative solutions to prototype and test. The context presented is entitled 'Where have all the bees gone?' and focuses on the emerging global problem of a shortage of insects to pollinate plants. Students will have their awareness of the issue raised by the use of video and text accessed online. Input for students to draw upon, will be provided in person or virtually, by experts, such as local beekeepers, biologists, or local authority environmental officers. Additional support from the school biology teacher will offer a source of information for both students and teacher as the work progresses. As the activity lends itself to group work, after initial input, the teacher establishes four groups of students, each being required to complete further investigation and come up with its own design brief. (This means that the teacher has less individual activities to know about and support.) In this scenario, proposals will range widely. They could include physical products, for example manufactured habitats to support insect activity and well-being; systems and devices to allow scientists and others to monitor insect activity, or information campaigns to influence and encourage individuals, groups, and industry to act responsibly and take steps to cease harmful environmental practice. The teacher provides access to resources that are both of interest to all but increasingly focus on the individual task or sub task in a group. Responsibility is given to individuals to record the part that they play in the process. This along with their participation in the final presentation of the concept will contribute to their assessment.

What are we to make of Andy's position on enhancing the possibility of creative activity through tasks that require designing without the follow through of producing fully functional prototypes. His example deals with a significant global problem and provides the learners with opportunities to conceive solutions that are realistic and can be justified. Confronting such global problems is inevitably daunting for learners and can easily lead to feelings of hopelessness and impotence. Yet here we have an example which enables young learners to tackle a global problem and develop viable solutions; a process leading to optimism and empowerment. It is worth noting that learners might revisit this task in the context of the GCSE contextual challenge and move to a position where they do actually produce a fully functional prototype for use within their local community.

Curriculum considerations

Too much time spent talking?

One of the difficulties sometimes faced when encouraging a class to discuss how values should inform their design & technology activities is that some learners who are particularly keen on making activities resent the time spent talking and withdraw their attention. How might you and colleagues address this situation?

Assessing values

Should you assess learners' value positions? If a learner expresses a value position at odds with those expected to be held, how should their position be assessed? Should the quality of their supporting arguments, as opposed to the value position itself, be the focus of the assessment?

Managing open starting points

The open starting point approach described above involves the teacher orchestrating a class discussion such that the learners identify design and make tasks that they consider worthwhile and to which they can commit. Constraining the discussion to ensure that the tasks are not over ambitious may result in learners losing ownership of the activity. Insufficient guidance, however, may lead to tasks that are beyond the learners' capabilities. Discussion with colleagues about how to address this dilemma will be important.

Relationships with other subjects

Developing a relationship through sharing formative assessment techniques

The usual suspects for relationships with design & technology are science and mathematics and this will be considered in the following section *Collaboration through STEM*, but before this it is worth asking whether design & technology might form a relationship with other subjects by using the same or similar formative assessment techniques? Learners need to become familiar with the way they are being assessed and given feedback, but if there are significant differences in the way this takes place in different subjects learners may become confused and are unlikely to see a bigger picture of how assessment is helping them improve across the board. It will be important to avoid a one-size-fits-all approach that forces in-appropriate assessment methods onto a subject. But it is easy to see the advantages if such sharing of assessment practice were possible. English teachers (and humanities teachers in general) use the idea of drafts of extended pieces of writing that are improved over time as successive drafts receive feedback and are edited in response. Some English teachers provide formative assessment on drafts using a minimalist technique called 'dot marking'. When using this approach, the teacher circulates the class with two highlighters – one orange, the other blue. Orange is used to indicate where an objective or part thereof has been met or demonstrated; the blue is for the student to 'try something new', to challenge their thinking and edit their work at that point. There are several variations:

- Just mark with orange or blue and walk away encouraging the learner to find and correct the specific error(s) or edit(s) required.
- Mark the work and prompt, i.e., 'spelling', 'vocabulary', or 'sense'.
- Mark the work and question the learner further. 'Which objective have you met here? / What else might you need to include in order to … ?', etc.

In design & technology extended writing is relatively rare as annotated sketching or bullet point lists are often the preferred way of working. However, the writing of performance evaluations of items designed and made by the learners does require extended writing. The idea of a draft might be important here, but a difficulty could be that often such evaluations get rushed as they are at the end of extended tasks when time is tight. However, having to write a draft which is then improved might give such writing more status and hence time. For this approach to be successful it is necessary that the teacher has a very clear set of expectations with regard to a written performance evaluation and has shared these with the learners.

Pause for thought

Might the dot marking approach be used when giving feedback on annotated sketches. Preliminary sketches are, well, preliminary and rarely reveal all that is needed to appreciate and develop emerging design ideas. Could using orange and blue dots to indicate what can stand and what needs development be possible?

Collaboration through STEM

It is very important that any form of curriculum collaboration between science, mathematics, and design & technology respects the legitimate differences between the subjects as well capitalising on areas of common interest. Science and design & technology are so significantly different from one another in their learning intentions that to subsume them under a 'science and technology' label is both illogical and highly dangerous to the education of young people. It is vital that in collaborating through STEM the integrity of the collaborating subjects is maintained. In simple terms science is concerned with *observing, exploring, and explaining* phenomenon in the natural world, whereas design & technology is concerned with *intervening* in the made and natural worlds often, though not always, using phenomenon revealed by science.

One way to maintain integrity is to plan on the basis of the utility-purpose model proposed by Janet Ainley and colleagues (2006). They argue that it is possible to engage the utility of some subjects in pursuing the learning purposes of others. Hence it should be possible to capitalise on the utility of mathematics and science in pursuing the learning purposes of design & technology. If one considers that a fundamental purpose of design & technology is for young people to learn how to make genuine design decisions then it is not difficult to see how such decisions can and ought to be informed by learning in mathematics and science. It is important that such decisions are genuine and authentic design decisions and not simply technical decisions contrived to support learning in mathematics and science. Ainley and colleagues also argue that there is mutual benefit in this arrangement. In utilizing mathematics and science learners will become more adept at these subjects, whilst at the same time enhancing their ability in design & technology.

This approach may be called 'teaching in the light of STEM' in that it requires the teacher of a STEM subject to 'look sideways' in the curriculum to see what learners have already been taught in other STEM subjects and to plan their teaching to take advantage of and reinforce this learning. Importantly such an approach is *not disruptive of the normal timetable*. It simply requires the teacher to know about what has already been taught in other subjects.

Of course, the challenge is to demonstrate the enhanced achievement in all the subjects involved. Three levels of impact evaluation are as follows:

Short term

Evidence can be collected from:

Lesson observation
Feedback from teachers
Feedback from pupils.

Medium term

Evidence can be collected from:

Assessment data
Option choices.

Long term

Evidence can be collected from:

Public examination results
Career choices and employment, further education, higher education destinations.

A subject leader in design & technology can play a significant role in supporting this evaluation to reveal the impact of such collaboration on the learning in all three subjects. Working with SLT she can influence the following:

- Which data will be collected in the short, medium, and long term?
- How to collect and collate this data

- How to interpret the data
- How to use the data to develop further or abandon the practice of 'teaching in the light of STEM'.

Pause for thought

If your department adopted a 'looking sideways in the light of STEM' approach in some of the work carried out and monitored its impact, what might be the results?

- Will it improve SLT's understanding of design & technology?
- Will it influence the value they give to design & technology?
- Will it improve science and mathematics teachers' understanding of design & technology?
- Will it influence the value they give to design & technology?

Serendipity

There will be occasions, hopefully very rare, when a teacher without design & technology teacher training or expertise will be timetabled to teach the subject. This is not an ideal situation, and the teacher will need a lot of support from other members of the department. But it does provide the opportunity for a teacher from outside the department to see first-hand what teaching design & technology is all about and appreciate its educational value. This experience might reveal links between the teacher's main teaching subject and design & technology and lead to curriculum collaboration. Similarly, the timetabling of a design & technology teacher to teach a different subject, say science, might lead to curriculum collaboration. Indeed, sometimes just having to take a cover lesson in another subject can bring insights that lead to collaboration.

Curriculum considerations

Assessment methods as a pathway to link with other subjects

The way design & technology might be assessed is discussed in detail in chapter 6, and in the above we have suggested that the way other subjects assess may be of use to design & technology. It is possible that the way design & technology is assessed might be useful to other subjects.

Maintaining subject integrity

The integrity of design & technology is important, and it is essential that links with other subjects do not compromise this.

Identifying the benefits of links

It is important that any links formed with other subjects are of mutual benefit and that this benefit can be demonstrated.

Summary

The chapter began with a discussion of the philosophy of technology using the ideas of Carl Mitcham that technology may be considered as artefacts, activities, knowledge, and volition along with possible attitudes towards technology. Technology as a controlling force in our lives was considered using the thinking of Kevin Kelly, Jacques Ellul, and Thomas Hughes. The philosophy of design was discussed next, exploring designing as an activity which shapes the made-world exemplified through a series of vignettes and the work of six iconic designers: Charles and Ray Eames, Milton Glaser, Margaret Calvert, Zaha Hadid, and Jony Ives, finishing with a critique of design activity which has led to designing for a small minority that is resulting in consuming the Earth's resources at an unsustainable rate and causing irretrievable damage to the world's ecosystems. The place of values in design & technology was considered next noting that any designing and making activity will embrace technical, social, economic, moral, environmental, and aesthetic values. The nature of and distinction between substantive and disciplinary knowledge was then discussed at length with the role they played in different learning activities explored. The interweaving of skills, knowledge and understanding and values within design & technology was discussed next with a focus on how starting points for the activity might affect this. Finally, the relationship with other subjects was considered from three perspectives: assessment methods, meeting the STEM agenda, and serendipitous curriculum encounters.

References

Ainley, J., Pratt, D., & Hansen, A. (2006) Connecting engagement and focus in pedagogic task design, *British Educational Research Journal*, 32(1): 23–38.
Barlex, D., & Steeg, T. (2017) *Big Ideas for Design & Technology*, https://dandtfordandt.wordpress.com/working-papers/big-ideas-for-dt/.
Berners-Lee, M. (2019) *There Is No Planet B*, Cambridge: Cambridge University Press.
Chochinov, A. (2009) In Pilloton, E., *Design Revolution*, London: Thames & Hudson.
Creativity in Crisis (2002) Report from a joint seminar held 10 September 2002 convened by Nuffield Design and Technology Design and the Design and Technology Association
de Vries. M. (2005) *Teaching about Technology* Dordecht, The Netherlands: Springer.
Ellen MacArthur Foundation, https://www.ellenmacarthurfoundation.org.
Ellul, J. (1964) *The Technological Society*, New York: Vintage.
Hallström, J. (2022) Embodying the past, designing the future: technological determinism reconsidered in technology education, *International Journal of Technology and Design Education*, 32: 17–31.
Harlen, W. (Ed) (2010) *Principles and Big Ideas of Science Education*. Hatfield, Herts: Association for Science Education.
Hughes, T. (1994) *Technological Momentum*, in Merrit Roe Smith & Leo Marx (Eds.), *Does Technology Drive History?* Massachusetts: MIT.
Kelly, K. (2010) *What Technology Wants*, New York: Penguin.
Lawson, B. (2004) *What Designers Know*, Oxford, UK: Elsevier.
Layton, D. (1993) *Technology's Challenge to Science Education*, Buckingham: Open University Press.

Mitcham, C. (1994) *Thinking Through Technology. The Path Between Engineering and Philosophy*, London: Chicago.

Nuffield Key Stage 3 Design & Technology Project, https://dandtfordandt.wordpress.com/resources/nuffield-ks3-dt-resources/.

Polak, P. (2007) *Design for the Other Ninety Percent*, in C. E. Smith (ed.), *Design for the Other 90%*, New York: Cooper-Hewitt, National Design Museum, Smithsonian Institute.

Ropohl, G. (1997). Knowledge types in technology, *International Journal of Technology and Design Education*, 7(1): 65–72.

Smith, C. (2011) *Design with the Other 90%: Cities*, New York: Cooper-Hewitt, National Design Museum, Smithsonian Institute.

Recommended reading

Banks, F., & Barlex, D. (2021) *Teaching STEM in the Secondary School*, Oxford: Routledge.

Dakers, J. R., Hallstrom J., & de Vries, M. J. (Eds.) (2019) *Reflections on Technology for Educational Practitioners Philosophers of Technology Inspiring Technology Education*, The Netherlands: Brill Sense.

Leonard, A. (2010) *The Story of Stuff*, New York: Simon and Schuster.

Martin, M. (2020) Values in Design and Technology, in Alison Hardy (Ed.), *Learning to Teach Design and Technology in the Secondary School*, Oxford: Routledge.

Myatt, M. (2018) *The Curriculum Gallimaufry to Coherence*. Woodbridge: John Catt.

Pilloton, E. (2009) *Design Revolution*, London: Thames & Hudson.

Von Mengersen, B., & Wilkinson, T. (2020) Question-Think-Learn: A pedagogy for Understanding the Material World, in Williams, P. J., & Barlex, D. (eds.), *Pedagogy for Technology Education in Secondary Schools*, Switzerland: Springer.

3 Important issues

Any curriculum has to operate in the context of its time and confront issues of significance in that time. Design & technology is no exception; the following five issues are particularly noteworthy. Each will be dealt with in turn.

- Decolonising design & technology
- Gender in design & technology
- Disruption
- Global warming
- Pollution and waste

Decolonising design & technology

Decolonising education is the process in which we rethink, reframe, and reconstruct the curricula and research that preserve the Europe-centred, colonial lens. This challenges a curriculum that has its roots in colonial epistemology, which centres and upholds the British Empire and the forms that it takes today. What this can look like in schooling is a white-washed retelling of the history of empire that speaks only to its 'successes', whilst omitting its evils, the voices of the oppressed, and the lasting legacy of imperialism today. Hence decolonising the curriculum can be seen as being of particular relevance to the history curriculum and involves acknowledging the stories and histories of countries which were impacted by the Empire. But decolonising the curriculum does not stop with history, and this section deals with decolonising the design & technology curriculum.

Before we consider decolonising our subject, it is important to define 'race' and 'ethnicity'. Erin Blakemore, writing in the *National Geographic* magazine (Blakemore, 2019) makes the following important points substantiated by reference to peer reviewed academic papers.

- Race may be defined as "a category of humankind that shares certain distinctive physical traits". Ethnicities may be more broadly defined as "large groups of people classed according to common racial, national, tribal, religious, linguistic, or cultural origin or background".

DOI: 10.4324/9781003008026-3

- "Race" is usually associated with biology and linked with physical characteristics such as skin colour or hair texture. "Ethnicity" is linked with cultural expression and identification. Importantly both are social constructs.
- Neither race nor ethnicity is detectable in the human genome. Humans do have genetic variations, some of which were once associated with ancestry from different parts of the world. But those variations cannot be tracked to distinct biological categories. Genetic tests cannot be used to verify or determine race or ethnicity.
- Though race has no genetic basis, the social concept of race still shapes human experiences. Racial bias fuels social exclusion, discrimination, and violence against people from certain social groups. In turn, racial prejudice confers social privilege to some, and social and physical disparities to others and is widely expressed in hierarchies that privilege people with white skin over people with darker skin colours.

There is considerable diversity within and across race and ethnicity in our society giving rise to a range of descriptors as identified by the UK government (see https://style.ons.gov.uk/house-style/race-and-ethnicity/). Certain descriptors are to be avoided: Black, Asian and minority ethnic (BAME), or Black and minority ethnic (BME) because these highlight some groups and not others, for example, Black and Asian people are specifically included but not people of a mixed ethnicity. Inconsistencies in their use mean it is unclear whether or not these terms include White minority groups, and user research has found the acronyms BAME and BME were not well understood by users. The terms "minoritized people or people from minoritized backgrounds" has been suggested by David Gillborn (2008).

A key question for us in considering decolonising our subject thus becomes, 'How might a design & technology curriculum enhance or diminish the engagement and success of learners from minoritized backgrounds?' In chapter 1 we identified four justifications for teaching all young people design & technology: personal empowerment, preparation for citizenship, cultural transmission, and preparation for work, particularly in STEM occupations. Each of these justifications are equally appropriate for all young people whatever their race or ethnicity. For this to be achieved it is essential that all learners 'feel at home' within the design & technology curriculum echoing the point made by Maya Angelou in *All God's Children Need Travelling Shoes*: "The ache for home lives in all of us, the safe place where we can go as we are and not be questioned".

Multiple factors contribute to making the design & technology curriculum a safe place as envisaged by Maya Angelou, a place where all learners can be themselves and thrive in their learning. But for learners from minoritized backgrounds, there are particular concerns. How does it feel to identify oneself or be identified as coming from a minoritized background? Such identities are seldom homogeneous. But they are significant especially if identifying as, or being identified as, a minoritized learner becomes synonymous with stereotypical teacher expectations which are sometimes but not always low.

Akala (2019) describes in heart rending detail how he was treated at primary school by teachers who seemed unable to respond positively to a highly intelligent and articulate minoritized learner. His personal history indicates that one teacher was suggesting that minoritized learners in England today should be grateful to iconic White figures such as William Wilberforce for abolishing slavery. Even at the age 7 he could see that the statement

'William Wilberforce abolished slavery', a two-century old human trafficking industry, as stated by his teacher, was ridiculous and that the abolition of slavery was a hard won and torturous business involving multiple stakeholders over time with the roots of this activity still playing out in our society today. This example reveals poor subject knowledge on the part of the teacher leading to the promulgating of inaccurate information about abolition. This is a stark reminder that if we are to decolonise the design & technology curriculum, teachers will need to revisit and revise the subject knowledge that informs the curriculum. The following example is relevant and instructive. In both science and design & technology lessons the advantages of replacing filament lamp bulbs with LEDs is often discussed with reference to those involved in the original development of the filament lamp (Panel 3.1). How often in such lessons does Lewis Howard Latimer get mentioned?

Three points are worth making here with regard to the revisiting and revising of the design & technology curriculum in the context of decolonization:

- There are historical inventions that are relevant to the design & technology curriculum and that were achieved by or with the help of inventors from minoritized backgrounds, and more of these should feature in our design & technology curricula.
- Many such examples are not widely known about in society as a whole, by teachers or by learners (irrespective of their ethnicity), so misconceptions about who can be an inventor are widespread across parents, learners, and teachers.

Panel 3.1 The light bulb – an example where a Black inventor has been written out of the popular history

The light bulb shouldn't be credited to one inventor. It was a series of small improvements on the ideas of previous inventors that have led to the filament light bulbs that until recently were used almost universally in our homes. In the public consciousness it is Thomas Edison who is credited with the invention of the light bulb, but as with many inventions it was a team of people who were involved. When Edison and his researchers at Menlo Park came onto the lighting scene, they focused on improving the filament, first testing carbon, then platinum, before finally returning to a carbon filament. By October 1879, Edison's team had produced a light bulb with a carbonized filament of uncoated cotton thread that could last for 14.5 hours. They continued to experiment with the filament until settling on one made from bamboo that gave Edison's lamps a lifetime of up to 1,200 hours. This filament became the standard for the Edison bulb for the next 10 years. Edison's team also made other improvements to the light bulb, including creating a better vacuum pump to fully remove the air from the bulb and developing the Edison screw (which is now one of the standard socket fittings for light bulbs). What is less generally known is that Lewis Howard Latimer (September 4, 1848 – December 11, 1928), a minoritized American working with Hira Maxim, a rival of Thomas Edison, had invented a modification to the process for making carbon filaments which aimed to reduce breakages during the carbonization process. This modification consisted of placing filament blanks inside a cardboard envelope during carbonization. He later became an important member of Edison's team. Latimer also developed a forerunner of the air conditioner called 'Apparatus for cooling and disinfecting' and pursued a patent on a safety elevator which prevented the riders from falling out and into the shaft.

For more information about Lewis Latimer visit https://www.lewislatimerhouse.org. For more information about the development of the light bulb visit https://www.energy.gov/articles/history-light-bulb#Incandescents.

- Co-operation between design & technology, science and history teachers could speed up the rectification of this inaccuracy in our respective subject curricula.

It is worth noting the work of the Aspires Project (Archer *et al.*, 2020). This extensive and long-term piece of research into learners' science identity and aspiration revealed the significance of the dominant educational and social representations of science which included masculine science and clever science indicating that science was seen as being really only for men and clever men at that. If minoritized learners don't see themselves in the design & technology curriculum, then it does not provide for them Maya Angelou's safe place in which they can be themselves and thrive.

The Aspires Project recommended that dominant representations should be challenged, so it is worth mentioning the book *Superheroes Inspiring Stories of Secret Strength* (Thakur, 2021), (Figure 3.1).

The introduction by Stormzy reads as follows:

> When I was younger, I used to MC in the school playground and in my local area, spitting with my friends and telling stories. Music has always been a huge part of my life, but at the time, I didn't understand that it was a talent – that it was my superpower and it made me unique.
>
> Growing up in South London as a young Black man from an under privileged background, there weren't many role models that I could aspire to be like. There came a moment when that changed, and I realised that I could turn my superpower into something extraordinary. I was at home watching Channel U and saw other people that looked like me – artists making waves in the music scene and being successful. It was then that I was inspired to start my own journey (page 1).

There then follows 51 double-page spreads each celebrating a minoritized person superhero identifying their power and the tool they use to execute that power. Each spread is divided into a page of text and a page with an arresting illustration of the superhero, providing high impact visual representation.

In challenging the dominant representations in the design & technology curriculum the following examples of minoritized people being highly successful are good starting points.

Harry Bhadeshia

If you travel from the UK to France via the channel tunnel, your carriage is riding on rails made of a particular kind of steel that Harry Bhadeshia invented. He has also developed the world's strongest armour – called 'super bainite' – in part through the discovery of a steel that seemed to sing. He has done all of this and more by applying physics and mathematics to predict what shapes will be made by crystals in metal, under certain conditions and with certain elements added or taken away. He arrived in London in 1970 after his Indian parents were forced to leave their home in Kenya by political changes. As a young teenager he has worked his way up from technician, through part-time study, to become the University of Cambridge's Tata Steel Professor of Metallurgy. See Harry's story at https://www.youtube.com/watch?v=jZUiTRTsynA.

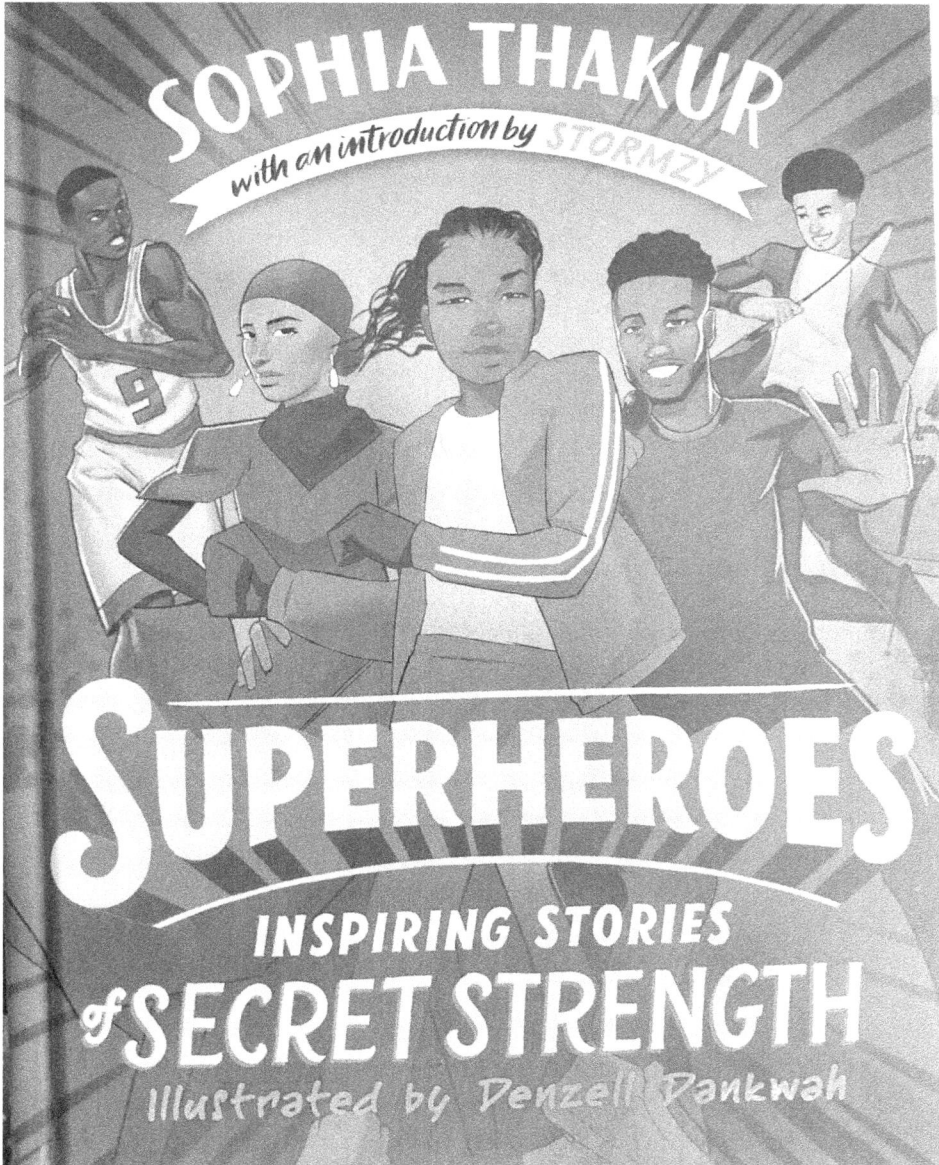

Figure 3.1 A book that challenges dominant representations

Jo Shien Ng

Jo Shien Ng works to develop more and more sensitive electrical components called 'avalanche photodiodes' used in everything from satellites that look at the Earth from space, to body scanners in hospitals and airports. She does this by applying an understanding of the behaviour of materials developed through secondary and further education at a Chinese school in Malaysia, and a degree and PhD at the University of Sheffield, UK. She explains that she is not intimidated by being often the only female scientist in technical meetings – her expertise is clear: "What I say goes". See Jo Shien's story at https://www.youtube.com/watch?v=mmqnI3C9qIM.

Elsie Owusu

Architect and Specialist Conservation Architect, interior and urban designer, Elsie has a wide expertise in transport and infrastructure, as well as the issues facing emerging economies. Passionate about contemporary architecture and city planning, she is particularly fascinated by their relationship to the arts in general, and the specific work of individual artists.

Elsie is also director of ArchQuestra, which provides the best of British architecture, art, and engineering to support emerging economies. You can find out more about Elsie and her company Elsie Owusu Architects at http://www.owusu.uk/index.html.

Karim Rashid

Karim Rashid is an Egyptian-born and Canadian-raised industrial designer. His designs include buildings, luxury goods, furniture, lighting, surface design, brand identity, and packaging. *Time* magazine has described him as the "most famous industrial designer in all the Americas". He is noted for saying, "For the longest time design only existed for the elite and for a small insular culture. I have worked hard for the last 30 years trying to make design a public subject". You can find out more about Karim and his work at https://www.karimrashid.com.

It is encouraging to note that AQA (2022) has added 12 new minoritized designers to their GCSE Design and Technology (8552) specification ready for first teaching in September 2022.

Akala (2019, p. 35) notes that there are some who believe that if we don't talk about it, then issues around race will simply disappear. Nothing could be further from the truth as he demonstrates with this paragraph.

> *In reality, the idea of race has been one of the most important ideas in the modern world, it has underpinned centuries of enslavement, justified genocide and been used to decide the demarcation lines between who lives and who dies, who gets to access rights of citizenship, property, migration and the vote. To not want to debate, discuss and deal with an idea that has been so impactful reveals a palpable lack of interest in humanity, or at least certain portions of it.*

Pause for thought

It is essential that we think about learners' design & technology identity and aspirations and devise ways to enhance this with special consideration for minoritized learners who might find that they cannot 'see themselves' in our current curriculum offerings. One way for teachers to do this is to read about the minoritized experience. Two books which are worth considering are shown in Figure 3.2.

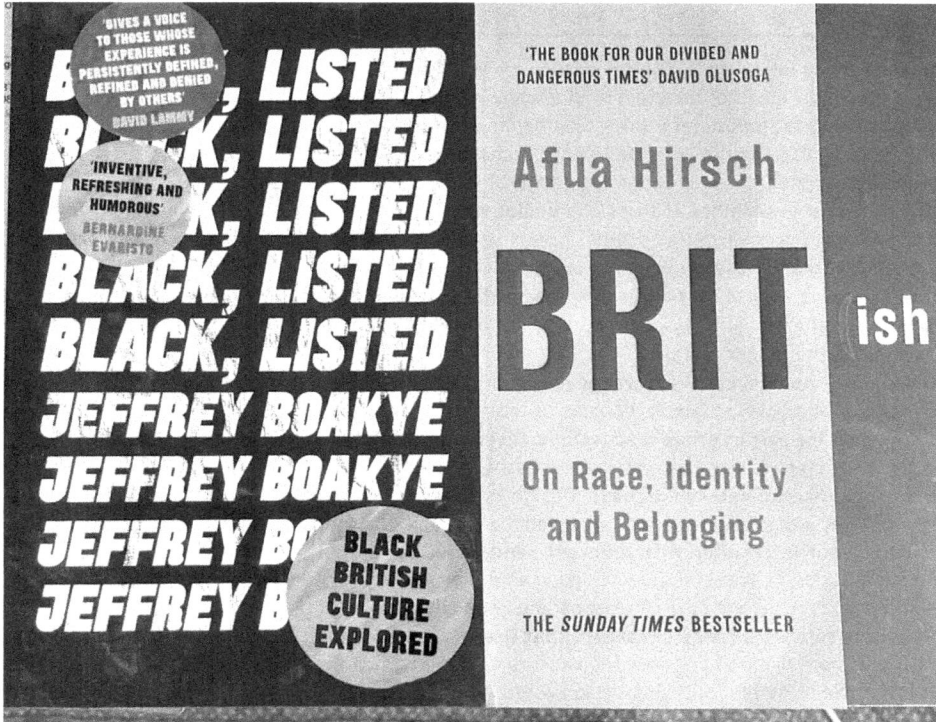

Figure 3.2 Two important books relevant to decolonising design & technology

These may not provide comfortable reading, particularly for those who are unfamiliar with the history of minoritized people, but it is essential that voices such as those of Jeffrey Boakye and Afua Hirsch are heard. Reading about the subject is not enough, what such authors have to say needs to be discussed and debated by design & technology teachers. Such conversations will not always be easy, and there will almost certainly be disagreements as different points of view are discussed. It will be important to embrace the complexity of the situations under discussion as to deny this will not reveal their truth. What is imperative is that as we engage in those conversations, we are able to 'disagree well' which will entail listening to the views we might disagree with without becoming angry and a willingness to change our mind.

Gender

In chapter 1 we identified four justifications for teaching all young people design & tech-nology: personal empowerment, preparation for citizenship, cultural transmission, and pre-paration for work, particularly in STEM occupations. Each of these justifications are equally appropriate for both boys and girls, yet we find that this isn't always reflected in girls' career choices or society's expectations of how young women or young men should operate in the world. Many of the influences contributing to gender stereotyping are outside our control

Panel 3.2 Ten classroom practices to support both girls and boys in design & technology

1 **Use everyday language**. Technical jargon can be intimidating for many learners. Avoid it and make sure that you only introduce technical language once the context is understood.

2 **Avoid asking for volunteers**. Boys may be more likely to raise their hands, call out answers, and volunteer to take part in activities. Other techniques, such as individual whiteboards or selecting students at random, can broaden the range of students participating.

3 **Ensure equal availability of tools and equipment.** Boys often dominate the equipment while girls hang back and concentrate on written work. To avoid this, especially when resources are limited, you can assign roles or use single-sex groups.

4 **Use examples that show how technical knowledge and understanding links to their experience.** This is useful for all learners, but research shows that girls in particular tend to appreciate context and seeing the bigger picture.

5 **Use gender-neutral contexts whenever possible.** Try to avoid using examples that focus on stereotypically male or female hobbies or interests.

6 **Allow time for pair or group discussions.** Give time for learners to discuss answers to challenging questions before asking them to share ideas with the class.

7 **Challenge discriminatory language.** Design & technology is for everyone. School policy should require that sexist language is unacceptable and tackle the attitudes behind it.

8 **Monitor your interaction with different genders.** You might be surprised at the ratio of different genders asking or answering questions in your class. Keep a note yourself or ask a colleague or learner to observe one of your lessons and keep count.

9 **Regularly refer to a range of careers that use design & technology-based knowledge and skills.** Girls are more likely to consider their future career when choosing their options. Emphasise the transferable skills that studying design & technology helps to develop.

10 **Ensure that your students are exposed to a diverse range of design & technology practitioners**. Be wary of giving your learners the impression that design & technology is only for those who are 'practical' achievers. Emphasise that design & technology is for everyone, irrespective of their background.

but we can, in our classrooms, take steps to challenge them. The Institute of Physics has made a list of 10 classroom practices that supports both girls and boys across STEM subjects which we can adapt specifically for design & technology as shown in Panel 3.2.

The personal empowerment achieved through studying design & technology provides young people with, amongst other things, practical problem-solving abilities. In the recent past these have been gendered in that it was seen, for example, as in setting up and maintaining a domestic environment the norm was for men to be responsible for activities involving resistant materials and related tools and equipment whilst women dealt with tasks involving fabrics such as dress making, furnishings, and washing and ironing. In a broad and balanced design & technology curriculum, both boys and girls will develop skills sets than enable both to operate successfully across this divide.

There is no doubt that technologies current, new, and emerging are having a significant impact on our lives often giving rise to questions and disputes that are contentious. Preparation for citizenship enables individuals to contribute significantly and intelligently to such debates and is a core function of an education in design & technology and this applies equally to both boys and girls. An individual's ability to respond to challenges facing the world should in no way be curtailed by their gender. Appreciation of the grand narratives of technology that explain to some extent the way we have lived in the past, are living now and might live in the future provides all young people with a sense of personal possibilities in how they envisage and might contribute to a future worth wanting. This cultural transmission underpins the way in which young people look at the world and identify their place in it. In celebrating the individuals who have played a significant part in developing and implementing technology in the past and present, it is essential that the role of women is given a high profile if girls at school are to see themselves as being engaged and involved in the future.

Hilda remembers hearing a colleague describe a conversation between herself and her father when discussing subject choices at A level in the 1960s. Hilda's colleague wanted to take A level mathematics to which her father replied, "What's the point in that; you can't be an engineer". Things have certainly changed for the better between then and now, but in many technical fields there is still a preponderance of men. This is often portrayed through articles under the broad heading of Women in STEM. *New Scientist* regularly includes a promotional supplement about this. The following from the issue published on 25 June 2022 is worthy of note. Across the piece a range of STEM industries are considered including energy, manufacturing, health care, Formula 1 racing, aerospace, national security, and medical device development with each featuring a woman who has been successful in these fields providing positive role models for students. In each case there are enthusiastic profiles and comments from these women.

Elizabeth Donnelly, CEO Women's Engineering Society, makes some useful observations:

- Research from Engineering UK (March 2022) shows that 16.5% of the engineering workforce are female compared to 10.5% in 2010.
- The critical decisions around GCSEs shouldn't inadvertently make it harder for girls to eventually move into STEM related occupations by having opted out of STEM related subjects early on.
- Quoting Marian Wright Edelman, Founder and President of the Children's Defense Fund, "You can't be what you can't see" emphasising the importance of role models.

It is worth noting that there is an acknowledged shortage of engineers in the UK with 50% of employers expecting to find a shortage of suitable candidates for engineering roles in 2019, up from 34% in 2017 (Cole, 2019). Increasing the number of women entering the engineering profession could go some way to reducing this deficit.

Natasha Engel, Chief Executive of Policy Connect, is less sanguine noting that whilst women make up half the population, only 14.5% of the engineering workforce are female (16.5% according to Engineering UK), so clearly a long way to go. She also points out that the general public see manufacturing as involving dirty overalls and loud machines and the sector needs to address this poor perception issue. Her plea is that if we want to meet net zero by 2050, more young people, especially women, need to become engineers and for that to happen manufacturing urgently needs a rebrand.

Nicola Brittain, Chief Editor of WISE, writes about unconscious bias making the strong point that recognising that this exists is insufficient; and that training should be used to raise awareness of the role many of us play, albeit unwittingly, in perpetuating stereotypes. This relates strongly to the Institute of Physics' list of 10 classroom practices that supports both girls and boys across STEM subjects referred to earlier.

The importance of design & technology in providing an experience that can mirror that of working in a STEM career is worthy of note here. And with this in mind we turn to a Thought Piece from Ulrika Sultan, who has carried out significant research into girls and technology education.

Gender for design & technology teachers – *A Thought Piece by Ulrika Sultan*

Ulrika Sultan is an educator, and researcher at Örebro University, Sweden.

The main issue that I struggle with is why we are so keen on sorting our pupils in binary. Binary as in boys and girls instead of seeing them as individuals. What would happen to the way we are thinking if we saw Carrie and Mohammed as individuals first and not as biological sex first? I know I am generalizing, but when we (teachers, researchers, and society) talk about education, we often fall into the gendered trap. We do it because that is how our society is shaped. From the first day a child is born, we ask – is it a boy or a girl? And so, it continues. We carry bias and stereotypical images of girls and boys that will shape whom we think is more interested in one subject than another. We carry these images not because we are bad people but because we, too, are constructions of the society and context we live in.

It is worth considering 'gender stereotypes'. These are widespread views or preconceptions about attributes, characteristics, or the roles that are, or ought to be, owned by or performed by girls, boys, women, and men. For example, one gender stereotype of boys is that boys are naturally interested in technical matters and will go into technical careers; the corollary of this is that such interests and career paths are unlikely for girls. For girls, one gender stereotype is that they are naturally sensitive and nurturing and will go into the caring professions. The corollary of this is that such qualities and career paths are unlikely for boys. Such gender stereotypes are harmful when they limit a person's ability for personal growth to pursue a specific career and/or make choices about their lives.

However, using these gendered spectacles does lead to some interesting thoughts. In many western countries, girls outperform boys when assessed for knowledge in STEM. Why is this? We can argue that they are not seen or expected to be a part of that world and hence overperform to prove themselves. For example, in Sweden, a report from the Association of Swedish Engineering Industries showed how choosing to study technology is a complex choice for girls.

My conversations with girls indicate that they say they feel the pressure of needing to have more knowledge and interest in technology compared to boys, who because of gender stereotype expectations can choose to study the subject even without expressing any interest. This is telling us boys feel more welcomed to studying technology, so much so that they do not even have to show interest or knowledge in it. So, what can we do? Changing bias, norms, and stereotypes is hard. But the first step is to be aware of them. When aware, it can be called out and shifted, and we can make a push forward to a more inclusive, non-stereotyped world.

Links to resources for further thinking and practical actions are given in Panel 3.3 below.

Panel 3.3 Resources for further thinking and practical action with regard to gender

Online resource for possible lessons in challenging societal biases:
The Unstereotype Alliance. This is a thought and action platform that seeks to eradicate harmful stereotypes in all media and advertising content, https://www.unstereotypealliance. org/en.

Research providing a practical checklist:
Dierickx, Eva; Luyckx, Kato; Ardies, Jan. *Are my technology lessons for girls? The gender sensitive education checklist (GSEC) for teaching science and technology,* <https://ojs.lboro.ac. uk/date/article/view/3199>.

Videos for more insights on our biases and stereotypes:
Girl toys vs boy toys: The experiment - BBC Stories.
The Experiment: Are you sure you don't gender-stereotype children in the toys you choose for them? https://youtu.be/nWu44AqFOiI.

A Gendered World Makes a Gendered Brain, Gina Rippon TEDxCardiff
Professor Gina Rippon explains the role that neuroscience can play in helping us better understand gender and sex differences, or the lack of them. Gina Rippon's research involves state-of-the-art brain imaging techniques to investigate how the brain interacts with its world, and what happens when this process goes wrong, https://youtu.be/2s1hrHppl5E.

What are we to make of Ulrika's Thought Piece? Our first response must surely be to take up her challenge of becoming more aware of gender stereotypes, and when meeting them in the content of our curriculum and the way we teach, adapt our practice accordingly. This will require us to interrogate our practice at different levels. Some of the changes to be made will be obvious, others will require more subtle thinking and nuanced responses. A case in point is the idea of activities being gender neutral. A more subtle and perhaps more effective approach might be to introduce activities in ways that were gender sensitive such that both boys and girls are enabled to cross the gender stereotype divide. Viewing the world through a critical eye, another important feature of our subject can be subject to gender stereotyping. It is well known that girls tend to respond more positively and creatively to technical challenges when these are placed in context. The drawing of systems boundaries in developing solutions, for example, can widen contextual considerations (Banks & Barlex, 2021)

Enabling boys to appreciate context constraints and opportunities associated with technical challenges would be a powerful way of challenging gender stereotypes.

Disruption

It is generally agreed that the successful introduction of new technologies into a society has an impact on that society, but some technologies have a more significant and often long-term effect on society in general across the globe. Such technologies are termed 'disruptive'. The introduction of the moveable type printing press in 1450 is a good example. At that time the impact of being able to quickly print multiple copies of posters, leaflets, pamphlets, and books spread quickly across Europe and then across the rest of the world. Now given the speed of global communication the impact of disruptive technologies can be even more rapid. The McKinsey Global Institute (Manyika *et al.*, 2013) has suggested some features that mark out a technology as having the potential to be disruptive. Each feature is exemplified below through the impact of the popularisation of photography at the beginning of the 20th century.

- They upset the status quo, for example, overturning existing hierarchies and offering the possibilities of both more and less democratic hierarchies.

   The advent of an easy-to-use camera accompanied by an inexpensive service to develop the negatives and produce black and white prints by George Kodak gave the general populace access to photography which had hitherto only been available to rich people with specialist knowledge.

- They alter the way people live and work, for example, increasing or decreasing employment opportunities, changing the knowledge and skills required for certain kinds of employment, shifting the expectations of education systems and altering relationships.

   Enabling ordinary people to take photographs altered the way people worked in providing employment for darkroom technicians who processed the film and the way people lived in providing a popular hobby.

- They reorganise financial and social structures, for example, by redistributing financial rewards towards those who are deploying these technologies.

   The Eastman Company became financially very successful in a market that had not previously existed and enabled the employment of photographers in many different industries.

- They lead to entirely new products and services.

   Cameras for the domestic market became more sophisticated as people learned more about photography and wanted to take better photographs leading to the development of the single lens reflex camera, the use of light meters, light meters becoming integrated into the cameras and the availability of coloured film.

Note that the success of the Eastman and Kodak Companies has not been indefinite. The rise of digital photography (ironically first developed by Kodak engineers) has all but eliminated the use of cameras with film that require developing so we have an example of a new technology displacing a technology that was in its day disruptive.

The authors, working with Nick Givens, have identified, and discussed nine disruptive technologies we consider highly suitable for inclusion in the secondary school curriculum (Barlex, Givens, & Steeg, 2020). These are listed with brief descriptions in Table 3.1.

Table 3.1 Disruptive technologies suitable for inclusion in the secondary school curriculum

The technology	*The description*
Additive manufacture (AM)	AM involves fabricating physical objects in successive thin horizontal layers, according to digital models derived from CAD designs, 3-D scans, or video games. Such printing can take place at different scales from nano structures to complete buildings and may involve a wide range of materials: human tissue, electronics, and food as well as traditional industrial product materials.
Artificial intelligence (AI)	AI can be categorized at three different levels. First is 'narrow' AI that specializes in one area, e.g., the AI that plays games such as chess or Go better than humans. Some AI are used in collaboration with humans, in the judicial system, for example. The second and third levels are concerned with more general ability. 'General' AI can perform as well as a human across the board, i.e., it is AI that can perform any intellectual task that a human can. Such AI is yet to be developed. Third is 'super intelligent' AI, i.e., an AI that performs better than human brains in practically every field.
Augmented reality (AR)	Augmented reality (AR) is a live, direct or indirect, view of a physical real-world environment whose elements are augmented (or supplemented) by computer generated sensory input such as sound, video, graphics, or GPS data.
Big data	Big data is data that exceeds the processing capacity of conventional database systems. The data is too big, moves too fast, or doesn't fit the strictures of standard database architectures. It is collected by large corporations and governments (and increasingly open data from 'citizen' scientists) and using big data analytics it can give insights into the behaviour of potential consumers and citizens.
Programmable matter	Imagine a product made up of fine-grained computing elements (in much the way that you are made up of cells). The way these elements are programmed, including their response to physical stimuli, can affect the physical properties of the bulk object, such as shape, texture, colour, conductivity, transparency, and so on. This is programmable matter. Currently, the smallest programmable elements are ~10mm-sized, but there are active research projects aimed at driving this size down.

Table 3.1 Disruptive technologies suitable for inclusion in the secondary school curriculum (Continued)

The technology	The description
Internet of Things (IoT)	The Internet of Things (IoT) is the networking of physical objects, i.e., things that have embedded electronics, software and sensors which are connected to one another over the Internet and can exchange data. This allows extensive communication between the physical and digital worlds, enables remote control of devices across the Internet, and produces vast amounts of big data. The successive roll outs from 3G, 4G, and now 5G, each offering increased download speed and reduced latency, increases the significance of the IoT.
Neuro-technology	Neuro-technology is concerned with technologies that inform about and influence the behaviour of the brain and various aspects of consciousness. Current neurotechnologies include various means to image brain activity, stimulation of the brain by magnetism and electricity, measuring the electrical and magnetic brainwave activity, implant technology to monitor or regulate brain activity, pharmaceuticals to support neurotypical brain function, and stem cell therapy to repair damaged brain tissue. Recently measurements of brain activity have been used to control real world artefacts.
Robotics	A robot may be defined as "a machine that carries out a physical task autonomously using a combination of embedded software and data provided by sensors". This definition embraces relatively simple robots such as the Roomba vacuum cleaner to extremely complex robots such as the Google self-driving car.
Synthetic biology	Synthetic biology is the process of designing and creating artificial genes and implanting them in cells. In some cases, all existing genes have been removed; in others the new genetic sequences are introduced into the DNA of existing cells. It is far more than simply borrowing existing genes from nature. Synthetic biology is the process by which completely new life forms, i.e., life forms that have never previously existed, are created.

Where in the curriculum might disruption be taught?

It is of course important that the legitimate differences between the subjects are acknowledged, and one such difference is the knowledge base that informs the subject. Hence some of the disruptive technologies that we have identified have a stronger base in the design & technology curriculum than others whilst some might find their place in other subjects. In Table 3.2 we have allocated our chosen disruptive technologies to design & technology, science, and computer science but it is important to realise that this is not a hard and fast allocation as some aspects of most of the disruptive technologies could legitimately be taught in all three subjects.

We think it is important that teachers have the subject knowledge necessary to respond fluently and authoritatively when dealing with the complexities inherent in teaching disruptive technologies, but this should not mean that any one disruptive technology becomes locked in a subject silo. Although synthetic biology, for example, may be more expertly taught by science

Table 3.2 Distribution of disruptive technologies in STEM subjects

The technology	Taught in design & technology	Taught in science	Taught in computer science
Additive manufacture (AM)	✓		
Artificial intelligence (AI)			✓
Augmented reality (AR)	✓		
Big data			✓
Programmable matter	✓	✓	
Internet of Things (IoT)	✓		✓
Neuro-technology	✓	✓	
Robotics	✓		
Synthetic biology		✓	

teachers, there is no reason why the implications of synthetic biology, particularly the development of new organisms to produce new materials and new approaches to environmental management, cannot be considered in design & technology classes. The keys to success here are the conversations that take place between the science and design & technology teachers to ensure that any learning about synthetic biology in design & technology is underpinned by sound science. Similarly, an understanding of Big Data is probably better taught by the computer science teacher but the implications of Big Data, say, for new product development might well be considered in design & technology. Conversations between the teachers from the different subjects are essential for success. And it is important to remember that this is a 'two-way street'.

Categories of disruption

We think that three categories of disruption: incidental, intentional, and cultural are useful. **Incidental disruption** may be seen as the result of a new and emerging technology that was developed, as are most technologies, with the intention of solving a particular problem and/or providing financial gain for those who invest in the technology. It was not conceived or implemented with the express intention of causing disruption; but disruption, as defined by the McKinsey Global Institute, happened nonetheless. The example of the easy-to-use camera accompanied by an inexpensive service to develop the negatives and produce black and white prints described above falls into this category. There are some technologists who develop products with the **deliberate intention of disruption**. This is the case for Ken Gabriel who managed the development of an automated cancer therapy treatment from a starting point that used 17 different machines, took up to 22 days to develop the therapy from the blood, and cost up to $450,000 per treatment. He set his engineers the target of producing an automated system within a single piece of equipment within a x10 framework; that is, it was to cost ten times less and work ten times faster. He described this work as "intentionally disruptive" (Gabriel, 2019). **Cultural disruption** is perhaps the most thought provoking. The philosopher Christopher J. Preston has written at length in his book *The Synthetic Age* (Preston, 2018) about the way our development and deployment of technologies in recent years is fundamentally changing our relationship with Planet Earth, with nature and with what it might mean to be human. He identifies the following:

- the production of nanomaterials, the like of which cannot be produced in nature,
- the use of AI to solve immensely complex problems beyond the scope of ordinary humans, and
- the use of synthetic biology and neuro-technology to augment humans to the point where we become a new species, no longer homo sapiens. Yuval Harari (2014) coined the name "Homo Deus", to describe humans with almost God-like powers to capture this change.

We should recognise that some new or emerging technologies, singly or in combination, may impact on the biosphere on a global scale in ways that may result in profound social and economic disruption. Preston (2018, p. 173) makes an eloquent and compelling plea for the involvement of *all* citizens in deciding what technologies to develop and how they should be deployed. He writes:

> *Making big choices is always hard. Making irrevocable choices for the whole planet is unprecedented. But at this point, we have changed too much to stand back and do nothing. We need to look at as many of the various options as we can, talk about them, argue about them, investigate and research them as thoroughly as possible. Conducting this discussion thoughtfully, fairly, and inclusively is perhaps the worthiest, and certainly the most important political task of our time. It is also one that we can no longer shirk.*

Possible disruption in everyday life - the case of transport

Additive manufacture and transport

If it becomes possible to print the products that people want at a price they can afford, then they could be manufactured on sites near to where the customers live. The transport of goods across the globe via long supply chains would become much reduced if not eliminated. Where will this leave all those employed in maintaining the supply chain? In some cases, people might have 3D printers at home, in much the same way as some have 2D printers now and be able to print small domestic items for themselves. How likely is this to happen do you think?

AI and transport

It is a common feature of airports now that passengers use kiosks linked to AI systems to check in themselves and their luggage without any human intervention. At the moment there is a parallel process involving humans at check-in desks and other humans are on hand to help with kiosk problems faced by passengers. The trend here will almost certainly be to minimise if not eliminate the use of humans at air transport hubs. Where will this leave those currently employed in check in tasks? How will it affect the quality of passenger experience?

Robotics and transport

Autonomous vehicles (AVs) are set to become a thing of the present before too long. And it will not be just road transport that is affected. Autonomous ships and aeroplanes are on the horizon. The safety issues and related liability problems when accidents do occur are being solved. The resultant unemployment for transportation operatives is a serious concern and some of the second order effects are interesting. In some cities large amounts of land are taken up with providing parking for cars that are used for commuting. When AVs are used on an as needed hire basis for journeys such as commuting, such space will not be needed and this might transform the appearance of cities and deprive local authorities of the significant income from parking fees. Do you think autonomous transport will become a reality within the lifetime of the young people you teach?

The above and other issues concerning transport of disruptive technologies are considered in greater depth in *Teaching about Disruption* (Barlex, Givens, & Steeg, 2021).

Asking learners about transport

You might use the following questions to explore with your learners their mobility expectations:

How many of you expect to drive at:

- 17 years old,
- 18–22 years old
- Sometime in your 20s
- Not in the foreseeable future.

If you do pass your driving test, how many of you would:

- Buy a car as soon as possible
- Borrow a family car
- Hire a car by the hour once old enough
- Hire a car by the day once old enough.

How do you think you will move about in your daily life?

- Walk
- Cycle
- Scooter
- Motorcycle
- Taxi
- Car – petrol engine
- Car – electric engine
- Bus/underground/metro/tram
- Train.

When you get a job, do you see yourself working:

* Entirely at home
* Mostly at home sometimes at your employer's location
* Sometimes at home but mostly at employer's location
* Entirely at employer's location
* How will this affect your transport requirements?

Using technology life cycle

You will be well versed in helping young people consider the so called 'life cycle' of products and have used such teaching to engage students in the environmental impact of not only the manufacture of products but also their use and disposal as a critique of consumerism and the need to move from a linear to a circular economy (MacArthur, 2015). Works such as *The Story of Stuff* (Leonard, 2010) have become standard items in teacher education reading lists. Looking at the emergence of a technology, its adoption, and impact on society is less familiar territory but particularly relevant to our concern with disruptive technologies. The Gartner Hype Cycle (Gartner, 2015) is an attempt to chart the life of a technology. It provides a graphic representation of the maturity and adoption of technologies and applications, and how they are potentially relevant to solving real business problems and exploiting new op-portunities. In its general form it is shown in Figure 3.3.

The key features of the cycle labelled in Figure 3.3 are as follows:

Technology Trigger: A potential technology breakthrough kicks things off. Early proof-of-concept stories and media interest trigger significant publicity. Often no usable products exist, and commercial viability is unproven.

Peak of Inflated Expectations: Early publicity produces several success stories, often accompanied by scores of failures. Some companies take action; many do not.

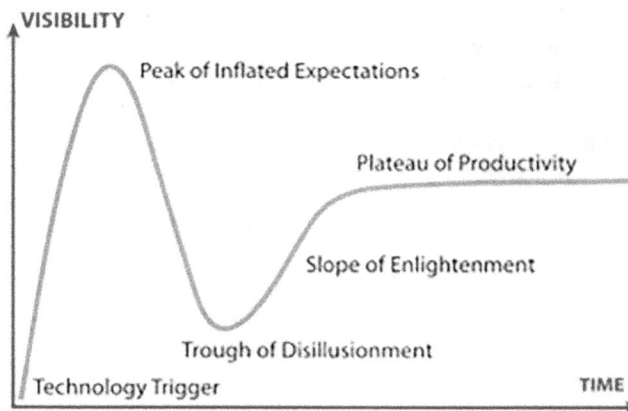

Figure 3.3 Gartner Hype Cycle in its general form

Trough of Disillusionment: Interest wanes as experiments and implementations fail to deliver. Producers of the technology shake out or fail. Investments continue only if the surviving providers improve their products to the satisfaction of early adopters.

Slope of Enlightenment: More instances of how the technology can benefit the enterprise start to crystallize and become more widely understood. Second- and third-generation products appear from technology providers. More enterprises fund pilots: conservative companies remain cautious.

Plateau of Productivity: Mainstream adoption starts to take off. Criteria for assessing provider viability are more clearly defined. The technology's broad market applicability and relevance are clearly paying off.

There are several ways you might engage learners. You could present the life cycle of a disruptive technology as a Gartner Hype Cycle within a case study and use 'pause for thought' and 'questions to answer' to engage the learners; essentially a comprehension exercise to develop technological perspective. Or you could provide information about a disruptive technology and require learners to work in groups to place the various pieces of information on the Hype Cycle curve. This is a more demanding activity and requires the learners to use their judgement. Or you could simply ask learners to investigate a disruptive technology and require them to present the results of their investigation as a Gartner Hype Cycle curve. This is a much more demanding approach. In any of these activities you could use an historical example where the life cycle of the technology is well known, e.g., the printing press or the radio, a contemporary example, or one of our disruptive technologies, in which the life cycle is far from complete. Our expectation is that this activity will intrigue learners.

Pause for thought

The importance of a bigger picture

The way that new and emerging technologies play out must be put into the context of the impact we are having on all other life forms on the Earth and on the behaviour of the planet itself. There is no doubt that human technological activity is the major cause of climate change. This disruption of planetary behaviour goes far beyond the commercial disruption envisaged in the McKinsey criteria for disruption. Aloc Sharma, summit president of COP 26, has stated unequivocally that more must be done to hit the targets agreed in Glasgow and failure would be "an act of monstrous self-harm" (Rowlattt, 2022). Some if not all of the disruptive technologies identified in Table 3.1 will have a key role in responding to climate change so it is important that this is explored in design & technology lessons.

It is in teaching critique, discussed in chapter 5, that you might consider disruption and as part of considering the consequences of technology discussed in chapter 4.

AI Stop Press

When Torben and Hilda in collaboration with Nick Givens developed their thinking on disruptive technologies they found that whilst there was agreement that AI had the potential for disruption, there was little in the way of interest in it from design & technology teachers as they concentrated their attention on disruptive technologies such as robotics and additive manufacture. As we were about to submit this manuscript this changed. In March 2023 key figures in artificial intelligence under the auspices of The Future of Life Institute signed an open letter warning of potential risks and say the race to develop AI systems is out of control (Vallance, 2023). The letter, which includes in its signatories Elon Musk, CEO of SpaceX, Tesla, and Twitter; Steve Wozniak, co-founder, Apple; and Yuval Noah Harari, author and professor, Hebrew University of Jerusalem asks that development be halted, temporarily warning of the risks future, more advanced systems might pose. It argues that AI systems with human-competitive intelligence can pose profound risks to society and humanity. Others are more sanguine (McCallum, 2022). For example, Martha Lane Fox has warned against becoming "too hysterical or hype-driven" over AI and that we should look more carefully at what is actually happening and how we can mitigate the risks and double down on the opportunities. She argues that there is no point in sitting here saying "AI going to destroy the world"; technology is speeding up and we have to decide whether we're going to digitise in a way that is ethical, that is inclusive, and that is sustainable. She is adamant that it is essential to get more diversity involved in developing the appropriate legislation.

In the months preceding the above, the use of the Chatbot ChatGPT in education caused concern. University students were using it to write coursework essays and were getting good marks! What to do about this is still under discussion. To explore what this might mean for design & technology, Hilda asked ChatGPT to describe a *design for a small moving toy that is powered by an electric motor and will appeal to a girl aged ten*. The result delivered almost immediately is shown in Panel 3.4. Admittedly the design proposal embraces some stereo-types, but refining the questions asked to include specific preferences of an identified user of the toy would overcome this. Iterations of questionings might become a useful skill for learners who wish to use AI in this way. Realising the proposed design would be challenging and require significant technical knowledge and understanding, a set of relevant making skills and access to a wide range of materials and components. This would probably be beyond all but the most

Panel 3.4 ChatGPT design proposal

---

1 Size and shape: The toy could be designed to be around 4–5 inches long, with a sleek and elegant cat-like shape.
2 Materials: The body of the cat could be made of soft-touch silicone material to give it a smooth and tactile feel.
3 Movement: The electric motor would power the cat to move forward and backward, while also making the tail move back and forth in a realistic cat-like way.
4 Eyes: The cat's eyes could be designed to light up with a soft LED glow, which will make it appear more life-like and appealing to young girls.
5 Colours: You could design the cat in a variety of colours, such as pink, purple, or light blue, to make it more attractive and personalized to a girl's preferences.
6 Sound: You could also add a small speaker to the toy, which would emit soft cat-like purring sounds, meows, and other cat-like sounds that would make the toy more interactive and realistic.
7 Power source: The toy could be powered by a rechargeable battery that could be charged using a USB cable, making it convenient for the user to keep it charged.

---

accomplished KS4 learners. But as a starting point for developing and negotiating learners' design proposals, it is an intriguing possibility. If learners used ChatGPT to identify possible issues embedded in a contextual challenge, would this invalidate their course work?

Note that Annalee Newitz (2023) is sceptical with regard to the likes of ChatGPT approaching artificial general intelligence rivalling the intelligence of humans. Along with many others Annalee notes that the AI is not aware of what it is doing and sees those producing such AI as doing this for commercial gain in that once we are convinced by the dystopian hype that it is a necessary adjunct to human activity, we will be charged for the privilege of using it.

Global warming

It is generally agreed across all nations that we face a climate crisis and the way to tackle this is to achieve net zero, a situation in which there is a balance between the carbon dioxide emitted into the atmosphere and the amount of carbon dioxide absorbed from the atmosphere. It is important to achieve net zero as quickly as possible to limit the global temperature rise to 1.5°C. Higher than this and the climate changes caused by global warming become much more severe. This piece describes why this is important, what is being done to achieve net zero and its relevance to those teaching and learning design & technology. There is no doubt that the concentration of carbon dioxide in the atmosphere has increased dramatically since the beginning of the industrial revolution, and this was fuelled literally by the burning of coal initially and then oil and gas. A graph illustrating this using highly reliable data taken from *Sustainable Energy without the Hot Air* by David MacKay (2009) is shown in Figure 3.4.

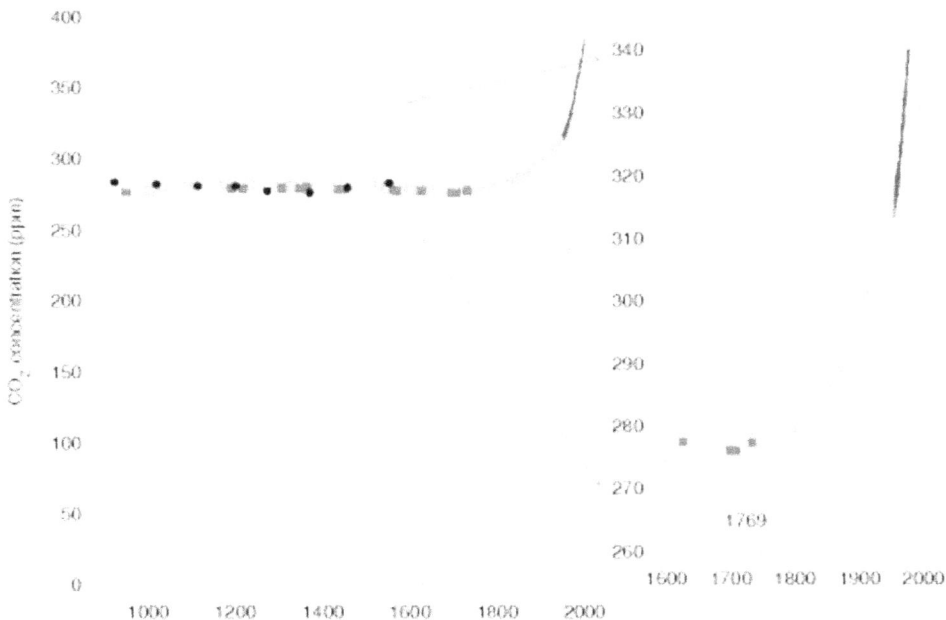

Figure 3.4 The rise in CO_2 concentration (MacKay, 2009)

> ## Pause for thought
>
> *Sustainable Energy without the Hot Air* by David MacKay is available free to download at www.withouthotair.com. David uses quotations at the beginning of some of his chapters as provocations to further thought. Here are some examples:
>
> * *We live at a time where emotions and feelings count more than truth, and there is a vast ignorance of science.* (James Lovelock)
> * *Nature cannot be fooled.* (Richard Feynman)
> * *Every gun that is made, every warship launched, every rocket fired signifies, in the final sense, a theft from those who hunger and are not fed, those who are cold and are not clothed. This world in arms is not spending alone. It is spending the sweat of its labourers, the genius of its scientists, the hopes of its children.* (President Dwight D. Eisenhower, April 1953).
>
> Might these be interesting starting points for curriculum discussions in your design & technology department?

Climate change and global warming

The weather in any location is likely to vary over a year according to the season and local conditions. Climate is the average weather in a place over many years. Climate change is a shift in those average conditions. The rapid climate change we are now seeing is caused by humans using oil, gas, and coal for their homes, factories, and transport. Fossil fuels are made up of hydrocarbons, and when these burn they release greenhouse gases (GHG) mostly carbon dioxide (CO_2). These gases trap the sun's heat and cause the planet's temperature to rise. The world is now about 1.1°C warmer than it was in the 19th century, and scientists are convinced that this temperature rise has been caused to a large extent by the increased amount of carbon dioxide in the atmosphere. The amount of CO_2 has risen by 50% as shown in Figure 3.4. The influence of human activity on the world has led to scientists calling the period of time that we are now in the Anthropocene and the effects that human activity is having as anthropogenic. Anthropogenic (human made) GHG have two main sources – the burning of fossil fuels which generate CO_2 and the rearing of animals for meat and dairy consumption which produce large quantities of methane. The amount of CO_2 in the atmosphere was maintained naturally before the impact of GHGs. The forests on the planet contribute significantly to maintaining this balance by the process of photosynthesis in which carbon dioxide is removed from the atmosphere to become part of the fabric of the trees that make up the forest. Hence deforestation to provide pasture for cattle and land for crops such as palm oil reduces the ability of the planet to remove CO_2 from the atmosphere and contributes to global warming.

The effect of climate change on the world

Climate change has and will continue to have different effects across the world. According to the UN climate body, the Intergovernmental Panel on Climate Change (IPCC) (BBC, 2022), if global temperature rise cannot be kept within 1.5°C, the following changes will take place:

- Extreme rainfall will make the UK and Europe vulnerable to flooding. And at the same time extreme temperatures will also increase the risk of wildfires, as seen in Europe in 2022 where France and Germany experienced about seven times more land burnt between January and the middle of July 2022, compared with the average (see Horton & Palumbo, 2022, for more details).
- Extreme heatwaves and widespread drought will affect countries in the Middle East.
- Rising seas will cause island nations and considerable mainland coastal resources (domestic, agricultural, commercial, and industrial) in the Pacific regions to disappear.
- Many African nations are likely to suffer droughts and food shortages. For example, East Africa in 2022 faced its fifth season of failed rains which put up to 22 million people at risk of severe hunger (see UN World Food Programme, 2022, for more details).
- The western US is likely to experience drought conditions whilst other areas will experience more intense storms.
- Australia is likely to suffer extremes of heat and increases in deaths from wildfires and storms.
- Hotter temperatures also mean that previously frozen ground will melt in places like Siberia, releasing greenhouse gases trapped for centuries into the atmosphere, further worsening climate change.
- In other regions, extreme rainfall is causing historic flooding, as seen recently in China, Pakistan, and Nigeria (see Le Page, 2022, for more details).

It is clear that no country is exempt from the effects of global warming, but it is important to note that people living in the global south are likely to suffer the most as they have fewer resources to adapt to climate change. And there is anger and frustration in these nations as they have produced the least greenhouse gas emissions. This is discussed later in the section *Climate justice*.

How can we be sure?

The work of the IPCC has been essential in providing the best possible scientific evidence on climate change. The IPCC is the United Nations body for assessing the science related to climate change. Thousands of people from all over the world contribute to the work of the IPCC. For the assessment reports, experts volunteer their time as IPCC authors to assess the thousands of scientific papers published each year to provide a comprehensive summary of what is known about the drivers of climate change, its impacts and future risks, and how adaptation (how countries can change the way they behave to limit the impact of climate change) and mitigation (how countries can change the way they behave to contribute less to climate change) can reduce those risks. This open and transparent review by experts around the world is an essential part of the IPCC process, to ensure an objective and complete assessment and to reflect a diverse range of views and expertise. Through its assessments, the IPCC identifies the strength of scientific agreement in different areas and indicates where further research is needed. The IPCC does not conduct its own research. The analysis of research into emissions of GHG by the IPCC has shown that they have increased steadily between 1990 and 2019 (IPCC, 2022) as shown in Figure 3.5.

Pause for thought

Given the importance of science in detecting climate change and understanding its effects, how might the way climate change, its effects, and implications is taught in design & technology be linked to how these features are taught elsewhere in the curriculum, in science, RE, and geography, for example?

Governments' actions

COP is an abbreviation for Conference of Parties and in this case the conferences assess progress in dealing with climate change. The first such conference took place in 1995 and there has been one such conference every year since. In 2015 at COP 21 in Paris the participants adopted an agreement which created a general path towards climate action. Any final text of a COP must be agreed by consensus. Countries agree climate change can only be tackled by working together, and in Paris in 2015 lots of countries made an agreement to keep global warming to 1.5°C. This Paris Agreement saw almost all the world's nations, for the first time, support a common strategy to cut the greenhouse gas emissions which cause global warming.

Adopted by 194 parties (193 countries plus the EU) in the French capital on 12 December 2015, the treaty came into force on 4th November 2016. This is what was agreed:

- To "pursue efforts" to limit global temperature rises to **1.5°C**, and to keep them **"well below" 2.0°C** above pre-industrial times.
- To limit greenhouse gas emissions from human activity to the same levels that trees, soil, and oceans can absorb naturally – known as **net zero** – between 2050 and 2100.
- Each country to set its own emission-reduction targets, reviewed every five years to **raise ambitions.**
- Richer countries to help poorer nations by providing funding, known as **climate finance**, to adapt to climate change and switch to renewable energy.

Are they keeping their word?

Georgina Rannard & Esme Stallard of the BBC have produced an analysis of national CO_2 emissions (Rannard & Stallard, 2022), see Figure 3.6.

a. Global net anthropogenic GHG emissions 1990-2019 (5)

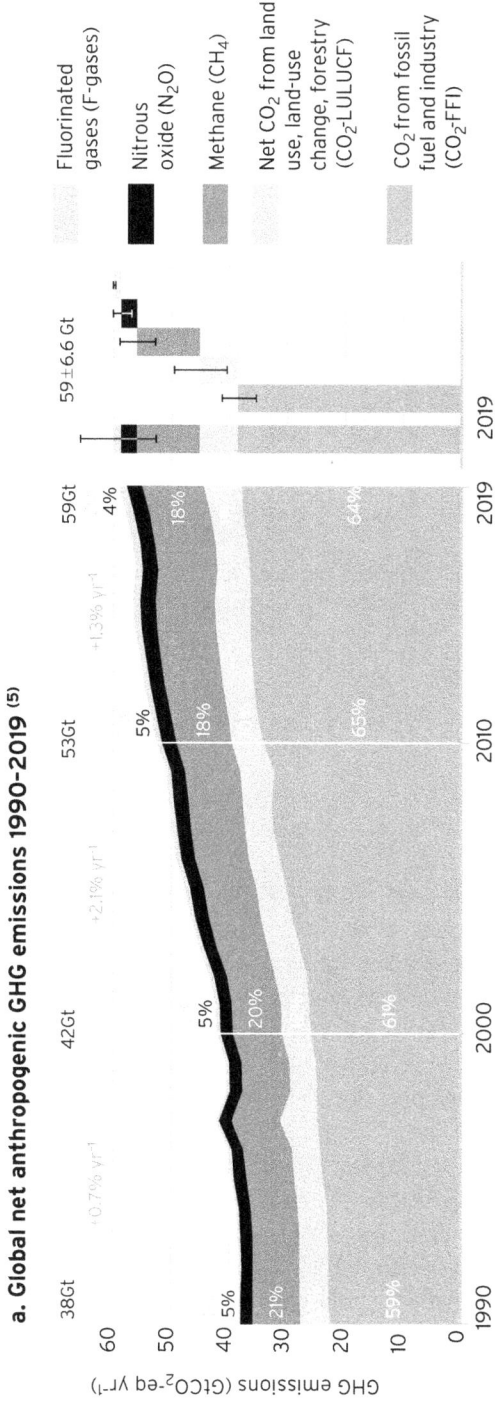

Figure 3.5 GHG emissions are increasing

Source: IPCC, 2022: Summary for Policymakers. In: *Climate Change 2022: Mitigation of Climate Change. Contribution of Working Group III to the Sixth Assessment Report of the Intergovernmental Panel on Climate Change* [P.R. Shukla, J. Skea, R. Slade, A. Al Khourdajie, R. van Diemen, D. McCollum, M. Pathak, S. Some, P. Vyas, R. Fradera, M. Belkacemi, A. Hasija, G. Lisboa, S. Luz, J. Malley, (eds.)]. Cambridge University Press, Cambridge, UK; Figure SPM.1, Global net anthropogenic GHG emissions (GtCO2-eq yr-1) 1990-2019, Panel a. Global net anthropogenic GHG emissions 1990-2019, p. 11.

How are countries doing?

Country	Emissions per person (CO2e 2021)	Climate money committed to other countries* (USD, billions, 2016-2020)	Share of electricity from coal (Jan-Jul 2022)	Tree cover change (2010-2020)
China	▬▬▬	0.00	69%	9%
US	▬▬▬▬▬	5.47	20%	1%
EU	▬▬▬	105.00	15%	2%
UK	▬▬	3.78	2%	5%
India	▪	0.00	79%	4%
Brazil	▬▬▬	0.00	5%	-3%
Australia	▬▬▬▬▬	0.87	51%	3%

*Developing nations Brazil, India and China not required to pledge climate finance. Source: Australian government, Brazilian government, CAT, China Global Times, Climate Change Home News, CSE, Donor Tracker, EIA, EU, European Commission, Government of India Ministry of Power, IEA, ODI, Reuters, UK government, UNFCCC, and World Bank.   **B B C**

Figure 3.6 Emission data for a range of nations (from Rannard & Stallard, 2022)

Their commentary on individual countries makes interesting reading. Panel 3.5 shows some extracts.

There is evidence in these extracts that all these nations are trying to some extent to have policies and practices that combat global warming but a combination of domestic political issues and the impact of the war in Ukraine has led to mixed success and limited international cooperation. With this in mind the development from COP 26 of the Beyond Oil and Gas Alliance (BOGA) (Beyond Oil and Gas, 2022) is relevant. This is an international alliance of governments and stakeholders working together to facilitate the managed phase-out of oil and gas production. Core members are Wales, Quebec, Ireland, France, Greenland, and Sweden, with Denmark and Costa Rica taking the lead. The alliance aims to elevate the issue of oil and gas production phase-out in international climate dialogues, mobilise action and commitments, and create an international community of practice on this issue. They report that if we are to have a reasonable chance of avoiding dangerous climate change by 2050, we can burn no more than 42% of current oil reserves and 41% of current proven gas reserves. Yet governments' production plans and projections for 2030 would lead to burning around 240% more coal, 57% more oil, and 71% more gas than would be consistent with limiting global warming to 1.5°C. Clearly this needs to change so the outcomes of COP 27 are crucial and these will be discussed later.

Panel 3.5 Comments concerning individual country emissions (from Rannard & Stallard, 2022)

Concerning the USA
The US made a huge leap forward this year when it passed sweeping new laws to confront climate change. But it is not all good news. A senior US politician controversially visited Taiwan which could seriously affect international climate negotiations. And in response to the energy crisis, President Joe Biden released 15m barrels of oil from reserves on to the market and approved new leases for oil and gas drilling. The US has also not delivered its fair share of finance to support developing countries suffering the most from climate change.

Concerning the UK
The UK hosted COP26, secured major global pledges, and showed itself to be a clear international climate leader. Only 2% of its electricity is generated using coal. But the UK is going to COP27 "weaker" with "disappointing" leadership, the infamous U-turn by Prime Minister Sunak to attend COP 27, and the global energy crisis also led the UK to back-track on commitments to end new oil and gas extraction in the North Sea and close down coal-powered stations.

Concerning the EU
The European Union is historically progressive on tackling climate change, but Russia's invasion of Ukraine and the impact on energy supplies to Europe have undermined that. Extending the lifeline of coal-fired power plants has led to an increase of about 2% in the first six months of 2022. But the return to investing in fossil fuels is probably a "temporary setback" and the EU could take this opportunity to make itself energy secure by investing in renewables. A new plan, the REPowerEU plan, aims to increase the EU's share of renewable energy in 2030 from 40% to 45%.

Concerning India
India is one of the few countries to have published updated climate targets in 2022. It promises to reduce emissions intensity by 45% by 2030. It also wants 50% of installed energy to be renewable. But India's plan to reopen 100 coal mines (coal is the most polluting fossil fuel) could be a barrier to those ambitions. However, as in other countries, this can be seen as a short-term measure to cope with the energy crisis.

Concerning Brazil
Brazil holds one of the keys to fighting climate change – its massive Amazon rainforest, the lungs of the planet, soaks up huge amounts of carbon. Luiz Inácio Lula da Silva, the newly elected president, has said, "Brazil is ready to retake its leadership in the fight against the climate crisis". This is in direct contrast to the views of the previous president, Jair Bolsonaro, who championed more mining in the Amazon leading to a 48% increase in deforestation in 2021. Historically, Brazil has used hydropower to provide large amounts of green energy, but a drought in 2021 drained its dams. In response, it invested in oil and gas, with predictions that its use of oil will increase by 70% by 2030. But it is hoped that solar energy will compensate for the loss of the nation's hydropower.

Concerning Australia
The new Prime Minister Anthony Albanese has accelerated climate plans, ending a decade of backsliding. The country submitted new targets promising to reduce emissions by 43% by 2030, a big leap forward from its previous target of 26%. But this only seems like significant progress because of how far behind Australia was. Australia's states have led the way in increasing renewable energy, but the country remains in the top five producers of coal in the world. And although Australia promised at COP26 to end deforestation, it was classed in 2021 as the only developed country that is a hotspot for tree loss; nearly half of forests in eastern Australia have been destroyed.

Concerning China
China has a complicated role in global climate action. Unlike countries in the developed world, it is not responsible for historical greenhouse gas emissions. But it is now a major polluter because of its very rapid economic growth, it burns half of the coal in the world, and is reluctant to cut back because of energy shortages. However, China is also by far the biggest investors in renewable energy. A quarter of newly registered cars in China are electric. They are making big efforts and setting demanding targets, including peaking its carbon emissions by 2030. And it has big ambitions to address carbon emissions with tree planting. In May, President Xi Jinping pledged to plant 70 billion trees by 2030.

In the light of Rannard and Stallards' comments about the UK, it is worth noting that in October 2021 the UK government published its strategy for getting to net zero through a ten-point plan (HMG, 2021) as follows:

- "Advancing offshore wind
- Driving growth of low-carbon hydrogen
- Delivering new and advanced nuclear power
- Accelerating the shift to zero-emission vehicles
- Green public transport, cycling and walking
- 'Jet zero' and green ships
- Greener buildings
- Investing in carbon capture and storage
- Protecting our natural environment
- Green finance and innovation".

Some of these are discussed in the section *Technology to the rescue?*

Tipping points

There is the possibility that some of climate changes taking place in response to the emission of anthropogenic GHGs may give rise to tipping points. These are conditions beyond which changes in a part of the climate system become self-perpetuating. These changes may lead to abrupt, irreversible, and dangerous impacts with serious implications for humanity. Recent research (McKay *et al.*, 2022) presented an updated assessment of the most important climate tipping elements and identified the following impacts:

- Greenland ice sheet collapse
- West Antarctic ice sheet collapse
- Collapse of ocean circulation in the polar region of the North Atlantic
- Coral reef die off in the low latitudes
- Sudden thawing of permafrost in the Northern regions
- Abrupt sea ice loss in the Barents Sea.

Their analysis indicates that even global warming of 1°C, a threshold that we already have passed, puts us at risk by triggering some tipping points. In addition, one of the authors, Ricarda Winkelmann, notes that many tipping elements in the Earth system are interlinked, making cascading tipping points a serious additional concern. For example, if there are smaller or fewer ice sheets and sea ice, then less of the sun's energy is reflected leading to further global warming.

Climate justice

The IPCC has reported that although anthropogenic CO_2 emissions have grown in most regions this growth is not evenly distributed (IPCC, 2022). This is clearly shown by the bar chart in Figure 3.7.

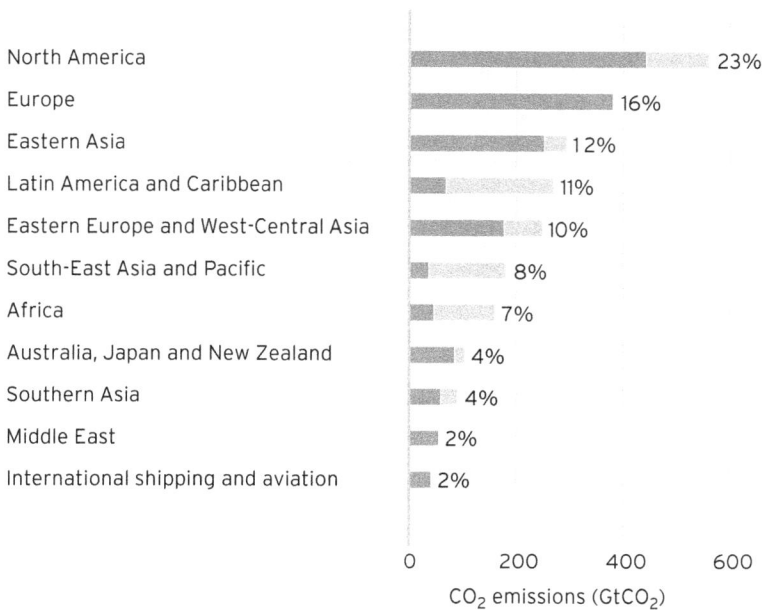

Region	%
North America	23%
Europe	16%
Eastern Asia	12%
Latin America and Caribbean	11%
Eastern Europe and West-Central Asia	10%
South-East Asia and Pacific	8%
Africa	7%
Australia, Japan and New Zealand	4%
Southern Asia	4%
Middle East	2%
International shipping and aviation	2%

CO_2 emissions (GtCO$_2$)

Figure 3.7 Historical cumulative net anthropogenic CO_2 emissions per region (1850–2019)

Source: IPCC, 2022: Summary for Policymakers. In: *Climate Change 2022: Mitigation of Climate Change. Contribution of Working Group III to the Sixth Assessment Report of the Intergovernmental Panel on Climate Change* [P.R. Shukla, J. Skea, R. Slade, A. Al Khourdajie, R. van Diemen, D. McCollum, M. Pathak, S. Some, P. Vyas, R. Fradera, M. Belkacemi, A. Hasija, G. Lisboa, S. Luz, J. Malley, (eds.)]. Cambridge University Press, Cambridge, UK and New York, NY, USA; Figure SPM.2, Regional GHG emissions, and the regional proportion of total cumulative production-based CO_2 emissions from 1850 to 2019, Panel b. Historical cumulative net anthropogenic CO_2 emissions per region (1850–2019), p. 14.

A particular problem facing the world is that many of the countries most affected by climate change are least able to deal with its consequences and contributed least to producing the emissions that are causing the climate change. Understandably vulnerable nations are exploring ways to make wealthy and historically high-emitting countries pay for the havoc their emissions have caused. They want what they see as climate justice. This is exemplified by Tuvalu, a country composed of nine small coral islands in the west-central Pacific Ocean. Kausea Natano, the prime minister of Tuvalu, said at the beginning of the COP 27 climate conference, "The warming seas are starting to swallow our lands, inch by inch. We, therefore, unite with a hundred Nobel peace prize laureates and thousands of scientists worldwide and urge world leaders to join the fossil fuel non-proliferation treaty to manage a just transition away from fossil fuels" (*Guardian*, 2022).

The situation is complicated as research by Philippe Le Billon, Nicolas Gaulin, and Päivi Lujala (experts in geography and environmental sciences at the University of British Columbia, Wageningen University, and the University of Oulu, respectively) shows. Their research (Marley, 2022) has revealed that a country's dependence on fossil fuels for revenue – and not the size of their reserves or industry – made them more or less likely to constrain production. Hence a country like France (high-income countries with fossil fuel reserves of little economic significance) and small countries like Vanuatu (no fossil fuel industry but highly vulnerable to climate change) are predisposed to join organisations like BOGA. But countries like Saudi Arabia, which use their vast fossil fuel revenue to finance new economic sectors, and poorer countries which have been unable to turn their fossil fuel wealth into prosperity, like many countries in sub-Saharan Africa, are not at all inclined to sign up to fossil fuel non-proliferation treaties. Le Billon, Gaulin, and Lujala (2022) argue that more countries could be persuaded into anti fossil fuel alliances if the world could agree terms for a transition to renewable energy that retrains workers, compensates lost revenue, and helps dirty economies diversify. They say, "An agreement over a managed fossil fuel phaseout will not only help reduce emissions, but also help producers move away from the harmful effects of fossil fuel revenue dependence".

The issue of what comprises climate justice will be discussed at length at COP27, and this is the first climate summit where the issue of loss and damage is on the agenda for discussion. This term refers to the effects of climate change which cannot be prevented or adapted to; the lives and livelihoods lost, the communities uprooted by sea-level rise, famine and extreme weather, the cultural and ecological heritage destroyed. These consequences mount and intensify with every increment of global temperature rise. A recent analysis suggests climate change will force 113 million people to relocate within Africa by 2050 (The Conversation, 2022).

Technology to the rescue?

Using carbon credits

Carbon credits create a market for reducing greenhouse emissions by giving a monetary value to the cost of polluting the air. Emissions become an internal cost of doing business and are visible on the balance sheet alongside raw materials and other liabilities or assets.

Consider a business that owns a factory putting out 100,000 tonnes of CO_2 emissions in a year. Its government enacts a law to limit the emissions that the business can produce and gives the business a quota of 80,000 tonnes per year. The factory can either reduce its emissions to 80,000 tonnes or purchase carbon credits to offset the excess. After costing up alternatives, the business decides that it is uneconomical or infeasible to invest in new machinery to reduce its emissions for that year. Instead, it chooses to buy carbon credits on the open market from organizations that have been approved as being able to sell legitimate carbon credits. Here are two scenarios in which the factory might purchase carbon credits:

1   One possible seller might be a company that will offer to offset emissions through a project in the developing world, such as recovering methane from a swine farm to feed a power station that previously would use fossil fuel. So, although the factory continues to emit gases, it would pay another group to reduce the equivalent of 20,000 tonnes of carbon dioxide emissions from the atmosphere for that year.
2   Another seller may have already invested in new low-emission machinery and have a surplus of allowances as a result. The factory could make up for its emissions by buying 20,000 tonnes of allowances from them. The cost of the seller's new machinery would be subsidized by the sale of allowances. Both the buyer and the seller would submit accounts for their emissions to prove that their allowances were met correctly.

Carbon capture technologies

A complete and sudden moratorium of burning fossil fuels is unlikely due to a) the pressures on some nations to continue burning fossil fuels and b) the desire of some nations to capitalise on so far unexploited fossil fuel deposits if only in the short term before alternative sources of energy are found. This will add to the CO_2 in the atmosphere. One way of mitigating this increase in anthropogenic CO_2 is to use carbon capture technologies. There are two types: carbon capture and storage (CCS) sometimes called carbon capture and sequestration and carbon capture and utilisation (CCU). CCS involves the capture of carbon dioxide (CO_2) emissions from industrial processes, such as steel and cement production, or from the burning of fossil fuels in power generation. This carbon is then transported from where it was produced, via ship or in a pipeline, and stored deep underground in geological formations from which it cannot escape. In this way the emission of GHGs can be prevented and the industrial and power generation processes no longer contribute to global warming. However, in reality nearly three-quarters of CO_2 captured annually is reinjected into oil fields to push more oil and gas out of the ground, a process called enhanced oil recovery, (EOR). This oil and gas are burned creating even more GHGs. (Robertson & Mousavian, 2022). CCU is the process of capturing CO_2 to be recycled for further usage. It differs from carbon capture and storage (CCS) in that CCU does not aim to, nor result in, permanent geological storage of carbon dioxide. Instead, CCU aims to convert the captured carbon dioxide into more valuable substances or products, such as plastics, concrete or biofuel while preventing the emissions of GHGs. CCU has the potential to reduce GHG emissions, but there are difficulties in putting it into practice. CO_2 is a very stable molecule, and attempts to make it react to produce new and useful materials require lots of energy, so care has to be taken that such energy is from sources that do not emit GHGs. Also, the profitability of the process will depend on the price of the CO_2 being utilised and this may vary according to market conditions. CCS and CCU are summarised and compared in Figure 3.8.

The Institute for Energy Economics and Financial Analysis (Salt, 2022) is sceptical as to the ability of carbon capture technologies to be effective reporting:

> *Given the status of technology and the balance of risks, there is significant evolution that carbon capture technologies need for them to be technically proven and commercially viable at scale, and therefore bankable. A key impediment to investment is the lack of availability and weak quality of data from the testing and operations of CCS across all applications, which makes the real technology, commercial readiness level, costs and cost competitiveness uncertain.*

However, the report does indicate that CCS may be the most viable pathway for deep decarbonisation of the cement industry. This is important as most future large infrastructure projects will rely heavily on the use of concrete.

Maintaining/extending natural carbon capture systems

Before human activity began to increase the amount of CO_2 in the atmosphere. a range of steady states of CO_2 concentration were achieved, depending on the global temperature, resulting in a climate in which most plants and animals, including humans, could thrive.

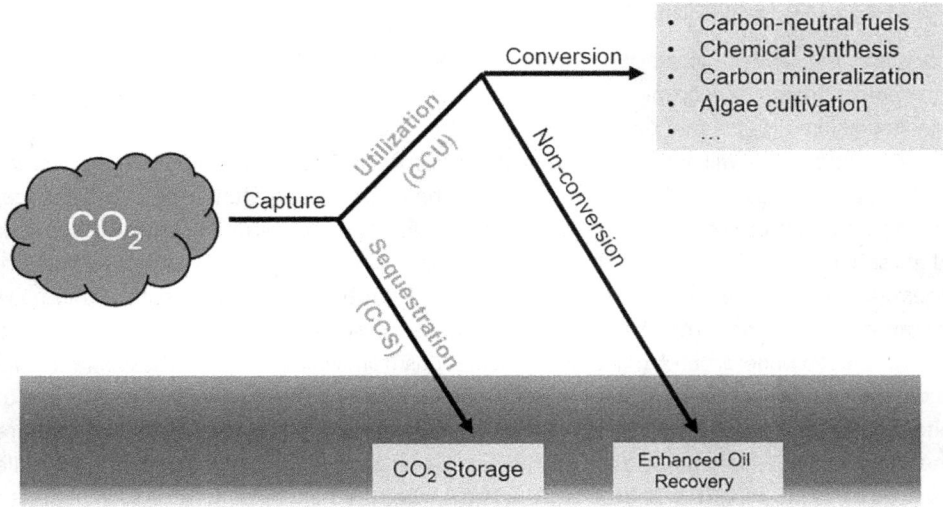

Figure 3.8 Comparison of CCS and CCU (taken from Wikipedia)

Source: https://en.wikipedia.org/wiki/Carbon_capture_and_storage#Carbon_capture_and_utilization_
(CCU)). See https://en.wikipedia.org/wiki/Carbon_capture_and_storage.

These steady states (between 200 and 300 parts CO_2 per million by volume) were achieved through competition between natural processes that produced and removed CO_2. CO_2 is removed from the atmosphere primarily through photosynthesis. Trees and other vegetation extract vast quantities of CO_2 from the atmosphere, and it becomes part of their living biomass. After death, some of this remains in the topsoil and subsoil as additional reserves of stored carbon. Hence it should be possible to enhance those natural processes that remove CO_2 and reduce the amount of CO_2 in the atmosphere. On land such techniques include reforestations, sustainable forest management, and improving the efficiency of photosynthesis in some plants through genetic engineering. Also, a considerable amount of carbon is captured and stored by the world's oceans and coastlands. This is referred to as Blue Carbon, and the carbon is captured through photosynthesis by a wide range of organisms that live in the sea and coastal wetlands including seaweeds, seagrasses, and mangroves. As the oceans cover 70% of the planet, there is increasing industry interest in exploiting Blue Carbon potential for climate change mitigation.

Sylvia Hurlimann makes a strong case for kelp sequestering carbon (Hurlimann, 2019) arguing that the kelp drifts away from the coastal regions where it grows out into the ocean where it sinks down towards the deep-sea floor, where the carbon is thought to be sequestered away from the atmosphere for centuries (and potentially up to millions of years). A commercial development of this natural process would seem to make sense. And one could imagine an investor who had developed a large kelp farm calculated to reduce CO_2 emissions by a large amount using this reduction in CO_2 as the basis for carbon credits, which she could sell to a business who wished to offset their CO_2 emissions. However, Gallagher, Shelamoff, and Layton (2022) urge caution in that they question the model by which seaweeds are thought to reduce CO_2 emissions arguing that in certain circumstances the way the ecosystems play out might result in the seaweed acting as a source of carbon rather than a sink.

Nuclear power

Fission and fusion explained

Nuclear fission creates energy through the decay of elements with heavy atoms such a uranium. This decay occurs spontaneously, and when a critical mass of the element is present a chain reaction occurs releasing large amounts of energy. The engineering task in a nuclear reactor is to control this chain reaction so that the energy is released steadily in a way that can be used to heat water to create high pressure, high temperature steam that can then be used to drive turbines that generate electricity. No GHGs are generated in the process so there is no contribution to global warming.

Nuclear fusion creates energy by mimicking what happens inside the sun. It uses small atoms, usually hydrogen and fuses them together to form heavier atoms. The total mass of the new atoms formed is less than the mass of the atoms that fused to form them, and the missing mass is released as enormous amounts of energy. The engineering tasks are first to create a container that can hold the miniature sun produced by the fusion reaction and then harness the energy produced to generate electricity.

Is fission sustainable?

The limiting resource for the production of electricity by nuclear fission reactors is the availability of the uranium that is required as fuel. Mackay (2009) has argued that if uranium is extracted from the sea as well as the land then there is sufficient available for fission power stations to operate for a thousand years given current rates of energy consumption.

What about nuclear waste?

Radioactivity is harmful to humans hence all radioactive waste produced by nuclear power stations needs to be stored such that humans are not affected by it now or in the future both short term and long term. Nuclear fission power stations generate radioactive waste of three kinds:

- Low level waste (about 90%) which contains small amounts of short-lived radioactivity and can be disposed of by shallow land burial.
- Intermediate level waste (about 7%) which contains radioactive atoms with half-lives of more than a thousand years, hence it has to be managed using long-term solutions. The waste is encapsulated in an inert material such as bitumen and concrete and stored above ground in steel drums for now in secure sites at the power station where it was generated. In the future it will need to be stored in deep underground storage although as little heat is generated it will not need to be cooled. As yet such deep underground storage sites have not been specified.

- High level waste (3% of the total waste) is very dangerous. This is waste with levels of activity concentration high enough to generate significant quantities of heat by the radioactive decay process or waste with large amounts of radioactive atoms with very long half-lives (more than a thousand years). It is usual to store this with cooling at the power station where it was generated for 40 years. After this disposal in deep, stable geological formations usually several hundred metres or more below the surface is the generally recognised option for disposal. As yet such deep underground storage sites have not been specified.

What about nuclear safety?

Accidents happen in all industries involved in power generation be they coal mining, wind farming, or oil and gas drilling, but the consequences of accidents in a nuclear power station are of a different category in that the materials leaked into the environment are extremely toxic, difficult to clean up, may find their way into the atmosphere, and be transported by wind hundreds if not thousands of miles from the site of the accident and last for thousands of years. In addition, the waste produced by nuclear power stations will need to be safely contained for a thousand years or more and this involves developing storage facilities in places that are deep underground and geologically stable, an engineering feat yet to be achieved. Some have argued that it is impossible to design 'accident immune' nuclear facilities particularly in the light of the extreme climate conditions being caused by global warming (Sovacool, 2011). Hence building, operating, and decommissioning nuclear power stations is not risk free but this risk has to be balanced by the consideration that nuclear power can provide a reliable continuous supply of carbon free electricity. At the time of writing the UK government has just confirmed that a new nuclear power station, Sizewell C, will be built in Suffolk with a state investment of £700 million. Both the Green Party and local residents have raised objections (Jolly, 2022).

Is fusion feasible?

Writing in the *New Scientist*, Thomas Lewton explored the timescale for designing, building and commissioning fusion power stations (Lewton ,2022). He notes that initiatives in the USA, Canada, and the UK are attracting significant investment with the optimistic promise in some cases of producing electricity continuously by the early 2030s with others being more sceptical believing that it will be the 2060s before such reactors will be producing appreciable amounts of electricity. The optimists base their view on the grounds that the physics of plasma containing is well understood and this will enable rapid innovative developments of the engineering required to use the contained plasma to generate electricity at a price consumers can afford. The pessimists argue that such engineering developments will take much longer noting that so far none of the fusion pilots have generated any electricity. It is hard to tell whether advances at big, state-funded fusion projects together with new technologies and reactor designs in development at private firms, really amount to a tipping point. What is certain is a) that there will be lots of start-ups, b) that some of them will fail, and c) that eventually (exactly when is unclear) some will be successful and the holy grail of affordable, carbon free, electricity from nuclear power will have been achieved.

Pause for thought

The science behind the various sorts of nuclear reactors both fission and fusion is fascinating and complex with the potential of considerable conceptual confusion for learners. It will be worth having a conversation with physics teachers in your school about how to provide an unambiguous picture and avoid misunderstanding.

A hydrogen economy

When hydrogen burns it combines with oxygen to produce heat and water; no GHG emissions at all. The problem in using hydrogen as an energy source is the way the hydrogen is obtained. At the moment there are three ways to do this commercially.

The first method is called steam reforming which reacts natural gas with steam to produce a mixture of hydrogen and CO_2 but without capturing the CO_2 produced. This sort of hydrogen is called grey hydrogen.

The second method is essentially the same but much of the CO_2 produced is captured and sequestered. This sort of hydrogen is called blue hydrogen.

The third method involves the electrolysis of water using electricity from renewable energy sources and produces no CO_2 at all. This is called green hydrogen.

At first glance it would seem that it is green hydrogen that we should be using, but the situation is complicated because at the moment green hydrogen is more expensive to produce than blue hydrogen and it is easier to produce large quantities of blue hydrogen than green hydrogen (see *Economist*, 2022a, for a more detailed discussion). The UK Government has developed a Hydrogen Economy Strategy (Crown, 2021) and has produced a roadmap for its development over the next ten years as shown in Panel 3.6. The strategy uses a twin-track approach to supporting both electrolytic 'green' and carbon capture (CCUS)-enabled 'blue' hydrogen production, alongside other potential production routes, which will enable the rapid growth of the sector while bringing down costs with the aim of providing 10GW in the 2030s. WorldData.info (2022) has estimated that the United Kingdom consumes approximately 309,000 GWh of electrical energy each year. The provision of 10GW electrical energy through a hydrogen economy would meet approximately 28% of this consumption which is significant.

Biofuels

A biofuel is a fuel that is produced over a short time span from plants or from agricultural, domestic, or industrial biowaste rather than by the very slow natural processes involved in the formation of fossil fuels such as oil. In theory biofuels should be carbon neutral in that all the CO_2 emitted when they are burned was extracted from the atmosphere when the plants that make up the biofuel were growing. In practice however the GHG mitigation of particular biofuels varies considerably, from emission levels comparable to fossil fuels in some scenarios to

Panel 3.6 Roadmap for the Hydrogen Economy as envisaged by the UK Government

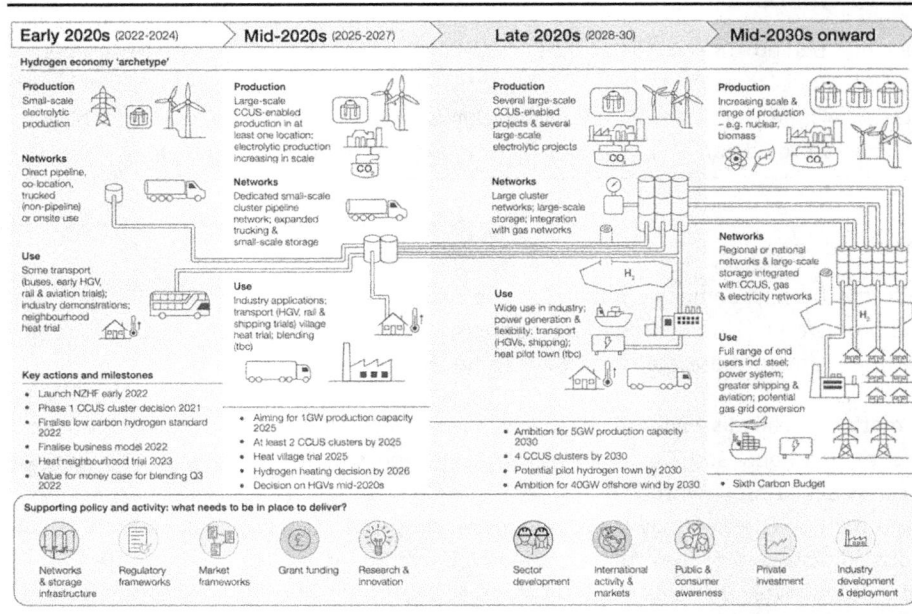

Early 2020s (2022-2024)	Mid-2020s (2025-2027)	Late 2020s (2028-30)	Mid-2030s onward

Hydrogen economy 'archetype'

Production
Small-scale electrolytic production

Networks
Direct pipeline, co-location, trucked (non-pipeline) or onsite use

Use
Some transport (buses, early HGV, rail & aviation trials); industry demonstrations; neighbourhood heat trial

Key actions and milestones
- Launch NZHF early 2022
- Phase 1 CCUS cluster decision 2021
- Finalise low carbon hydrogen standard 2022
- Finalise business model 2022
- Heat neighbourhood trial 2023
- Value for money case for blending Q3 2022

Production
Large-scale CCUS-enabled production in at least one location; electrolytic production increasing in scale

Networks
Dedicated small-scale cluster pipeline network; expanded trucking & small-scale storage

Use
Industry applications; transport (HGV, rail & shipping trials) village heat trial; blending (tbc)

- Aiming for 1GW production capacity 2025
- At least 2 CCUS clusters by 2025
- Heat village trial 2025
- Hydrogen heating decision by 2026
- Decision on HGVs mid-2020s

Production
Several large-scale CCUS-enabled projects & several large-scale electrolytic projects

Networks
Large cluster networks; large-scale storage; integration with gas networks

Use
Wide use in industry; power generation & flexibility; transport (HGVs, shipping); heat pilot town (tbc)

- Ambition for 5GW production capacity 2030
- 4 CCUS clusters by 2030
- Potential pilot hydrogen town by 2030
- Ambition for 40GW offshore wind by 2030

Production
Increasing scale & range of production – e.g. nuclear, biomass

Networks
Regional or national networks & large-scale storage integrated with CCUS, gas & electricity networks

Use
Full range of end users incl. steel; power system; greater shipping & aviation; potential gas grid conversion

- Sixth Carbon Budget

Supporting policy and activity: what needs to be in place to deliver?

Networks & storage infrastructure | Regulatory frameworks | Market frameworks | Grant funding | Research & innovation | Sector development | International activity & markets | Public & consumer awareness | Private investment | Industry development & deployment

negative emissions in others. Life cycle assessments of biofuels have shown that the level of emissions depends on the land use change required for their development. If no or little land use change takes place in growing the plants used for the biofuels, then the resultant fuels have lower emissions than fossil fuels. However, in some cases this reduction in emissions comes at a cost as the growing of the plants for biofuels may have other impacts such as loss of biodiversity, nearby water becoming acidified, and overly rich in nutrients.

The International Energy Agency (IEA) wants biofuels to make up 64% of the world demand for transportation fuels by 2050, in order to reduce dependency on petroleum. However, the production and consumption of biofuels are not on track to meet the IEA's sustainable development scenario (Rodionova *et al.*, 2017). From 2020 to 2030 global biofuel output has to increase by 14% each year to reach IEA's goal (IEA, 2021).

What about flying?

The *Economist* (2022b) notes that whilst travelling by air contributes about 2.5% of GHG, post-Covid air travel is increasing and the emissions are high profile, so the idea of a sustainable aviation fuel (SAF) is attractive. If it can be produced at an economic price it could simply replace the fossil fuels currently being used. There are several ways to produce SAF. Discarded cooking oils and animal fats, or biomass in the form of leftovers from forestry and agriculture can be used as starting points. The carbon dioxide produced when the SAF is burned replaces the carbon dioxide that was taken from the atmosphere when the starting materials were formed in the first place. A difficulty here is ensuring the supply of the raw materials; biomass as raw material is bulky, expensive to gather, transport, and store, and shortage of discarded cooking oils might require buying fresh oils that could otherwise be used as food. An alternative is to produce syngas (a mixture of carbon monoxide and hydrogen) which when subjected to high temperatures and high pressures in the presence of catalysts produces hydrocarbons that can be used for fuel. The carbon monoxide can be produced from carbon dioxide that is in the air or be produced in fermentation plants such as breweries and the hydrogen can by produced by electrolysis using electricity generated sustainably. The Swiss firm Synhelion uses solar energy to produce syngas as opposed to electricity and expects to be able to do this on an industrial scale and deliver SAF to the Lufthansa group. Synhelion are also working with CEMEX, a Mexican company that produces cement to capture the CO_2 from the process as a feedstock, to produce the carbon monoxide for syngas. A third approach is to use biotechnology and genetically engineer algae or bacteria such that they produce and excrete hydrocarbons that could be used as jet fuel. These are at the research stage only. The overall picture is that SAFs are beginning to be produced at an industrial scale and that with the help of government incentives they may make a significant contribution to the mitigation of air travel GHG emissions.

Pause for thought

Other transport related activities have large carbon footprints. For example, global transportation of goods through shipping, global cruising, manufacture of concrete, and steel essential for transport related infrastructure. Might it be worth asking learners to investigate these activities to discover the significance of their GHG emissions and consider what might be done to alleviate them?

Confronting the methane problem

The Natural History Museum (2022) describes the sources and the impact of methane as a GHG in its answer to the question, 'Is Methane a greenhouse gas?' as shown in Panel 3.7.

The Food and Agriculture Organisation of the United Nations (FAO, 2013) has argued that one way to reduce the amount of methane in the atmosphere is to improve the efficiency of animal farming at animal and herd levels. In the case of cows, for example, they argue that "the greatest promise involves improving animal and herd efficiency. This includes using better feeds and feeding techniques, which can reduce methane (CH_4) generated during digestion as well as the amount of CH_4 and nitrous oxide (N_2O) released by decomposing manure". Others are less sanguine. Jenny Kleeman (2020), for example, mounts a well referenced attack on eating meat including the following points:

- The global livestock industry produces more greenhouse gases than the exhaust from every form of transport on the planet combined.
- The use of antibiotics to make animals put on weight more rapidly and to prevent disease contributes to the development of medicine resistant superbugs.

Panel 3.7 Concerning the nature of methane as a greenhouse gas

---

Methane is a more powerful greenhouse gas than carbon dioxide, but there is far less of it in the atmosphere, and it does not stay there as long. Methane is more than 25 times as potent as carbon dioxide at trapping heat in the atmosphere over the course of a century, but it has an 'atmospheric lifetime' of around 12 years, whereas carbon dioxide molecules hang around for hundreds of years.

This means that if humans stopped adding any methane to the atmosphere tomorrow, within several decades all trace of the extra methane and its climate influence would be gone, whereas the same is not true for carbon dioxide. However, methane is still an important greenhouse gas because there are many human-caused sources of it. Methane today is responsible for about 0.5°C of total warming.

Methane is released during the extraction and transport of fossil fuels including coal, oil, and natural gas. It is also released by rice fields, the decay of food waste in rubbish dumps, and even cows – meaning the rise in beef consumption worldwide has increased methane emissions.

There are also natural sources of methane that are being released faster due to global warming itself. These include the melting of permafrost, the layer of previously permanently frozen ice within soil in polar and sub-polar regions. These methane emissions could in turn accelerate warming, leading to the release of more methane, and so on.

- A meat-eating diet is ridiculously inefficient as we are getting our energy from animals that get it from plants when we could get it directly from plants plus we only use a small amount of the livestock reared for food.
- Livestock farming uses huge amounts of water; it takes 43,000 litres to produce the feed, drinking water, and service water that ends up as one kilogram of beef.
- Livestock farming uses huge amounts of land; almost 80% of all the planet's agricultural land is being used to graze animals or grow their feed rather than grow plants for consumption.

Given that the production of meat, particularly beef, is bad for the planet and a very in-efficient process, the idea that we might be able to simply grow meat in bioreactors, using our knowledge of biotechnology is very appealing. Staring with a small sample of cells from an animal the cells are grown in a bioreactor such that they cling to an edible scaffold to create 3D tissue, i.e., meat. This meat is then harvested and turned into food products without the need to clear forests for grazing, raise herds of cattle on the cleared land, slaughtering and butchering their carcasses, etc., with the attendant environmental damage. This might be described as 'cellular agriculture' (Lawton, 2020). The similarity of the pro-ducts to conventional meat and public acceptance will play a large part in whether these endeavours are commercially successful, but one considerable advantage of cultured meat is that it is free from antibiotics. Recently the US safety agency, the Food and Drug Administration (FDA), has given approval for cell-cultured chicken produced in steel tanks by the firm Upside Foods, using cells harvested from live animals (McCallum, 2022). This is the first time a meat product grown in a lab has been cleared for human consumption.

Another approach is to develop plant-based meat substitutes with a carbon footprint 0.6 (kg CO_2 equivalent), water consumption 17 litres, and land use 0.31 square metre for an 85 g plant-based burger compared with a carbon footprint of 2.4 (kg CO_2 equivalent), water consumption 68 litres, and 6.2 square metres for an 85 g beef burger (Firth, 2018). This is no flash in the pan development. McDonald's now has on its standard menu in the UK a vegan burger made with a plant-based patty co-developed with Beyond Meat® featuring vegan sandwich sauce, ketchup, mustard, onion, pickles, lettuce, tomato, and a vegan alternative to cheese on a sesame seed bun (McPlant™, 2022).

Renewables

The weather in and around the UK is such that the sun doesn't always shine, and the wind doesn't always blow so the country cannot rely entirely on renewable energy to meet its total energy requirements. However, renewables can make a significant contribution to a mixed approach which will also include nuclear energy. Information from the National Grid (2022a) about the contribution of renewables to the country's energy use is summarised in Table 3.3.

The government in partnership with industry has already built significant numbers of onshore and offshore wind farms and has included more offshore farms in its future strategy. At the time of writing there is debate about increasing onshore windfarms. There are pros and cons for both offshore and onshore wind farms (see National Grid, 2022b) but at the moment the government seems more committed to expanding offshore wind farm capacity. In August 2022 Hornsea 2 become operational and is the largest offshore windfarm in the world. Future plans for wind energy generation include:

- Multi-purpose interconnectors (MPIs) which will allow clusters of offshore wind farms to connect simultaneously, plugging into the energy systems of neighbouring countries and making it even easier to share clean energy between countries.
- Floating wind farms which, unlike existing offshore wind farms, don't need to be fixed to the seabed, instead using anchors to keep them in place, similar to a boat. This means they can be positioned in much deeper sea areas, meaning there's more room for bigger turbines that generate larger amounts of power.

Table 3.3 Contribution of renewable energy to UK energy consumption

Renewable	Contribution
Wind power	26.1% of the UK's total electricity generation in the last three months of 2021, with onshore and offshore contributing 12% and 14%, respectively
Bio Energy (the burning of renewable organic materials)	12.7%
Solar power	1.8% – this represented a 24% increase compared to the last three months of 2020, due to a 0.7 gigawatt (GW) increase in installed capacity
Hydropower (including tidal)	2.1%
Total	42.7%

Source: National Grid.

•   Energy Islands which will act as state-of-the-art 'clean energy hubs', enabling the connection of offshore wind to multiple countries via MPIs, while also serving as a platform for the production and delivery of green hydrogen.

Solar power, generating only 1.8% of the UK's energy requirement is very much the poor relation compared to wind power. However, that might change if European Space Agency's plans to beam solar energy from space come to fruition. The technology is illustrated in Figure 3.9. The eventual aim is to have giant satellites in orbit, each able to generate the same amount of electricity as a power station (ESA, 2022). Pallab Ghosh (2022) reports that the US, China, and Japan are also advanced in the race to develop space-based solar power and are expected to announce their own plans shortly. Separately from the ESA proposal, in the UK the company Space Solar has been formed. It aims to demonstrate beaming power from space within six years and doing so commercially within nine years. The engineering needed will be impressive – the size of the orbiting solar panels is equivalent to 100 football fields! The game-changer has been the plummeting cost of launches, thanks to reusable rockets and advances in robotic construction in space and the development of technology to wirelessly beam energy from space to Earth also indicate that the idea can become a reality.

COP 27

The messages from the COP 27 climate summit in Egypt in November 2022 were mixed. (Cuff, 2022). On one hand significant progress has been made with regard to achieving climate justice in that after 20 years of campaigning by low-income countries that have increasingly suffered from the effects of climate change, high income countries backed plans for a compensation fund. Under the leadership of Pakistan all the developing countries united to negotiate an agreement for addressing loss and damage from human induced climate change. Details of how the fund will operate, including which nations will contribute, are still to be worked out. Nevertheless, this is an historic moment. On the other hand, there was significant disappointment in that overall little had been done to advance progress on cutting greenhouse gas emissions. The overarching agreement from COP 27 maintains the commitment to limit global warming to 1.5°C above pre-industrial levels. The UN says breaching this threshold would expose millions more people to potentially devastating climate impacts. Alok Sharma, COP 26 president expressed disappointment that the final agreement lacked any reference to ensuring that global emissions peak before 2025 and to further action to phasing down the use of coal and phasing out fossil fuels. He commented, "Friends, I said in Glasgow that the pulse of 1.5°C was weak. Unfortunately, it remains on life support". UN Secretary General António Guterres says it did not address the need for drastic reductions and the planet is still "in the emergency room". Experts say current policies set us on track for a rise of about 2.7°C so there is still much to do.

The personal response

Given the undoubted climate crisis, a key question is how individuals in the UK should **change the way they behave to limit the impact of climate** (adaptation) and **change the way they behave to contribute less to climate change** (mitigation). The podcast *A matter*

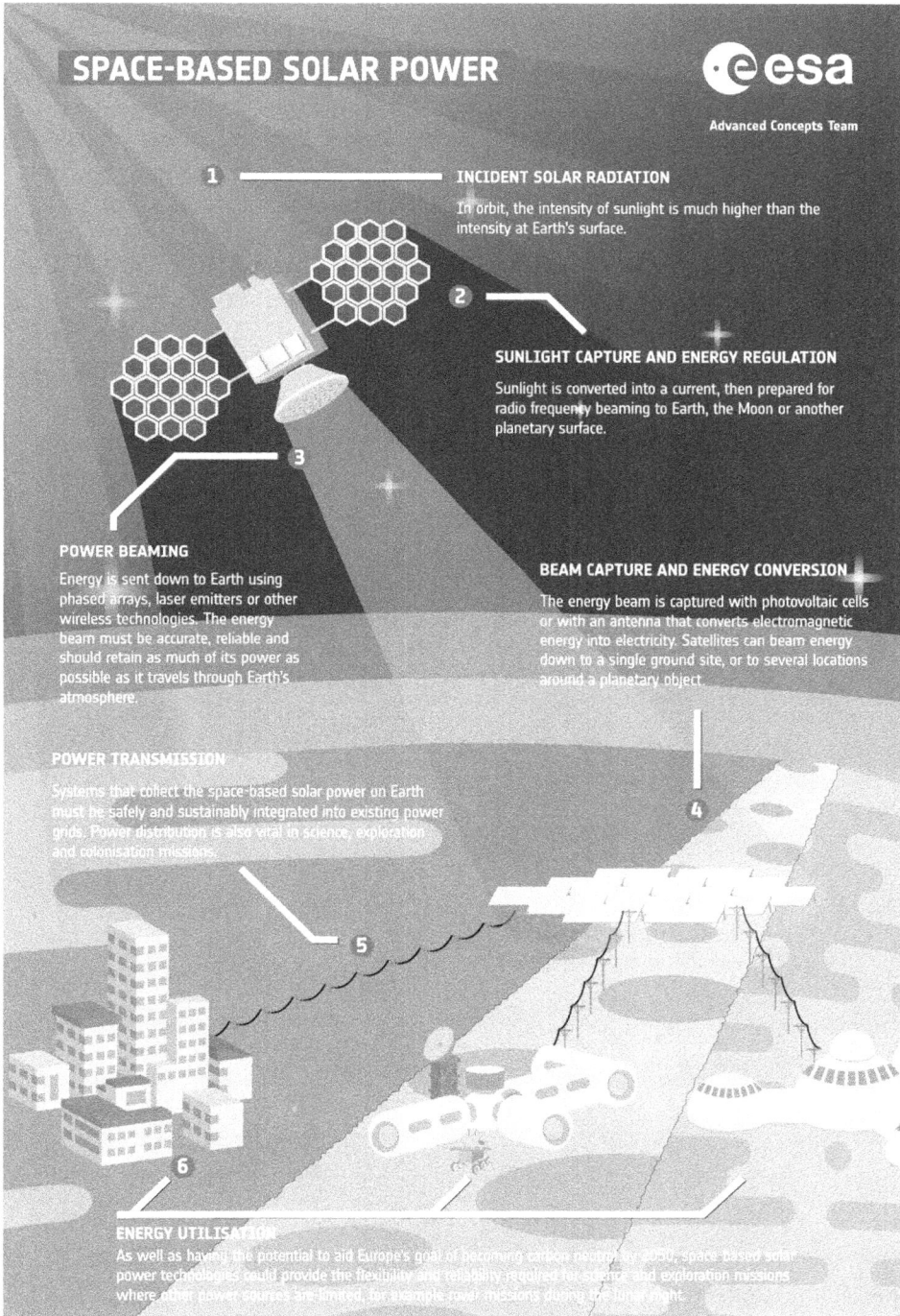

Figure 3.9 Space-based solar power as envisioned by the European Space Agency

of degrees (Stokes & Wilkinson, 2022) provides some useful guidance. They divide the guidance into three levels of response each with a dedicated episode.

The Personal Response (Episode 1) considers changes in our personal lives that have the biggest impact. This is mirrored by the work of Diana Ivanova, Clare Downing, and Aimee Eeles who have used the data from *Quantifying the Potential for Climate Change Mitigation of CONSUMPTION OPTIONs*, a peer reviewed paper published in the *Journal of Environmental Research Letters* (ERL) to identify top ten options for reducing carbon footprint. These are summarised in Figure 3.10.

The Professional Response (Episode 2) uses the slogan 'every job can be a climate job' to look at career changes that support climate goals at work; either by pushing for climate action at one's current workplace or recalibrating existing skill to enable a change of workplace in order to work directly in the climate field. And it is worth remembering that businesses in the climate field are likely to require very similar skill sets as businesses in non-climate fields.

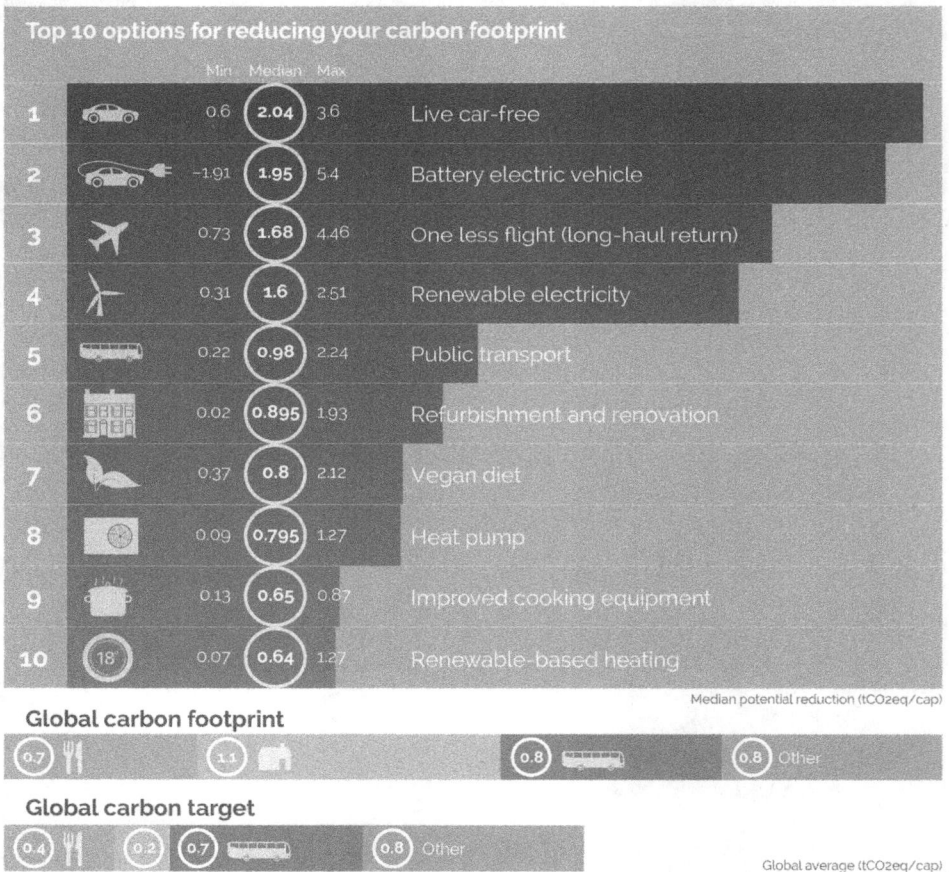

Figure 3.10 Top options for reducing your carbon footprint

Source: © Centre for Research into Energy Demand Reduction, 2020. Image based on Ivanova et al., 2020. doi: 10.1088/1748-9326/ab8589.

The Political Response (Episode 3) looks at how individuals can become politically active at local, regional, and national levels.

Responding to the question 'What can I do' at these three levels is useful as it empowers individuals and enables them to prioritise their activities and be in a strong position to discuss with other what they are doing and, if it seems worthwhile, to join with others in collaborative and/or community endeavours. This is important as doing 'something' that an individual or group can justify and carry out gives rise to hope and being hopeful in the face of the climate crisis is important as it helps sustain our efforts.

In the light of the above we turn to a thought piece by Dominic Nolan. Dominic is well placed to write about this issue as he is very much involved in Kyndryl's Carbon Literacy education programme which aims to empower employees to reduce their personal and professional carbon emissions.

Global warming for design & technology teachers – *A Thought Piece by Dominic Nolan*

Dominic Nolan is Corporate Social Responsibility Leader, Kyndryl UK & Ireland.

In October 2021 I read an article (Murray, 2021) about how organisations were using the Carbon Literacy Project (https://carbonliteracy.com/) to help their employees understand the impact of climate change and take positive action. At the time, I felt powerless in the face of the climate emergency, which is a challenge so huge that it's easy for the individual to believe that their actions can have no impact. However, the article explained how broadcasters, publishers, and arts organisations were using Carbon Literacy education to empower their staff to reduce their personal carbon emissions and collaborate to cut their organisation's CO_2emissions (CO_2e).

The Carbon Literacy Project was co-founded by Phil Korbel and Dave Coleman in 2012. Phil Korbel believes Carbon Literacy should become a core work competence, just like numeracy or digital literacy, and that everyone needs to get involved in the journey to net zero. To date, over 46,000 citizens in 18 nations have achieved Carbon Literate certification, via the Carbon Literacy Project, and pledged to save 167,000 tons of CO_2e (Carbon Literacy Project, 2022).

This inspired me to launch Carbon Literacy Education at Kyndryl, which is the world's largest IT infrastructure services provider serving thousands of businesses in more than 60 countries. Carbon reduction is a priority for all businesses, and Kyndryl has a goal to reach net zero greenhouse gas emissions by 2040, with employee education making up one of three key actions being taken to reach this goal (Taylor, 2022a).

At Kyndryl, we have developed our own Carbon Literacy education programme that provides employees with six hours of learning about the impact of climate change and how to reduce their carbon emissions. After the course, employees submit personal and professional carbon reduction pledges, which are independently assessed. Employees are certified Carbon Literate if their pledges meet the Carbon Literacy Project's standards.

One action Kyndryl employees take as part of the training is to measure their carbon footprint using the World Wildlife Fund's (WWF) environmental footprint calculator (https://footprint.wwf.org.uk/#/). Working out a carbon emission baseline is the starting point for any individual or organisation looking to reduce CO_2e and fight climate change.

Another great resource to help assess carbon footprints is the book *How Bad Are Bananas?* (Berners-Lee, 2020), which provides the carbon footprint of everything, from a pint of tap water (0.2g CO_2e) to cryptocurrencies, which emitted 68 million tons of CO_2e in 2019. The book also has a section on negative emissions and what we can do to remove CO_2. As Berners-Lee points out, it's not enough to reduce emissions if we are to limit global warming, we need to actively remove CO_2 from the atmosphere, which can include tree planting, marine planting, and soil carbon sequestration. Donating to an organisation, such as the World Land Trust, which is a registered charity, is an action that supports the protection and restoration of forests across the world that store carbon.

Faith Taylor, Kyndryl's Global Sustainability Officer, writes about rejecting the myth that individuals' actions don't make a difference (Taylor, 2022b). Like Faith, I believe that we have more power than we think, and all have a responsibility to support the journey to net zero; a journey that involves education, raising awareness across organisations and committing to taking action.

So, what are we to make of Dominic's Thought Piece? First it is empowering in that it celebrates what individuals may do in whatever walk of life they find themselves. Secondly, it endorses and emphasises the role of education in the fight against climate change which brings us naturally to the next section which considers the implications of global warming for design & technology.

What does this mean for design & technology?

In a very real sense design & technology as it operates in the world outside school is responsible for the climate crisis. One can view this as an extreme example of unintended consequences, but this would be to err on the side of generosity with regard to forgiving those who are responsible. The words of Gus Spence (Holtam, 2022), Dean of the Yale School of Forestry and Environmental Studies, are particularly relevant here:

> *I used to think the top environmental problems were biodiversity loss, eco system collapse, and climate change. I thought that with 30 years of good science we could address these problems. But I was wrong. The top environmental problems are selfishness, greed, and apathy – and to deal with those we need a spiritual and cultural transformation – and we scientists don't know how to do that.*

Selfishness, greed, and apathy – are Spence's words too harsh? And if they apply, even only to a limited extent, then what can the teaching of design & technology do in response. Firstly, we need to revisit the words of Jacob Bronowski (1973), adjusted to include all humans, in describing what it is about humans that makes us unique among living creatures:

> *The human is a singular creature. They have a set of gifts which make them unique among the animal: so that, unlike them, they are not figures in the landscape – they are shapers of the landscape … Among the multitude of animals which scamper, fly, burrow and swim around us, the human is the only animal who is not locked into their environment. Their imagination, their reason, their emotional subtlety, and toughness, make it possible for them not to accept the environment but to change it.*

So, it is our intrinsic nature that enables us to intervene in the world and change our surroundings. Teaching learners at school not only about intervention but also how to intervene is one of the two key features of design & technology education. In this book we have called this technological capability (see page 7). But as we have seen intervention is not without its perils. Hence the second feature, teaching technological perspective (see page 7), is an essential counterpoint to teaching technological capability. Taken together they provide a learning experience from which young people can draw hope for the future. The intertwining of capability and perspective provides the ability to envisage what might be possible with regard to a future worth wanting, an insight into how this might be achieved and a sensitivity to possible pitfalls along the way. Some of these pitfalls can be predicted, others not, but this sensitivity should enable us to respond flexibly and wisely as the future we are creating unfolds. Learning design & technology will empower the next generations who will go out into the world and meet the challenge of climate change with the very real expectation that they will be able to meet and overcome this challenge; overcoming the selfishness, greed, and apathy that has so far bedevilled our efforts.

Climate change stop press

As we were about to submit this manuscript it is clear that the impact of climate change is already taking place on our country and the wider world, and it is important to be informed of developments that will help the country adapt to its impact. The Climate Change Committee (CCC) is an independent, statutory body established under the Climate Change Act 2008. Its purpose is to advise the UK and devolved governments on emissions targets and to report to Parliament on progress made in reducing greenhouse gas emissions and preparing for and adapting to the impacts of climate change. Hence keeping abreast of reports from the CCC is an important means of staying in touch with the way governments in the UK are dealing with the impact of climate change. The most recent report from the CCC is critical of the way the government is putting in place the means to adapt to the impact of climate change. The key messages are:

- **The second National Adaptation Programme has not adequately prepared the UK for climate change.** Our assessment has found very limited evidence of the implementation of adaptation at the scale needed to fully prepare for climate risks facing the UK across cities, communities, infrastructure, economy, and ecosystems.
- **The impacts from extreme weather in the UK over the last year highlight the urgency of adapting to climate change.** The record-breaking temperatures seen in summer 2022 brought unprecedented numbers of heat-related deaths, wildfire incidents, and significant infrastructure disruption.
- **The next National Adaptation Programme must make a step change.** The next National Adaptation Programme (NAP3) must be much more ambitious than its predecessors and lead to a long overdue shift in focus towards the delivery of effective adaptation.

The full report is available at the CCC website (https://www.theccc.org.uk).

According to a report in the *New Scientist* (Cuff, 2023) the UK government is relying on five key endeavours to reach net-zero carbon emissions by 2050. There are:

- Decarbonising power – to be achieved by introducing new nuclear power stations, increasing solar and hydrogen power, and developing carbon capture from power stations still using fossil fuels plus a vast increase in off shore wind generation.
- Creating a market for greenhouse gas removals – capturing, storing, and/or utilising greenhouse gases will need to attract investment if it is to become commercially profitable but the technologies for this are in early stages of development.
- Decarbonising steel – can, in theory, be achieved by electrifying the process and using hydrogen to reduce the iron oxide to iron but at the moment there are no large-scale pilots in operation.
- Mass deployment of heat pumps – the CCC advocates a rapid increase in heat pump deployment but this will require the government to incentivise households to buy heat pumps and eventually ban new gas boilers.
- Electric cars – the government is requiring car manufacturers to increase the percentage of zero emission cars by 22% in 2024. To support the resultant increasing sales of electric vehicles, there needs to be 300,000 charging points across the UK by 2030. At the moment this roll out of charging points is behind schedule.

Following the developments of these key endeavours will be an important part of being au fait with the way the government is tackling climate change and should be discussed with learners as part of their technological perspective curriculum.

Pollution and waste

It is generally agreed that pollution is serious problem, and this section discusses this in the context of moving away from a linear economy towards the introduction of a circular economy. It includes a series of short case studies, a consideration of the personal response to the problem of pollution and a discission about key concepts necessary to understand the issues raised by pollution.

Planet Earth is the home to an amazing variety of life (from the microscopic: colonies of bacteria; to the macroscopic: herds of bison) and awesome natural phenomena, (invisible yet pervasive, visible, and spectacular) existing alongside the endeavours of humans which recently have begun to disrupt the harmony within which life and natural phenomena have co-existed for millennia. Initially we must acknowledge that on Planet Earth there is no such place as 'away' and a major contribution to this disruption is treating the planet as if there were. The development of national and international trading practices based on a linear economy is at the root of this. Linear economics may be expressed both eloquently and pithily by describing it as TAKE, MAKE, USE, and DISPOSE. Raw materials are taken from the Earth, developed into a variety of products that we use and when their useful life is over, these products are disposed of by 'throwing away'. This throwing away has two consequences. Firstly, given that most of the resources required to produce what we use are finite then there is the very real possibility that we will run out of essential raw materials. It has been estimated that if everyone on the planet consumed as much as the average US citizen, four Earths would be needed to sustain them (McDonald, 2015). Secondly the material that is thrown away has a damaging effect on the environment and many of the animals and plants living on our planet. This is termed pollution and in order to protect the planet we need to find ways to reduce and eliminate it. The *Story of Stuff* (Leonard, 2010) provided a ground-breaking account of the challenge we face, and her approach is still highly relevant. In this seminal book Leonard considered extraction, production, distribution, consumption, and disposal, describing the harmful effects of each stage and what might be done to alleviate these. The book gave rise to the *Story of Stuff Project* which is still very much alive with the strap line: *"We have a problem with Stuff: we have too much of it, too much of it is toxic and we don't share it very well. But that's not the way things have to be".* The website (https://www.storyofstuff.org/) and the regular electronic newsletters, although US focused, are well worth following.

Nature's way

A good starting point for considering ways to eliminate pollution is to consider the natural world in which nothing is ever 'thrown away'. All life forms exist as part of circular pathways in which the waste products from some organisms become the feedstock for others. This is described in a simplified form in Figure 3.11. The driving force behind nature's circular economy is the sun. Solar radiation is used by plants to grow and form their own biomass. When plants die this biomass is decomposed by micro-organisms in the soil and this in turn provides nutrients to support the growth of new plants. Some plants will be eaten by animals, and when these animals die a natural death, their bodies will be decomposed by micro-

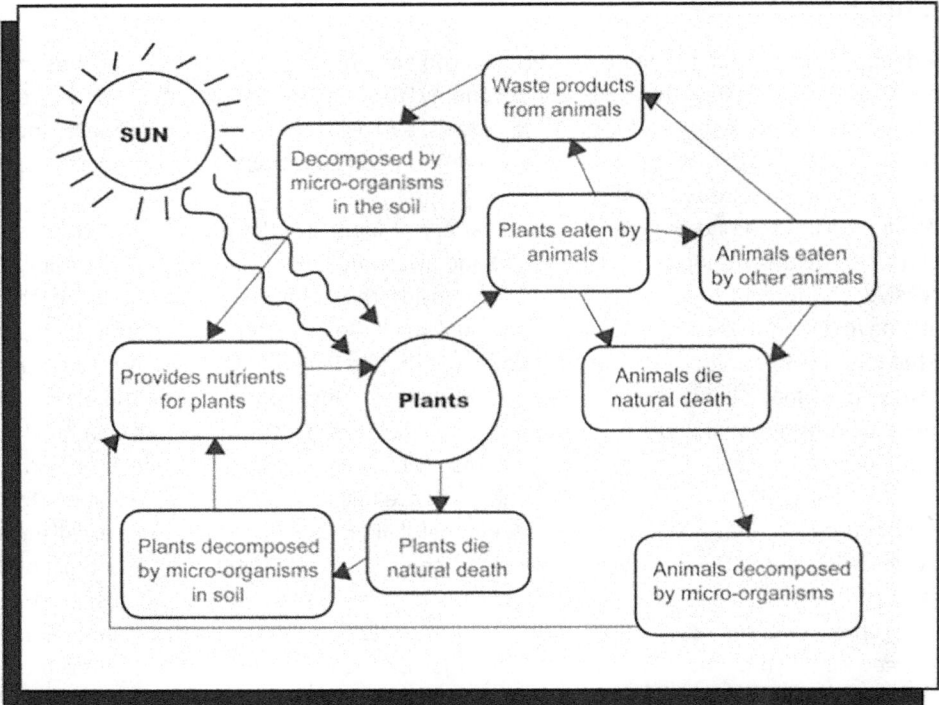

Figure 3.11 A simplified version of Nature's circular economy

organisms in the soil and provide nutrients for the growth of new plants. Some animals will be eaten by other animals, and when these animals die their bodies too will be decomposed by micro-organisms in the soil and provide nutrients for the growth of new plants. The waste products from all animals will be decomposed by micro-organisms in the soil and provide nutrients for the growth of new plants. And nature is bountiful in this process in that thousands of seeds and blossoms from a single tree might give rise to only one or two new trees, but the discarded seeds and blossoms will provide food for a host of creatures.

Mimicking nature

The Ellen MacArthur Foundation has been working since 2010 to develop models of economic activity which mirror as far as is possible the circular pathways in nature. The results are impressive and are being taken seriously by the business community. The timeline for her organisation shows just how active the Foundation has been since its inception. Three recent publications indicate the breadth and relevance of the Foundation's work:

- *The Nature Imperative: How the circular economy tackles biodiversity*
    - Published in November 2021
    - Available free to download

- *The Big Food Redesign Study*
  - Published in November 2021
  - Available free to download

- *Circular Design for Fashion*
  - Published in December 2021
  - Available from Amazon

Given the significance of the idea of a circular economy as a key method to tackle pollution and the depth and breadth of the work carried out by the Foundation, it is worth delving into the details of the model it has developed. The three key principles of a circular economy are shown in Table 3.4.

The biological and technical cycles are shown in Figure 3.12.

Concerning the biological cycle

Farming methods

Farms and other sources of biological resources such as forests and fisheries are managed in ways that create positive outcomes for nature. Farmers may draw on several different schools of thought, such as regenerative agriculture, restorative aquaculture, agroecology, agroforestry, and conservation agriculture, to help them apply the most appropriate set of practices to drive regenerative outcomes on their farms. Once food is harvested and

Table 3.4 Three key principles of a circular economy

Principle 1. Eliminate waste and pollution
Currently, our economy works in a take-make-waste system. We take raw materials from the Earth, we make products from them, and eventually we throw them away as waste. Much of this waste ends up in landfills or incinerators and is lost. This system cannot work in the long term because the resources on our planet are finite.

Principle 2. Circulate products and materials at their highest value
This means keeping materials in use, either as a product or, when that can no longer be used, as components or raw materials. This way, nothing becomes waste, and the intrinsic value of products and materials are retained. It is helpful to think about two fundamental cycles – the **technical cycle** and the **biological cycle.** In the technical cycle, products are reused, repaired, remanufactured, and recycled. In the biological cycle, biodegradable materials are returned to the earth through processes like composting and anaerobic digestion.

Principle 3. Regenerate nature
By moving from a take-make-waste linear economy to a circular economy, we support natural processes and leave more room for nature to thrive. Instead of continuously degrading nature, we build natural capital. We employ farming practises that allow nature to rebuild soils and increase biodiversity and return biological materials to the earth. Regenerative farming practises can significantly reduce greenhouse gas emissions from food production by reducing reliance on synthetic inputs and by building healthy soils that absorb rather than release carbon. By adopting circular economy principles, the food industry could halve its projected greenhouse gas emissions in 2050. By keeping products and materials in use, less land is required for sourcing virgin raw materials

---

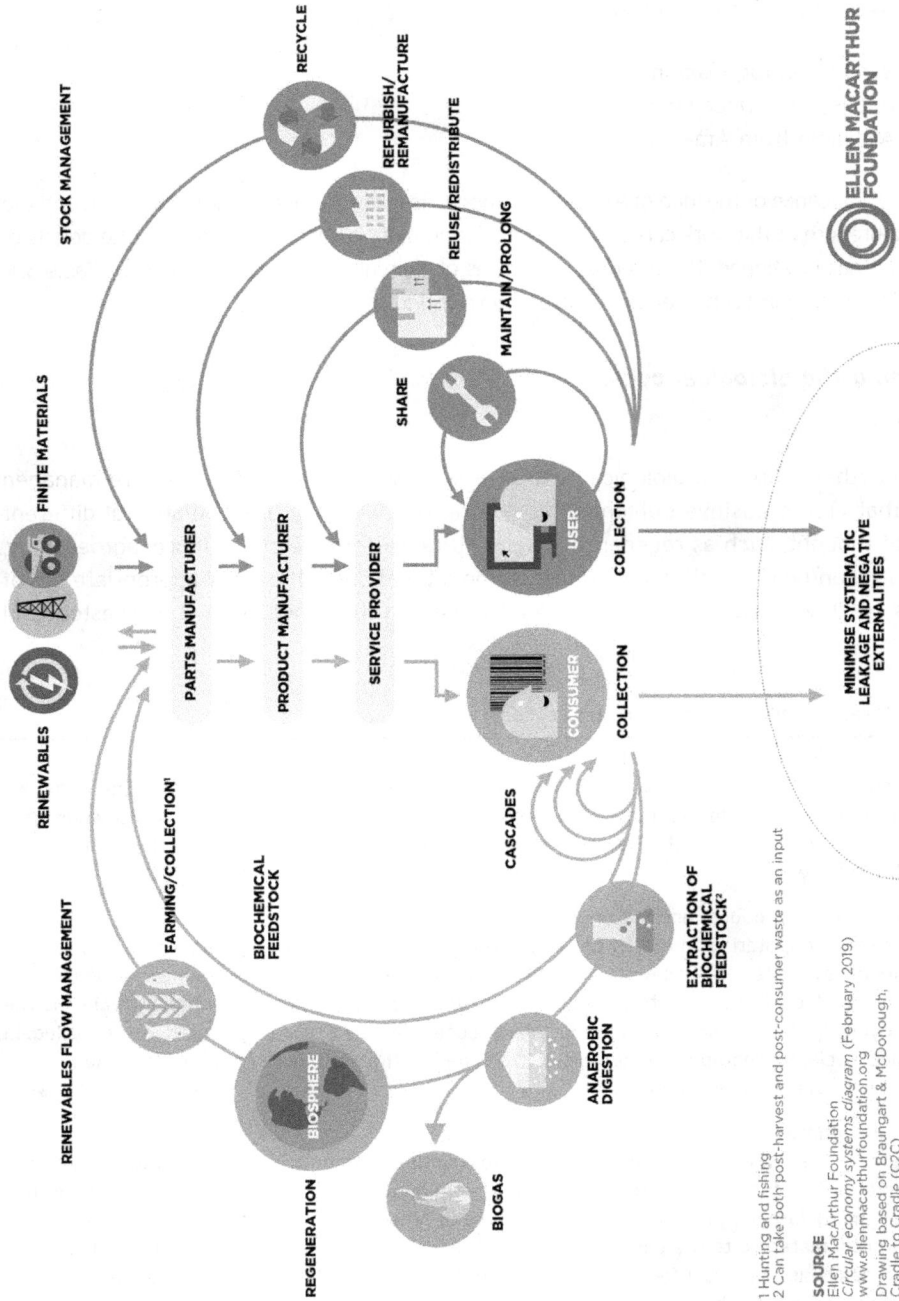

Figure 3.12 The biological and technical cycles as envisaged by the Ellen MacArthur Foundation

Source: Copyright © Ellen MacArthur Foundation, (Circular economy system diagram, 2019).

consumed, the nutrients in organic waste streams can be collected, and returned to the soil via processes such as composting and anaerobic digestion.

Composting and anaerobic digestion

Composting is the microbial breakdown of organic matter in the presence of oxygen. It can be used to turn food by-products and other biodegradable materials into compost, which can be used as a soil enhancer, returning valuable materials to farmland in place of artificial fertilisers. The process is biological and involves naturally occurring microorganisms, such as bacteria and fungi.

Anaerobic digestion also involves microorganisms, but in this case in the absence of oxygen. Anaerobic digestion produces biogas and a solid residual or 'digestate'. This digestate can be applied directly to the land or composted and used as a soil amendment. Biogas, made primarily of methane and carbon dioxide, can be produced from both composting and anaerobic digestion and used as a source of energy similar to natural gas. This type of energy recovery is part of a circular economy since it is a by-product of the process of returning organic material to the soil.

Cascades

These loops of the biological cycle make use of products and materials already in the economy. This could mean, for example, using food by-products to make other materials, such as textiles made from orange peel, or designing new food products using ingredients usually considered waste, like ketchup made from banana peel. It could also mean using the material for applications such as animal feed. When products or materials can no longer be used, they move to the outer loops of the biological cycle where they are returned to the soil.

Extraction of biochemical feedstock

Taking both post-harvest and post-consumer biological materials as feedstock, this step involves the use of biorefineries to produce low volume but high value chemical products. On top of this, biorefineries can produce a range of other valuable products from organic materials through a series of steps. These processes could consecutively produce, for example, high value biochemicals and nutraceuticals followed by bulk biochemicals.

Pause for thought

In the science curriculum your learners will study food chains and food webs. Might it be worth talking with science colleagues about this and how it relates to your teaching of circular economies?

Concerning the technical cycle

Most people regard recycling as a very important way to tackle pollution and save resources. However, in a circular economy recycling is very much a last resort used only when all other options for extending the useful life of manufactured items have been exhausted. Hence the inner loops in the diagram are activities that take place before recycling is initiated.

Sharing

Sharing is the first port of call in the technical cycle and, while not appropriate for all products in the economy, it has the power to dramatically increase the utilisation of many products. Power tools for example spend most of their time unused. Community tool libraries where people can borrow both hand and power tools are one way of sharing tools. And people are beginning to share wardrobes; for example, MsParis; a subscription/one time-based rental for women's designer wear. Users can choose between subscription based monthly rental/rent per day basis. The firm claims that the clothes are genuine and dry cleaned after they are returned by the customers.

Maintaining

Whilst sharing increases the intensity of product use, maintenance prolongs products' useful lives. Maintenance is an important way of keeping products at a high quality and guards against failure or decline. Servicing a car or repairing brickwork on a house are well known examples of maintenance but maintenance can be applied to most products that suffer wear and tear. For example, Clothes Doctor empowers people to look after their clothing by sharing knowledge about care and maintenance and providing a clothes mending service.

Reusing

Reuse keeps products in use in their original form and for their original purpose. Reusable packaging is one of the most effective ways of tackling packaging waste, particularly plastic, and is being adopted by businesses across industries, from food and drink, to cosmetics and home cleaning. Clothing is being reused; people are selling their unwanted clothing and buying clothes from resale platforms, often at a fraction of the cost of buying new. This displaces the need for a new item to be made and stops an unwanted item going to waste.

Redistributing

Redistribution is another way to keep products in use and stop them becoming waste. By diverting products from their intended market to another customer, the product is put to valuable use. For example, a fashion brand could redistribute unsold clothing from one store to another.

Refurbishing

Returning products to good working order is a way to restore their value. This could include repairing or replacing components, updating specifications, and improving cosmetic appearance. Refurbishing can be carried out by individuals on their own products, or by specialists. The Right to Repair movement aims to make changes to regulations so that products are designed in a way that makes it possible for users to repair them by themselves. There are countless examples of companies working to keep products in use through refurbishment. A good example is in the tech industry, where companies buy up used items such as mobile phones, refurbish them, and sell them on at a fraction of their original price.

Remanufacturing

Remanufacturing is done when products cannot remain in circulation in their current state and need more intensive work to be used again. Remanufacturing involves re-engineering products and components to as-new condition with the same, or improved, level of performance as a newly manufactured one. Remanufactured products or components are typically provided with a warranty that is equivalent to, or better than, that of the newly manufactured product. It may require more investment in plant and machinery than do the inner loops of the technical cycle, but it means that products and components do not become waste and can remain in the economy, representing a cost saving to businesses and customers.

And finally, recycling

Recycling takes place when a product can no longer be used and is beyond refurbishment or remanufacture or isn't suitable for those steps. It is the final way of keeping in use the materials from which the product is made so they don't become waste. With recycling, the embedded value of a product – the time and energy invested in making it – is lost, but the value of the materials is retained. Recycling transforms a product or component into its basic materials or substances and reprocesses them into new materials. Designing for recycling is important for all products in the technical cycle, but especially for items that are not suitable for the other steps in the cycle. These items include single use packaging which is itself only appropriate when it cannot be designed out and reusable alternatives are not possible.

Pause for thought

Designing products so that they can fit into a circular economy is necessary if society is to eliminate waste and its attendant pollution. In each loop of the technical cycle of a circular economy there are opportunities to design products such that they can enter into those loops. Might it be possible for your learners to redesign existing products so that they can enter into the loops of a circular economy?

Case studies

Plastics and a circular economy

Plastics are an interesting and very useful group of materials. They are composed of long chain molecules called polymers. These are made by joining together lots of very much smaller molecules called monomers. Depending on the nature of the monomer the plastics formed have different properties. Some are thermoplastics which when heated soften and melt and on cooling resolidify. Hence, they can be used in a wide range manufacturing processes such as blow moulding, vacuum forming, injection moulding and 3D printing. Some are thermosetting plastics and once formed do not soften and melt and if heated to a high temperature decompose. Some are elastomers which although solid are stretchy. These different sorts of plastic have useful properties which results in them being used to make a huge variety of everyday products in vast numbers. The problem of pollution arises when the useful life of these products comes to an end, and they are thrown away. Of the 24.5 million tonnes of plastic waste generated in Europe every year only 14% is recycled. The rest is incinerated (which leads to the emission of GHGs), buried in landfill (which is a waste of valuable material), or lost on land or sea (which often leads to the damage of wildlife). Recycling is currently achieved through a mechanical process which involves sorting, washing, drying, and grinding followed by heating and reforming into a new material which is of a lower quality than the original plastic (Dow, 2022). Rather than recycling plastics as they are, scientists are now beginning to develop ways to break down the polymers in plastic products into monomers that can then be repolymerised into useful plastics. This is called chemical recycling and it is possible to use catalysts to achieve this at low temperatures, so the process does not require a lot of energy. This is the beginning of plastics becoming part of a circular economy. Mura Technology have developed the Hydrprs^{TM} Process (see https://muratechnology.com/technology/). This starts by shredding waste plastic and removing contaminants such as glass, grit, metals, and stones. Then the shredded plastic is melted, pressurised and treated with high pressure, high temperature steam which breaks the plastic down into liquid hydrocarbons and gas very quickly. These are separated into various components that can be sold to petrochemical companies that use them in the manufacture of new plastics and other materials. Mura Technology are working with Dow, one of the world's leading chemicals and plastics manufacturers, to develop a new facility in Boehlen, Germany, which is predicted to recycle 120 kilotonnes of plastic per year using the Hydrprs^{TM} Process (Dow, 2022). This is an interesting example of the way plastics can become part of the circular economy in the future.

Rechargeable batteries and a circular economy

The days of cars that use the internal combustion engine are numbered and more, and more countries are developing the charging infrastructure that will allow electric cars to operate across longs distances mirroring the way that in the early part of the 20th century large numbers of petrol stations were built to support vehicles that used fossil fuels. But this transition to electric vehicles which use rechargeable batteries immediately creates the problem of what to do with the batteries once their useful life is over. Electronic waste is already a serious problem although there are attempts to situate electronic products that no longer work in a circular economy. An interesting example of this is the Mexican electronics recycling company, Recicla Electronicos Mexico S.a de C.V., which collects e-waste in order to refurbish and resell electronic products, disassemble electronic waste to obtain parts that can be resold and utilise parts in the development of new products for sale (de Vries *et al.*, 2023). And important legislation is being introduced. From July 2024 the carbon footprint of batteries in electric vehicles sold in the EU will need to be declared and by 2030 those batteries will have to contain minimum levels of recycled materials (*Economist*, 2022). This is where the developments of gigafactories are important. These are factories which are designed to produce rechargeable batteries in a way described as circular manufacturing.

The direct recycling process is the recovery, regeneration, and reuse of battery components directly without breaking down the chemical structure. By maintaining the process value in the original battery components, a lower-cost re-constituted material can be supplied to battery manufacturers. This is a great improvement on previous recycling processes which were much more energy intensive and produced materials of little use to battery manufacturers.

Fast fashion needs to slow down

Currently most of the textile industry operates on a linear economy model.

All features of this life cycle contribute to pollution but perhaps the most disturbing are the following.

• The scale of clothing production and the length of time garments are worn.

The world currently buys 62 million tonnes of apparel per year, some 100 billion items of clothing (Lawton, 2022). According to the Swedish Foundation for Strategic Environmental Research (cited in Lawton, 2022) the number of times items are worn before disposal is often low, e.g., dresses 27 times, T-shirts 30 times.

What can be done about this?

The rapid production of inexpensive clothing which consumers purchase and then discard after wearing for a short time only is a vicious circle leading to massive and increasing production. An advertising campaign to alter the attitude of consumers such that they are disinclined to change what they wear at such frequent intervals is one possible way forward. Also worth considering is increased care to extend useful life, known as refurbishing and discussed above.

• The way they are cared for during use.

The washing of clothing during use gives rise to microfibers which become distributed in the natural environment including the oceans where they are swallowed by many different species of marine animals including plankton which, as they are at the bottom of every food chain lead to them being ingested by many other animals.

What can be done about this?

This can be alleviated to some extent by modifying the washing process as suggested by the US Environmental Protection Agency (undated) as shown in Figure 3.13.

- End of life disposal; only a very small proportion of discarded clothes are ever recycled.

Only 1% of the world's textile waste is turned back into clothing (Lawton, 2022), the rest end up in landfill or are incinerated. This is largely due to the difficulty in recycling garments that are made of mixed materials, polyester, cotton, elastane, for example. Mechanical recycling degrades the fibres, lowering the value of the recycled materials and chemical recycling involving depolymerisation followed by repolymerisation is not that well developed although progress is being made.

What can be done about this?

New fabrics that are easier to recycle so that garments made from them can enter a circular economy are being developed. For example, Infinited Fiber, a Finnish company (see https://infinitedfiber.com), have developed a process which produces a fibre called Infinna. The process breaks down waste and captures its value at the polymer level. It takes piles of trashed textiles that would otherwise be landfilled or burned and transforms them into brand-new premium-quality fibres for the textile industry. Currently focusing on using cotton-rich textiles, the technology can also be used to turn other cellulose-rich materials – old newspapers, used cardboard, crop residues like rice or wheat straw – into the same fibre. Customers for the new fibre are the clothing brands H&M and Patagonia. Infinited Fiber's strap line captures the essence of their approach: *Nothing new needs to be grown when we make the most of what's already in circulation.*

Earthshot Initiatives

The Earthshot Prize, launched by the Royal Foundation and Prince William, is centred around five 'Earthshots', simple but ambitious goals for our planet, which if achieved by 2030 will improve life for us all, for generations to come (see https://royalfoundation.com/programme/the-earthshot-prize/).
   The five Earthshots are:

- Protect and restore nature
- Clean our air
- Revive our oceans
- Build a waste-free world
- Fix our climate.

Of particular relevance to this issue is 'build a waste-free world'. The prize winner was Notpla and a brief summary of their work is shown in Panel 3.8.

WANT TO REDUCE MICROFIBERS?

6 Simple tips to help reduce microfiber pollution:

Wash clothing less often.
This is perhaps the simplest and most effective method for reducing microfiber pollution.

Only wash full loads of laundry.
This results in less friction between clothes and reduces shedding of synthetic fibers.

Use microfiber-catching devices when you do the laundry.
Several technologies are available for purchase, including special wash bags and laundry balls designed to trap microfibers.

Wash laundry with cold water for a shorter period of time.
Studies have found that switching to a colder and shorter cycle can dramatically reduce microfiber shedding.

Install an external microfiber filter on your washing machine and dispose of captured microfibers in the trash.
There are several commercially available external lint filters to choose from.

Use a front-loading washer, if possible.
Top-load washing machines tend to produce more microfibers than front-loading machines.

For more information, visit neefusa.org

NEEF National Environmental Education Foundation

Figure 3.13 6 ways to reduce microfibre pollution

Source: Used with permission from The National Environmental Education Foundation (NEEF), NEEFusa.org.

Panel 3.8 Notpla, the winning entry in the 2022 Earthshot 'Build a waste free world' category

At Notpla the starting point is brown seaweed which has the advantages of being globally abundant and fast-growing, not requiring freshwater, land, or fertiliser plus it reduces ocean acidification and absorbs carbon.

Notpla extract the gelatinous material from the seaweed and use this to produce a variety of products including:

- Covering for food packaging that is grease and water resistance necessary for a wide variety of applications including hot, cold, wet, and dry foods. The containers are microwaveable, stackable, and leak proof. Importantly they are home compostable and bio-degrade quickly.
- Ooho, an edible bubble to hold liquids that replaces single use plastic items such as cups and bottles. The bubbles may be eaten as part of the drink or thrown away in a home compost where they biodegrade in a few weeks like fruit peel.
- Notpla paper made from the fibres and biomass left behind after the gelatinous part of the seaweed is extracted. It can be printed and used for packaging.

Visit https://www.notpla.com for full details.

Pause for thought

We think that the use of case studies like those above provide learners with an opportunity to learn about the important role played by design & technology in the world outside school. Those above have been written to inform teachers and will need some simplification if they are to be accessible to learners in school. You can find advice and guidance on writing case studies at https://dandtfordandt.wordpress.com/resources/technological-perspective-readers/.

The personal response to waste

In discussing the personal response to global warming we referenced the podcast *A Matter of Degrees* (Stokes & Wilkinson, 2022) and the three-fold approach they advocated is relevant to our response to waste. Firstly, we can make changes in our personal lives reduce waste and as far as possible behave in ways that become part of a circular economy. For example, in the case of clothing we can refurbish clothes to extend their useful life and we can 'buy better that lasts longer'. Secondly, we can raise the issue of waste where we work so that the amount of waste is reduced. Again, this will involve finding opportunities for the way materials are handled to become part of a circular economy. Thirdly, we can become politically active at local, regional, and national levels to support the development of circular economy approaches to the way people live and business functions. It is important that learners appreciate these three possible approaches so that they can discuss them with their families and encourage them to consider the way they live and work.

In terms of learners' own designing and making, Nick Givens (2022) has suggested that it is possible for learners to design and make in ways that engage with the problems of waste and the pollution it causes. He wonders whether learners might be challenged with designing and making textile products that maximise their durability, repair-ability, re-cyclability, and the reuse of recycled materials and components. He suggests that for physical durability learners could consider construction and strategic reinforcing to create products that can resist damage and wear. He extends durability to include emotional durability suggesting that learners might develop features to keep a product relevant and desirable to the user (or multiple users) over time. He also suggests that learners could be encouraged to design and make with recycled yarns, recycled fabrics, recycled fasteners and recycled embellishments.

Key ideas for the design & technology curriculum

Systems thinking

Systems thinking is important if learners are to understand the way linear and circular economies operate and the way materials might or might not become waste and cause pollution. Various materials flow through these economies and a useful way to track this flow and its consequences is through the use of systems thinking. The starting materials may be considered as inputs, what happens to them as processes which lead to various outputs. And thinking about the sub systems that make up the overall systems allows learners to drill down into more detailed thinking about what is happening. It will be important to define the system boundary as this will either limit or expand the scope of the thinking. In the case of a circular economy the concept of feedback is important as the output of some sub systems will become the input of other subsystems. Lag is another important idea as this deals with the time a system or subsystem takes to respond to various inputs. Systems thinking is dealt with in more detail in chapter 5.

Life Cycle Analysis

Life Cycle Analysis (LCA) is a way of thinking about the life of a product from the moment when the materials used to make it are extracted right up to the end of its useful life. Figure 3.14 shows the five stages in the life cycle. Understanding this diagram requires systems thinking. Each stage uses energy and materials as inputs and leads to emissions and waste as outputs. It is important to minimise the energy and materials used and the emis-sions and waste produced. It is also important to maximise the gains to be made from re-cycling materials once the useful life of the product is over. In the diagram the only element of circularity is the loop from recycling and disposal back to production. So, in this form the diagram mainly reflects a linear economy. In a circular economy there would be loops be-tween all adjacent stages. Despite this limitation it can lead to some interesting findings. Consider, for example, the washing machine. There is little point in reducing the energy used in producing or distributing washing machines as this is only a tiny fraction of the energy that is consumed by the washing machine over its normal working life. To make a washing machine more environmentally friendly, product designers need to develop low energy ways of washing clothes that use less water, less if any detergent, and less energy.

PRIMARY MATERIALS

```
                         ▼
ENERGY    ▷    ┌──────────────────┐    ▷    EMISSIONS
               │    EXTRACTION    │         AND WASTE
               └──────────────────┘
                         ▼
ENERGY    ▷    ┌──────────────────┐    ▷◁
               │   PRODUCTION     │
               └──────────────────┘
                         ▼
ENERGY    ▷    ┌──────────────────┐    ▷    EMISSIONS
MATERIALS      │  DISTRIBUTION    │         AND WASTE
               └──────────────────┘
                         ▼
ENERGY    ▷    ┌──────────────────┐    ▷    EMISSIONS
MATERIALS      │       USE        │         AND WASTE
               └──────────────────┘
                         ▼
ENERGY    ▷    ┌──────────────────┐
MATERIALS      │ RECYCLING AND    │
               │    DISPOSAL      │
               └──────────────────┘
                         ▼
```

WASTE

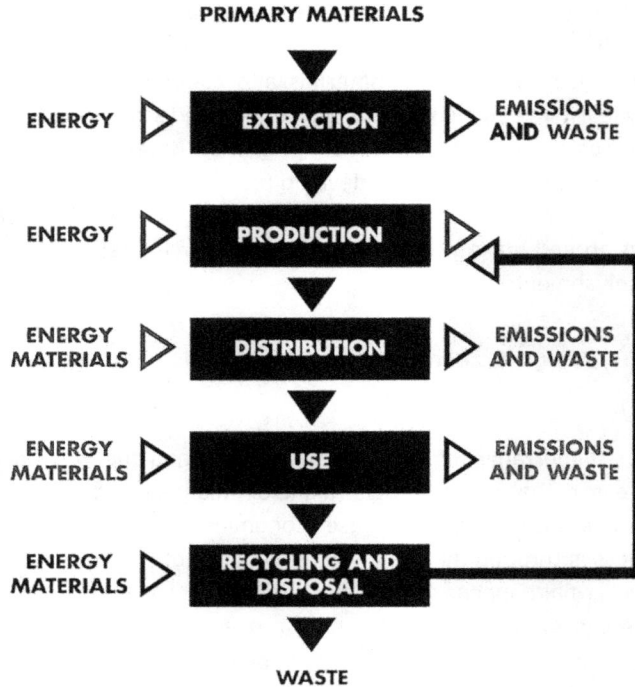

Figure 3.14 Life cycle analysis for a product in a mainly linear economy as a diagram

Challenging ownership – designing for sharing or leasing

Many of the items we use spend most of their time being un-used. DIY hand tools, which are used infrequently by their owners are an example and so are motor cars which spend many hours per day 'parked' as opposed to moving passengers. Devising schemes that allow people to share such items by borrowing them on an as needed basis from tool libraries or car pools are ideas that designers are exploring. The idea of leasing as opposed to owning is also being explored. The item to be used, a washing machine for example, is leased rather than being bought. The manufacturer (or distributor) retains ownership of the item and is responsible for its end-of-life disposal within a circular economy. The lessee uses the item until its useful life is over whereupon the item is handed back to the manufacturer. During its useful life, the item may undergo maintenance provided by the manufacturer to extend its useful life and also upgrades to improve its performance.

Design for circularity to minimise waste

A useful application of systems thinking is to consider any complex product as a series of interlinked sub-systems. The production of these sub-systems and their subsequent in-tegration into the final product may be seen in terms of their place in a circular economy such that their design enables maintenance and repair and replacement of sub-systems to extend useful life; further use of components and materials in defunct subsystems in other applications, and finally at the end of useful life when replacement of failing sub-systems is no longer feasible the materials and components in the sub-systems comprising the entire product can be recycled so that there is a little waste as possible. An adjustable desk lamp is sufficiently complex to be the subject of such consideration but not so complex as to be beyond the scope of learners in school. The lamp shade, bulb, bulb holder, springs, struts, switch, wiring, hinges, base, fixings, brightness controller, may be grouped into sub systems for the purpose of being part of a circular economy in the life cycle of the desk lamp. Such thinking need not take much in the way of curriculum time, but it will introduce learners to the implications of designing for circularity with, for example, the conflict between achieving ease of disassembly and robustness in use becoming apparent.

Pause for thought

It is worth exploring with colleagues the content of your design & technology curriculum with a view to finding out where and to what extent you teach these key ideas.

Summary

This chapter considered five issues that are, at the time if writing, of great significance for those teaching and learning design & technology. The section on decolonising gave prominence to providing role models to inspire learners from diverse backgrounds. The section of gender emphasised the challenging of stereotypes and included a Thought Piece from Ulrika Sultan. The section on disruption identified nine disruptive technologies to be taught in secondary school and included a Stop Press piece concerning the recent availability of the Chatbot ChatGPT. The section on global warming presented the evidence for and effects of the impact of human activity giving rise to greenhouse gases and national and international attempts to both adapt to and mitigate the impacts of climate change and included a Thought Piece by Dominic Nolan and a Stop Press piece concerning the recent pronouncements of the UK's Climate Change Committee which are critical of the way the government is putting in place the means to adapt to the impact of climate change. The section on pollution and waste considered in some detail the nature of circular economies including case studies and identifying relevant key ideas for inclusion in the design & technology curriculum.

References

Akala (2019) *Natives Race and Class in the Ruins of Empire*, UK: Two Roads.

AQA (2022) https://www.aqa.org.uk/news/new-diverse-designers-added-to-gcse-design-and-technology.

Archer, L., Moote, J., MacLeod, E., Francis, B., & DeWitt, J. (2020) *ASPIRES 2: Young People's Science and Career Aspirations, Age 10-19*, London: UCL Institute of Education.

Banks, F., & Barlex, D. (2021) *Teaching STEM in the Secondary School*, Oxford: Routledge, p. 22.

Barlex, D., Givens, N., & Steeg, T. (2021) Teaching about disruption: A key feature of new and emerging technologies, in Hardy, A. (Ed.), *Learning to Teach Design and Technology in the Secondary School*, 4th Edition, Oxon: Routledge.

BBC (2022) *What Is Climate Change? A Really Simple Guide*, https://www.bbc.co.uk/news/science-environment-24021772.

Berners-Lee, M. (2020) *How Bad Are Bananas? The Carbon Footprint of Everything*, London: Profile Books Ltd.

Beyond Oil and Gas Alliance (2022), https://beyondoilandgasalliance.com.

Blakemore, E. (2019 February) National Geographic, *Race and Ethnicity: How Are They Different?* https://www.nationalgeographic.com/culture/article/race-ethnicity

Boakye, J. (2019) *Black, Listed*, UK: Dialogue Books.

Bronowski, J. (1973) *The Ascent of Man*, London: BBC.

Carbon Literacy Project (2022) *Overview of Carbon Literacy*, https://carbonliteracy.com/about-us/

Cole, J. (2019) *What's the Reason for the Shortage of Engineers in the UK?* https://www.jonlee.co.uk/blog/2020/01/whats-the-reason-behind-the-shortage-of-engineers-in-uk?source=google.com.

Crown (2021) *Hydrogen Economy Strategy*, https://assets.publishing.service.gov.uk/government/uploads/system/uploads/attachment_data/file/1011283/UK-Hydrogen-Strategy_web.pdf

Cuff, M. (2023) The UK's Five Big Climate Bets, *New Scientist*, 8 April 2023.

Cuff, M. (2022) Mixed View on COP 27 Deal, *New Scientist*, 26 November, p. 7.

de Vries, M., Klapwijk, M. R., Gu, J., & Yang. C. (Eds.) (2023) *Maker Education and Technology Education: Reflections on Good Practice*, Leiden, The Netherlands: Brill Sense.

Dow (2022) *New Scientist*, 17 September 2022.

Economist (2022 Oct 29) *Inside the Gigafactory*.

Economist (2022a) *More than Hot Air*, July 30th, p. 22.

Economist (2022b) *Guilt Free Flying*, August 20th, p. 67.

Ellen MacArthur Foundation, extensive information about the Foundation and its work on circular economies, https://ellenmacarthurfoundation.org.

ESSA (2022) *Solaris*, https://www.esa.int/Enabling_Support/Space_Engineering_Technology/SOLARIS

FAO (2013) *Key Facts and Findings Sheet Derived from Tackling Climate Change through Livestock*, https://www.fao.org/news/story/en/item/197623/icode/.

Firth, N. (2018) *New Scientist*, 5 May 2018 (pp. 31–34).

Gabriel. K. (2019) Interview with Jim Al-Khalili, *The Life Scientific*, 12 March 2019, https://www.bbc.co.uk/programmes/m00035tc.

Gallagher, J.B., Shelamoff, V., & Layton, C. (2022) Seaweed Ecosystems May Not Mitigate CO2 Emissions, *ICES Journal of Marine Science*, 79(3): 585–592, 10.1093/icesjms/fsac011.

Gartner (2015) Gartner Hype Cycle, http://www.gartner.com/technology/research/methodologies/hype-cycle.jsp.

Ghosh, P. (2022) Esa mulls Solaris plan to beam solar energy from space, https://www.bbc.co.uk/news/science-environment-62982113

Gillborn, D. (2008) *Racism and Education Coincidence or conspiracy*, London: Routledge.

Givens, N. (2022) Private communication with the authors.

Guardian (2022) *Tuvalu first to call for fossil fuel non-proliferation treaty at COP 27*, https://www.theguardian.com/environment/2022/nov/08/tuvalu-first-to-call-for-fossil-fuel-non-proliferation-treaty-at-cop27.

Harari, Y. (2014) *Homo Deus a Brief History of Tomorrow*, London: Vintage.

Hirsch, A. (2018) *BRIT(ish)*, London: Vintage.

HMG (2021) Ref Net Zero Strategy Build Back Greener, October 2021, https://assets.publishing.service.gov.uk/government/uploads/system/uploads/attachment_data/file/1033990/net-zero-strategy-beis.pdf.

Holtam, N. (2022) *Sleepers Wake Getting Serious about Climate Change*, London: SPCK.

Horton, J., & Palumbo, D. (21 July 2022) *Europe Wildfires: Are They Linked to Climate Change?* https://www.bbc.co.uk/news/58159451).

Hurlimann, S. (2019) *How Kelp Naturally Combats Climate Change*, https://sitn.hms.harvard.edu/flash/2019/how-kelp-naturally-combats-global-climate-change/#:~:text=Coastal%20ecosystems%20sequester%20away%20surprisingly,seagrass%2C%20olive%20in%20rich%20soil.

IEA (2021) https://www.iea.org/reports/transport-biofuels.

IPCC (2022) *Summary for Policy Makers on Mitigation of Climate Change*, https://www.ipcc.ch/report/ar6/wg3/downloads/report/IPCC_AR6_WGIII_SPM.pdf.

Jolly, J. (2022) Sizewell C Nuclear Plant Confirmed with £700m Public Stake, https://www.theguardian.com/business/2022/nov/29/sizewell-c-nuclear-plant-confirmed-edf-suffolk-jobs-uk

Kleeman, J. (2020) *Sex Robots and Vegan Meat Adventures at the Frontier of Birth, Food, Sex & Death*, London: Picador.

Lawton, G. (2022) Can Fashion Really Go Green? *New Scientist*, 4 June 2022.

Lawton, G. (2020) *New Scientist*, 22 February 2020 (pp. 39–43).

Le Billon, P., Gaulin, N., & Lujala, P. (2022) *Phasing Out Fossil Fuels: Determinants of Production Cuts and Implications for an International Agreement*, https://direct.mit.edu/glep/article-abstract/22/4/95/113511/Phasing-Out-Fossil-Fuels-Determinants-of?redirectedFrom=fulltext.

Leonard, A. (2010) *The Story of Stuff*. London: Constable & Robinson Ltd.

Le Page, M. (2022) Last Shot. *New Scientist*, 29 October 2022.

Lewton, T. (2022) The New Age of Fusion, *New Scientist*, 22 October 2022, page 38–41.

MacArthur, E. (2015) Resources Developed by the Ellen McArthur Foundation, https://ellenmacarthurfoundation.org/resources/education-and-learning/teaching-resources.

MacKay, D. J. C. (2009) *Sustainable Energy without the Hot Air*, Cambridge, UIT Cambridge, www.withouthotair.com.

Manyika J., et al. (2013) *Disruptive Technologies: Advances That Will Transform Life, Business, and The Global Economy*, McKinsey Global Institute, https://www.mckinsey.com/business-functions/mckinsey-digital/our-insights/disruptive-technologies.

Marley, J. (2022) *COP 27: Which Countries Will Push to End Fossil Fuel Production? And Which Won't?* https://theconversation.com/cop27-which-countries-will-push-to-end-fossil-fuel-production-and-which-wont-193471.

McCallum, S. (2022) Nov 17, *Lab-grown Chicken Safe to Eat, Say US Regulators*, https://www.bbc.co.uk/news/technology-63660488.

McCallam, S. (2023) *Martha Lane Fox Warns Against Hysteria over AI*, https://www.bbc.co.uk/news/technology-65162257.

McDonald, C. (2015) *How Many Earths Do We Need?*, https://www.bbc.co.uk/news/magazine-33133712.

McKay, D., Staal, A., Abrahams, J., Winkleman, R., Sakschweski, B., Loriani, S., Fetzer, I., Cornell, S., Rockstroms, J., & Lenton, T. (2022) Exceeding 1.5°C Global Warming Could Trigger Multiple Climate Tipping Points, *Science*, 337(6611), https://www.science.org/doi/abs/10.1126/science.abn7950

McPlant^{TM} (2022), https://www.mcdonalds.com/gb/en-gb/product/vegan-mcplant.html.

Murray, J. (2021) *From Corrie to Car Ads, Carbon Literacy Training Pushes Climate to the Fore*, https://www.theguardian.com/environment/2021/oct/02/from-corrie-to-car-ads-carbon-literacy-training-pushes-climate-to-the-fore.

National Grid (2022a) *How Much of the UK's Energy Is Renewable?* https://www.nationalgrid.com/stories/energy-explained/how-much-uks-energy-renewable

National Grid (2022b) *Onshore vs Offshore Wind Energy: What's the Difference?* https://www.nationalgrid.com/stories/energy-explained/onshore-vs-offshore-wind-energy.

Natural History Museum (2022) *Is Methane a Greenhouse Gas?*, https://www.nhm.ac.uk/discover/quick-questions/is-methane-a-greenhouse-gas.html

Newitz, A. (2023) The Chatbot Apocalypse, *New Scientist*, 18 March 2023.

Preston, C. J. (2018) *The Synthetic Age*, Cambridge Massachusetts: The MIT Press.

Rannard, G., & Stallard E. (2022) COP27: *What Have Global Leaders Done on Climate Change in 2022?* https://www.bbc.co.uk/news/science-environment-63458945.

Robertson, B., & Mousavian, M. (2022) *The Carbon Capture Crux: Lessons Learned*, https://ieefa.org/resources/carbon-capture-crux-lessons-learned

Rodionova, M.V., Poudyal, R.S., Tiwari, I., Voloshin, R. A., Zharmukhamedov, V. H., Nam, G., Zayadan, B. K., Bruce, B. D., Hou, H. J. M., & Allakhverdiev, S. I. (2017) Biofuel Production: Challenges and Opportunities, *International Journal of Hydrogen Energy*, 42(12), 23 March 2017: 8450-8461, https://www.sciencedirect.com/science/article/abs/pii/S0360319916334139?via%3Dihub.

Rowlatt, J. (2022) *COP 26 Chief: Leaders Must Do More to Honour Climate Promises*, https://www.bbc.co.uk/news/uk-scotland-61457983.

Salt, M. (2022) *Carbon Capture Landscape 2022 – Still Too Early to Confidently Fulfil Promises*, https://ieefa.org/resources/carbon-capture-landscape-2022-still-too-early-confidently-fulfil-promises.

Sovacool, B. (2011) *Second Thoughts about Nuclear Power*, https://web.archive.org/web/20130116084833/http://spp.nus.edu.sg/docs/policy-briefs/201101_RSU_PolicyBrief_1-2nd_Thought_Nuclear-Sovacool.pdf.

Stokes, L., & Wilkinson, K. (2022) *Podcast*, https://www.degreespod.com/?utm_source=densediscovery&utm_medium=email&utm_campaign=newsletter-issue-211.

For the Personal Response, see https://www.degreespod.com/episodes/season-3-episode-1

For the Professional Response, see https://www.degreespod.com/episodes/season-3-episode-2.

For the Political Response, see https://www.degreespod.com/episodes/season-3-episode-3.

Swedish Foundation for Strategic Environmental Research (MISTRA), https://www.hb.se/en/research/research-portal/funders/the-foundation-for-strategic-environmental-research---mistra/.

Taylor, F. (2022a) *Becoming Carbon Literate: A Climate Education*, https://digitalisationworld.com/blog/57138/becoming-carbon-literate-a-climate-education.

Taylor, F. (2022b) *3 Ways Kyndryl Embraced Sustainability and Carbon Net Zero Goals*, https://www.kyndryl.com/gb/en/about-us/news/2022/12/sustainability-carbon-net-zero-goals-kyndryl.

Thakur, S. (2021) *SUPERHEROES Inspiring Stories of Secret Strength*, UK: Penguin.

The Conversation (2022) *Climate Change Will Force Up to 113m People to Relocate within Africa by 2050 – new report*, https://theconversation.com/climate-change-will-force-up-to-113m-people-to-relocate-within-africa-by-2050-new-report-193633?utm_medium=email&utm_campaign=Imagine%20058%205pm&utm_content=Imagine%20058%205pm+CID_80649b3cf4125fac777ce9023fab6385&utm_source=campaign_monitor_uk&utm_term=force%20113%20million%20people%20to%20relocate.

United Nations Environment Programme (2020) *Sustainability and Circularity in the Textile Value Chain: Global Stocktaking*, https://wedocs.unep.org/handle/20.500.11822/34184

UN World Food Programme (2022) *Horn of Africa 'Cannot Wait': WFP Scales up Assistance as Historic Drought Raises Famine Threat*, https://www.wfp.org/news/horn-africa-cannot-wait-wfp-scales-assistance-historic-drought-raises-famine-threat.

US Environmental Protection Agency (undated) *What You Should Know about Microfibre Pollution*, https://www.epa.gov/sites/default/files/2020-07/documents/article_2_microfibers.pdf.

Vallance, C. (2023) *Elon Musk among Experts Urging a Halt to AI Training*, https://www.bbc.co.uk/news/technology-65110030.

WorldData.info, https://www.worlddata.info/europe/united-kingdom/energy-consumption.php on 24.11.2022.

Recommended reading

Decolonising design & technology

Akala (2019) *Natives Race and Class in the Ruins of Empire*, UK: Two Roads.

Gender in design & technology

The discussion on gender in design & technology deliberately adopted an over simplified view focusing on the binary male/female gender divide. For a more nuanced and wider discussion of gender see:

Barker, Meg-John, Scheele, Jules (2019) *Gender: A Graphic Guide*, London: Icon Books.

Disruption

Preston, Christopher J. (2018) *The Synthetic Age*. Cambridge, Massachusetts: The MIT Press.

Global warming

Berners-Lee, M. (2020) *How Bad Are Bananas? The Carbon Footprint of Everything*. London: Profile Books Ltd.

Pollution and waste

Leonard, A. (2010) *The Story of Stuff*. London: Constable & Robinson Ltd.

4 Planning your design & technology curriculum

In the way a curriculum plays out, very little happens by accident. Sometimes it is the dead hand of previous practice that holds sway and a curriculum stays more or less the same as it has been for the past few years except for a few minor tweaks here and there. In the hurly burly of a busy school this approach is understandable but not really defendable. It is the aim of this chapter to enable you to plan your design & technology curriculum in a way that meets the significant changes faced by the subject, is true to the intrinsic nature of the subject, and leaves open the possibility of change in the light of the way your curriculum acts out. This chapter deals with six major topics:

1   Content
2   Resources
3   Activities
4   Planning for breadth, balance, and progression
5   Organisation and strategy
6   Ofsted.

Content

In chapter 2 we introduced the concept of Big Ideas for design & technology. These can be presented diagrammatically as in Figure 4.1. In this section we will explore further the nature and significance of these when planning your curriculum. Each of the Big Ideas of design & technology will be considered in turn.

Fundamental Nature of D&T

In the 1960s and '70s Jacob Bronowski produced a remarkable series of television pro-grammes, *The Ascent of Man*,[1] and a book of the same title (Bronowski, 1973). In this work he captured the uniqueness of humankind as the following quotations indicate:

> *Man is a singular creature. He has a set of gifts which make him unique among the animal: so that, unlike them, he is not a figure in the landscape – he is a shaper of the landscape (p. 19).*

DOI: 10.4324/9781003008026-4

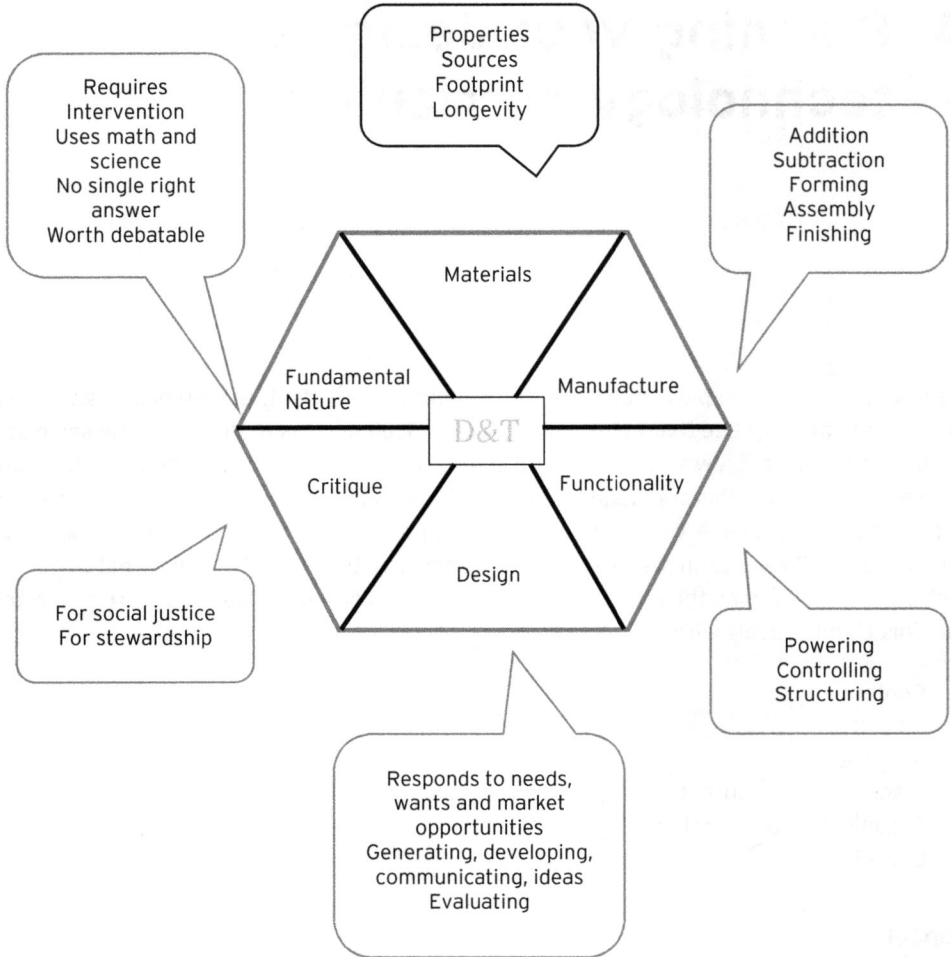

Figure 4.1 The Big Ideas **of** and **about** D&T represented as a diagram

> *Among the multitude of animals which scamper, fly, burrow and swim around us, man is the only animal who is not locked into his environment. His imagination, his reason, his emotional subtlety and toughness, make it possible for him not to accept the environment but to change it (p. 20).*

> *But he has what no other animal possesses, a saw of faculties which alone, over three thousand million years of life make him creative. Every animal leaves traces of what it was; man alone leaves traces of what he created (pp. 36-37).*

Bronowski's elegant description of humans' unique ability to envisage what might exist in the future and intervene in the world to bring this vision into reality not only provides a powerful justification for design & technology in the school curriculum but also identifies five key features that the subject must embrace if it is to be true to its intrinsic nature.

1   The activity requires imagination; learners will be required to use their mind's eye to conjure up alternatives to that which currently exists. Learners will ask, *'What needs to be different?'*

2   This imagination will need to be informed by values that enable learners to justify the worth of their proposals. The worth of any particular proposal will be debatable. Learners will ask, *'We can, but should we and why?'*

3   In imagining and developing solutions, learners will use knowledge, understanding, and skills from across and beyond the school curriculum with the application of science and mathematics often being particularly relevant. Learners will ask, *'What will it be useful to know and how can I find out?'*

4   Any intervention will inevitably be accompanied by unintended consequences and learners will need to be sensitive to such possibilities. Learners will ask, *'Who wins and who loses?'*

5   In responding to a particular problem or situation, learners will generate many possible solutions, some of which will be better than others. There will be no unique, single right answers. Learners will ask, *'What might I change to improve my proposal?'*

Pause for thought

Where in your design & technology curriculum at KS3 and KS4 are learners enabled to ask and answer the questions identified above?

Where in your curriculum could you include thinking about these questions?

Materials

If a learner does not understand the word 'properties', then it will be very difficult for them to make and justify decisions about which material to use for a particular purpose in a proposed design or to understand the reasons why one material was chosen by a professional designer. The whole notion of fitness for purpose is underpinned to a large extent by understanding what is meant by 'properties'. In simple terms the properties of a material tells us about what that material is like and how this information can be used to differentiate what that material is like compared to other materials. Properties of solid materials can be divided into different categories:

- mechanical properties which include strength, stiffness, hardness, and density
- electrical properties such as conductivity, and its opposite, resistance to current flow
- thermal properties such a conductivity and thermal capacity
- optical properties such as colour and transparency
- chemical properties such as reactivity and resistance to corrosion and degradation.

The behaviour of all solid materials can be described in terms of these properties. Using this information about properties to decide which material to use is one of the ways in which design & technology becomes intellectually challenging. The fledgling designer has to deal with the difference between declarative and normative knowledge, as described below. Consider a learner having to decide whether the material she has in mind will be stiff enough and strong enough for a component in her design proposal. When her design is in use the component must be sufficiently stiff such that it does not bend out of shape and sufficiently strong that it does not break. She can know how strong and stiff a particular material is; that's declarative knowledge (or 'knowing that'). Whether this strength and stiffness is that required by her design is a matter of judgment; and making this judgement requires normative knowledge (or 'knowing how') in that she must compare the behaviour of the material she thinks is stiff and strong enough with the behaviour of other possible materials and decide which is best. The situation gets more complicated when the learner widens the scope of considerations to include working properties, (there's little point in choosing a material that you cannot produce in the correct shape and form). And the scope can, and should, be widened further still to consider the source of the material chosen; where it comes from, and the working conditions of those who produce it, and the carbon footprint of the production process and the extent to which it is a finite as opposed to a renewable resource. A further consideration can be the extent to which the overall design enables the materials within it to become part of a circular economy mitigating some of the footprint and finite resource considerations. The extensive complexity of the decisions to be made soon becomes overwhelming, and in most cases professional designers (and learners) rely on precedent using thinking that goes along the lines, 'Well other designers have used this or that material for a similar purpose and it performs well so it's likely to work for my design too'. This approach has stood the test of time, but there is now the need to question such precedent-based decisions in the light of the stewardship and social justice challenges facing the world.

So, in planning your curriculum it will be important to introduce learners to a range of materials and their associated properties and regularly ask the question, 'This is what they have usually been used for but are these the best choices for today and the future? What might we use instead?' Learners can do this when considering the life cycle of particular products; they can critique the design choices that have been made by professional designers and engineers. They can also do this on their own designs when engaged in designing without making activities. It is perhaps more difficult to do this in designing and making activities as the material choices are often limited and based to a large extent on what materials are affordable and the decisions are often made by teachers. This raises the important point that the materials made available to learners in design and make activities should have a good environmental impact 'pedigree' which immediately questions the use of materials derived from fossil fuels or requiring significant fossil fuel use in their genesis. Over time learners will build up a repository of knowledge about a range of materials and will be able to use this knowledge to make decisions about the suitability of a material for inclusion in an existing design or design proposal. It will be important for learners to visit and revisit this knowledge bank so that they become increasingly familiar with its contents and importantly understand it in terms of the Big Ideas about materials – properties, sources, footprint, and longevity.

Pause for thought

How will you ensure that learners understand the relevance of particular properties with regard to the performance of a material within a design?

Manufacture

It is possible to provide a list of ways in which making can take place. Here is an example:

- By subtraction (removal of material to achieve a desired shape or form)
- By addition (addition of material to achieve a desired shape or form)
- By forming (changing the material to a desired 3D form)
- By assembly (joining pieces together)
- With finishing (treating the surface of the material).

Note that this list does not indicate how the making takes place or which tools are used but instead provides a conceptual framework for making to which the detail of particular processes and tools can be added as a learner progresses. As learners progress, they will need to become familiar with an increasingly wide range of hand tools, machine tools, and digital manufacturing devices, some of which are used in commercial activity as well as being available in school. This familiarity will need to be accompanied by increasing competence in using some of these items in their own making. There is immediately a tension here between breadth and depth. The wider the range of items included the less actual time there is 'on the tools' with any individual item for learners to practice and become competent in their use. You can use a sequence of making without designing activities to develop basic competencies and provide extension activities for those learners who develop competence more quickly than others in their class. The conceptual framework for making can be extended to include the various tools and processes. Here is an example:

- Subtraction (the removal of material to achieve a desired shape or form).

This may be achieved with the following tools: scissors, knife, saw, drill, file, plane, lathe, mill. The exact type of tool to be used will depend on both the material being worked and the final shape that is required. In some cases, both hand and machine tool versions are available. So, if learners are to be autonomous in a designing and making activity, they will be faced with a wide range of choices when trying to decide how best to produce the particular piece of material required for their designs. They will need to consider the most appropriate starting form and exactly how best to hold the material during the making process. They will also need to mark out the material so that they know where to apply the tool's cutting edge. As learners become more experienced, they will be able to make these decisions almost intuitively, but in the process of developing this high level of capability, it will be necessary for the teacher to bring the decision-making process to the fore. One way to do this is to ask questions as indicated below:

OK so you need to make it shorter – what will you use to do that?
OK a saw – what sort of saw?
OK a tenon saw – how will you know where to cut?
OK you'll mark it out – what will you use?
OK a tri square and a pencil – how will you hold it while you cut it?
OK a sawing board – great you've got it sussed!

Malcolm Welch's Thought Piece in chapter 6 expands on the important role of questioning.

It will be necessary to develop each feature of the conceptual framework for each of the materials you want learners to use. This will entail identifying the tools, equipment, and other resources that are used in each feature of the conceptual framework for each of the materials. It will be important to be realistic in this exercise to ensure that this aspect of your curriculum isn't so broad that it cannot be taught successfully in the time available. Examples of such possible developments for timber, metal, plastic, and paper and board are shown in Tables 4.1, 4.2, 4.3, and 4.4. Note that for the sake of simplicity tools and equipment for marking out have been omitted.

Textiles are more complex than the other materials because there are processes in which the textile material itself is manufactured which is generally not the case for other materials. Knitting, weaving, crocheting, macrame are examples. In some cases, the material manufacture is carried out in such a way that the resultant material is in the form of a textile item,

Table 4.1 Tools, equipment, and other resources used for manufacturing with timber

			TIMBER	
Subtraction	Addition	Forming	Assembly	Finishing
Hand saws Machine saws Chisels Planes Rasps Hand drills Machine drills Lathes Routers	Specially made formers with clamps to hold veneers in place while adhesive sets for laminating	Steam box or hot water bath for steam bending	Parts to be joined are generally produced by subtraction. They may be joined mechanically with pins, nails, screws and knock down fittings and chemically using adhesives to hold pieces together and joints in which pieces interpenetrate each other. During assembly it is sometimes necessary to use clamps or cramps and on occasions specially made jigs	Smooth surfaces created by planning, use of abrasive papers by hand and by machine (belt and disc) may then be further treated with polish, stain, preservative, varnish, or paint

Table 4.2 Tools, equipment, and materials used for manufacturing with metal

METAL				
Subtraction	Addition	Forming	Assembly	Finishing
Hand saws	Three means of	Crucible,	Parts to be joined	Smooth surfaces
Machine	additive	furnace, and	generally produced	created with
saws	manufacture are	mould for	by subtraction.	abrasive papers by
Files	Direct metal	casting	They may then be	hand and by
Hand drills	laser Sintering	Press and die	joined	machine (grinding
Machine	Selective laser	for stamping	mechanically with	wheel) and polishing
drills	melting		machine screws	may then be further
Taps and dies	Electron bream		and nuts, or	treated:
Lathes	melting		riveting and	lacquering painting
Milling	Not usually found		chemically by	dip coating
machines	in schools but		soldering, brazing,	case hardening (steel)
	widely used in		or welding	anodising (aluminium)
	industry			

Table 4.3 Tools, equipment, and materials used for manufacturing with plastic

PLASTIC				
Subtraction	Addition	Forming	Assembly	Finishing
Hand saws	3D printer	Strip bender	Adhesive tapes	Polishing by hand
Machine saws		Vacuum former	Liquid adhesives	using abrasive
Hand drills		Blow moulder		pastes
Machine drills		Injection		
Files		moulder		
Use of abrasive papers by		Moulds for		
hand and by machine (belt		casting		
and disc)				
Guillotine				
Taps and dies				
Milling machines				
Knife cutting machine (vinyl				
cutter)				
Milling machine				
Laser cutter				

knitting booties or jackets for babies, for example. The development for textiles is shown in Table 4.5. Note that all the tables are exercises in giving substance to a simple conceptual structure for manufacture. You may wish to assign various elements to different categories in the light of how you view learning about manufacturing. You may wish to delete certain elements as unsuitable for your situation. Or you may choose to add elements. The key point is that you have at your fingertips an organising principle that allows *you* to structure your

Table 4.4 Tools, equipment, and materials used for manufacturing with paper and board

PAPER AND BOARD				
Subtraction	*Addition*	*Forming*	*Assembly*	*Finishing*
Scissors	Press to loin	Stylus for	Parts to be joined may	Often carried out
Craft knife	several sheets	creasing	be produced by	before assembly
Roller cutter	together while	before	subtraction or	the surface may be
Compass cutter	adhesive sets to	folding by	forming. They may	decorated by
Guillotine	provide greater	hand	be joined	printing, painting,
Hole punch	strength and		mechanically using a	drawing or block
Die cutter	stiffness		stapler or hole	printing
Knife cutting			punch plus split pins	Textured rollers may
machine			and chemically with	be used to give
(vinyl cutter)			adhesive tapes and	textured surface
Laser cutter			sprays or adhesive	Single sheets may be
			in liquid or stick	laminated for
			form	protection

Table 4.5 Tools, equipment, and materials used for manufacturing with textiles

TEXTILES				
Subtraction	*Addition*	*Forming*	*Assembly*	*Finishing*
Scissors	Needle and thread or	Needle and	Needle and	Electric iron and ironing
Roller cutter	sewing machine	thread for:	thread for	board (used
Guillotine	for embroidery,	Pleating,	sewing by	throughout
Die cutter	appliqué, and	Gathering	hand	manufacture to
Laser cutter	quilting	Darting	Sewing machine	remove creases)
Heat cutter		Shirring	Glue	Many processes are used
			Needles for	to 'finish' a fabric
			knitting,	before final assembly:
			crochet, and	Dye bath and dyes for
			macrame	dying
			Hand loom for	Heat press for
			weaving	sublimation printing
			Rollers and mats	Screen and squeegee for
			for felting	screen printing
				Dyes and blocks for
				block printing
				Wax heating pot and
				tjanting tool for batik
				Sprays and brushes to
				apply finishes to
				achieve flame
				resistance, water
				resistance etc.

curriculum. In deciding on the tools, equipment, and materials that you wish to include in your manufacturing concept map you may find the Tools Chooser Chart and the Fabric Decoration Chooser Chart useful (Nuffield Foundation, 2000).

The teaching of making is considered in more detail in chapter 5 including a Thought Piece by Matt McLean. How to devise a curriculum that makes more demands on learners as they move through your programme of study is considered in more detail later in this chapter under the section *Planning for breadth, balance, and progression*.

Pause for thought

How might you change the *Tools, equipment, and materials used for manufacturing* tables in the light of your own situation?

Providing learners with products that are made up of several different parts and asking them to think about how each part was manufactured is one way to help learners understand manufacture. Which products might be appropriate?

Functionality

All designed artefacts have to 'work' in one way or another. They have to perform in a particular way to achieve their function. For simple artefacts this functionality can be achieved relatively simply – a basic torch functions by means of an electrical circuit including a battery, bulb, and an on/off switch. The more complex the artefact the more complicated the means of achieving the function becomes. Controlling the lights on a stairway such that they can be turned on or off at both the top and the bottom of the stairs incorporates and extends the simple torch circuit. If the circuit is required to include voice activation the circuitry becomes even more complex. Note that in order for these circuits to work an energy source will be needed. In the case of the torch a battery, in the case of the stair lights energy will be supplied by the National Grid and in the case of the voice activated system a battery and the National Grid will be used. Your learners will almost certainly be required to learn and understand about energy in their science lessons, and it is important that what they learn about there and in design & technology presents a coherent and consistent view of a difficult concept if they are not to become confused. The potential for confusion and how to avoid this is discussed in some detail in *Teaching technical understanding* in chapter 5.

A summary of the ways in which functionality can be achieved are shown in Tables 4.6 and 4.7 below.

For any artefact its way of working needs to be supported by some form of framework or enclosure and this will involve designing the artefact so that it meets structural requirements such as:

- stiffness so the artefact won't deform when being used,
- strength so the artefact won't break when being used,
- stability so that if free standing the artefact won't topple over.

Table 4.6 Ways of achieving functionality

Type of system	Examples	Energy source sources that might be used in design & technology to power products
Mechanical	Compound gear train in salad spinner Cam driven rise and fall figure in a child's toy Chain drive in a bicycle	Human effort from food
Electrical	Electric motor in, e.g.: • simple moving toy • rotary display system	Chemical battery. Could be single use or rechargeable using: • sunlight via solar cell
Electronic	A range of actuators (motors, lights, sounders) in, e.g.: • simple plant watering system • safety lamp for cyclist or walker • an alarm system	• human effort via a mechanical charger, • mains electricity
Programmable	A range of actuators (motors, lights, sounders) in, e.g.: • Hydroponic system • Robot arm • Automatic curtain closer	

Table 4.7 Structural inadequacies

Inadequate strength	Inadequate stiffness	Inadequate stability
The wire supporting the hanging basket has broken because it wasn't strong enough.	The shelf is bowing because it isn't stiff enough. It hasn't broken yet, so it is just strong enough.	The table lamp is tipping over because it isn't stable enough

In summary the functionality of a technical artefact will involve three features: powering, controlling, and structuring. In designing and making such artefacts learners should consider each of these features. As the complexity of the artefacts they design and make increases the way in which each of these features is considered should become more sophisticated. This is considered in more detail later in this chapter under the section *Progression*. Functionality is considered in more detail in chapter 5 in the section *Teaching technical understanding*.

Pause for thought

Providing learners with an artefact that works in a particular way and asking them to identify different ways that it could work is one way to engage them with functionality. Which artefacts would be appropriate?

Design

Enabling learners to design is perhaps the most challenging aspect of design & technology. The sorts of design decision that learners are expected to make are considered in detail later in this chapter in the section on designing and making tasks 132. Teaching designing is considered in detail chapter 5 (from page 176). Here we will restrict the discussion to identifying four key ideas central to designing.

1   Designing is sometimes thought of as imagining a 'something', for 'somebody', in a 'situation' – a triple S approach. The 'something' being conceived will be dependent on the needs and wants of the person or people in a particular situation. Hence a key idea is that designing should be in response to the needs and wants of a person or group of people.

2   An alternative way to think about design is as a commercial activity within a variety of different markets and that by scrutinizing a particular market a designer might identify a gap in the market that might be filled through as yet new and unknown products and associated services. Once such products are realised, they often give rise to new markets in which further new products and services might arise. Devising improvements to existing products may also be seen as identifying a gap in the market. Hence a key idea is that designing can be in response to market opportunities. It is important to realise that responding to market opportunities is only likely to be successful if the designed outcome meet peoples' needs and wants.

3   Designing requires that the designer to generate new ideas and then develop them to the point where they can be shared with key stakeholders: potential users, companies that might manufacture them, and businesses that might promote and sell them. This requires designers to develop a range of communication skills; firstly with themselves to support the internal dialogue that enables the details of the design to be clarified, secondly with others who might be involved in the designing, members of a design team, thirdly with those who might use the product or service, and fourthly with key stakeholders responsible for manufacturing, selling, and promoting the design. Hence a key idea is that designing will involve generating, developing and communicating design ideas.

Within this process of generating and developing design ideas, the designer will need to use two important devices. The first is the design brief. This may be open in which case the exact nature of the item to be designed has yet to be decided. Or a closed brief in which nature of the item to be designed has been given. In responding to either of these sorts of brief the designer also has to develop a specification for the item which defines key requirements that the designed item must meet. As the designer makes design decisions to clarify the detail of the emerging design each of these decisions must be compared with the requirements of the specification to ensure that these are being met. This leads us to the fourth key idea – evaluation.

4   Throughout the process of generating and developing design ideas the designer is evaluating the worth of the design ideas as they emerge. At the end of the process when a working prototype of the design is available it is possible to carry out further evaluations by engaging with key stakeholders and eliciting their views – the user, the manufacturer, the seller. This may be positive and endorse the design decisions made, in which case the design can move into production. Or the feedback may be negative in which case some of the design decision will have to be reconsidered. Hence a key idea is that throughout any design activity evaluation is an essential activity.

Donald Schön (1983) in his seminal work, *The Reflective Practitioner*, identified two important activities relevant to designing: reflection *in* action and reflection *on* action. The evaluation described above relates strongly to the former. But it is important to bear in mind the latter in which designers reflect back on the whole designing process and ask themselves why they did what they did, what might they have done differently, and what are the implications of the answers with regard to their developing practice. In teaching your learners to design it will be important to help them reflect on their actions as designers.

Pause for thought

To what extent are teachers and learners in your school able to reflect *in* and *on* their practice?

Critique

The previous section highlighted the importance of reflection and in terms of developing learners' capability this reflection finds itself in the guise of evaluating from two perspectives. Firstly, the efficacy of the item being designed and made: did it do what it was designed to do, did it appeal to the intended user, did it meet the requirements of other stakeholders? Secondly how well the whole designing and making process was expedited with a view to identifying areas of improvement such as quality of making skills, exploration of alternative design possibility, time management. These areas of evaluation are important, but they do not constitute critique. Critique requires that we stand back and ask not, 'Did the design do what it was supposed to?' but, 'Is what it was supposed to do worth doing?' and 'What are its consequences?' Two important perspectives to enable this consideration of worth and consequence are social justice and stewardship of Plant Earth. Regarding social justice, it is important that learners are taught that all people should be able to live in freedom from hunger and fear, have shelter from harm, and should have opportunities to pursue happiness and make the best of their lives. Regarding stewardship of Plant Earth, it is important that learners are taught that the way humans have behaved in the past 200 years has compromised the well-being of Planet Earth and all the creatures that are living there now and in the future. This mistreatment of the planet has resulted in global warming (see chapter 3 for a discussion of this topic) and an important starting point for reversing global warming is critique. Critique is treated in more detail in the sections *Teaching critique* and *Critique through considering the consequences of technology* in chapter 5.

Pause for thought

Critiquing may lead young people to become despondent about the quality of their future lives. How might your curriculum provide an antidote to this?

Resources

This piece is divided into three sections: Physical resources – focussing particularly on the need for their organisation, Human resources – dealing in some depth with utilising teams, and Intellectual resources – using the idea of teachers' personal subject constructs as a way of thinking about this.

Physical resources

One of the main aims of design & technology teaching is for learners to develop capability. The availability of resources plays a key role in this, but this must be underpinned by the expectation that learners will, if given the opportunity, be capable. This means that it will be perfectly acceptable for learners to make decisions and take action based on those decisions. In some cases, the actions will require teacher approval but in many cases they will be autonomous. This has serious implications for the way teachers need to organize and maintain the learning environment. It means that learners will have open access to materials, components, tools, and equipment. In most cases they will be able to collect what they need, as they need it, use it, and return it. In some cases, particularly scarce resources may need to be booked in advance. But it is essential that decisions once taken can be acted upon if learners are not to become dispirited and demotivated. There are issues of organisation and trust here. From an organisational point of view, for example, tools need to be displayed in ways that makes them easy to access and easy for the teacher to see if any are missing. From a trust point of view learners are expected to use the display system sensibly so that no tools go missing. It will be necessary to have high expectations here and train learners in how to behave. Given a well-organised workshop or design studio with appropriate materials, components, tools, and equipment available with trustworthy learners there are two more essential considerations for this situation to enable learners to develop capability. The first is their knowledge, understanding, and skills relevant to the particular task in hand. If these are lacking, then the decisions they make will be flawed and their use of the physical resources available will be poor. Hence it is necessary that the teacher identifies the knowledge, understanding, and skills needed and ensures this has been taught. In some cases, this may have been covered in previous units of work and all that is necessary is a reminder or a short recap session. The availability of short video clips demonstrating particular skills is useful here. In other cases, it might be new to the learners in which case some explicit teaching will be necessary. How this might be achieved is discussed in *Activities* later in this chapter. The second is that the teacher should maintain the motivation for capability through insight into learners' interests and concerns ensuring that activities are relevant, urgent, important, and attractive.

Pause for thought

Some might argue that the situation described above is idealistic and not feasible. It certainly aims high. Consider to what extent you are able to achieve this in your school. If you decide that you can't, try to identify particular areas of shortfall and consider what you might do to change these. It might be something as simple as the need for better labelling of component trays or something much more fundamental like the trustworthiness of learners for example in which case the remedy will lie in discussions with SLT as this may well be a school wide problem in lessons where there is practical activity.

Phil Holton enjoyed many years as a highly successful design & technology teacher, head of department and senior leader before he moved to his present position. In his Thought Piece he questions the prevailing orthodoxy of the physical resources needed by our subject.

Physical resources as a legacy approach – *A Thought Piece by Philip Holton*

Philip Holton is Senior Strategy Manager for Pearson UK Schools with 15 years in design & technology education.

Design & technology has long protected an assumption that it needs large amounts of physical resources (materials, components, tools, or equipment) to be taught effectively. Designers in industry usually operate without such resources to inform what is to be made. But designers do have the capability to make creative and informed choices for the solutions they design, without the need to be surrounded by a large range of physical resources. In my view this is the design capability we as educators should be aiming for in our students.

This is not to say that physical resources are never necessary, but they can at a minimum be limited, inexpensive, and easy to work (see Figure 4.2). Design capability with these sorts of physical resources will come from direct experience and will be best achieved by students where the barriers of moving between ideas and made outcomes are as low as possible, with progressive increases in challenge, and 'learning through connections' that provide a trajectory through increased sophistication.

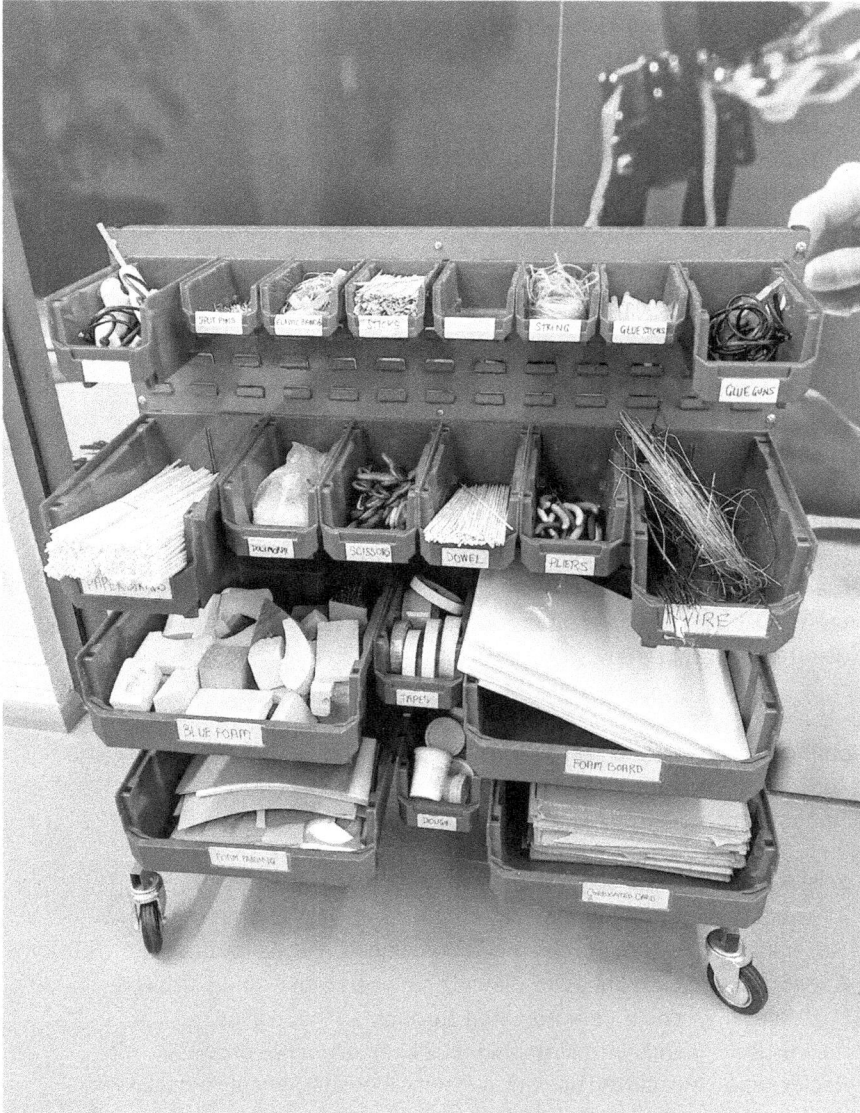

Figure 4.2 Physical resources suitable for design activity in secondary schools

In 2021 and 2022 the GCSE requirement for students to produce a "high quality final prototype" was replaced by a proof-of-concept model which inevitably was made to less exacting standards using easy to work materials, as students were completing coursework requirements remotely at home. They no longer had access to the physical resources usually available in their D&T departments. They were in fact operating in much the same way as designers in industry. They needed to appreciate the properties of the materials they had available (both intrinsic and working) and use this knowledge to create proof-of-concept models which needed to demonstrate connections to potential physical resource decisions through form and function to be a valid outcome. Hence this activity is not a barrier to learning to design.

To enable students to use this approach to designing requires a KS3 curriculum in which students learn about the use of simple physical resources to produce proof of concept models in a progressive way such that the breadth of physical resources available widens as the bar of design complexity is raised, and they move through the key stage.

How might this look?

1   Teach students about physical resources through practical experience making connections to other similar physical resources. Connections would include shared features and characteristics.
2   As a teacher you can require the students to respond to increases in challenge by means of greater complexity, more creative opportunity, and independent choice of physical resources.
3   Once a student is capable of using any physical resource (without risk of injury to themselves/others), they are permitted to do so freely.
4   If a physical resource is similar to others, only physically engage with one, then teach students about the differences to the others so that they are in a position to use them appropriately.

Here is an example.

Commence connections learning with Year 7 students who are able to use scissors as a tool to cut paper.

The connections journey is as follows:

1   Scissors operate the same way as shears.
2   All sheet materials (paper, metal, etc.) have similar characteristics.
3   The limitations of scissors when cutting complex shapes introduces a craft knife.
4   A craft knife can be linked to die-cutting when repetition is desired.
5   The craft knife could be automated through a vinyl cutter.
6   Die cutting expands into stamping, blanking, or embossing.
7   Replacing a vinyl cutter tip with a laser widens the sheet material list.
8   Laser cutters operate like plasma and waterjet cutters.
9   The numerical control associated in 2D processes, with the addition of a third dimension, introduces 3D printing.

Whilst in this example, students are making the connections between physical resources, a moment is reached where the physical resource is not required to be in the workshop for those learning connections to be appreciated. Students will be able to look at their proof-of-concept model and identify resistant materials that could be used, and the manufacturing processes required for a higher quality prototype.

Students typically increase their aspirations for made solutions as they get older. By teaching through connections, students have the awareness of how to resolve technical issues by experimenting with physical resources. At some point some students will have learned enough from their experiences to be able to design without recourse to physically producing a proof-of-concept model – iterating between design ideas in their minds eye and those they produce on paper or on screen. What we as D&T teachers need to decide is, what physical resources and associated learning give students the fundamental understanding they need to reach a point where connections take over, and they have the capability to design as do those designers who work in industry?

In summary when considering physical resources my suggested approach requires:

1 Teaching through connections
2 Planning for progression
3 Awarding students their freedom
4 Enable discussion of the proof-of-concept model in terms of high-quality prototype requirements.

What are we to make of Phil's Thought Piece? Are his ideas the thin end of a thick wedge leading to the loss of making skills in the design & technology curriculum or are they a way forward that might in the right circumstances enable learners to design, and when the time is right be given access to the making and material resources required to turn their proof-of-concept models into high quality prototype. Hilda remembers visiting a resource centre in Malta some years ago which was extremely well equipped in terms of modern manufacturing facilities and supplies of materials with the full-time presence of a highly skilled technician. Initially the facility was being used to provide CPD for teachers. We wonder if such a facility, perhaps in the guise of a maker space, might be made available as a scarce resource for those learners who, through making connections, were now able to be taught how to realise a high-quality prototype.

Human resources

This section will build a picture of the human resources in a design & technology department and the way they can be organised to create highly effective teaching and learning. It begins by focusing on the individual teacher, widens out to include technicians and teaching assistants, and widens further still to consider how the contribution of these 'actors' can be enhanced by a team approach.

The individual teacher

Individual teachers play a pivotal role in the fabric of a design & technology department. It is individual teachers who implement the schemes of work. However well planned, the execution is down to the individual teacher and it is important that they are allowed to bring their own particular flair to the teaching. Whilst a department might want to establish an orthodoxy of approach this should not lead to uniformity of teaching. It is individual teachers who engage and inspire learners and communicate the worth of the subject to parents and carers. So, providing an environment in which individual teachers can flourish is very important. There are many well-known and effective features to this environment. Regular conversations with colleagues who act as mentors, paired observations with colleagues giving each other useful commentary and feedback, instructional coaching and regular CPD.

The technicians and teaching assistants

Design & technology being a practically based subject with a large amount of project-based work can require significant material preparation in addition to planning lessons. Without technician support for material preparation, teacher time to prepare everything for lessons is inevitably stretched. There are many tasks that a technician's role can fulfil which add significantly to the effectiveness of lessons and learning. Below is a list of just some of the core tasks.

- Preparing and cutting materials for units of work
- Preparing packs of components for units of work
- Preparing demonstration resources
- Maintaining and servicing equipment in workshops
- Checking and ordering materials and components required
- Ensuring health and safety within the department
- Providing printed and display materials

Increasingly the technical expertise of technicians is being channelled in a more learning support role. Working with and under the guidance of the design & technology class teacher technicians can be used in class to support both teachers and learners in the following ways:

- Demonstration of specialised tools and equipment to a small group of learners
- Overseeing of a potentially hazardous task as each learner in the group undertakes the task, e.g., casting.
- Support for a disabled learner to use specially made jigs and holding devices, enabling them to access the curriculum.

To some extent the role of the teaching assistant (TA) can overlap that of the technician in that a TA might get a workshop ready for lessons and clear away materials and equipment after lessons. Collaboration between technicians and TAs in this work enables lesson changeovers to go more smoothly. But the role has much wider dimensions. Key activities are:

- Helping learners who need extra support to complete tasks; hence it is important that the TA is familiar with the unit of work being taught.
- Helping teachers to plan learning activities and complete records.
- Supporting teachers in managing class behaviour and looking after learners who are upset or have had accidents.

The involvement of both technicians and TAs in a team approach to teaching and learning is discussed further in the following section.

A team approach

Later in this chapter, four ways of teaching design & technology are identified and discussed (see page 136). If these ways are used across the department such that different teachers are teaching a unit of work based on a particular approach there are significant advantages to adopting a team approach, so that the expertise of all those teaching can be incorporated into the planning, teaching, and assessment of that unit. Such an approach might involve all members of the department and provide explicit support for those who will be teaching those lessons. But to be successful adopting such a team approach will need to be well organised. One way of organising and hence supporting a team approach is outlined in Table 4.8 below. Used successfully the team approach will exploit and grow the individual expertise and the collaboration skills of those working in the department. On some occasions this will require the head of department to take on particular roles to show how they might be carried out. But this will not always be the case, and there will be occasions when the head of department will support others to take centre stage.

A key feature of this approach is that it enables those teaching and supporting teaching to share the load and take on different levels of responsibility at different times. But the use of such an approach does require considerable effort and organisation and on-going 'maintenance' if it is to be successful. The authors' experience is that those departments that have committed themselves to this approach find that it enhances considerably the quality of the teaching and learning and the collegiality amongst all members of the department.

Another sort of team

In some cases, there are problems that need expertise from outside the design & technology department. In such cases knotworking is a useful approach in which a group of people can come together to do various strands of activity to tackle a particular task or problem. Knotworking, the tying and untying of a knot from separate threads of activity, is not linked to any specific individual or fixed organisational entity, such as a department, as centre of control or authority. Rather the 'knot' brings together interested participants from different

Table 4.8 An approach to organising and supporting a team approach

Stage	Team activity
Stage 1 First full department meeting	The department meets to discuss the requirements of the learning activity and identifies the knowledge, understanding, skills, and values that will be learned through the activity. This gives the learning activity clarity. One teacher assumes the role of leader and is responsible for producing the package of core learning materials and suggestions for the next meeting. This may involve writing new materials or utilising those already within the department.
Stage 2 Second full department meeting	The package is discussed and constructive criticism made. The activity leader is now in a position to produce the core set of resources which may include a PowerPoint presentation and materials for students (as hard copy handouts or electronic resources on the school VLE).
Stage 3 Involvement of the technician	The activity leader discusses the requirements with the technician (hand tools, machine tools, computing facilities, software, consumable materials, components, etc.) to ensure availability and gives the technician a clear overview of the topic. The activity leader then writes the technician notes for the activity with the assurance that no impossible demands will be made.
Stage 4 Teacher notes for all	The activity leader then writes the teachers' notes that can be used as a reference by all those who will teach the activity.
Stage 5 Teaching team meeting	All those who will teach the activity meet together to discuss the best way to use the core resources developed so far and to develop further resources to enhance the learner experience. This would probably include homework assignments, case study reading, extension work suggestions, help sheets, feedback prompts, joint presentation planning. It is very important that all those teaching have the necessary expertise with the tools and equipment to be used. Those with a high level of competence and subject knowledge can act as mentors to those less familiar with the activity.
Stage 6 Involvement of the teaching assistant (TA)	If one or more TAs are to be present during the teaching of the unit, then it is important to see them as a team member and involve them in the development of the resources and the teaching plans. They will have insight into the needs of particular learners and how these might be met.
Stage 7 Liaison with the technician	During the teaching of the activity, it is important that liaison is maintained with the technician so that equipment and materials are readily available throughout the activity.
Stage 8 Liaison with the TA	During the teaching of the activity, it is important that liaison is maintained with the TA so that the progress of learners in their care is maintained.

Table 4.8 An approach to organising and supporting a team approach (Continued)

Stage	Team activity
Stage 9 Third full department meeting	Assessment of various sorts will have taken place throughout the activity and at the end of the activity using evidence that has been produced by the learners. All those who have taught the activity can take this evidence along with their experience of having taught the activity and evaluate its success to a full department meeting. This serves three important functions. It allows for improvement in the next iteration of the learning activity. It provides the basis of CPD for individual team members such that they each become more rounded design & technology teachers. It keeps all members of the department familiar with the curriculum.

communities of practice to solve a particular problem. At a school Hilda introduced to Young Foresight as an attempt to re-ignite creative thinking, the knot was created not only from teachers of design & technology but also from art and design, science as well as two STEM ambassadors, engineers from a local camera company. The knot supported the development and implementation of Young Foresight. Once the initiative was established and up and running, the 'knot' was untied as it had served its purpose. Knotworking is a useful technique for cross curriculum collaboration as it recognises that there are a range of stakeholders who can all contribute to the different strands of activity needed.

Pause for thought

To what extent do those working in your design & technology department see themselves as being part of one or more teams?

The introduction of more team planning and collaborative teaching can improve the quality and impact of the learning experiences in a design & technology department but there may be drawbacks to a team approach such as:

- Disagreement within teams
- Loss of individual teacher autonomy
- Possibility of some staff making limited contributions
- Possibility of some staff dominating
- Personality clashes within teams.

How might these difficulties be overcome?

Paul Mburu has significant experience and expertise in the management of design & technology departments, so it is to his Thought Piece we now turn.

Developing teams as a key leadership strategy – *A Thought Piece by Dr Paul K. Mburu*

Paul K. Mburu is Head of Design & Technology Department, Harlington School.

One of the keys to successful leadership of design & technology departments is fusing the work of department staff who include specialist subject teachers, technicians, and assigned teaching assistants to create a developmental platform to improve practice. This task is one of the many that is performed by heads of department of design & technology, who are seen as middle leaders in schools (Bennett *et al.*, 2003). Not only are these leaders entrusted with improving the attainment of pupils in their departments, they also facilitate the quality of learning and development of the members of staff in their unique design & technology department social contexts (Mburu, 2022). The emphasis on context is important because 'subject departments' environments shape but are also shaped by individuals' (Douglas, 2015, p. 14). Individual members of staff perform a crucial part in the work of departments and how they perceive and participate in this role is important.

Accordingly, departments such as those of design & technology have become settings in which teachers as professionals share views and collaborate. Heads of departments enhance this collaborative working by promoting collegiality (Bennett, 2006) to create an all-encompassing team. Collegiality entails heads of departments building collaborative cultures in their departments and extending the same to the other stakeholders (Leithwood, 2012; Hardy, Gyekye, & Wainwright, 2015). The design & technology department contexts present an opportunity for building a rich diverse team given the nature of the subject. The various specialist teachers of subjects that make up design & technology, the technicians of the different subjects (in design & technology) and assigned teaching assistants afford an excellent opportunity for team approach.

One element of sustaining and developing a team approach in design & technology is the understanding the head of department has about their role. For example, on the authors' recommendations on Table 4.8, I suggest that using available tools within the department would enhance the practice of others by developing and creating opportunities that encourage a team approach. Achieving this goal requires the use of tools in a developmental way to build collegiality as opposed to the other ways of working. Examples of such tools in a design & technology department context would include joint planning time, specialist subject knowledge, department led work scrutiny, and lesson

observations. Consequently, the head of department consciously steers the members of staff in the department to see their interactions as a way of working towards developing each other's practice. This would in turn improve teaching and learning in the department.
    Practical actions for heads of departments

- Implement measures that create an environment where the sharing of good practice is seen as developmental rather than judgemental.
- Encourage members of staff in the department to draw upon experiences gained from working in other teams.

What are we to make of Paul's Thought Piece? It is tempting for a Head of Department to adopt the role of problem solver supreme and use their experience to dictate the curriculum and in the hurly burly of a busy department that is trying to improve teaching and learning this may well provide short-term solutions to immediate problems. The risk here is that this turns into an on-going sequence of 'firefighting' with little if any long-term improvement. Paul makes an eloquent plea for Heads of Department to develop teams in which the participating members contribute to curriculum development, and in so doing support one another's' professional growth resulting in improved teaching and learning. Senior leaders are generally well disposed to the idea of developing departmental teams although this will always take extra time and effort. Discussing how best to achieve this with those senior leaders having responsibility for design & technology will always be worthwhile.

Intellectual resources

The DEPTH (Developing Professional Thinking) Project described teachers' personal subject construct as consisting of three related features: subject knowledge, pedagogic knowledge, and school knowledge (related to the way subject knowledge is specific to schools) (Banks & Barlex, 2021). The authors paraphrased this as: know your stuff, know how to teach your stuff, and know how to teach your stuff in your school and illustrated this as three overlapping circles (Figure 4.3). This is not a Venn diagram and the central overlap of the three circles may be seen as teachers' personal constructs of the subject. We think that this provides a useful starting point for considering intellectual resources. The first two categories can stand as they are, but it is important to note that the idea of school knowledge should be seen to embrace, local, national, and international perspectives from the past and in the present which influence the way the subject is valued and taught in schools.

Keeping up to date with advances in subject knowledge

The Design & Technology Association provides a variety of professional development courses that deal with particular aspects of subject knowledge with many of these being available on-line. They are inevitably highly focused dealing with specific areas. They are

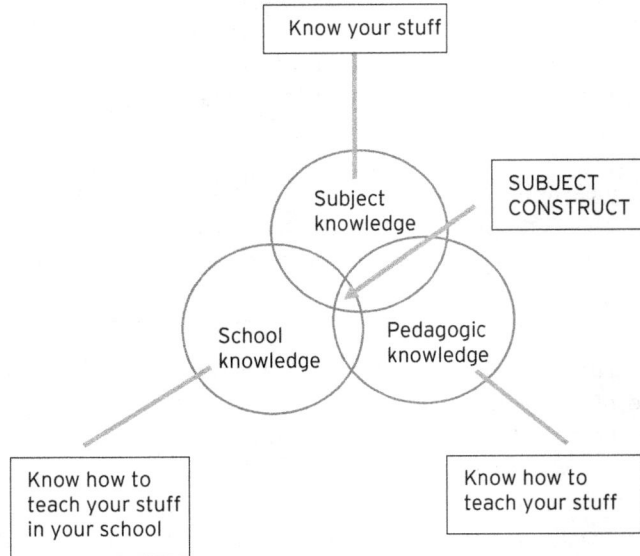

Figure 4.3 The DEPTH model for a teachers' subject construct

obviously useful, and it is important to monitor their offerings to find courses that meet your situation's particular requirements. Details can be found at the *Training and events section* of the Association's website. For any such training attended by an individual teacher, it is important that other members of the department and the curriculum benefit. Hence it will be important for the attendee to provide a feedback session to the department as part of the professional development.

It is also important to develop an ethos of being generally up to date with the developments taking place in science and technology in the world outside school which are relevant to the design & technology curriculum. These are often reported in magazines such as *New Scientist* (£55.00 per annum with a website at https://www.newscientist.com), *MIT Review* (monthly cost £8.00 with a website at https://www.technologyreview.com), *Wired* (monthly cost £3.50 with a website at www.wired.co.uk), *Ingenia* (monthly and free from the Royal Academy of Engineering; see https://www.ingenia.org.uk), and *Make* (see https://makezine. com). The actual magazines can be housed in a departmental library, and links to all the magazine websites can be made available on the department website. This availability is probably insufficient to engage the teachers in the department with the contents so it will be important to find ways to bring relevant articles to the attention of staff. One way to do this is to assign the reading of one or two magazines to individual members of staff and have a regular subject knowledge update slot at department meetings. The significance of the pieces identified with regard to the curriculum can be discussed and ways in which they might be used identified. In some cases, summaries of the items might be made available for learners to read and discuss with parents or carers as homework. In other cases the items can become the basis for a technological perspective reader (see https://dandtfordandt. wordpress.com/resources/technological-perspective-readers/) enabling consequences of technology lessons to consider the latest in technological developments. In some cases, the items are just interesting in their own right with regard to the sort of knowledge that design & technology teachers should have at their fingertips. In some cases, they cover a topic of considerable significance that can inform your teaching of key issues. In some cases, they might provide useful background reading to a design and make task. Here are examples of all types taken from the 4th June 2022 issue of *New Scientist*:

Summarise for homework reading – *Micromachine can climb through body* (p. 23).
Basis for a technological perspective reader – *Driverless cars could force other road users to drive more efficiently* (p. 16).
Interesting in its own right – *3D-printed tourniquets could help save lives* (p. 10).
Informing the teaching of a key issue – *Can fashion really go green? An exploration of how fast fashion damages the environment and what sustainable fashion might look like* (pp. 38–45).

Background reading for a design and make task – if learners are exploring the behaviour of spinning tops in order to design their own then the possible use of a giant centrifuge to launch satellites might be intriguing – known as *SpinLaunch* (p. 12). This piece would need simplification and interpretation for both for KS3 and probably KS4 and would be challenging reading for KS5 as it stands, but so interesting.

Keeping up to date with advances in pedagogic knowledge

Technology education now features in the listings of several well-regarded academic publishers, some of whom are developing series devoted to the subject. Examples are shown in Panel 4.1. It is worth being on their mailing lists so that your department can keep up with their publications and can buy those volumes of particular interest. In some cases, they are expensive, but the authors know of some departments which have obtained funds from their governing body to make such purchases. Also, it is usually possible to buy electronic copies of particularly relevant chapters.

Developing and maintaining school knowledge across a broad perspective

This is perhaps the most challenging area of intellectual resources as it is broad, nebulous, and volatile. It involves 'looking' in three directions: backwards to be aware of the history of our subject, contemplating the subject's current position, and forwards to gauge where it might be going. Inevitably the resources used to look in these different directions will overlap to some extent and some of the resources already identified as useful in keeping up to date with advances in subject knowledge and pedagogic knowledge will also be valuable.

Looking backwards
The National Curriculum was introduced in England in 1988 by the then Minister of Education Kenneth Baker through the Education Reform Act and there followed a series of reforms and amendments. These included the Dearing Review under the then Minister of Education

Panel 4.1 Publishers and their technology education publications

Routledge	**Springer**
Debates in Design and Technology Education (2nd Edition)	Contemporary Issues in Technology Education Series including:
Edited by Alison Hardy	
Copyright Year 2023	*Applications of Research in Technology Education Helping Teachers Develop Research-Informed Practice*
Learning to Teach Design and Technology in the Secondary School (4th Edition)	Edited by P. John Williams and Belinda von Mengersen
A Companion to School Experience	Copyright Year 2022
Edited by <u>Alison Hardy</u>	
Copyright Year 2021	*Teaching and Learning about Technological Systems Philosophical, Curriculum and Classroom Perspectives*
Teaching STEM in the Secondary School (2nd Edition)	Edited by Jonas Hallström and P. John Williams
Helping Teachers Meet The Challenge	Copyright Year 2022
Frank Banks and David Barlex	
Copyright Year 2021	*Pedagogy for Technology Education in Secondary Schools Research Informed Perspectives for Classroom Teachers*
Mentoring Design and Technology Teachers in the Secondary School	Edited by P. John Williams and David Barlex
A Practical Guide	Copyright Year 2020
Edited by Suzanne Lawson and Susan Wood-Griffiths	
Copyright Year 2020	*Explorations in Technology Education Research Helping Teachers Develop Research Informed Practice*
	Edited by P. John Williams and David Barlex
Sage	Copyright Year 2019
STEM in the Primary Curriculum	
Edited by Helen Caldwell and Sue Pope	*Contemporary Research in Technology Education Helping Teachers Develop Research-informed Practice*
Copyright Year 2019	Edited by P. John Williams and David Barlex
	Copyright Year 2017
Brill Sense	*Critique in Design and Technology Education*
International Technology Education Studies including:	Edited by P. John Williams and Kay Stables
	Copyright Year 2017
Design-Based Concept learning in Science and Technology Education	
Edited by <u>Ineke Henze</u> and <u>Marc J. de Vries</u>	*Teaching about Technology An Introduction to the Philosophy of Technology for Non-philosophers*
Copyright Year 2021	Marc J. de Vries
	Copyright Year 2016
Reflections on Technology for Educational Practitioners	
Philosophers of Technology Inspiring Technology Education	*The Future of Technology Education*
Edited by <u>John R. Dakers</u>, <u>Jonas Hallström</u>, and <u>Marc J. de Vries</u>	Edited by P. John Williams, Alister Jones, and Cathy Buntting
Copyright Year 2019	Copyright Year 2015

Gillian Shepherd in 1995, a new version in 1999 under the then Minister of Education David Blunket, further reforms under the then Minister of Education Ed Balls in 2008 followed by an Expert Panel Report in 2011 (DfE, 2011) set up by the then Minister of Education Michael Gove leading to a new version of the National Curriculum for England in 2013 (National Curriculum, 2013). The Expert Panel raised serious doubts as to whether design & technology should be a National Curriculum subject, arguing that it lacked the disciplinary coherence associated with the more established school subjects. Fortunately, the design & technology community were able to convince Michael Gove otherwise. Winston Churchill is reputed to have said, "The farther backward you can look, the farther forward you can see". Hence appreciating the past of our subject will be important in guiding its future. The extent to which the statutory requirements for teaching design & technology will change in the future is unclear but given the advances being made in both science and technology it is important that changes are made to embrace these developments and take into account the lessons of past developments.

Contemplating the subject's current position

Awarding organisation specifications are an obvious way of monitoring the requirements of GCSE, GCE, and other qualifications. Comparisons of their requirements and procedures can also give useful information as to differences in their interpretations of the knowledge, understanding, skills, and values. To some extent this gives a snapshot of the subject's current position but it is a limited view as it comes from within the community of practice. The work of organisations such as the Education Policy Institute can give a much less re-stricted view which is why their commentary on the state of the subject is particularly useful. The findings are summarised in Panel 4.2 (Educational Policy Institute, 2022). Alison Hardy's

Panel 4.2 Summary findings of the Educational Policy Institute report
A spotlight on design & technology study in England
Trends in subject uptake and the teacher workforce

The research, which is the first study to comprehensively examine trends in the subject over the last ten years, shows that 44% of students took design & technology GCSE in 2009, but this fell by half to just 22% of students in 2020.

Entries for students at A level have also declined over the same period, as more students now opt for vocational engineering qualifications. The analysis finds that GCSE students attending free schools and sponsored academies are less likely to enter design & technology, while at A level, students in independent schools are most likely to enter the subject.

The report also uncovers significant local and regional variation in design & technology take up, with entries in local authorities ranging from nearly 40% of pupils taking design & technology at GCSE in Herefordshire, to just 4% of pupils taking the subject at GCSE in Middlesbrough.

Choosing design & technology as a subject at GCSE level is shown to be particularly critical to continuing study in the subject at 16–19 level. Of those who did not study design & technology at GCSE, less than 2% opted to take up the subject at the next stage of education.

This shows that without the option or encouragement to begin studying design & technology an early age, students are far less inclined to pursue design & technology subjects at a higher level of education.

The study identifies several developments that have coincided with the considerable decline in take up. Between 2011 and 2020, the number of design & technology teachers fell by half from 14,800 to 7,300, with the government failing to meet its design & technology teacher recruitment targets. Significant school accountability reforms such as the EBacc and Progress 8, and qualifications reforms, such as the introduction of new GCSEs, also occurred during this period.

The new findings on the state of design & technology come as the government continues to roll out a series of major reforms to vocational education in England, including the introduction of T levels, apprenticeship reforms, and Institutes of Technology.

---

podcasts (Hardy, 2022) also provide useful relevant commentaries through conversations with those involved in the subject – teachers, academics, professional association figures. There are over 100 such conversations available including one with Tony Ryan, Chief Executive of the Design and Technology Association, about the EPI report (Ryan, 2022). And this podcast reminds us that the Design and Technology Association provides, through its various publications, commentary and snapshots of the subject's current position. Full details are available at the Associations website (https://www.data.org.uk). On a broader educational front, it is worth someone in the department being a member of the Chartered College of Teaching. The College's journal *Impact* covers a wide range of important topics and although these rarely if ever focus specifically on design & technology what they have to say about other subjects is often relevant. For example, the spring 2022 edition contained a raft of articles concerning cognitive science and curricular planning, none specific to design & technology but all relevant.

There are various social media groups dedicated to design & technology. For example Design and Technology Teachers (see https://www.facebook.com/groups/DTteachers) and Product Design Surgery (see https://www.facebook.com/groups/productdesignsurgery) and these provide a useful forum for seeking advice and exchanging views. It is important to be aware that in any such group, one can find oneself in an echo chamber amplifying the views of those with the loudest and most persistent voices.

It is important to consider the curriculum politics operating in your school in contemplating the subject's current position as this will enable you to situate your own position in the wider national one. A particularly useful book here is *Huh Curriculum Conversations between Subject and Senior Leaders* (Myatt & Tomsett, 2021). It is difficult for senior leaders to meet a subject's requirements in terms of staffing, ancillary support, timetable time, KS4 option arrangements if they lack a fundamental understanding of the nature of the subject and its teaching and learning requirements. *Huh* goes a long way to overcoming these difficulties and enabling the subject to enhance its standing in the curriculum and facilitate useful cross curricular collaboration.

Looking forwards

Predicting the future of design & technology is fraught with difficulties and to a degree there are influences completely outside the control of teachers, schools, and the education system that will exert change. But it is important to remember that teachers' visions for the future of the subject are important and can certainly influence the future of the subject in the schools where they teach and perhaps further afield if their practice is seen by the wider community as innovative and transferable to other schools. In chapter 7 there is a discussion of the nature and possible content of department vision and mission statements for design & technology. Through such statements colleagues in a department working together can forge the future path of the subject in their schools. Such paths will need to take into account the local situation, but they should not be overly limited by this; the paths should aspire towards a better understanding of the subject by key stakeholders and an improved subject experience for both teachers and learners.

Teacher visions for the subject need to be informed by more than their local conditions which is why it is important to look further afield to what is happening elsewhere in England and in other jurisdictions. The Researching D&T podcast, set up by Alison Hardy, promises to be a useful resource here (see https://open.spotify.com/show/2I6zGCD5s4InwoRTjQvLVB) in which those engaged in research into design & technology discuss the relevance of their findings to curriculum planning, classroom practice, and assessment. On a wider front, the researchED series of conferences are of significance (see https://researched.org.uk). ResearchED conferences bring together many parties affected by educational research – e.g., teachers, academics, researchers, policy makers, teacher-trainers – in order to establish healthy relationships where field-specific expertise is pooled usefully. At a researchED event, there are usually 6-7 rounds of sessions. Each session is 40 minutes long. Attendees build their own day using the timetable and programme that is released a couple of weeks before the day of the event.

An international conference that is of particular relevance to design & technology is the PATT conference. PATT (Pupils Attitudes Toward Technology) is an international organization based in the Netherlands that promotes research in technology education. They conduct conferences around the globe. These have occurred annually for the past 30 years and take place in different parts of the world. PATT is best described as an international community of technology education colleagues (researchers, teacher educators, teachers) who are interested in educational research as a support to developments in technology teaching. PATT is open to all. There is no membership. The proceedings for the PATT Conference can be found at this website https://www.iteea.org/conference-proceedings. A particularly interesting feature of the conference is that it encourages and supports presentations from teachers.

Pause for thought

Developing, maintaining, and extending the intellectual resources of your department is a substantial and on-going undertaking. It is important that each individual teacher can take part in this endeavour. It is important that the particular intellectual resources do not become compartmentalised in certain individuals with the result that if they leave the department these resources are lost. To what extent does your department have a plan for developing, maintaining, and extending intellectual resources and to ensure that they become embedded within the department.

Activities

This section will consider a range of teaching approaches for design & technology. It is important to have a range as this provides variety to lessons and, more importantly, each different approach is particularly adept at teaching different aspects of the subject. Over time a programme of study utilising a sequence of these different approaches will provide a broad and balanced 'diet' that deals effectively with teaching all aspects of both substantive and disciplinary knowledge.

Designing and making tasks

This is often seen as the heartland of design & technology education, although it does not reflect the reality of commercial activity in the world outside school, where those who design artefacts are usually not those who manufacture them.

David Barlex has described the decision making that pupils need to undertake when they are designing and making as involving five key areas of interdependent design decision (Barlex, 2007), shown diagrammatically in Figure 4.4:

- Conceptual (overall purpose of the design, the sort of product that it will be)
- Technical (how the design will work)
- Aesthetic (what the design will look like)
- Constructional (how the design will be put together)
- Stakeholder (users, buyers, sellers, manufacturers).

The interdependence of these areas is an important feature of making design decisions, as change of decision within one area will affect some if not all of design decisions that are made within the others. It is the juggling of these various decisions to arrive at a coherent design proposal that can then be realised to the point of a fully working prototype that provides the act of designing and making with intellectual rigour and educational worth and makes it an essential part of design & technology education.

The Nuffield Design & Technology Project coined the term "Capability Task" for designing and making tasks. Through attempting such tasks learners develop and reveal their design & technological capability. The Project was very clear as to the need for this activity to be

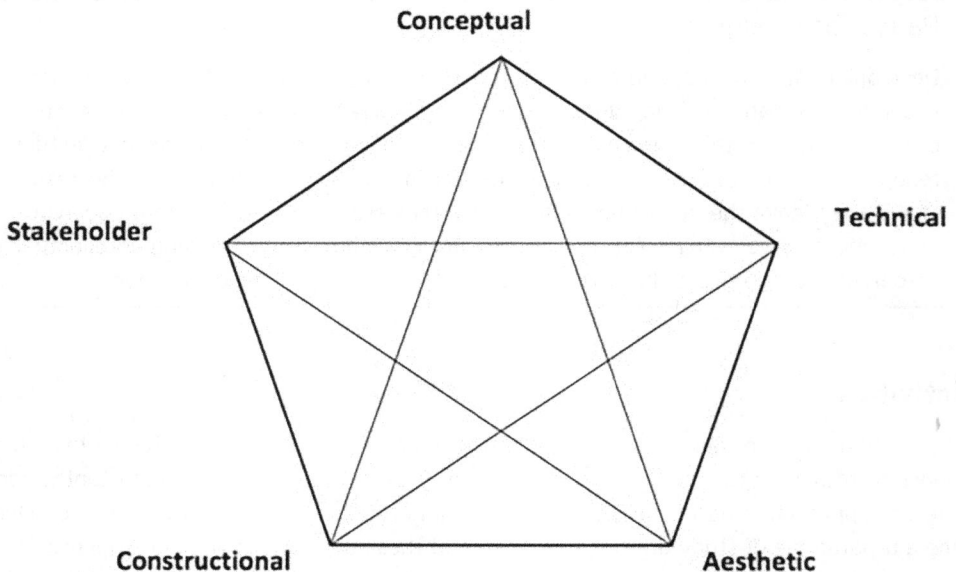

Figure 4.4 The Design Decision Pentagon

underpinned by two broad areas of knowledge: *knowledge **of** the problem* and *knowledge **for** the solution*.

Knowledge **of** the problem

Knowledge of the problem is always specific to the problem being addressed and needs to be found by exploring the situation in which the problem is embedded. It cannot be "looked up" in a general design & technology reference text. Because the scope of this knowledge can't be predicted (and thus can't be taught) in advance of exploring the design context, Neil Gershenfeld has described the acquisition of this kind of knowledge "Just-in-Time" learning (Gershenfeld, 2005). A good example of the power of "Just-in-Time" learning arises when learners are engaged with a designing and making task for young children. They realise that to understand the specific needs and wants of the children they are designing for they need to know more about, for example, the particular reading abilities of these children which might be different to their age expected reading ability. Learners can be taught general strategies for observing situations and identifying the needs and wants of people in those situations. But they have to utilise these strategies for themselves when learning about pertinent aspects of a particular context – just in time – to help them understand the nature of the design decisions they will need to make. And, of course, this is an iterative process, with learners revisiting the situation as they use strategies to find out more about the requirements their design proposals must meet.

Knowledge **for** the solution

Knowledge for the solution can be more easily predicted and acquired through the learner being taught in that, for any domain of design & technology, the basic knowledge does not change as the design task changes. Gears, for example, behave in the same way, in terms of principles, whether they are used in a child's toy, a lawn mower or a motorcar, although the detailed arrangement and robustness of the gearing system developed to operate in these artefacts will be different.

Teaching a design and make task

The way you teach a designing and making task will depend on the answers to the following questions:

- Do I want the learners to use learning from other subjects?

Effective links with other subjects will not happen by accident. Only a few learners will naturally make connections with other areas of the curriculum. To ensure that the majority make good use of other subjects, it is best to choose knowledge from a definite subject that lends itself to links with the design and make task and then to teach the task with this in mind.

- How open should I make the brief?

At Key Stage 3 the teacher is expected to provide learners with the brief. The more open the brief, the wider the range of products that learners in your class will want to design and make. It is important that the brief is not so open that you cannot support different learners' attempts at designing and making. It is equally important that the brief is not so narrow that all learners end up designing and making very similar products. It is essential that the individual signature of each learner can show through the work.

- How do I ensure good design ideas?

You have to decide on the range of ideas that it is best to get from the class. Do you want just one from each learner or lots? It is particularly important that that each learner receives feedback on their ideas. This is much more manageable if you limit the number of ideas they are asked to produce. If each learner is asked to produce one idea on a large Post-it® note, the notes can be displayed and each learner can hear feedback from the rest of the group. In this way all learners receive feedback and can adapt their ideas accordingly.

- How complex should the specification be?

More capable learners should be working to more ambitious specifications than less capable learners. You can use the same framework for specification with all learners in a class, but you can negotiate the detail with individual learners, which is a good way to achieve differentiation.

- How will learners model solutions?

Decide on the diversity of modelling that is appropriate and manageable. How many different sorts of modelling will be happening in your class to produce prototype products – just sketching, 3D mock-ups, working models, and/or computer images?

- How do I ensure they stay on track?

Once the design ideas are more fully developed it is still important that they are scrutinised. This process can be more dynamic if learners work in pairs, taking alternate roles of client and designer. The client has the specification and the designer the prototype product (in whatever form this has been developed). The client has to question the designer about the prototype. You can provide questions or expect the learners to make them up. It is important that this feedback informs the final design.

- What sort of written feedback do I give?

You can give three-point feedback to each learner based on their flatwork and any prototypes they have produced. Give a comment:

* about the design, either overall or on a point of detail

*   about the production, such as where particular care is necessary
*   to motivate, personal to the learner.
•   How do I ensure quality making?

It is important that learners are able to make their designs. You have to decide on the range of tools, equipment, materials, and components they can use and the amount of help you can give. You may need to demonstrate or set up specialist making stations. It might be important to encourage learners to help each other.

•   How will I organise final evaluation?

There are several different strategies for final evaluation:

•   Comparison of performance against specification;
•   User response;
•   Performance in the light of wider issues (winners and losers or appropriateness).

These can be carried out by individuals, in pairs or small groups, and sometimes through general class discussion. You will need to ensure that learners are taught these methods of evaluating and given the opportunity to use them in a variety of ways.

•   How do I organize a progress review?

It is important to enable learners to reflect on the efficacy of their learning and the progress they have made. Small group discussion between learners of the following questions will help individuals write a short progress review. And these are likely to contain information that is useful in finding ways to improve the teaching.

•   What did you enjoy most?
•   What did you find easy?
•   What did you find difficult?
•   What did you get better at?
•   Were you able to help other learners?
•   Were other learners able to help you?
•   What could you have done better?
•   How could you have done this better?

Resource tasks

To ensure that learners had the practical and intellectual resources with which to be capable, the Nuffield Project devised a series of "Resource Tasks" which could be used to teach a wide range of substantive and disciplinary knowledge. For example: design strategies, technical knowledge and understanding, and making skills. Resource Tasks are short practical activities to make learners think and to help them to learn the knowledge and skills they need to design and make really well. The style of the learning is active and responsive. Learners may have to explain, design, construct, investigate, and/or test. The learning intention for any one task is narrow but some tasks meet several learning intentions. It is the learning through Resource Tasks that enables young people to make sound design decisions. One might describe some Resource Task learning as "Just-in-Case" learning; learning that is likely, but not inevitably, to be useful in the future. A learner might choose not to use what they have learned about, for example, mechanisms, by avoiding mechanical solutions altogether. However, one important aspect of Just-in-Case learning relating to knowledge for the solution is that it can enable Just-in-Time learning. If a learner knows nothing or very little about a particular area of knowledge and realises that some knowledge about this might be useful for a solution to a design problem, then it is a very steep just-in-time learning curve. If, however, the learner knows something about the area, through some just-in-case learning, extending this knowledge just-in-time becomes much more feasible. Ian Leslie's main argument in *Curious* (2014) is particularly pertinent: the more you already know the easier it will be to find out about what you don't know and need to know. The Resources Tasks can be used to support individual Just-in-Time learning; an individual learner can choose to use appropriate tasks to develop knowledge as it is required.

Designing without making tasks

Designing without making is an approach developed extensively by the Young Foresight[2] project as the means to improve the ability to communicate design ideas, cultivate creativity and enable collaboration in design & technology lessons. Patricia Murphy of the Open University carried out independent evaluations of designing without making and showed that young people do not necessarily require "something to take home" (Murphy, 2013). Learners responded enthusiastically to working collaboratively to develop design ideas providing they knew at the outset that that they would not be going to make their designs. In fact, this 'not requiring to make' was welcomed by the learners, as it released them from the constraints of the materials and equipment available in their school workshops.

An important feature of this approach is that learners themselves decide on the need or want they will address and make conceptual design decisions accordingly, which provides ownership and motivation. The learners do, however, have to justify their ideas in terms of feasibility; meeting needs and wants, acceptability to society, and marketability. In moving from an initial idea to its clear representation learners can use and practice their drawing skills and use this representation when they present and justify their idea to the rest of the class. This focus on designing develops significant disciplinary knowledge.

Making without designing tasks

Making without designing also has a place in the pedagogy. Imagine an activity in which Year 7 learners make (and then fly) a kite. The teacher has provided the plans for the kite and, if followed faithfully, they are known to produce a kite that flies well. What might a learner learn from making a simple kite? They would certainly learn making skills involving textiles and resistant materials. Given the nature of kites there is the possibility of teaching about forces in structures as well as key aspects of health and safety, e.g., not flying near electricity pylons, avoiding cuts from taut string, and preventing being pulled over. If learners are given a choice of materials, there is the possibility of carrying out investigations into their properties and using the results to decide on which materials to use – both for the fabric and the frame. So, this making without designing activity is very rich in learning both substantive and disciplinary knowledge. Additionally, acquiring making skills is almost certainly highly enjoyable for the learners. It is worth noting that a short making without designing task can act as a Resource Task to support a designing and making task.

Considering consequences of technology tasks

The opportunity for learners to consider the consequences of a technology and its impact on society in general and their lives in particular is an important element of design & technology. Critique is one of the Big Ideas that underpin the subject. It is through learning to critique that young people will be enabled to partake in and contribute to on-going debates about what we do with the technology at our disposal. A simple 'winners and losers' analysis, to identify the impact of a product or technology on those who it might affect, is a very powerful way of engaging young people in considering consequences. Identification of 'winners and losers' featured in both the Nuffield Design & Technology Project and Young Foresight. A more structured approach to considering consequences is the reflective reading of case studies which describe and discuss a particular technology and its impact on the world. Such studies can easily be based on news items so that they have topicality and immediacy. The authors have developed a selection of such cases under the broad heading of Technological Perspective Readers[3] based on BBC News items. Activities to encourage discussion and reflection are embedded in the readers to help learners become active in critiquing.

We note that it is fairly straightforward to assess each of these four types of activity, providing the teacher is clear about the learning intentions underpinning the activity.

In summary, any 'grand plan' for a design & technology curriculum will need to give each of these four activities appropriate significance. Depending on the age and stage of the learners' design & technology experience, the relative significance of these components may vary within each year of the course. But there is a strong case that each should be present, to some degree, within each year.

While we have emphasised the learning value of these four approaches to teaching design & technology others have pointed to learners' huge enjoyment of the practical activity of making and suggested that it is this alone which earns the subject its place in the curriculum. While we agree that making is a very important aspect of the subject, we are adamant that if this is seen as the sole reason for its inclusion in the curriculum then the status of the subject will remain low. This is not to deny the power of making, particularly successful making, which can increase a learner's confidence and self-belief.

Pause for thought

Here is an example of a Year 7 Scheme of Work organised in terms of the four ways of teaching discussed above.

Term 1	Term 2	Term 3
Make without Design Learners will make, fly & investigate a kite	*Design without Make* Learners will design an item that utilises the new material QTC *Considering consequences* Learners explore their own understanding of robots and AI, consider whether automation will take jobs away from people, whether robots might help the disabled and consider winners and losers with regard to self-driving cars?	*Designing and Making* Learners will design and make a moving toy that is powered by a small electric motor, taking into account the user of the toy and design a toy that a) moves in a way that will appeal to the user, b) has an appearance which pleases the user, c) can incorporate a range of special effects, e.g., light and sound, that will give the toy more play value for the user.

Reflect on the extent to which this Scheme of Work covers the substantive and disciplinary knowledge required for Year 7 and discuss your thoughts with colleagues.

Planning for breadth, balance, and progression

The messy nature of progression is discussed in chapter 6 in terms of the possible un-evenness of learners' responses to the different ways teaching, considered previously in this chapter, and topics within any of these ways of teaching. In this section the discussion will focus on the intention for progression, breadth, and balance that departments can build into their schemes of work (SoW). In developing a robust scheme of work, it will be important to ensure that your SoW meets the main educational intentions of the subject which were clearly identified in chapter 1: technological capability and technological perspective. In broad sweep terms achieving progress in technological capability will require learners to use their knowledge, understanding skills and values in increasingly complex ways. They will become more creative as their confidence in dealing with uncertainty and taking intellectual risks increases. Previously in this chapter technological capability was described in terms of the number and type of design decisions a learner makes in a de-signing and making task (page 132). In developing progression, the teacher should increase the opportunities for learners to make more, harder, and different design decisions across time by providing more open design briefs and allowing the learner to devise their own design briefs from given contexts. As learners progress in technological capability, they will show *greater independence* and *better time management*. It will be important for the tea-cher to devise activities where there are opportunities for learners to demonstrate such qualities. whilst at the same time providing 'safety nets' for those learners for whom this is too great a challenge. Learners develop technological perspective by considering the economic and social impact of particular technologies and artefacts on both groups and individuals and their environmental impact on both the made and natural worlds. Progress in *technological perspective* will require learners to develop an understanding of unfamiliar technologies and to develop critical skills in challenging value positions. In developing progression, the teacher should begin with relatively simple artefacts used by learners and their families and move to considering more complex technologies and artefacts that will require systems thinking for their critical evaluation.

Any scheme of work will of necessity be sequential and the order in which the various Big Ideas (discussed in chapter 2 and earlier in this chapter) are introduced and revisited can be used to ensure breadth, balance, and provide progression. To illustrate this, a possible scheme of work has been developed in the following way. It is presented as a sequence of different sorts of learning activities across each term and these learning activities have been audited against the inclusion of the Big Ideas discussed earlier in this chapter. The SoW is also scrutinised with regard to the overall authenticity of the experience across each year by considering whether the learning reflects the fundamental nature of the subject. The resulting SoW is shown in shown in Panel 4.3.

In terms of breadth inspection reveals that all the Big Ideas are 'visited' across each year of Key Stage 3 and in Year 10. Regarding balance, it is necessary to look at the frequency with which the Big Ideas occur. Inspection reveals the following:

- Materials is visited three times in Year 7, three times in Year 8, twice in Year 9, and three times in Year 10.
- Manufacture is visited three times in Year 7, three times in Year 8, three times in Year 9, and three times in Year 10.
- Functionality is visited three times in Year 7, three times in Year 8, three times in Year 9, and three times in Year 10.
- Design is visited twice in Year 7, three times in Year 8, three times in Year 9, and three times in Year 10.
- Critique is visited twice in Year 7, three times in Year 8, three times in Year 9, and three times in Year 10.

This inspection reveals that all the Big Ideas are visited frequently and to similar extents indicating that balance has been achieved.

In terms of overall authenticity, the SoW is strong in that the very nature of the learning activities chosen embrace the nature of the subject which requires intervention to produce a range of possible responses of debatable worth, using knowledge from other subjects including math and science.

Our remaining concern is progression, and this will depend to a large extent on the detailed content of the teaching. Rather than presenting a detailed description of the possible content in the SoW shown in Panel 4.3, we think it is more useful to consider a general approach which may be applied to any SoW. Knowledge of materials, manufacturing, and functionality are aspects of substantive knowledge and a general approach to identifying what progression for any one of these Big Ideas might look like is as follows. It involves three steps.

Panel 4.3 A possible scheme of work for Years 7, 8, 9, and 10

Scheme of work for Year 7

Year & term		Materials	Manufacture	Function	Design	Critique	Overall authenticity
Year 7 Learning Activities							
Term 1	MwoD, make, fly, & investigate a kite	MwsD exploring the use of low relief vacuum forming	➤	➤	➤ structure			STRONG
Term 2	DwoM including CC using a new & emerging technology Possibly QTC	DMA concerning containing Design and make a container that can be formed from one or two nets and will hold one or two favourite small items safely and that, from its appearance, reflects the importance and nature of the contents. *Note the DMA will contain small tasks to provide learning likely to be useful for the 'big' task plus CC case studies.*	➤	➤	➤ structure	➤	➤	
Term 3	DMA concerning moving toys Design and make a moving toy that is powered by a small electric motor, taking into account the user of the toy and design a toy that a) moves in a way that will appeal to the user, b) has an appearance which pleases the user, c) can incorporate a range of special effects, e.g., light and sound, that will give the toy more play value for the user. *Note the DMA will contain small tasks to provide learning likely to be useful for the 'big' task plus CC case studies.*		➤	➤	➤ structure power control	➤	➤	

Key
DwoM = Design without Make   MwoD = Make without design   MwsD = Make with some design
DMA = Designing and making assignment   CC = Considering consequences

Scheme of work for Year 8

Year 8 Learning Activities

Year & terms			Materials	Manufacture	Function	Design	Critique	Overall authenticity
Term 1	DwoM using a new & emerging technology Possibly aerogels and/or memory alloys	MwoD, make, play with, & investigate spinning tops / MwsD using the laser cutter and the 3D printer to produce simple body adornment	❯	❯	❯ control (?)	❯	❯	STRONG
Term 2	DMA concerning lighting. Design and make a light that is suitable for use in a particular situation. The device will be constructed from easy to work materials and technical components. It will be powered by a battery, controlled by switches, and use LEDs for illumination. *Note the DMA will contain small tasks to provide learning likely to be useful for the 'big' task plus CC case studies of relevant technology in society.*		❯	❯	❯ structure power control	❯	❯	
Term 3	DMA, concerning carriers. Design and make a carrier that meets the needs of a person (who may be the learner) who has to carry particular items. The carrier will be constructed from textiles and flexible sheet materials. *Note the DMA will contain small tasks to provide learning likely to be useful for the 'big' task plus CC case studies of relevant technology in society.*		❯	❯	❯ structure	❯	❯	

Key
DwoM = Design without Make MwoD = Make without design MwsD = Make with some design
DMA = Designing and making assignment CC = Considering consequences

Scheme of work for Year 9

Year 9 Learning Activities

Year & terms		Materials	Manufacture	Function	Design	Critique	Overall authenticity
Term 1	DwoM using a new & emerging technology Augmented reality (?)	Robotics, MwoD, programme & CC of robots and AI to our society		>	> control	>	>	STRONG
Term 2	DMA concerning the exploitation of a phenomenon Design and make an item that exploits a scientific phenomenon such as magnetism and/or electromagnetism that is of benefit to an identified user. *Note the DMA will contain small tasks to provide learning likely to be useful for the 'big' task plus CC case studies.*	>	>	> structure power(?) control (?)	>	>	
Term 3	ConCh concerning shelter Identify and explore a situation in which there is the need for shelter. Devise and produce full-scale prototypes that meet this need using a combination of textiles, flexible sheet materials, easy to work resistant materials, plus technical components. *Note the DMA will contain small tasks to provide learning likely to be useful for the 'big' task plus CC case studies.*	>	>	> structure power(?) control (?)	>	>	

Key
DwoM = Design without Make MwoD = Make without design MwsD = Make with some design
DMA = Designing and making assignment CC = Considering consequences ConCh = Contextual Challenge

Scheme of work for Year10

Year & terms			Materials	Manufacture	Function	Design	Critique	Overall authenticity
Year 10 Learning Activities								
Term 1	DMA Heath Robinson Challenge How many forms of movement can you get from a rotating shaft?	MwsD Exploring electronic circuits for sensing	ConCh Exploration Identify and investigate places that require exploration. Develop prototype products that could carry out such exploration. *Note the ConCh will contain small tasks to provide learning likely to be useful for the 'big' task plus CC case studies.*	≫	≫	≫ structure control	≫	≫	STRONG
Term 2	CC Linear or Circular? Arguing for changing the way we do business	MwsD Exploring energy generation and storage	ConCh Living spaces Explore the living space needs of different individuals. Develop models that show how such needs might be met in the context of a low carbon economy. *Note the ConCh will contain small tasks to provide learning likely to be useful for the 'big' task plus CC case studies.*	≫	≫	≫ structure power control	≫	≫	STRONG

Scheme of work for Year10

Year & terms			Materials	Manufacture	Function	Design	Critique	Overall authenticity
Term 3	MwsD Exploring materials and structures	ConCh concerning Protection Identify and explore activities in which participants need protection. Develop prototype product that supply this protection. *Note the ConCh will contain small tasks to provide learning likely to be useful for the 'big' task plus CC case studies.*	›	›	› structure	›	›	STRONG
		ConCh for GCSE NEA						

Key
DwoM = Design without Make MwoD = Make without design MwsD = Make with some design
DMA = Designing and making assignment CC = Considering consequences ConCh = Contextual Challenge

First, identify the dimensions of progression, probably no more than three. In the case of materials this might be 1) the idea of properties and the extent to which learners may be taught about the different sorts of properties that materials might exhibit; 2) expanding the idea of properties to embrace the environmental and societal impacts of different materials; and 3) learners' actual experience of handling a range of different materials so that they are able to use them in their own designing and making.

The second step is to look at the teaching in each year and ask if each of the three features of progression have been included (if any are missing then these will need to be included).

The third step is to compare the content of each year with that of the following year to ascertain whether the way each feature is dealt with is more demanding in terms of the learning. This increased demand might be in terms of expanding the knowledge base without requiring any new ideas to understand this 'new' knowledge or it could require a more sophisticated understanding of existing knowledge, i.e., what has already been taught.

For designing and critiquing a different approach is necessary as these are aspects of disciplinary knowledge. In the case of designing, we have seen earlier in this chapter that learners' designing may be seen in terms of making decisions about five interrelated features: conceptual, technical, aesthetic, constructional, and stakeholder (see Figure 4.4 and associate text). It is the extent to which learners are required to make these decisions and their intrinsic complexity that will provide for progression. Again, there are three steps.

Step 1 involves identifying where in the designing and making tasks the learners are required to make design decisions other than conceptual decisions. As a learner moves across Key Stage 3, the balance should change from the teacher making most of these design decisions to the learner making most of them. In some cases, the teacher might provide a range of possible decisions. For example, she might indicate that the way the design might work could be mechanically or electrically and if mechanically this might be by clockwork or by energy stored in a stretched elastic band. Step 2 requires scrutiny of the complexity of the design decisions being made. For example, in Year 7 the design of a lighting circuit might involve a simple series circuit containing a light bulb and on off switch. In Year 9 the design of a lighting circuit might involve parallel circuits with several LEDs, each independently controlled by on off switches. The complexity of the design decisions made should increase across the Key Stage. Step 3 requires scrutiny of the extent to which learners are involved in conceptual decisions, i.e., deciding on the sort of item they are designing. Designing without making tasks require that learners make such decisions. However, it is more difficult to enable this in designing and making tasks but very important that by the end of Key Stage 3 learners are involved to some extent in making conceptual design decisions for themselves. Ways to do achieve this are discussed in chapter 2 and the Thought Piece by Andy Mitchell.

In the case of critique, it is important to remember that we want learners to question the very terms of reference for designed outcomes. Critique is *not* concerned with whether a design does what it was supposed to but, firstly, what are the consequences of the design in action with regard to social justice and stewardship of Planet Earth, and secondly is what it was supposed to do worth doing? In terms of proposed designs learners need to ask, 'We can, but should we?' The approach here requires just two steps. The first step requires scrutiny of the activities in the SoW that purport to involve critique to check that they do in fact require critique and not simply evaluation. Assuming that they do, then the second step to achieve progression needs to look at the complexity of the critique required. Critique involves identifying the impact of a design on different stakeholders. At the beginning of Key Stage 3 considering the impact on a single stakeholder might well be sufficient. Later in the Key Stage multiple stakeholders should be considered, and by the end of Key Stage 3 and into Year 10 the conflicting requirements of different stakeholders should be considered.

Pause for thought

Hilda and Torben have discussed the contents of Panel 4.3 at length. Hilda thinks that it is very much an 'art of the possible' approach, whereas Torben thinks it could perhaps have more hi-tech components. What do you think?

Once a department has developed a SoW that meets the requirements of breadth, balance, and progression and appears to be working well, it is tempting to adopt an 'if it isn't broken then don't try to fix it' approach leading, over time to a lack lustre and pedestrian experience for learners. What steps might be taken to avoid this?

Organisation and strategy

Sound departmental organisation invariably revolves around maintaining workshop and design studios in good order so that the teachers and classes using the rooms are able to tackle both practical and written work efficiently and effectively as well as engage in discussions and watch demonstrations. This is discussed in some detail previously in this chapter in the section *Physical resources* and also in chapter 5. This requires all the items in regular use to be arranged and organised consistently. Here we depart from Oscar Wilde's criticism that "Consistency is the last refuge of the unimaginative" and suggest that as far as possible there should be a consistent approach with regard to the locations of tools, materials, and equipment such that once teachers and learners are accustomed to using one workspace well they will be able to use others just as easily as similar resources for teaching and learning will be in equivalent or similar locations similarly organised. The role of department technicians is essential in setting up and maintaining this good order but of course they cannot do this if teachers using the rooms do not play their part in ensuring that the learners use the various organisational systems that are in place to maintain the necessary good order.

In an ideal world, each teacher would be in their 'own' space for all the lessons they teach, but this is difficult to achieve and with some rooms being assigned a permanent specialist function impossible to achieve. However, the number of teachers using a particular studio or workshop should be kept to a minimum. In this way teachers have a considerable vested interest in keeping 'their' room in good order and developing ownership of the spaces in which they teach. This also allows teachers to give the room a personal touch by displaying and varying visual materials that create interest without compromising the overall good order that needs to be maintained.

At Key Stage 3 some departments operate on a 'circus' basis with learners spending a relatively short period of time with a specialist teacher before moving on to another specialist teacher, and so on throughout the school year. In this approach a learner may, across a year, spend five six-week periods each with a different teacher. The argument to support this is that each teacher is an expert in their particular field – graphics, resistant materials, textiles, electronics, CADCAM, etc. – and the learners benefit from the teacher expertise. The need for similar organisational systems across the different areas of learning spaces is strong if learners are not to spend valuable time becoming familiar with different organisational systems. The argument against this approach is that it is difficult for the teachers to get to know the learners any single class. The teacher is just beginning to establish a rapport with the class and understand and respond to individual learner's needs, and it is time for the learners to move on. Some departments operate on a completely different approach and a class of learners is assigned to a single teacher who teaches across the specialist areas. The argument for this approach is that the teacher can over the year build up a strong rapport with the class, gain significant insight into individual learner's needs, and understand the progress being made by the learners with regard to the subject as a whole. However, this approach does require that teachers support one another in developing expertise outside their individual areas of expertise. It is important that if this system is introduced, it is accompanied by time and resources to support this professional development. Proponents of this approach argue that it is worth providing this time and resources as over time all the teachers in the department will gain significant expertise across all areas of expertise. As with the circus approach a consistent approach with regard to the locations of tools, materials, and equipment across the teaching spaces is necessary.

Pause for thought

If your department is considering moving away from a circus arrangement, what key considerations do you think should be discussed by the department to identify the necessary changes? Over what length of time should the alternative approach operate in order to give it the chance of success? How might the department evaluate the effectiveness of the move?

Once a department is well organised in terms of its day to day running and implementing the teaching, learning, and assessment needed by the SoWs in place, it is important that this is scrutinised in terms of the strategic planning required for the department to be able to continuously improve its offerings to learners. The short-term improvements required can be achieved by the end of unit reviews as discussed earlier in this chapter. But medium- and long-term improvements will require members of the department to stand back and critique the work of the department in terms of the ways it might need to change in order to meet its vision and mission statements. Such statements are discussed in some detail in chapter 7. Suffice it to say here that such critique might for example suggest change regarding making more use of learner voice, or engaging more widely with local industry, or communicating the nature and worth of the subject more deeply to parents and carers, or modernising the teaching of systems and control or developing a research informed approach to teaching. These are significant changes and will require time and effort from those taking them forward. It will be important to discuss any such intentions with the SLT and agree how they fit into a five-year development plan. The SLT will be able to provide both support and guidance in these endeavours and ensure that they mesh with other departments' plans and the school's overall development.

Pause for thought

If your department wishes to develop some long-term strategies to inform its development over, say the next five to ten years, what series of meetings might be necessary to begin this process?

Ofsted

The detailed arrangements for the inspection of schools can be found in the Education Inspection Framework Guidance document (HMSO, 2021).

Inspectors use a 4-point grading scale in all inspections to make the principal judgements:

- grade 1 – outstanding
- grade 2 – good
- grade 3 – requires improvement
- grade 4 – inadequate.

Inspectors make graded judgements on the following areas using the 4-point scale:

- quality of education
- behaviour and attitudes
- personal development
- leadership and management.

In this section we will focus mainly on the inspection of the quality of education. The method used by inspectors to find out about the curriculum offering is as follows.

Top-level view: inspectors and leaders start with a top-level view of the school's curriculum, exploring what is on offer, to whom and when, leaders' understanding of curriculum intent and sequencing, and why these choices were made.

Deep dive: then, a 'deep dive', which involves gathering evidence on the curriculum intent, implementation, and impact over a sample of subjects, topics, or aspects. This is done in collaboration with leaders, teachers, and learners. The intent of the deep dive is to seek to interrogate and establish a coherent evidence base on the quality of education.

Bringing it together: inspectors will bring the evidence together to widen coverage and to test whether any issues identified during the deep dives are systemic. This will usually lead to school leaders bringing forward further evidence and inspectors gathering additional evidence.

It is in the deep dive that design & technology subject leaders and teachers will be most involved, and the three features of intent, implementation, and impact explored by the inspectors.

Concerning **intent**; according to the guidance:

- Leaders should construct a curriculum that is ambitious and designed to give all learners the knowledge and cultural capital they need to succeed in life.
- The curriculum should be coherently planned and sequenced towards cumulatively sufficient knowledge and skills for future learning and employment.
- There should be the same academic, technical, or vocational ambitions for almost all learners.
- Learners should study the full curriculum by being taught a full range of subjects for as long as possible, 'specialising' only when necessary.

Concerning **implementation**, according to the guidance:

- Teachers should have good knowledge of the subject(s) and courses they teach, and leaders provide effective support, including for those teaching outside their main areas of expertise.
- Teachers should present subject matter clearly, promoting appropriate discussion about the subject matter they are teaching. They should check learners' understanding systematically, identify misconceptions accurately and provide clear, direct feedback. In doing so, they respond and adapt their teaching as necessary, without unnecessarily elaborate or differentiated approaches.
- Over the course of study, teaching should be designed to help learners to remember in the long term the content they have been taught and to integrate new knowledge into larger concepts.
- Teachers and leaders should use assessment well, for example, to help learners embed and use knowledge fluently or to check understanding and inform teaching. Leaders should understand the limitations of assessment and not use it in a way that creates unnecessary burdens for staff or learners.
- Teachers should create an environment that allows learners to focus on learning. The resources and materials that teachers select – in a way that does not create unnecessary workload for staff – should reflect ambitious intentions for the course of study and clearly support the intent of a coherently planned curriculum, sequenced towards cumulatively sufficient knowledge and skills for future learning and employment.

Concerning **impact**, according to the guidance:

- Learners should develop detailed knowledge and skills across the curriculum and, as a result, achieve well. Where relevant, this is reflected in results from national tests and examinations that meet government expectations, or in the qualifications obtained.
- Learners should be ready for the next stage of education, employment, or training. Where relevant, they gain qualifications that allow them to go on to destinations that meet their interests, aspirations and the intention of their course of study. They read widely and often, with fluency and comprehension.

In discussing **intent** with inspectors, a good place to start is with an overview of the curriculum from Years 7-10, similar to that described and discussed previously in the section on progression, breadth, and balance. Initially it will be important to point out to the inspectors the way that you have used the Big Ideas of design & technology to ensure that the curriculum has a clear intention to teach significant amounts of knowledge, understanding, skills, and values pertinent to the subject. In discussing **implementation**, it will be important to point out the way that four clearly identified ways of teaching are used to teach the knowledge, understanding skills, and values identified as the content to be taught. It will be important to discuss with the inspectors how the interplay between the Big Ideas and the teaching leads to learners developing both technological capability and technological perspective. You should be able to demonstrate the progression that is taking place in the learning of the individual Big Ideas as discussed in the previous sections as well as the overall progression in capability and perspective also discussed in the previous section. With regard to capability, the range and sophistication of the design ideas developed by the learners should be apparent, and it should be clear that the nature of the designing and making tasks set make more demands as the learners move from year to year. Also, it should be clear that as learners get older, they get the opportunity to explore contexts and identify their own design briefs. With regard to perspective, the increased sophistication with which learners are expected to discuss the impacts of technology on society with regard to both social justice and stewardship issues should be apparent. Across a year it should be clear that deployment of the different sorts learning activities covers a sufficient breadth of Big Ideas that overall the learning experience is authentic with regard to the two major intentions of the subject; developing technological capability and technological perspective.

In order to gauge **implementation** the inspectors will observe individual lessons and it will be important that you, and those teaching these lessons are fully conversant with a) the particular type of learning activity of which the lesson is a part, b) the place of that lesson in the sequence of lessons that comprise that activity, and c) the place of the activity in the sequence of activities that comprise the scheme of work for that year. Being au fait across the piece, as it were, will enable you and other teachers to talk with the inspectors about the curriculum in both broad sweep terms and at the finer grained level of individual learner's development. It will be important that the lessons observed show the characteristics of good teaching in the context of the design & technology being taught: proper pace, good questioning with appropriate wait times, effective demonstration and sound modelling, effective teacher – learner interactions, useful peer-to peer-learning. Details of how to teach various aspects of design & technology in the light of how learning occurs are discussed in some detail in chapter 5 and it will be important that you and other teachers are able to describe and justify the approaches to teaching taken in the departments scheme of work.

In order to gauge **impact** inspectors will collect some data through lesson observation and it is here that observing teachers giving feedback 'in the moment' as described in chapter 6 will provide evidence in real time of the progress being made as learners respond to this feedback. Effective feedback in the moment builds strong relationships between teachers and learners developing the confidence in learners to ask for help when they are unsure and enabling teachers to help learners overcome their difficulties. Inspectors will also look at samples of flat work and 3D outcomes along with associated assessment records. It is here that 'end of a task' feedback, as described in chapter 6, provides a significant record of the progress being made by each learner along with the support they are receiving to maintain or extend progress.

With regard to behaviour and attitudes

The behaviour and attitudes of learners as revealed in design & technology lessons will contribute to the inspector's overall view of behaviour and attitudes across the school. Workshops and design studios are by the very nature of the activities taking place therein potentially dangerous so it will be important to have established safe practice as the norm. The lesson spaces should be physically safe in terms of the way learners handle materials, tools, and equipment. But in addition, they need to be safe across other features. They need to be intellectually safe such that learners are encouraged to take risks with regard to their design thinking so that they develop ideas that are unusual and innovative. They need to be emotionally safe in that learners can manage the feelings of uncertainty and insecurity that can accompany thinking outside the box. They need to be socially safe in that learners know they will receive support and encouragement from both peers and teachers when they tackle tasks they find difficult and get appropriate help when they think they are failing. Vera John-Steiner (2000) has written compellingly about the benefits of creative collaboration arguing convincingly that those collaborating achieve far more than is possible through their individual efforts. If safety across these four features is achieved, then design & technology lesson spaces have the potential to become home to communities of practice where creative collaboration is the norm and learning thrives.

With regard to personal development

Two features of personal development are particularly relevant for design & technology. The way in which learners respond to contextual challenges will almost certainly involve discovering and developing interests and talents and in developing technological capability they will become more resilient, confident, and independent.

With regard to leadership and management

The professional improvement of teachers' subject, pedagogical and pedagogical content knowledge is seen as a key feature of good leadership and management. The compelling case for working in teams made earlier in this chapter, particularly by Paul Mburu's Thought Piece provides an interesting opportunity for leaders to support professional development of design & technology staff.

Pause for thought

Might it be worth using intent, implementation, and impact as a framework for any substantial review or evaluation your department undertakes of elements of the curriculum? For example you might ask, in the case of this unit of work, what learning were we trying to achieve (intent), how did we go about it (implementation), and to what extent were we successful (impact)?

Summary

This chapter began by considering the *Content of the curriculum* in terms of the Big Ideas of and about design & technology in the light of the writing of Jacob Bronowski. Next *Resources* were considered in terms of physical resources, focussing particularly on the need for their organisation including a Thought Piece by Philip Holton, human resources dealing in some depth with utilising teams including a Thought Piece by Paul Mburu, and intellectual resources using the idea of teachers' personal subject constructs as a way of thinking about this. The third part of the chapter considered *Activities* identifying and discussing in some depth designing and making tasks in the light of the necessary design decisions, resource tasks, designing without making tasks, making without designing tasks, and considering the consequences of technology tasks. The fourth part considered *Planning for breadth, balance, and progression* and how this might be achieved in a SoW through developing the demands of different learning activities across time and considering the extent to which they embraced the Big Ideas of and about design & technology. *Organisation*, in terms of the regulation of the resources in learning spaces, and *strategy*, in terms of planning for the medium- and long-term growth and maintenance of the curriculum, were considered in the fifth part. The final part considered the *Ofsted Inspection Framework* and how a department might respond in discussing each of these features: intent, implementation and impact.

Notes

1 At the time Bronowski was writing the term 'man' was used to denote the whole of humanity not only those of a male sex.
2 Young Foresight learning resources are available free to download at https://dandtfordandt. wordpress.com/resources/young-foresight/
3 Technological Perspective readers are available, free to download, at https://dandtfordandt. wordpress.com/resources/technological-perspective-readers/

References

Banks, F., & Barlex, D. (2021) *Teaching STEM in the Secondary School*. Oxon: Routledge.

Barlex, D. (2007) Assessing capability in design & technology The case for a minimally invasive approach, *Design and Technology Education: An International Journal*, 12.2, 9–56.

Bennett, N. (2006) *Making a Difference: A Study of Effective Middle Leadership in Schools Facing Challenging Circumstances*. Nottingham: National College for School Leadership.

Bennett, N., Newton, W., Wise, C., Woods, P. A., & Economou, A. (2003) *The Role and Purpose of Middle Leaders in Schools*. Nottingham: National College for School Leadership.

Bronowski, J. (1973) *The Ascent of Man*, London, BBC.

DfE (2011) *Expert Panel Report*, https://www.gov.uk/government/publications/framework-for-the-national-curriculum-a-report-by-the-expert-panel-for-the-national-curriculum-review.

Douglas, A. (2015) *Student Teachers in School Practice: An Analysis of Learning Opportunities*. Basingstoke: Palgrave Macmillan.

EPI (2022) *A Spotlight on Design and Technology Study in England Trends in Subject Uptake and the Teacher Workforce*, https://epi.org.uk/publications-and-research/a-spotlight-on-design-and-technology-study-in-england/.

Gershenfeld, N. (2005) *FAB The coming revolution on Your Desktop – From Personal Computers to Personal Fabrication*. New York: Basic Books.

Hardy, A. (2022) Podcast, https://dralisonhardy.com/podcast/.

Hardy, A., Gyekye, K., & Wainwright, C. (2015) *What Do Others Think Is the Point of Design and Technology Education?* http://irep.ntu.ac.uk/id/eprint/18559/1/219822_PubSub2185_Hardy.pdf.

HMSO (2021) *Education Inspection Framework Guidance*, *23 July 2021*, https://www.gov.uk/government/publications/education-inspection-framework/education-inspection-framework#contents.

John-Steiner, V. (2000) *Creative Collaboration*. New York: Oxford University Press.

Leithwood, K. (2012) *The Ontario leadership framework 2012 with a discussion of the research foundations*, https://www.education-leadershipontario.ca/application/files/2514/9452/5287/The_Ontario_Leadership_Framework_2012_-_with_a_Discussion_of_the_Research_Foundations.pdf.

Leslie, I. (2014) *Curious*. London: Quercus.

Mburu, P.K. (2022). Leadership Perceptions in Design and Technology Education. In: Williams, P.J., von Mengersen, B. (eds.), Applications of Research in Technology Education. *Contemporary Issues in Technology Education*. Springer, Singapore. 10.1007/978-981-16-7885-1_2.

Myatt, M., & Tomsett, J. (2021) *Huh Curriculum Conversations between Subject and Senior Leaders*. Woodbridge: John Catt Educational Ltd.

National Curriculum (2013), https://www.gov.uk/government/collections/national-curriculum.

Nuffield Foundation (2000) *Chooser Charts*, https://dandtfordandt.wordpress.com/resources/nuffield-ks3-dt-resources/chooser-charts/.

Ryan, T. (2022) *TD&T103 Talking about the EPI Report with Tony Ryan*, https://dralisonhardy.com/tdt103-talking-about-the-epi-report-with-tony-ryan/.

Schön, D. (1983) *The Reflective Practitioner: How Professionals Think in Action*, New York: Basic Books.

Swailes, R. (2019) Choose it, use it, put it away. In O. Caviglioli (ed.), *Dual Coding for Teachers Woodbridge*, UK: John Catt Educational.

Recommended reading

Myatt, M., & Tomsett, J. (2021) *Huh Curriculum Conversations Between Subject and Senior Leaders*. Woodbridge: John Catt Educational Ltd.

5 Teaching design & technology

This chapter deals with seven topics:

- How learning happens in design & technology which considers how the findings of cognitive science may be used to inform design & technology teaching.
- The teaching of technical understanding which deals with power, control, and structures and considers how these engage with science learning and systems thinking.
- The teaching of making which focuses on the role of demonstration and the need for practice.
- The teaching of designing exploring particularly the role of classroom talk between learners and teachers.
- The teaching of critique which can take place in different sorts of pedagogy.
- Digital designing and making exploring the opportunities it provides and the need for balance with manual designing and making

How learning happens in design & technology

It's rare to visit a school that hasn't embedded an approach to teaching based, to a greater or lesser degree, on current understandings of cognitive science. Often these teaching models build on one of the popular encapsulations of cognitive science ideas, such as Lemov's Teach Like a Champion (2021), Rosenshine's principles (2012), Sherrington & Cavigioli's Walkthrus (2020-2022), or the guidance provided by the Education Endowment Foundation. This section of the book isn't going to rehearse these core ideas; each of the references above provides an excellent introduction to any reader for whom they might be new. Rather, it aims to build on these models of how learning happens in a few directions, by exploring:

- some limits of the models,
- how these models might be best used in the distinctive situation of learning in design & technology,
- other understandings of cognition that are less talked about in secondary education but that may be especially pertinent to learning in design & technology; in particular '4E cognition' (embodied, embedded, enactive, and extended cognition).

DOI: 10.4324/9781003008026-5

Limits of cognitive science models

Every teacher clearly holds a mental model of how learning happens, whether implicitly or explicitly (how could one operate in a classroom otherwise?). For teaching to be reflective, it is better for the model to be explicit, as Sherrington has argued (2020). Seasoned teachers have sometimes argued that all this 'new' cognitive science stuff is 'just common sense'. We take this to mean that it chimes with the implicit models that they have built up through experience, which is reassuring; it would be surprising and worrying if teacher expertise on enabling learning and research into how learning happens *didn't* generally agree with each other. For the less-seasoned, especially student teachers and those early in their career (i.e., those who have not yet had time to build deep expertise) having explicit access to a good model is a game-changer.

However, as one often hears, 'All models are wrong; some models are useful' (Box, 2005). Clearly this applies as much to models of how learning happens as to any other. Willingham (2021) has provided a simplified model of how learning happens that is widely used as a foundation for the models of learning that schools and teachers are using (Sherrington's model, noted above, builds from Willingham's simpler model). In a recent interview (TES, 2023) Willingham makes the following observations:

> Take the working memory model – it is very successful in accounting for a lot of data. But it is probably wrong.
>
> [... *he then outlines an 'altogether different model'* ...]
>
> Yet I still use that box model. Why? Because it is really complicated to explain the other. And they make identical predictions for the classroom, and the difference doesn't matter for the classroom.

In addition to models being inherently limited in this way, they are also subject to being misinterpreted and misapplied (one hears the phrase 'lethal mutations' currently used rather a lot in relation to cognitive science models (Jones & Wiliam, 2022)). Sometimes this arises from teachers being required, across a whole school, to follow a particular practice, for example starting every lesson with retrieval practice, without being given a solid understanding of what underlies the practice. In the case of retrieval practice the underpinning idea is that the act of retrieving information from memory reinforces the ability to retrieve that information in the future. This is often claimed to be one of the most robust findings of cognitive science. So, in many schools it is now mandated for all lessons to start with retrieval practice to improve the quality of learning. But an episode of retrieval practice as a 'Do Now' activity at the start of a lesson could be undermined by, say, the teacher simply giving out the answers after the register has been taken, rather than systematically checking learners' responses. In such a case there is no certainty that retrieval has taken place (learners may simply have waited for the answers to be given out) and, if it has not, memory won't have been strengthened.

In another example, even well-done retrieval practice at the start of a lesson may not be helpful in the context of that lesson's learning objectives. Perhaps it would be better to spend those valuable first minutes of the lesson setting the scene with an intriguing starter designed to establish curiosity and desire to understand more. Equally, in many design & technology lessons a core objective is to develop a particular manipulative skill. This may well happen in a context where constraints of time or equipment mean that, for this objective to be met, the teaching and subsequent practice of the skill needs to get going rapidly at the lesson start. Perhaps retrieval practice in this context would simply get in the way of a successful lesson outcome. Or perhaps retrieval practice would sit more naturally at the lesson end, or as a lesson break-point mid-way through.

Teachers are highly qualified and knowledgeable professionals. To get the best out of them, schools need to ensure that not only are they well-informed about what cognitive science suggests for good teaching practice, but also that they are allowed to use the high-level skills that their qualification as a teacher has equipped them with. For example, the QAA Level 7 (QAA, 2014) (Masters level, a level that all UK teachers are qualified to) descriptors include the ability to: 'demonstrate self-direction and originality in tackling and solving problems, and act autonomously in planning and implementing tasks at a professional or equivalent level'.

So, having a model of how learning happens is necessary, as is the understanding that such models are provisional. At the same time a teacher needs to have a clear understanding of the kinds of knowledge (e.g., substantive and disciplinary) that are the Big Ideas in their subject. And they need insight into the ways that the learning model and the Big Ideas can be best brought together in the context of the learners they are teaching (such as their age and prior knowledge) and the school they are teaching in (such as the resources available and the social and cultural context). The conclusion here is that, as well as properly understanding what underpins any practice developed from a model of learning, teachers need to have the freedom to use it thoughtfully and flexibly as experts in the subject, their learners, and their school. This is discussed in more detail in chapter 4 in terms of teachers' personal subject constructs as consisting of three related features: subject knowledge, pedagogic knowledge, and school knowledge (related to the way subject knowledge is specific to schools).

Applying strategies from cognitive science models in design & technology

The strategies discussed here use elements of Rosenshine's Principles of Instruction as a structure, though, as noted above, other cognitive toolboxes commonly used by schools suggest the same or similar strategies, even if the terms used may differ. Not all of Rosenshine's Principles are discussed here, rather the focus is on those where we might expect the nature of design & technology to suggest application that is distinct from the approach in other subjects.

There is an additional and very useful perspective on these ideas, one whose conclusions inform what follows, which is that of 'key pedagogies' in design & technology, as described by McLean (2020). These are summarised as:

> activities such as direct instruction (e.g. teacher demonstrations of practical skills), those to promote design thinking (e.g. avoiding design fixation, iterative design, etc.), critical thinking (e.g. questioning, product analysis/evaluation, etc.) and collaboration

(e.g. group work, peer feedback, etc.). The aim being to develop the dispositions, values and attitudes of pupils that frame how they view and experience the world around them from a design & technology perspective.

Review material daily, weekly, monthly

This seems to be one of the most widely adopted of these Principles and is a required lesson element in most of the schools Hilda and Torben visit. The key for making this effective for design & technology teachers is, of course, in understanding the range of types of knowledge that can be included in the review. Design & technology is concerned with developing technological capability and technological perspective and the knowledge that young people have to learn and understand to achieve this has been discussed at some length in both chapter 2 and chapter 4. Suffice it to say here that this knowledge embraces both substantive and disciplinary knowledge and planned reviewing can embrace these in the light of the learning activities taking place. Such reviewing can easily embrace knowledge for the solution but reviewing knowledge of the problem is more complex as this depends on the way the problem is being envisaged by the learner (see chapter 4, page 133).

Present new material using small steps

Here it is important to think broadly about what the term 'material' means in a design & technology context. As in the section above, this needs to apply to all the forms of knowledge that we hold important in design & technology. So, it will include not only introducing declarative knowledge, such as the properties of materials, but also supporting the development of new critical skills through activities such as product analysis or the development of skills with a large sensorimotor component such as safe cutting, perspective drawing, or effective soldering.

Whatever the focus of your teaching, you need to think about how to break down new concepts and procedures into small steps that, once brought together, will lead your learners to mastery.

Scaffold new skills

This links strongly to the 'small steps' section above, since it is at the point when learners are being introduced to new material that support is most needed.

Scaffolding, along with its complementary notion of fading (carefully removing the scaffold supports so that learners become confident in using the skill independently) is well-established as an idea in teaching, but, as ever in design & technology, needs to be applied to the broad range of skills that make up design & technology activity.

Some scaffolding techniques can be adopted from other subjects; for example, writing frames to support the development of a product specification or a critique of a product or class of technology. Similarly, scaffolds for introducing equations can be adapted from those used in the teaching of science and maths.

Where we can't draw on practice from elsewhere in the curriculum, there are usually subject-specific scaffolding tools available from within the design & technology community. Most design & technology teachers are familiar with tools such as 'SCAMPER' (an acronym for seven techniques; (S) substitute, (C) combine, (A) adapt, (M) modify, (P) put to another use, (E) eliminate, and (R) reverse) and '4×4' (used to scaffold collaborative creative design thinking) and 'ACCESSFM' (an acronym for aesthetics, consumer, cost, environment, size, safety, function, and materials; used to scaffold product analysis). What often seems to have been overlooked is that there exist rich sources of further scaffolded tasks that cover a wide range of aspects of design & technology that are (or perhaps should be?) commonly, taught. In particular:

- The KS3 Design & Technology National Strategy, Module 4: Teaching the subskills of designing (HMSO, 2004).
- The KS3 Strategy Resource Tasks from the Nuffield Design & Technology materials (Nuffield Foundation, 2000).

But scaffolding should extend beyond these kinds of tasks to encompass and support the teaching of any new material, including 'practical' skills (we are using scare quotes because all design & technology teachers know that these kinds of things are never simply practical, all have an intellectual component), such as using a saw to create a particular kind of wood joint, using an electronics breadboard, learning to use a new software tool, or using a sewing machine safely.

Pause for thought

It might be worth discussing with colleagues the extent to which the department uses scaffolded tasks and the extent to which this scaffolding is faded as learners become adept at using the learning independently.

Provide models

This too links closely to 'small steps' as well as 'scaffolding' discussed in the sections above.

In discussions about applying this principle, the technique most often discussed is that of 'worked examples' with references to the development of mathematical techniques such as applying equations in science lessons. Certainly, there are times when design & technology teachers need to teach the use of equations and the approaches used by mathematics and science teachers are well-honed and should be adopted, firstly because they are tried and tested and secondly because this avoids confusing learners through adopting a different approach. But the idea of modelling stretches well beyond this with design & technology teaching. It can, it should, be applied to any context where new skills are being taught; including all those discussed in the previous section on scaffolding. And because providing scaffolded materials (for example, a SCAMPER worksheet) by itself is not enough – learners must be shown how to apply the technique and how the provided materials support them in doing so. And they may need to be shown how to apply the technique (depending on its complexity) in small steps with consolidation in between. In many contexts it is also appropriate to provide a physical model that learners can refer to when working. This might be a deconstructed tote bag showing how the elements fit together, a range of development nets for 3D shapes that learners can examine or a carefully annotated example of how to use Ohm's law to calculate the appropriate resistor for an LED circuit.

Note that what this principle calls modelling also encompasses the wide range of activities usually known as demonstrating in design & technology practice.

Practice

To quote Rosenshine directly: "It is not enough simply to present students with new material, because the material will be forgotten unless there is sufficient rehearsal".

Once new material has been introduced in appropriate small steps, with scaffolding and models provided, learners need the opportunity to practice. A kind of scaffolded support for practice is suggested by Rosenshine whereby initial practice is strongly guided to ensure that well-founded understanding and capability is established. This requires the use of carefully structured examples, with an appropriate incline of difficulty introduced as confidence grows, allied to close supervision of the activity to ensure that errors are caught. During this practice a teacher should be looking for a high success rate; Rosenshine suggests that around 80% is appropriate. This is not in any way a law of nature, but much less suggests that learners haven't fully mastered the material, much more indicates that it is time to move on to more independent practice.

The examples of practice that Rosenshine uses, also the examples that most commentators on his work use, are largely based on research in mathematics education. That doesn't, at all, invalidate his recommendations, but it does mean that we design & technology educators need to carefully think through the actual implementation of practice in the very different range of activities and types of knowledge (discussed in previous sections above) that we wish our learners to master.

4E cognition (embodied, embedded, enactive, and extended cognition)

We talked earlier in this chapter about the limits of models. A key limitation of the standard cognition model (as exemplified by Sherrington, 2022) is that, apart from the brain, eyes, and ears, it largely ignores the fact that humans have bodies. And in the context of a subject like design & technology (amongst many others of course), this seems a significant omission, given that so much of the work we engage learners in requires the thoughtful and controlled use of their bodies.

Fortunately, the body hasn't been ignored generally in cognitive science, and there is an interesting strand that brings the link between the body and cognition into focus, using the ideas of embodied, embedded, enactive, and extended cognition (4E cognition); in brief these ideas argue that cognition isn't limited to just the brain (though clearly the brain is pretty important!).

Briefly, what these terms mean:

Embodied: Cognition can't be fully described in terms of what goes on in the brain. Rather, it engages one's bodily structures and processes. For a simple example, it has been found that if you prevent people from moving their arms, they find it much harder to explain something.

Embedded: Cognition is not even separated from the environment. Rather, it engages with physical, social, and cultural aspects of the world. Most of the ideas we have don't spiring unbidden from the depths of our brain, instead we draw ideas from, and develop them within, interactions with all kinds of elements of the environment. These include other people, books, and videos but also nature and the built environment. Both of your authors know that much of our understanding has been built on, and during, discussions with each other and many other people as well as through extensive reading.

Enactive: Enactive cognition involves not only your neural processes but also the things that you do. For example, very often a designer needs to sketch out an idea (in 2D or 3D) before they can fully understand it.

Extended: Cognition is generally extended outside the body into both other biological beings and non-biological devices. These enable thinking that would be very hard to achieve using only one's own mental capacity. This is probably intuitively true for most people in the 21stC; where would you be without the extended memory that is your phone?!

These ideas come into play naturally in very many design & technology teaching contexts. Here are two broad considerations.

In designing

As noted above, generally the only way to articulate design ideas is through the development of models in physical space, outside of the brain. These can take the form of sketches, waving your hands about in explanation to someone else, 3D models, and so forth. Generally, there is an iteration of development whereby the designer articulates ideas in physical space, then considers them, thinks about them, then articulates further in physical space. The teaching of designing is discussed at greater length later in this chapter (see page 176) and considers this from the perspective of design decision making developed by Barlex (2007) and the mind – hand iteration developed by TERU at Goldsmiths (Kimbell *et al.*, 1991). As well as these ideas being useful to teachers, it could be helpful to clearly articulate them to our learners, so that they have some insight into why we ask them to work in particular ways (such as not accepting their very first design idea). Interestingly, this also resonates with an approach to teaching and learning known as **constructionism**; first articulated by Seymour Papert (Papert & Harel, 1991) as the idea that learning is more effective when people are active learners while creating tangible objects in the real world. An idea that seems to match well with the kinds of approaches to learning that often take place in design & technology.

In making

In almost every situation making requires tool use. And tool use can be hard to teach, mainly because an expert tool user (the teacher) uses tools so intuitively that it is hard to break the process back down to the key steps. It's not uncommon to hear phrases such as 'you have to *feel* when it's right', which, while undoubtedly true, aren't very helpful to the novice. It may be easier to teach a tool technique that you have recently learned than one with which you have years of experience. What the idea of extended cognition allows us to see is that this is because your cognitive system has expanded to 'take in' the tool you are using; your brain, your body *and* the tool acting as parts of a single cognitive system. You don't any longer think, while you are using it, of the hammer or the soldering iron or the needle as something separate from you. Perhaps knowing this doesn't make the teaching (or learning) of a skill any easier, but it might make the difficulties easier to understand and the necessity for practice to support the development of a skill clearer. The teaching of making is discussed at greater length later in this chapter (see page 172) and considers the roles of demonstration and practice. There is also a Thought Piece by Matt McLean devoted to this topic.

Pause for thought

Might it be worth discussing with colleagues how to use the 4E ideas of learning as a way of explaining to parents, school leadership, and governors how young people learn design & technology?

Teaching technical understanding

The purpose of teaching technical understanding in design & technology is to provide learners with sufficient understanding to be able to make technical design decisions. Technical and scientific knowledge do not, in design & technology, have inherent value, rather they are valuable for what they allow the learner to achieve through designing and making. For learners at the beginning of Key Stage 3 it is usual for the teacher to limit the range of these decisions so that learners can become familiar with individual elements of technical understanding before being put into situations where they are required to decide between different technical options. This section will consider three elements of technical understanding: powering, controlling, and structuring. All three of these lean heavily on concepts from science; powering requires knowledge of energy, controlling involves understanding ideas from both mechanics (such as gear ratio, moments, etc.), and electricity (voltage, current, resistance, power) and structuring brings in the need to know about forces. These all involve potentially tricky ideas, and it is easy for learners to develop misconceptions particularly as this knowledge learned in science will often need to be re-configured to be useful in design & technology. So, a first step in planning your teaching about how various devices are or might be powered, controlled, or structured should be to discuss the teaching with science teacher colleagues to establish a shared vocabulary, a knowledge of the level of understanding learners are expected to gain in, say, KS3 and a shared approach to supporting conceptual development (useful models, examples, etc.). It is important to note that of the technical terms that learners need to understand many are Tier 2 words (BESA, 2022). These have a technical meaning that may be different from, though sometimes related to, everyday uses of the word.

Powering

Powering any item requires an energy source of some kind. The nature of energy is studied in science lessons. It is a slippery idea and re-configuring the science learning to be useful in design & technology is fraught with the potential for misconceptions. So, a first step in teaching about how various devices are or might be powered is to discuss the teaching with science teacher colleagues to establish a shared vocabulary. 'How are we going to make it work?' is a key question that enables learners to speculate on possibilities. There are two broad categories of possibilities. The first category includes items that store energy and can release this energy in ways that will 'make something work'. These include strained materials such as coiled springs and stretched or twisted elastic bands. In these cases, once the energy stored initially has been 'used up' more energy can be transferred into them so they can be used again by, for example, rewinding the spring in a clockwork motor. The source of this 'new' energy is that stored in the muscles of the winder derived ultimately from the food the winder has eaten. Note that the term 'used up' is a little suspect in that energy can be neither created nor destroyed but it can be transferred and transformed. Electrical batteries can also be seen as energy stores, the energy being used to drive electric currents through circuits. In some cases when this store is depleted the battery is of no further use, but some batteries are rechargeable and can be used multiple times over. The second category consists of phenomena from which energy may be drawn on an as needed basis. This includes moving air, moving water, and solar radiation. In all these cases there have to be devices that capture the energy and turn it into a form that is useful. For example, wind turbines produce rotary motion which can be used to drive turbines to generate electricity. Solar cells generate electricity directly. In both cases this electrical energy can then be used to power electric devices or stored for future use.

Conversations between learners and learners and teachers about how energy sources work and which to choose for a particular design will make fascinating listening as they are likely to reveal learners' understanding of the energy concept. It's worth inviting science colleagues into lessons to 'listen in'. In practical terms, learners might be introduced to powering by 'stored energy' in designing and making a simple elastic band powered water toy and to powering by electrical energy in designing and making a variety of battery powered products. The aim will be that by the end of Key Stage 3 or the beginning of Key Stage 4 learners should be in a position to choose between these different forms of powering and with this confidence consider other forms of powering – moving air or water, falling weights, coiled springs, or flywheels. This understanding of powering can be used to inform learners' wider understanding of the way power is derived from natural sources and may be stored for future use as is the case hydroelectric power and rechargeable batteries.

Controlling

This section will limit itself to considering mechanical control, electrical control and electronics, and programmable control.

Systems diagrams

It has become common when teaching about control systems to make use of a 'systems' approach and, in particular, of system block diagrams. These are often represented as shown in Figure 5.1.

Note that this is a *generalised* diagram; it shows the key elements of a block diagram; diagrams of real systems will make use of these elements as necessary, as is described later.

Figure 5.1 A generalised system block diagram

The key elements are:

- Arrows: these indicate, as labelled, the signals in the system. Signals are physical entities that can be measured, for example, a light level, a sound level, a voltage level, and so on. The signal labelled 'Input' shows those coming from the environment outside of the system that effect the system. Those labelled 'Output' are the signals produced by the system and represent the effect of the system on the environment around it. The nature of the internal signals depends on the kind of systems being represented. In a mechanical system they might be forces, or rotational speeds or directions. In an electronic system they are generally voltages.
- Blocks: these represent elements that change signals; these might be changes in the type of signal, the size of a signal, or changes brought about by combining signals (such as in a logic gate). Input blocks are those that take a signal from the outside world and turn it into the systems 'internal' signal, output blocks do the opposite, taking internal signals and creating a signal from the system that can be 'seen' (measured, etc.). Process blocks change the state of internal signals.

For a more thorough treatment of these ideas, see Steeg (2003). However, it is worth noting that many texts written for learners, both books and online resources, not to mention GCSE support materials, often deal with these ideas poorly, non-explicitly, or plain wrongly. This leads to both teacher and learner confusion and undermines the potential usefulness of system block diagrams as a design and analytical tool.

Mechanical control

Mechanical control involves using assemblies of technical components that can achieve one or more of the following:

Changing the type of movement (from rotating to reciprocating for example which can be achieved using a cam and slide follower)

Changing the direction of movement (from clockwise to anticlockwise for example which can be achieved using gears)

Changing the axis of motion (which can be achieved using bevel gears)

Increasing the output force and decreasing speed (which can be achieved using gears or pulleys)

Increasing the output speed and decreasing force (which can be achieved using gears or pulleys).

An effective way to communicate the myriad possibilities afforded by assemblies of mechanical components is via a chooser chart which presents the possibilities in visual form. In this way learners can see what is available in terms of what they want a mechanism to achieve, and they can choose the one that is most appropriate for their situation (Nuffield Design & Technology, 2000a). Of course, it is easier to make these decisions if the actual mechanisms themselves are available so that learners can explore them 'hands on'. Hence Torben and Hilda advocate the use of chooser charts consisting of 3D models. We have to say that we are not the first to suggest this. Christopher Polhem (1661–1751), sometimes referred to as the Swedish Leonardo DaVinci and without doubt a technical genius, developed a mechanical 'alphabet' composed of some 80 different working models and encouraged his students to learn about mechanisms by 'playing' with them. Such models can be made from technical kits such as Meccano, Lego, and Fischer Technic, and some schools create their own sets of mechanical components for display using a laser cutter. These are put on display boards in workshops and design studios for inspection and handling by learners. Constructing mechanisms from technical components is without doubt quite challenging but, in the absence of technical kits, packs of wheels, axles, gears, pulleys and cams along with wooden lollipop stick and paper fasteners for levers are available from education suppliers. Hence learners can construct their own mechanical systems to be part of their designs.

System diagrams can be used to support both the teaching of how mechanical systems work and the design of mechanical systems as an element of a wider design activity. An example of using systems diagrams to support idea development might be, after an explanation of how bevel gears work, to ask learners to examine and use an eggbeater and create a system diagram that describes its behaviour (see Figure 5.2). The mechanical system clearly has two parts; a large gear driven by the handle and a pair of small bevel-type

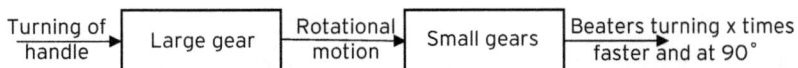

| Turning of handle → | Large gear | Rotational motion → | Small gears | Beaters turning x times faster and at 90° |

Figure 5.2 An egg beater and associated systems diagram

gears that drive the two beaters. This can be explored in terms of the different speeds of the two elements and/or in terms of the different axes of rotation. In either case there are just two relevant blocks in a system diagram: an input block and an output block. (This is a clear example of a system where a process block is not required.)

Once pupils are designing their own mechanical systems – for example in the context of designing an automaton – they can combine their understanding of the use of system diagrams with chooser charts to support their design thinking. A design idea might be expressed as shown in Figure 5.3.

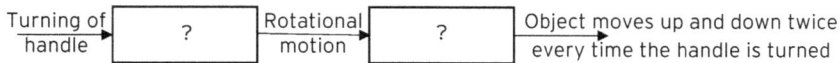

Figure 5.3 A system block diagram for the design of an automaton

A chooser chart can then be consulted to help with the necessary design decisions about which might be the most appropriate mechanisms to use to achieve the stated design aim.

Electrical control

Within an electrical circuit learners may want to include components that provide the following functions:

Give a signal (by using an LED)
Provide illumination (by using a lamp)
Provide rotary movement (by using an electric motor)
To make a sound (by using a buzzer)

To control these components learners will need to use switches for the following purposes:
To hold a component on or off while the switch is being activated (single pole push to make or break switches)
To set a component on or off (singe pole single throw switch)
To turn one component on and another component off (singe pole double throw change over switch)
To reverse the direction of current flow (singe pole double throw change over switch).

As with mechanisms there is a chooser chart available describing the various options (Nuffield Design & Technology, 2000b) and as with mechanisms, providing a set of circuits for learners to explore and become familiar with the way various switches may be used is an effective way of enabling them to develop the circuits they need in their design proposals. The technical performance of the switch is only one consideration. As learners become involved in more sophisticated product design, they will need to consider where on a product's exterior any switches might be located and also the physical nature of the switch – push, slide, toggle, or rocker. These aren't trivial decisions as they will govern how easy or difficult the product is to use for the intended users.

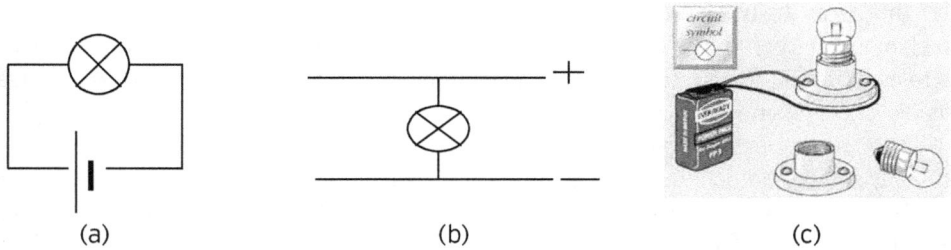

(a)　　　　　　　　　　　(b)　　　　　　　　　　　(c)

Figure 5.4 a: How the circuit is drawn in science; b: How the circuit is drawn in design & technology; c: What the circuit looks like

In devising the electric circuits they need, learners may start with a circuit diagram and immediately there are hurdles to be overcome. The first is that the symbols used in such diagrams do not always look like the component they represent. The second is that a convention used for drawing circuits in science lessons is subtly different from that used in design & technology lessons. Circuit diagrams in science are drawn as a means of explaining what is happening in the circuit (and thus emphasise the circularity of the circuit) by drawing in a symbol for the battery, how this is connected to the other components, and how these are connected to each other as shown in Figure 5.4a. In design & technology lessons, the circuit diagram may well be drawn as in Figure 5.4b, which does not include the battery but has a top positive 'rail' and a bottom negative 'rail' with components strung between them. This brings to the fore the practical idea of generally needing to add elements of a circuit in parallel to existing components to ensure they have the full system voltage across them.

So, it will be important to clarify this with learners. And neither of these representations look much like the actual circuit itself (see Figure 5.4c); for that learners need to produce a layout diagram. None of this is particularly difficult but unless it is addressed learners can become confused. And if a circuit fails to work learners can become demotivated so they need to be able to fault find (see chapter 7, pages 252/3 for a brief discussion).

Even with a clear circuit diagram as a guide, learners can find it hard to replicate the physical circuit when this needs to be laid out, as a part of a product of some kind; the physical layout is unlikely to be as neatly arranged as the diagram, with, for example, a battery kept at some distance from the active components for usability purposes. Here physical modelling of the circuit with a circuit simulator, such as TinkerCAD, can be very helpful. This is explored further in the section on 'Digital Designing and Making' (see page 186).

One of the great things about working with simple electric circuits at secondary level is the wide range of ways of connecting components that is available. In addition to 'traditional' insulated wires, there are conductive inks and paints that can be applied to card, certain plastics and wood, various kinds of copper tape and braid that will adhere to most surfaces including flexible ones and conductive threads and fabrics (as well as accessories such as conductive Velcro) that allow circuits to be combined with textiles products (e-textiles). These possibilities mean that a wide range of possible materials can be used as both substrates for circuits and the product material. Or to look at in another way; pretty much any material used in design & technology (metals being an exception for obvious reasons) can easily and cheaply incorporate electric circuits.

We won't discuss the use of system diagrams in this context because, generally, the kinds of electrical circuits that learners will design will tend to be pretty simple and more clearly described using a circuit diagram.

Electronics and programmable control

The distinction between an 'electric' and an 'electronic' circuit can seem obscure; our simple way of distinguishing these is that an electric circuit becomes electronic as soon as any kind of 'active' component is introduced. Active components can be anything from transistors through to integrated circuits ('chips') including programmable components such as microcontrollers; these are components that can use either voltage or a secondary current to control the flow of current in a circuit. Active components exploit the properties of semiconductors such as silicon. Other components, such as resistors and capacitors and most sensors and actuators (see below) are called 'passive' components.

Electronics and programmable control (based on microcontrollers) are in the KS3 National Curriculum for design & technology and are also present in design & technology GCSE specifications. However, we are also aware, based on the work we do with schools (though we are not aware of any current research to support this view), that many schools offer little if any practical curriculum experience in this area. We believe this due to simple lack of expertise and resources available to schools; we think most design & technology teachers would agree that this is a key area of the subject and would like to see it having a higher profile. Following the direction of the National Curriculum and GCSE specifications, most of those schools that do teach any electronics between 11–16 build this teaching around the use of one or other of the available educational microcontroller systems. Accordingly, this will be the focus of what follows.

When learners are designing and making a simple electronic product, they will probably need to devise a circuit which includes a sensor or switch which detects a change of some sort, a processor in the form of a microcontroller, which is programmed to respond to the sensors and send control signals to one or more actuators (output devices) which provide signals back into the environment. This can be summarised in a system diagram as in Figure 5.5.

What this approach offers is a rich environment for allowing learners to make meaningful design decisions. These fall into two areas. Firstly, in terms of hardware the choices about physical components can be limited to a reasonable set of sensors and actuators, while the

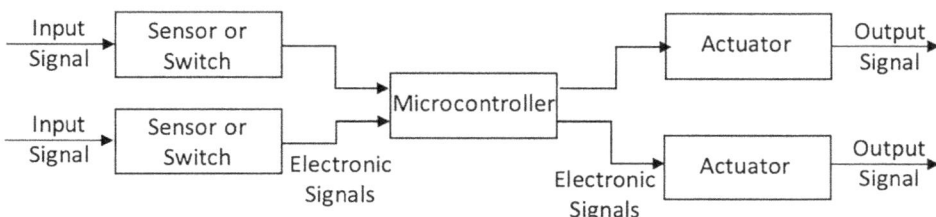

Figure 5.5 A representative system block diagram for a microcontroller

microcontroller is a fixed and known asset that is the same for all learners (and completely reusable). Secondly the 'process' aspect of the design is entirely based in software, allowing individuals to respond in a wide range of ways, and at different levels of complexity, without accruing any extra component costs.

Sensors

Inexpensive sensors are available to detect environmental changes including in temperature, light level, rotation, and moisture. Switches can be used to detect pressure/touch (see notes on switches under 'Electrical Control', above) as well as magnetic fields (reed switches) and motion (tilt switches). Modern microcontroller systems can, in addition, provide easy access to what may seem advanced solid-state sensors such as accelerometers, gyroscopes and compasses as well as radio communications systems.

Actuators

The required output signals might include:

- light, for example via one of a wide range of sizes and colours of LED, including arrays, multicolour LEDs, and programmable LEDs such as NeoPixels.
- sound, for example using a simple buzzer, or a piezo sounder to produce a range of notes.
- motion, for example using a motor, electromagnet, or solenoid. Most of these will need some kind of separately powered driver circuit, since a microcontroller is limited to relatively small currents to drive output devices. However, solar motors and servo motors can be driven directly from some microcontrollers (check your system's requirements!).

This information can be summarised in appropriate chooser charts, built around the input and output devices you intend to make available to learners for a particular scheme of work. The Sensing with Electronics Chooser Chart (Nuffield Design & Technology, 2000c) gives a flavour of what this might look like, bearing in mind that this particular chart doesn't reflect developments in technologies that have happened since its publication.

Microcontrollers

Several microcontroller systems are either designed for use in schools, or very accessible to school age learners. These are the tools that allow, in the words of the KS3 National Curriculum, learners to be taught to apply computing and use electronics to embed intelligence in products. In fact, there is almost an embarrassment of suitable tools, and this has been highly influenced by the presence of Computing as a high-profile curriculum subject. Within that subject there is no requirement to engage with what is often called **physical computing** – that is the development of computer systems that engage with the physical world. However, physical computing does provide a rich context for teaching many areas of the computing curriculum and it is common to find microcontroller systems being used in computing departments. This means that, as we noted earlier in relation to liaising with science departments about science content in design &technology, that planning for the teaching of physical computing with design & technology should be discussed with the computing department. Partly this is about establishing a shared understanding of vocabulary, expectations of learner outcomes and useful conceptual models, examples, what computer language(s) should be employed and so forth. But, in addition, there may be (should be) the opportunity to share taught content between the two departments with, for example computing focussing on computing concepts and design & technology employing these ideas in the context of designing and making 'intelligent products' in rich contexts.

Going into detail comparing different microcontroller systems is beyond the scope of this book, but it is probably helpful to note that, at the time of writing the most widely used microcontroller systems in secondary schools is almost certainly the micro:bit[1]. Also used are Crumble[2] (designed for primary use but popular at KS3), PICAXE[3], and Genie[4] (though it is our sense that the use of these has diminished in recent years). Others we know that are in use in some schools include Arduino[5], the RP2040[6], and the Raspberry Pi[7] (though we note that this last is not a microcontroller, but a single board computer capable of running Linux and Windows – albeit with excellent support for physical computing).

Most of these allow for both 'Block' programming (i.e., using jigsaw like blocks to assemble programs) as well as text-based programming languages. Deciding on progression from the former to the latter might well be one of the discussions that you have with the computing department to ensure learners are provided with a coherent set of experiences as they develop their programming understanding. However, it is worth noting that block software might be appropriate for use in design & technology even at KS5. It is a matter of 'horses for courses'.

The range of possible physical computing contexts is close to infinite; however, we offer as a set of suggestions the following design and make physical computing contexts:

- Design and make a device that can explore the environment in a small stream.
- Design and make a small weather station that can collect data concerning temperature, pressure, light levels, and rain fall.
- Design and make a plaything to engage and amuse young children on a long car journey.
- Design and make an electronic dice to be used in a snakes and ladders game to be played by children aged between 4 and 6 years.
- Design and make a device that will keep small valuable items at home safe from theft.
- Design an anti-theft system to be installed in a small jewellery box.
- Design and make a communication device that utilises the ability to receive and transmit infrared signals.
- Design and make a device that enables parents to listen in on a sleeping child to ensure they are breathing normally and not in distress.

Product design aspects of electronics

The use of electronic and programmable circuits in design & technology will always exist in a design context and will involve the marrying of circuitry with other materials. We have noted above (under 'Electrical Control') the wide range of materials that can be used as circuit substrates allowing elegant integration of circuitry and product. Many microcontrollers are equipped with connection points that allow for flexibility in making connections including soldering, the use of conductive thread, conductive tape and braids, and even conductive paints. Some more sophisticated designs will require the development of additional circuitry to be added to a microcontroller and possibilities here include the use of breadboards (mainly for prototyping), stripboard (a printed circuit board (PCB) with a predesigned grid of holes), or purpose made PCBs. Designing a simple PCB is not especially hard (electronic design software is just CAD software optimised for circuit design), though we are aware that the facility to make PCBs has disappeared from many design & technology departments. In addition, learning to use this software and spending time in circuit design clearly adds considerably to the task. Traditionally school PCBs were made using a chemical development process; this apes the process used in industry but does involve the use of hazardous (and messy) chemicals. An alternative is to use a milling machine, which, while it has its own risks, is generally much more manageable in a design & technology department – and may well make employment for a machine that the department already owns. Finally, it is remarkably cheap to have PCBs made to order in China, though shipping times generally extend into weeks. However, we know of schools that do use this route to getting custom PCBs made where appropriate.

Of course, there is more to designing an electronic product than devising the internal circuitry and learners will also need to consider the product casing and style and how this incorporates a sound user interface, allows for user maintenance and repair and other product design aspects. These aspects of the task are also summarised in the Sensing with Electronics Chooser Chart (Nuffield Design & Technology, 2000c).

Structuring

Fundamental to understanding how structures 'work' are two concepts. The first involves understanding materials and this has been dealt with in some depth in chapter 4 as one of the Big Ideas of design & technology. The second is the concept of force. In simple term force may be thought of as a push, a pull or a twist. Within structures these manifest themselves in the following ways:

- *Tension*: This is where a part of the structure is being stretched by pull forces. Parts in a structure that resist tension are called **ties**. Ties can be made of flexible materials such as string or rope or rigid materials such as wood.
- *Compression*: where a part of the structure is being squashed by push forces. Parts in a structure that resist compression are called **struts**. Struts must be made of rigid materials.
- *Torque:* where a part of the structure is being twisted. Parts in a structure that resist torque must be made from rigid materials.
- *Shear*: where a part of the structure has two forces acting across it, in different directions so as to create a cutting action across it. Parts in a structure that resist shear must be made from hard, rigid materials.

- *Bending*: where a part of a structure is held firm at one or both ends and force is applied to the rest of it. Parts in a structure that resist bending are called **beams**. One side of a beam has to resist compression whereas the other side has to resist tension. Beams must be made of rigid materials.

When looking at a structure learners should be taught to identify the various structural elements within the structure and the forces they need to resist if the structure is to be robust. The Nuffield Structural Elements Chooser chart (Nuffield Design & Technology, 2000d) describes the different structural elements that learners will see in the structures around them such as houses, blocks of flats, religious buildings, commercial centres, bridges, arches. They might also see pylons, mobile phone masts, and windmills. Encouraging learners to look at the made world in terms of structures and the forces operating on and within them is part of developing their technological perspective. And there will be occasions when they will need to design and make structures for themselves. In most cases these will be small but the same structural parts will be present and will behave in the same way in terms of the forces acting in and on them. It may seem a stretch to use the same ideas about structures for both very large and rather small items, but the work of Jon Parker described in chapter 7 (see page 253) shows how useful this can be in enabling learners to develop innovative designs.

An important area in which there can be conceptual confusion in thinking about structures is the distinction between *strength* and *stiffness* (more Tier 2 words!).

- The strength of a material is related to how difficult it is to break.
- The stiffness of a material is related to how difficult it is to bend.

A material can have stiffness or strength, or both or neither. Steel, for example, is both stiff and strong, nylon is strong but not very stiff, concrete is weak in tension but strong in compression, jelly is neither stiff nor strong.

The strength of a part in a structure can be increased by making that part thicker. A part in a structure can be made stiffer by increasing the depth of that part. Parts that are deep are much more difficult to bend. You and your learners can experience this by trying to bend a plastic ruler. When held 'flat' such a ruler is easy to bend but when held 'edge wise' it is much more difficult to bend. When learners are designing shell forms to act as enclosures for technical components the deployment of different struts, ties, and beams within the shell can make a difference to the robustness of the form and the way the technical components might be organised. Questions along the lines of, 'If you put the switch on the top here, when I push it the top starts to buckle – what can you do about that?' can lead to very interesting conversations. It is worth considering some textile products as being 'soft' structures. Made of fabrics of various types including netting they can resist tension but not compression. In combination with resistant materials the fabric parts often transfer forces to the resistant material parts as in kites and tents where the fabric parts are in tension and the framework parts are in compression.

And to reiterate, as with teaching about electricity, it is important to talk with both math and science teacher colleagues about the way they teach forces and deal with Tier 2 words.

Teaching making

A fundamental teaching activity in design & technology is the demonstration of making skills. This sees the teacher as expert, modelling and explaining both physically and linguistically the technique to be taught. Often such demonstrations are 'front loaded' in that they take place well before they are likely to be needed in project work. This usually involves the teacher carrying out a particular making activity in front of the whole class with the intention that the learners will know what to do after the demonstration when it is their turn to try out the activity. The teacher usually comments on key points as she does so such as how to hold the tool being used; how to ensure that the work piece is firmly held and does not move as the tool is applied, to keep hands and fingers well out of the way of any cutting edges, how to stand so that the person using the tool is stable, and the effort required to use the tool is minimal. There is always a lot to remember and for the learners they are seeing what is happening the opposite way around to the teacher who is doing the demonstration so there is not only the task of remembering what the teacher has said but also turning the mental image of what the learner has seen through 180° to acquire the tool users view of the operation. One way to overcome this difficulty is to use a visualiser placed behind the teacher so what the teacher sees as they carry out the demonstration is what the learner sees on a large screen adjacent to and slightly above the teacher. This not only has the advantage of providing the learners with the tool users view but also of ensuring that all the learners in the class have a clear view of the operation. This is often not the case when learners are crowded around the teacher's bench. Often the teacher will not only comment on what they are doing, e.g., notice that I am holding the chisel like this taking care to keep my fingers behind the cutting edge, but ask questions about 'why' they are doing what they are doing or 'what do you think would happen' if questions, e.g., If I held the chisel like this what might happen? This question-based commentary is much more powerful than admonitions to 'notice how I am …' or 'when you do this you must make sure that …' as they require the learner to think about the actions being carried out by the teacher as opposed to simply observing them. This is in accord with Barak Rosenshine's principles of instruction: more effective teachers ask more questions, involving more learners and taking more time to explain, clarify and check for understanding. But understanding why you have to do what you have to when making is not the same thing as actually being able to do it although it is an important step on the way. Hence as part of a demonstration, some teachers ask a learner to come to the front and try for themselves while the class watches and the teacher comments on what the learner is doing. Hilda has always felt that this is somewhat unfair, putting the learner on the spot when he or she hasn't had time to practice the skill, but she can see that it has the attraction of revealing what one of the learners in the class might or might not have remembered in how to carry out the activity. Providing the commentary is kindly then it is perhaps a useful addition to the demonstration before learners move off to try it out for themselves. The teacher has been modelling the activity and wants the learners to carry it out as closely to the way she has done it as possible. There is usually a wide variation in response; some learners will have grasped how to tackle the activity and will be able to carry it out well whilst others will struggle. It is here that the teacher must move around the room observing how each learner is performing and intervene to correct mistakes. Sometimes this correction requires just a few words, e.g., don't push so hard, do it gently like if you are stroking the wood with the saw. Sometimes there has to be a firm and loud interjection if it looks as if a learner is about to hurt himself, e.g., 'Stop right now!' Sometimes it is necessary for the teacher to adjust the way a learner is holding a tool and this requires physical contact between the teacher and the learner. This must be done carefully in a way that does not interfere with the learner's personal space.

At the end of a demonstration and the follow up observation of learners practice of the technique it will be important to bring to the attention of the class those features of the skill that were carried out well and those that were not so that the latter might be addressed next time the skill is being used. If miniature cam recorders are available for teachers to wear, then it is possible for this session to show good and bad points but it is important that this is done in ways that are kindly and do not embarrass learners.

There are times when the way a group of learners are tackling a design and make task indicates that it would be useful for them to be shown a particular technique. One might call this a 'just in time' approach. Here is an opportunity to carry out a demonstration without the disadvantages of the whole class demonstration and for the learners to take turns in emulating what the teacher does in a short space of time with appropriate commentary from the teacher and their peers. And there will be times when it is necessary to demonstrate a technique to a single learner perhaps because they missed the class demonstration or their work has taken them in a direction where that skill, not demonstrated to the class so far, is required. In both the small group and single learner demonstrations, the learners benefit from the individual attention of the teacher, but it is important for the teacher not to get so immersed in the activity that she loses sense of what is happening with the rest of the class.

There are cases where what is being demonstrated requires close up observation; some sewing techniques and soldering components into a circuit board are good examples. Here the visualiser can be particularly useful, focusing in close on details that only the demonstrating teacher is able to see. There are of course innumerable videos on YouTube showing how to carry out many techniques, they are usually accompanied by a commentary and often include close ups of features difficult to see. These have the potential to be very useful as a way of reminding learners of skills they have already been taught but care should be exercised in letting learners watch such video clips and then try out new techniques for themselves without at least a conversation with their teacher visiting salient points.

It is often quoted that it takes 10,000 hours of practice to make an expert. This idea can be traced back to a 1993 paper written by Anders Ericsson, a Professor at the University of Colorado, called *The Role of Deliberate Practice in the Acquisition of Expert Performance*. It highlighted the work of a group of psychologists in Berlin, who had studied the practice habits of violin students in childhood, adolescence, and adulthood. All had begun playing at roughly five years of age with similar practice times. However, at age eight, practice times began to diverge. By age 20, the elite performers had averaged more than 10,000 hours of practice each, while the less able performers had only done 4,000 hours of practice. The psychologists didn't see any naturally gifted performers emerge and this surprised them. If natural talent had played a role, it wouldn't have been unreasonable to expect gifted performers to emerge after, say, 5,000 hours. Anders Ericsson concluded that "many characteristics once believed to reflect innate talent are actually the result of intense practice extended for a minimum of 10 years".

This research has some implications for the level of skill that we can expect from learners who often receive only two hours design & technology per week, and within this there is much more to learn than physical performance skill. Practice is obviously necessary if learners are to acquire the muscle memory that leads to coordination of hand and eye to carry out techniques well enough for the classroom. And the more learners practice the better they will get but we need to be realistic about how good they will get and ensure that the complexity of the making skills being taught is not so great that the amount of practice time required is unlikely to be available.

Pause for thought

In your design & technology curriculum what is the sequence of making skill acquisition? Are they in an order of complexity? How much demonstration and practice time do you allow for each? Is there much spread across a class of learners with regard to level of making skills achieved? Generally, do what the learners make over time indicate an improvement in making skills?

Matt McLain has done significant research into demonstration in design & technology and it is to his Thought Piece we now turn.

Demonstration; a pedagogy for teaching making - *A Thought Piece by Matt McLain*

Matt McLain is Senior Lecturer in Education and Professional Learning, School of Education, Liverpool John Moores University.

I first became interested in this area of design & technology pedagogy when, as a teacher, I noticed the challenges of students observing demonstrations of fine motor skills involved with the fabrication and assembly of electronic circuits. Before discovering visualisers, which now seem to be ubiquitous in the modern classroom, I began using a cheap webcam to project what I could see onto board. The effect was transformative, with students' attention seemingly transfixed where previously there had been distraction. Although as human beings we are predisposed to observe and replicate (i.e., learn new skills), our short-term memory is not perfect and not being able to see what the demonstrator is trying to show can risk misunderstanding and confusion to arise. This can be addressed during guided practice, following a demonstration, but a better demonstration (facilitated by suitable learning technologies) enables the teacher to focus on the students who most need help – identifying and addressing misunderstandings before they become habitual. As Hilda and Torben point out above, true competence requires many hours of deliberate practice, which is not going to take place in design & technology lessons – even over the period of primary and secondary schooling! Therefore, we must ask ourselves to what purpose are we demonstrating making skills. Is it for students to become accomplished in craft skills for their own sake? Certainly not! Or is it to open children and young people's minds (and bodies) to new experiences that they may develop in the future? Maybe. However, the place of making in design & technology is primarily about realising design ideas – giving students practical ways to solve problems, using their hands, and aided by tools and equipment.

My research into demonstration highlights its use (and limitations) as a signature pedagogy in design & technology. It is a deliberately restrictive teaching method, where the teacher models and explains a process or procedure, drawing on their subject expertise. Teachers use it where they want (and expect) students to replicate a process, or procedure, with a degree of accuracy and precision. It is, therefore, less suitable as a method for facilitating creativity or innovation, where students are expected to come up with their own ideas and solutions. This calls for a form of teacher modelling and explaining, which is more expansive and open-ended; that shows students how to think more divergently. Demonstration (and making) should be intelligently used in the wider context of design & technology activity, with an awareness of the inherent benefits and limitations; and in support of growing autonomy through project-based learning, where students engage in ideating, realising, and critiquing. The purpose of demonstration in design & technology – alongside other signature methods – is to open up possibilities in students' design thinking and doing, rather than to develop high levels of practical craft skill in a narrow disciplinary area as an end goal. As such, I encourage design & technology teachers to demonstrate to build students design capability, enabling them to use a range of tools, equipment, materials, and components to bring their ideas to life and use their knowledge in action.

What are we to make of Matt's Thought Piece? We think it is a provocative challenge to see making skills as a gateway to enhanced design skills in that it encourages learners to think about the possibilities afforded by particular making skills to achieve certain design outcomes. As an example, Hilda remembers a learner, who having learned about the simple process of cutting strips of soft wood to equal length and using PVA to glue them together side by side to create a piece of sheet material, used this technique to saw a small sheet of plywood into strips and then glue them together to create a striped piece of sheet material.

Teaching designing

There is something unrealistic about teaching designing if by 'teaching' one is thinking in terms of a 'transfer' of knowledge and understanding from the teacher to the learner by means of explaining, questioning, and demonstrating. As in learning to ride a bicycle, no matter how much one explains or demonstrates how to do it, the only way to learn is to get on the bicycle and try. Torben and Hilda see designing as 'intellectual cycling'; you have to do it to learn how. A first question, therefore, is what does a learner have to do when they are designing?

Models of designing

David Barlex (2007) adopted an approach which uses the idea of the learner making related design decisions in five domains: conceptual – what the design will do, technical – how it will work, aesthetic – what it will look like, constructional – how it will be made, and stakeholder – who it is for. These decisions will create the final design. Note that the decisions are not made independently of one another. Hence these areas of design decision can be represented visually, with each type of design decision at a corner of a pentagon and each corner connected to every other corner. This is shown in Figure 5.6. This inter-connectedness is an important feature of making design decisions. A change of decision within one area will affect some, if not all, of the design decisions made within the others. For example, a change in the way a design is to work will almost certainly affect what the design looks like and how it is constructed. It may also have far-reaching effects in changing some of the purposes that the design can meet and who might be able to use it.

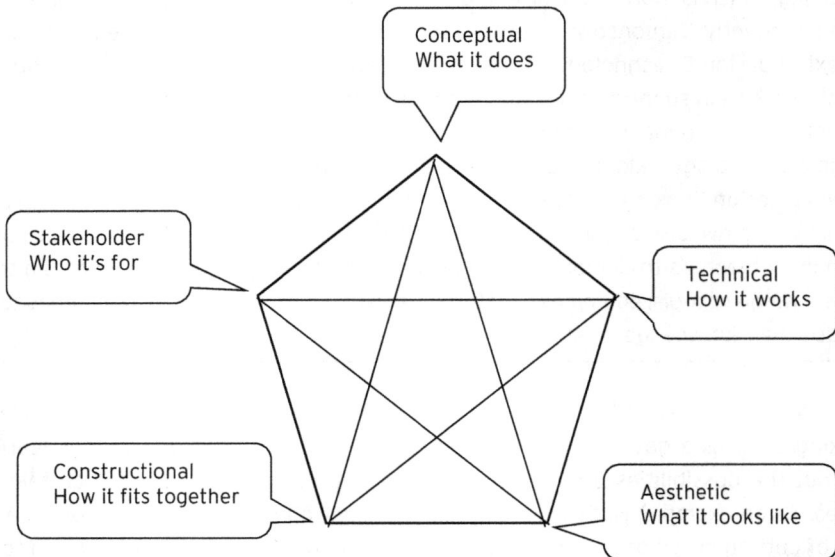

Figure 5.6 The design decision pentagon

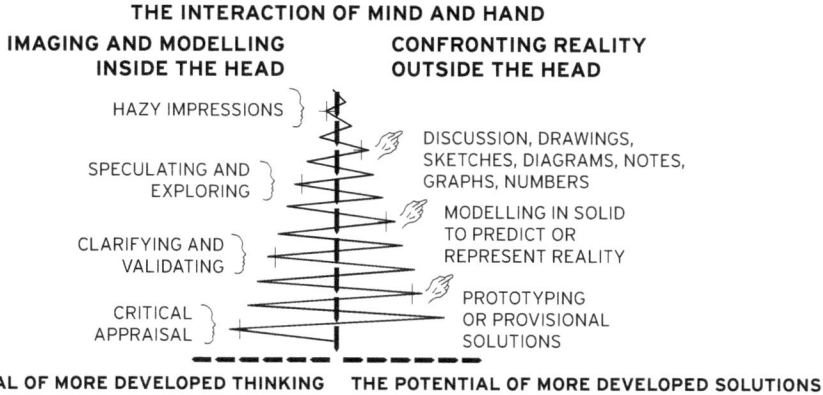

Figure 5.7 The APU model of designing

The model developed by the APU in the 1990s is shown in Figure 5.7 and describes designing as the interaction of mind and hand considering ideas that are inside the head and how these are developed outside the head by a variety of activities with on-going iteration between inside and outside the head as the design is developed and clarified.

It is easy to see how at each vertex of the decision pentagon the learner is carrying out the iterations described by the APU model and can be overlaid on the APU model with the decisions being made becoming more precise as the iteration between hand and mind advances from hazy to critical appraisal.

The role of conversations

Elegant though these models are in describing what might be going on in learners' minds and what they do in response, they don't grasp the nettle of describing what the teacher should be doing to enable designing in a designing and making activity. The importance of some preliminary learning through Resource Tasks is discussed in chapter 4 but here we are concerned with teacher activity once the designing and making task is under way. Surprisingly perhaps, it is talking that's important. The realisation of the significance of talk in learning is not new. Robin Alexander (2006) argued convincingly for the importance of classroom talk that is based on dialogue. He noted that, "children, we now know, need to talk ... in order to think and learn ... talk is arguably the true foundation of learning" (p. 9). He also argued that it is not only dialogue between the teacher and learner that is important, but also that dialogue between learner and learner has an essential part to play in learning.

Malcolm Welch and David Barlex carried out research that indicated the crucial role of talking in what teachers should be doing in a designing and making task (Welch & Barlex, 2009, 2010). As part of a three-year study entitled *Learning to Design*, teacher-learner and learner-learner discourse was analysed. In one particular case study, a teacher used a three-part sequence. In Part 1 the teacher asks a question about the work in hand.

In Part 2 the learner responds and in Part 3 the teacher comments on the answer in ways that either endorse the actions the learner is taking or suggests an alternative path. On occasions the teacher used a 'reflective toss', a three-part sequence consisting of a learner statement in response to a teacher question, a follow-up teacher question and additional learner statements. The reality of such dialogue in the classroom is that sometimes it is over very quickly but that at other times it can take a many-part sequence to help the learner move on in their designing and making. Importantly, this approach takes account of the learner's voice and provides guidance without the learner losing ownership of the task in hand.

Kay Stables (2020) has suggested that teachers will need a range of pedagogies in order to support learners in their designing and making including the following:

- pedagogies of *speculation*: that support learners to consider 'what if', 'what might be', 'how could'
- pedagogies of *imaging and modelling*: that support learners to test their speculative ideas by bringing them into some form of reality
- pedagogies of *materiality*: that enable learners to understand and develop knowledge and skills in bringing ideas into physical being
- pedagogies of *need-to-know*: that enable learners to have the confidence and competence to acquire knowledge, skill, and understanding as the needs in their design tasks arise
- pedagogies of *critiquing*: that allow learners to make thoughtful decisions and judgements, based on values and ethics
- pedagogies of *collaboration*: that support learners to develop skills in working with and for others.

Enacting each of Kay's suggestions requires communication between the teacher and learners. Across a class this is made up of myriads of conversations that take place rapidly. This requires the teacher to be fluent in engaging in these conversations, move swiftly from conversation to conversation, responding in ways that are appropriate to the issues faced by the learners and adopt those pedagogies identified by Kay (and perhaps others) as and when they are needed. The precise detail of each conversation will depend on where the learner is in their designing and making task and the teacher appreciating the strengths and weaknesses of the learner's capability which gives insight into what might or might not be a feasible way forward for that particular learner.

In response to Kay's suggested pedagogies, it is possible to identify a range of strategies to support designing that can be taught through short, focused tasks. If learners have been taught these, the teacher can use conversations during a designing and making task to enable learners to revisit this learning and apply it effectively. Here are three examples:

1   In being speculative, a learner might use attribute analysis to develop more ideas: *'Okay so you've hit a brick wall with ideas; why not try attribute analysis and see where that gets you. I'll be back in five minutes to see how you're getting on'.*

2   In the case of critiquing design proposals, the teacher might suggest using a winners and losers analysis: *'You might want to think about how your idea will affect various people, Remember that winners and losers task we did with the target chart. Give that a whirl and let me know how you get on'*.

3   In supporting imaging and modelling the conversation might go like this: *'I can see you've tried to draw the shape of the handle but it's not really clear to me what it's like. Yeah I know it's tricky to get the shape right on paper. Remember that plastic we used for modelling? That's right polymorph. Why not use that to get some shapes that work?'*

Pause for thought

Does your department have in its resources a range of such pedagogic tools which teachers can deploy as they teach learners to design? If not, it might well be worth developing some and building their use into your curriculum. A starting point for such development might be the Nuffield Strategy Resource Tasks available free to download at https://dandtfordandt.wordpress.com/resources/nuffield-ks3-dt-resources/strategy-resource-tasks/.

It is not only conversations between teachers and learners that are important during a designing and making task. The case studies carried out by Malcolm Welch and David Barlex (2009, 2010) revealed that when learners were fully engaged with a collaborative designing and making task the talk was almost always on task, centred around the decisions they needed to make but was often limited in the extent to which various options of ways forward were explored. Even so the influence of the conversation on the designing and making was significant. Naill Seery (2020) has taken the idea of learner – learner conversations and their significance in his work on the social and cognitive interaction between teachers and learners. He acknowledges that to the uninitiated a design & technology workshop in which young people are tackling a range of designing and making projects appears chaotic. But his research shows that this is not the case and that underlying this apparent chaos is a network of social interactions which 'grows' the knowledge available to the learners enabling them to make difficult decisions about the details of their emerging and as yet unresolved design proposals. This knowledge is not evenly distributed amongst the learners; serendipity plays its part in who knows what, but the skilful teacher orchestrates the social interaction to ensure that the workshop is a place in which communication between learners is the norm, invariably on task and beneficial. This requires the teacher to develop trust between herself and the learners and between the learners. Establishing the design & technology workshop as such a collaborative creative community of practice does not happen quickly and the teacher will need to nurture this over a significant period of time.

> **Pause for thought**
>
> Might the learning taking place through social interaction during an extended designing and making task be revealed by asking a class the following question: 'Okay, now what more do we know and understand about X or Y given our experience and conversations in the designing and making project we've just tackled?' Hopefully the responses would make explicit the learning that is taking place within the class and provide the opportunity to make this more widely available. It could also be used to convince those who have a limited view of the learning that takes place in design & technology education lessons, often seeing it as limited to making with little if any cognitive gain.

To return to the bicycle riding analogy, the regular use of a variety of pedagogic tools built into the curriculum and used by the teacher enables the learner to become fluent at designing, mirroring the way that wobbling during the first attempts at cycling is gradually eliminated as the learner cyclist develops confidence and a sense of balance.

Teaching critique

In design & technology we are used to learners evaluating the items they have designed and made themselves and also items designed and made by others in the world outside school. Such evaluation usually revolves around questions like these:

* Did the item do what it was supposed to, i.e., did it meet its specification?
* Were the users able to use it as intended?
* Did it delight the user?

There is nothing wrong with these questions as far as evaluation is concerned but they sit within the limited paradigm of 'if designers design what users need and want and can afford to buy then all is well in the world'. But this sort of thinking is inadequate for critique. Here we ask the learners to step back and ask:

* Not, 'Did it do what it was supposed to do?' But ...
  * 'Is what it is supposed to do worth doing?' And ...
  * To what extent does it contribute to a future worth wanting? And ...
  * 'What are the unintended consequences of it doing what it was supposed to do'? And ...
  * 'To what extent will these consequences compromise the well-being of Planet Earth and the creatures that live there now and in the future?'

Using questions like these leads learners to adopt a more historical perspective on design asking questions such as:

* We could, and we did – what were the consequences?

Of course, it is easy to be wise after the event. No one could have predicted the consequences of petrol driven transport or the availability of hydrocarbon-based plastics. But given that we now see the consequences of these technological innovations it perhaps behoves us to be more circumspect and get learners to ask:

- We can, but should we – what might be the consequences?

It is important that in design & technology education, we take a stand against the status quo, a deterministic view that as far as technology is concerned and its manifestation through design, what will be will be. Such a view is not fruitful with regard to developing technological perspective (discussed in chapter 1). Through technological perspective future citizens will be able to makes sophisticated judgments about various aspects and phases of technological developments including what technologies should society develop now and in the future. Such an approach is enshrined in the precautionary principle which argues that if an activity raises threats of harm to human health or the environment, precautionary measures should be taken even if some cause-and-effect relationships are not fully established scientifically. In this context the proponent of an activity, rather than the public, should bear the burden of proof.

  In chapter 4 we identified four ways of teaching design & technology, and all of these can to some extent embrace teaching learners to critique. The most obvious candidate is 'considering the consequences of technology', but there are definitely possibilities within 'designing without making' and 'designing and making' activities. Even when learners are 'making without designing', following given instructions, there are opportunities for critique. We will deal with each in turn.

Critique through considering the consequences of technology

Here are two learning activities that develop critique.

- Identifying winners and losers

This activity involves using the target chart shown in Figure 5.8. The item being considered (this might be a product, a range of products, or a technology) is placed in the centre of the chart. Consideration of the immediate impacts of the item gives rise to a list of groups and individuals who will be affected by these impacts. Those who are directly affected are written in the inner circle, those indirectly affected are written in the outer circle. Then these entries are classified as either winners (those who benefit from the item) or losers (those for whom the item causes some form of detriment). Giving one colour to the winner segments and a different colour to the loser segments gives an immediate visual picture of the winner loser balance although care must be taken in the interpretation of this as it does not, of itself, give any indication of the size of the groups involved or the severity or otherwise of any impact. If time is short, the teacher may decide to 'cut to the chase' and produce a filled-in version of the chart and use that to stimulate discussion about the impacts that might be caused by the item under consideration. An effective way to stimulate discussion around a completed chart is to assign some learners the role of 'winners' and other learners the role of 'losers'. The task then facing the learners is for the winners to justify why it is permissible for them to win at the losers'

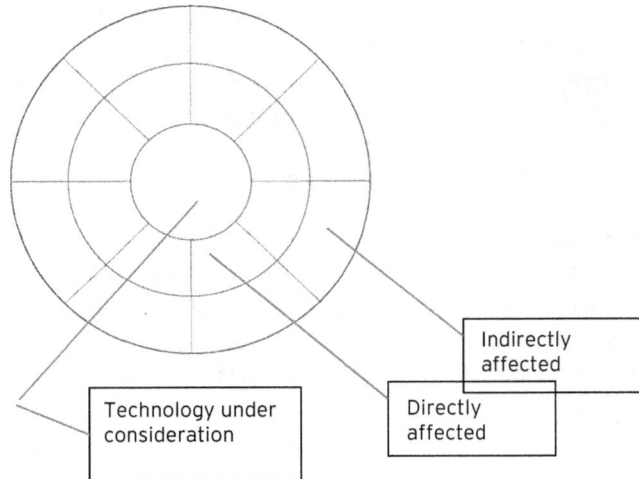

Figure 5.8 Winners and losers target chart

expense, and the losers to argue for some form of recompense from the winners. It is worth noting here that learners will need to understand something about social justice in deciding who wins and who loses so it is worth prefacing the activity with some explicit teaching about this ensuring that learners are introduced to the idea that in a just world, all people should be able to live in freedom from hunger and fear and have shelter from harm. They should have opportunities to pursue happiness and make the best of their lives.

•   Writing design fictions

Design fictions are devices to critique future possibilities by creating a story world in which the learner creates an object that represents a particular technology that will act out in the story world. This is literally a prop that enables a story to unfold through the imagined interaction of the prop and the story world. The teacher might create a story world and present it to the class or work with the class in creating one. The teacher will need to ensure that the learners are sufficiently au fait with the reality the prop represents for imagined interactions between the technology and the story world to be feasible. For example, the story world might involve driving for a living and the technology being considered autonomous vehicles. Learners will need to know something about autonomous vehicles before they begin to write their story. The teacher may decide that they should find this out through independent group research or that it would be fairer to give a short presentation to the class so that there is a level playing field. What will happen in the story world once there are autonomous vehicles? The story the learners write may take many forms: a written story, a comic book, a story board, a script for a play, an animation, a short video clip in which learners describe what is happening in the story. Whatever the form, the teacher has a key role in asking the learners about the implications of what is happening in the story which will engage learners in discussion and debate about the rights and wrongs of the situation in the story world.

Critique through designing without making

The Young Foresight Project introduced the idea of designing without making with four points of questioning for learners to use in developing their designs.

1   The technology that is available for use

This should be a new and/or emerging technology and learners should be concerned primarily with how the new product or service will work. They should not concern themselves with manufacture.

The key question here, 'Is the proposal feasible?'

2   The society in which the technology will be used.

This will be concerned with the prevailing values of the society, and what is thought to be important and worthwhile. This will govern whether a particular application of technology will be welcomed and supported.

The key question here, 'Will the proposal be acceptable to society?'

3   The needs and wants of the people who might use the product or service.

If the product does not meet the needs and wants of a sufficiently large number of people then it will not be successful.

The key question here, 'Is it something people are likely to need or want?'

4   The market that might exist or could be created for the products or services.

Ideally, the market should be one with the potential to grow, one that will last, and one that adapts to engage with developments in technology and changes in society.

The key question here, 'Is there, or could there be a market for the proposal?'

These four points were presented to learners in the form of a tetrahedron as shown in Figure 5.9. In tackling the design challenge learners worked in groups of three or four.

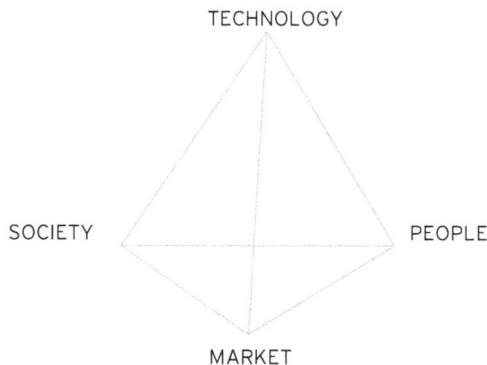

Figure 5.9 The designing without make tetrahedron

As learners develop their proposals the teacher asks them to comment on the key questions and gives feedback on their answers. This can often lead to discussions with the teacher and amongst the group of learners developing the proposal. By giving Question 2 a high profile, the teacher can engage the learners in critique. What is or is not acceptable to society depends on the values held by people in that society. Sometimes there are groups in society who challenge prevailing values, and this may lead to change. Asking learners to identify prevailing values and whether they are in agreement develops their ability to critique.

Critique through designing and making, and making without designing

Learners usually evaluate the products that they design and make and those they make without designing at the end of the activity. In the case of making without designing the evaluation will probe the level of skill shown by the learners. In the case of designing and making the evaluation will probe the extent to which the product met its intentions. The teacher can extend both these evaluation sessions to include critique by posing the idea that the product was very successful, selling across the world in millions, and requiring learners to answer the following questions:

- What materials and components have you used? Where did they come from? How were they obtained? What would be the impact of providing the materials and components for your product on a large scale both on the planet and the people working to provide them?
- What manufacturing methods did you use? What methods would be used in industry? What is the impact of these methods on those who make the product? What is the impact on the people and places near where the manufacturing takes place?
- If the product is sold across the world, how does it reach those who buy it? What is the environmental impact of this transportation?
- Once the useful life of the product is over how easy is it to disassemble and recycle the different materials and components?
- What changes might you need to make to your design if your product was to become part of a circular economy?

Answering these questions starts to enable learners to consider the consequences of consumerism, something that was discussed earlier in the section on the philosophy of design in chapter 2. Answering these questions extends learners' field of vision into the world outside school. The questions are not easy to answer and will require learners to research in order to know about industrial and commercial practice. This can take place as a homework activity with follow up discussion when the learners return to their next design & technology lesson.

Pause for thought

Critique may lead learners to identify what is wrong in the world without giving them much in the way of how such wrongs might be addressed. One way to address this is to frame the critique against a backdrop of 'a future worth wanting' and identifying the changes that need to be made to work towards this. Learners can then discuss how their own personal actions might contribute to these changes.

James Pitt contributed significantly to the Nuffield Design & Technology Project in enabling learners to consider values and has worked for the Ellen MacArthur Foundation. Hence, he is well placed to extend our thinking on critique.

Some wider considerations – *A Thought Piece by James Pitt*

James Pitt is Honorary Professor of Education at the Amur State University of Humanities and Pedagogy, Russia.

Critical thinking is fundamental to our nature as conscious beings. In an ideal world learning the basic skills of critiquing would be at the heart of any curriculum. Yet all too often schools are more oriented towards 'delivering' a compulsory curriculum that has been centrally defined, and training students to 'perform well' in standardised tests. Sadly, what can be measured in standardised tests is often so-called 'knowledge' which can be learned and reproduced in the form of teacher-generated propositions.

I put the words 'delivering', 'perform well', and 'knowledge' in inverted commas as I believe they have little to do with real education. Consider the Latin root of 'educate' which means to draw out. Every learner or every group of learners (for learning is both a personal and social enterprise) has a latent capability to make sense of the world and their experiences, in a never-ending cycle of action and reflection. This is very different from trying to get students to amass facts. Yet so much of what is taught in schools is geared towards just that.

One of the delights of design & technology is that it is an area of learning in schools with no obvious boundaries. In evaluating a design one can go into ethics, 'Is the world a better place for this?' This leads us to ask, 'Better for whom?'. This takes us into metaethics – 'On what basis or bases are we asking if the world a better place?' These questions encourage

---

us to consider how society is not a homogenous bloc, and that different people have differing interests and different ideas about what is the common good.

We can begin to unravel some of these competing interests through critique. We can examine who are the dominant groups in society who influence common sense, or what people take for granted as being good or desirable. These are the people that Antonio Gramsci (Burke, 1999, 2005) calls the organic intellectuals – at any one time it might have been the church, temple or mosque, or the government, or the established media, or the influencers. We can examine how peer pressure can shape how we evaluate products and technologies. Through critiquing, education becomes a force for self-awareness and freedom.

Paulo Freire (1970), that giant of education from Brazil, contrasts banking education with liberating education. The former is similar to depositing knowledge in a bank (the learner's mind), the latter as empowerment and social, political, and personal understanding. The product of banking education is uncritical students who neither want, nor are capable of, challenging the status quo. This is what our schools, colleges and universities produce. The aim of liberating education is to bring about the 'artisans of a new humanity' (Segundo, 1973, 1974) who can and will be genuinely creative. Through critique, design & technology can play its part in contributing to liberating education and help young people develop a vision of a future worth wanting and the abilities to achieve this.

Critiquing products, systems and technologies is central to design & technology learning. It can be used as a vehicle for encouraging radical thinking. It can be an antidote to mindless populism, uncritical consumption, and echo-chamber prejudice. And thank goodness, it can be justified – even required – in terms of a statutory duty to teach citizenship and British values.

For additional reading, see Pitt and Webster (2021).

What are we to make of James' Thought Piece? His vision of the significance of critique and its central role in design & technology may be seen by some as idealistic but given the situation in which we find ourselves; locally, nationally, and globally it provides a useful and effective counterpoint to the oft quoted and limited economic utilitarian justification for our subject.

Digital designing and making

Digital or manual?

There has long been discussion within design & technology about the merits and risks of introducing digital technologies to support designing and making. Broadly, the merits come from providing access to tools that allow for greater precision and complexity in the outcomes that learners can produce. The risks are that important cognitive and physical knowledge and skills related to the acts of sketching and precision drawing, the use of hand tools and machine tools and, more broadly, physical engagement with materials are lost.

There is also a question of engagement; some argue that the activity of physical making is what attracts many to the subject. Others point to the poor quality of many 'handmade' learner outcomes and point to the increased satisfaction that comes from producing a high-quality product with the aid of digital tools. Our position is that a curriculum that ignores what digital tools can offer will be impoverished, equally, one that relies exclusively on them (for example a school where the whole of KS3 design & technology is reduced to teaching CAD with limited elements of CAM – a genuine case we know of) is, we hope clearly, missing the point of the subject. A more subtle trap to avoid is what Bilkstein (2013) calls the'keychain trap'. This is where learners, enthused by the quality of what comes out of a laser cutter or 3D printer, end up mass-producing artefacts, often found in online file stores, for which they have had no personal engagement in the design. The learning attached to such activity is minimal. A slightly more remote risk, we think, is that a school invested heavily in CAD/CAM could become re- luctant to 'waste' the expenditure and end up, perhaps inadvertently, limiting pupils' oppor- tunity to experience a broad range of making experiences. We take the stance that physical work with materials and digital tools can work in harmony in design & technology teaching, with careful planning, to create rich and meaningful learning experiences. In what follows we attempt to outline some of the ways this can be achieved. As a book can so quickly go out of date there are risks in mentioning specific software and hardware tools, so we generally avoid that in what follows. However, we break this rule where we think it's helpful.

Digital designing

A broad view of digital designing is required; it stretches beyond what can be narrowly thought of as CAD (i.e., 2D and 3D design) and should also include a wide range of modelling tools. These can be used to support design thinking and the making of design decisions in areas that include visual, structural, mechanical, electrical, and electronic modelling.

Visual modelling

A wide range of software encompassing word processors, vector and bitmap drawing, and dedicated 2D CAD software can be used as design tools to help learners explore their 2D thinking. Inevitably time is required to learn how to use these effectively. One way to short cut this process can be to use (and develop) learners' hand drawing and sketching skills as a starting point. These can then be scanned into an appropriate file format and used either as the final design for output to manufacturing, or as the starting point for more development work. For 3D modelling, schools are in the envious position that most of the 'industrial' 3D tools are available with educational licences that are either free or very cheap. Many of these also run in the browser (so that remote servers do the hard work). This means they do not require especially powerful computers at the user end. Each of these applications has its enthusiastic supporters in the design & technology community, but, in our view, have broadly similar capabilities with a depth that generally goes way beyond what most learners are going to require (compare Word; perfectly good for everyday word processing, with features that most of us never use but that are great to have available in certain situations). If you can use one 3D design environment, you will generally be able transfer those skills to another one without too much difficulty.

TinkerCAD[8] is noteworthy in offering an introductory approach to 3D design that is friendly enough for primary-age pupils to use while not insulting for introductory work with secondary pupils. Importantly it aids the development of mental models for how 3D CAD works that make it a useful steppingstone to more advanced work with the commercial level tools. As with 2D modelling, it can be far quicker to develop and iterate models using cheap physical materials such as card; the approach you choose to use with learners at any particular point in a design process will depend on your learning aims.

Structural modelling

For 2D modelling, various free structural modelling tools that run in the browser allow 2D structural modelling to take place[9]. These generally offer more than enough capability for any work exploring structures pre-16. 3D modelling is supported by the 3D CAD tools mentioned in the previous section. This is probably best classed as advanced use and is unlikely to be required pre-16 except in exceptional cases. We think this is definitely a case where the digital tool is best used as an adjunct to work with physical models (whether these use simple materials such as card or spaghetti, or structural modelling kits). The physical engagement allows the development of an intuitive sense of how structures 'work' that that can then be enhanced using the precision of the digital tool.

Mechanical modelling

As with structural modelling, there is a range of free online tools that allow various kinds of mechanical model to be explored in 2D[10]. These tools generally also allow for designs to be saved in relevant CAD formats, allowing a smooth path from design to manufacturing. And the same 3D CAD tools already discussed also offer sophisticated mechanical modelling. As with their structural modelling tools, we feel these count as 'advanced' for most designing and making purposes pre-16.

For learning about mechanisms, we advocate the use of 'physical chooser charts' discussed at length in Teaching technical understanding (see page 161). Development of a virtual mechanisms chooser charts in 3D CAD software is an interesting avenue to explore, though we're not aware of anyone having done this yet. When designing a bespoke mechanical system, it is better for learners to use cheap modelling materials such as card or thin ply along with readily available technical components to iterate towards a workable solution before turning to digital tools to help refine and realise their ideas.

Electrical modelling

This is an area where we think that digital tools provide some real advantages over the physical circuit modelling kits that have long been available in schools, predating the computer era (at least in the science department). TinkerCAD is once again a prime example of a free and powerful tool. Take the case of learners tasked with designing an electrical circuit that will be incorporated into a product. A simulation of this circuit can achieve the following:

- It supports the development of a working circuit; if it doesn't 'work' in the simulation you can be sure it won't work in real life. And vice versa. Unlike a physical kit, the batteries will always be fully charged and the connections reliable.
- The simulation elements can be easily moved around, and the wires stretched. This allows the learners to match the simulated layout to the intended physical layout.
- The learners can be required to demonstrate a working simulation before moving on to the physical implementation.
- The simulation layout can be used as a template to guide the construction of the physical circuit as it is incorporated into product.

The combination of these features provides a set of scaffolds that increase the likelihood of learners ending up with working circuits; non-working circuitry being a major reason why some design & technology departments may avoid this kind of work. And, of course, such an approach can support the development of electrical circuits incorporated into a wide range of materials including e-textiles and sheet materials (e.g., using copper tape and conductive ink), as well as those based around soldering wires.

Electronic modelling

As noted previously, working with electronics now means the use of physical computing through some kind of microcontroller system. Of necessity this involves developing a program to run on the microcontroller. All recent microcontroller systems include an option to program using a Blockly (or Scratch) style graphical interface as well as the ability to progress to text-based languages such as Python. Adding to the friendliness of the graphical programming at the introductory level is the ability to simulate the developed program on-screen thus providing rapid feedback about the effectiveness of the code just written. Some environments go a step better and allow the learner to virtually attach components to the microcontroller that are then simulated along with the running code on the device. The best example of this, at the time of writing, is the combination of the micro:bit with TinkerCAD, but we anticipate similar tools becoming available for other popular microcontroller systems.

The availability of simulation is a powerful tool to support design thinking and development. However, it does not obviate the need to move back into the physical world at the appropriate point in the development cycle. Microcontrollers are designed for physical computing, which does mean working in the real physical world – which always provides additional challenges on the path to a working system. The move in design & technology from electronics product development based on discrete components to the use of programmable systems has brought a range of advantages that, we hope, will help reinvigorate this neglected area of the curriculum. These include:

- the ability to simulate a control program before trying it out in 'real life'.

- the ability to easily change a control program. This allows product development and refinement to take place without imposing any necessity for additional components.
- it allows learners to develop highly personal and individual products on the same platform thus standardising costs and equipment organisation.
- previous control programs can be adapted for a new situation, or shared, or developed from code found online, improving development times.
- the need to bring a wide range of technical aspects of design & technology together since even a computer-controlled system has to respond to real sensors and control real actuators.

Digital making

Digital making is, inevitably, closely coupled to digital designing in that to use a computer-controlled machine you need to send it an appropriate digital file, created using some kind of design software. There is a wide range of computer driven tools available to schools. These include paper printers, vinyl cutters, plotters, laser cutters, 3D printers, embroidery and sewing machines, knitting machines, 2D/2½D millers, 3D (and also higher dimension) millers, lathes, plasma cutters, and water cutters. Though we note that, at the time of writing, some of these, especially towards the end of the list are pretty rare in educational settings. This book isn't the right place to get into the detail of the pros and cons of these machines; technology moves fast and there is plenty of information and advice available online. Instead, we discuss a few issues that schools planning to develop digital making in the curriculum might consider.

What machines are likely to be most useful in what teaching contexts?

It is a saying within the maker movement that people join a maker space because of the 3D printers but stay because of the laser cutters. We think many teachers will recognise the wisdom of this. If you have 250 pupils in Year 8, who will all follow the same curriculum units, what digital making tool is most likely to be able to contribute usefully? Clearly, it will be one that allows reasonably high rate of production. The setting of a Year 11 NEA is very different, and it might be much more plausible to include tools whose throughput is lower but allows for more complex outcomes. SEND learners provide an interesting case to consider. Since one of the strengths of digital making is precision, there is a strong argument for it particularly being made available to learners whose making skills are limited, or who have other special needs, though not, of course, to the exclusion of work with hand tools.

What are the practical implications of incorporating digital making into curriculum units?

Organising the effective use of machinery whose availability is limited is always a challenge, however, it is one that most design & technology teachers must manage every day. There are, for example, rarely sufficient machine tools for every learner. Is it possible that only some individuals have their work produced digitally, but everyone can see both the process and products of digital manufacturing and compare them to hand produced items? Alternatively, the whole class could observe the production process, but the actual making of most individuals designs are made either while learners are doing other work or at another time (often with technician help). An aspiration might be to aim towards a place where learners can make an informed choice between manual and digital making. This suggests that learners need to be taught explicitly about the relative strengths and weaknesses of each and can weigh such things as individuality and speed against precision or mass manufacture.

What professional development plans do you need to include in your budgeting for new technology, for both teaching and support staff?

Every new item of equipment comes with the need to learn how to use it effectively. All staff (teaching and support) who will be expected to include the tool in their teaching need to be provided with the time to learn how to use both the software and hardware elements effectively. This may sound like an overly obvious piece of advice. But it is more common than we might like to admit in public to find, in schools, new but dusty digital tools that haven't been used because of a lack of professional development time to enable their effective deployment.

To summarise, these are some questions that you could ask in preparation for the introduction of a digital tool:

1 Are staff fully familiar with the hardware and software that you are going to use?
2 Have you evaluated the appropriateness of the hardware and software for your teaching purpose? This includes all relevant risk assessments.
3 Have you considered the limitations imposed by the actual equipment that is available to you?
4 Have you planned how the room will be organised and how learner access to hardware and software will be arranged?
5 Have you thought through the ways in which the digital tool can support your teaching and learning objectives?
6 How will your assessment of learning be affected? What criteria will you use to assess digital designing and making as opposed to manual designing and making.

Artificial intelligence (AI)

We are writing this book at a time when some new developments in AI have led to a surge of public interest in the technology's potential as well as the possible risks it poses. There is also a great deal of misunderstanding about how AI works. However, perhaps more than any other thing we have written about here, anything we say is likely to be read in the context of yet further rapid change. And yet it would be strange to completely ignore this technology. We make the following points.

Firstly, we think that the 'I' in AI leads to unhelpful mental models, not least in the minds of the young people we teach. It is more accurate (based on how these technologies actually work) to think of current AI as being in the same space as autocorrect or predictive text on your phone. The basic principle is the same, the differences are twofold. Firstly, AI draws on a vastly broader range of texts (or graphics, or videos, etc.) to inform the associations it makes as it creates responses. Secondly, it uses much more complex engines to help it make these associations; this is the 'deep' in 'deep learning'. The result is a quality of response that can be quite astonishing. However, these responses will always be limited by the resources it has been able to digest. Given that these resources are broadly the materials available on the Internet, it is important that the various purveyors of these tools work extremely hard to suppress violent, racist, sexist, homophobic, and similar responses.

Secondly, and because of the above, the responses provided by AI systems come with no guarantees of accuracy. There is no way for an AI to independently check the accuracy of the information it provides. Topics that are uncontentious are more likely to lead to accurate responses since the texts that feed the responses are likely to provide a unified view, based on a paradigm accepted by the relevant established community of practice.

In addition to the text-based tools that are currently causing a stir there are tools that create, based on textual prompts, 2D and 3D CAD drawings, design sketches, video sequences, etc. These are currently quite primitive, but we expect the quality to improve to the point where they attain a quality similar to the textual systems (and with all the same limitations). In our view banning these tools and branding their use as cheating is unhelpful. Compare with spell checking tools; we generally don't see their use as cheating but rather, for many people, they are liberating. At the same time individuals do need a reasonable ability to spell accurately, if only to intelligently select between homophones. A better approach is to incorporate their thoughtful use into the flow of design activity, seeing them as an assistive technology whose output can be helpful, but also needs critical engagement. This way our learners can benefit from the strengths of these tools while at the same learning about their limitations.

The use of AI in design & technology is discussed further in chapter 3 (see page 57 AI Stop Press)

Moving forward with digital design & technology - *A Thought Piece by Ed Charlwood*

Ed Charlwood is National Lead Practitioner for design & technology at the Oasis Learning Trust, Co-founder of Badgeable.org.

It is my reflection that the arguments presented above neatly encapsulate some of the fundamental struggles that design & technology has wrestled with for many years, namely; with an ever-growing body of subject knowledge, what do we closely hold onto as 'core' and what do we de-emphasise?

The case for digital designing and making is, I believe, compelling and it is even there in the name of the subject – the T in D&T. If we can agree for the sake of brevity that hands-on experiences are engaging and important but at the same time that 'craft' is no longer the domain of design & technology then the question is how do we think about and leverage the opportunities afforded by digital technologies to improve learner agency and help them to use these tools to create and implement 'better' solutions in the challenging context that may schools currently find themselves in: lack of teachers, tiny budgets, reducing timetable allocations and high expectations of outcomes.

The trajectory of digital design tools like Tinkercad, Onshape, and Fusion 360 is that they are becoming ever more powerful, more usable (improved UI/UX), more accessible (browser and cloud based) and more affordable (if not free). It is reasonable to say that with a few sign-up steps all students now have free access to industry standard software that they can run on almost any device. Many of these have built-in tutorials and learning pathways (although the quality of these can be variable). I would argue that the only thing stopping students from realizing the potential of these tools is the mindset of teachers and furthermore that many of these tools offer a unique equality of provision and opportunity.

I believe teachers should see digital design tools as a fundamental pillar of a 'good' design & technology education alongside others like sketching and modelling and that we should be thinking about ways to design our curriculum with CAD *and* hands-on experiences, not as CAD *or* hands-on.

The ability to move a 2D sketch into 3D CAD, develop and test solid models and export 2D working drawings and photorealistic renderings reflects industrial practice.

Digital manufacturing tools have their own particular advantages and issues to consider. The plummeting cost of low-cost, high-quality 3D printers is remarkable and with some careful classroom management these can become fundamental tools in a modern design & technology workshop. Laser cutters clearly have a speed advantage but are expensive. With careful task design 3D printers *can* be used by large classes, for example, by including manufacturing constraints like print time or material usage. Students can also simulate print settings like layer height or infill to make informed decisions and they can also use tools like 'cut' to quickly test specific features of a larger design, for example, isolating a few millimetres of a screw thread to test for tolerance.

The use of digital designing and making technologies in schools should move beyond teaching them in isolation, rather embedding them at the core of the design & technology curriculum they sit within, and should be thought of as incredibly powerful tools that, with thoughtful pedagogy developed around learning principles, can provide incredible teaching and learning potential.

Suggested practical actions:

- Map your current curriculum offering for opportunities to interleave CAD and CAM. For example, if you already make finger joints in a softwood, you could extend or reframe the task by including a CAD design task to create and simulate forces on a 'digital joint' like these by Jochen Gros, http://winterdienst.info/50-digital-wood-joints-by-jochen-gros/, and furthermore you could then laser cut or 3D print scale models to test like this https://cults3d.com/en/3d-model/various/japanese-dovetail. Also plan for progression over time, considering Ebbinghaus's Forgetting Curve.
- Review your current CAD offering and challenge any assumptions you may have about alternative tools. For example, Tinkercad may look a little 'primary school' but is incredibly powerful as this gallery of work shows: https://www.tinkercad.com/users/gZrHtBpg1Rb-zdp189.
- Consider becoming CAD-agnostic. Plan for the competencies you'd like to foster and then match the tools to them, considering that the landscape of both CAD and CAM is shifting so you should be prepared and ready to move from one platform to another.
- Look at the tutorials and learning pathways that software companies offer, to avoid reinventing the wheel.
- Reach out to other educators who are like-minded: https://the-innnovation-association.mn.co/share/1XBIOwqJfybSBBhe?utm_source=manual.

Further reading:

- Approaches to teaching CAD, based on learning science principles *(part 1)*, https://mrcharlwood.blogspot.com/2023/03/approaches-to-teaching-cad-based-on.html.
- *Makers: The New Industrial Revolution* by Chris Anderson: https://www.goodreads.com/book/show/13414678-makers.
- *Build: An Unorthodox Guide to Making Things Worth Making* by Tony Fadell: https://www.goodreads.com/en/book/show/59696349.
- Anker, Bambu, Prusa, Creality: 3D printers suddenly have a need for speed: https://www.theverge.com/2023/4/13/23681219/anker-bambu-prusa-creality-3d-printer-speed-arms-race.
- Teach to use CAD or through using CAD: An interview study with technology teachers: https://link.springer.com/article/10.1007/s10798-022-09770-1.

What are we to make of Ed's Thought Piece? His vision of the place of digital designing and making in design & technology is both inspiring and compelling but it does come at a price. That price is that many design & technology teachers will need to relinquish long held and cherished beliefs as to the significance of craft practice in the subject. This will not be easy and will involve considerable soul searching for some. It is important to remember that Ed is not advocating throwing the 'craft baby' out with the bath water but a measured approach in which 'hands on' and 'bits on' work in harmony. And this change will only be accomplished with the availability of significant and sustained professional development.

Summary

Initially this chapter considered the applications of cognitive science to the teaching of design & technology. Then it discussed how three separate, but related aspects of technical understanding might be taught. These were powering, controlling and structuring noting that learning in the science curriculum is relevant here and the need for conversations between science and design & technology teachers. Next it discussed the teaching of making and included a Thought Piece on demonstration from Matt McLain. The following section dealt with the teaching of designing with a particular emphasis on the role of classroom talk. The penultimate section dealt with the teaching of critique identifying ways this might be achieved within different pedagogies. The section included a Thought Piece by James Pitt who advocated the teaching of critique to develop radical thinking in learners. The final section dealt with digital designing and making, the balance required with manual making, and the potential contribution of AI tools. The section included a Thought Piece by Ed Charlwood which advocated promoting the use of digital tools.

Notes

 1 https://microbit.org
 2 https://redfernelectronics.co.uk/crumble/
 3 https://picaxe.com
 4 https://www.genieonline.com
 5 https://www.arduino.cc
 6 https://www.raspberrypi.com/documentation/microcontrollers/rp2040.html
 7 https://www.raspberrypi.com
 8 https://www.tinkercad.com
 9 E.g., Civils.ai Free Structural Analysis Calculator: https://civils.ai/1/free-structural-analysis-calculator
10 E.g., For gears, Gear generator: https://geargenerator.com/

References

Alexander, R. J. (2006). *Towards dialogic Teaching: Rethinking Classroom Talk* (3rd ed.). Cambridge, UK: Dialogos.
Barlex, D. (2007) Assessing capability in design & technology The case for a minimally invasive approach. *Design and Technology Education: An International Journal*, 12.2, 9–56, Design & Technology Association: Wellesbourne.
BESA (2022) Using vocabulary tiers to improve literacy, https://www.besa.org.uk/news/using-vocabulary-tiers-to-improve-literacy/.
Blikstein, P. (2013). Digital fabrication and 'making' in education: The democratization of invention. In J. Walter-Herrmann & C. Büching (Eds.), *FabLabs: Of Machines, Makers and Inventors* (pp. 203–221). Bielefeld, Germany: Transcript Publishers.
Box, G. (2005) https://en.wikiquote.org/wiki/George_E._P._Box.
Burke, B. (1999, 2005) Antonio Gramsci, Schooling and Education, *The Encyclopaedia of Informal Education*, http://www.infed.org/thinkers/et-gram.htm.
Education Endowment Foundation, https://educationendowmentfoundation.org.uk.

Freire. P. (1970) *Pedagogy of the Oppressed* (English edition), Harmondsworth: Penguin.

HMSO (2004) *The KS3 Design & Technology National Strategy, Module 4: Teaching the subskills of designing,* https://www.designtechnology.org.uk/resource-shop/ks3-dt-national-strategy-module-4-teaching-the-subskills-of-designing/.

Jones, K., & Wiliam, D. (2022) *Lethal mutations in education and how to prevent them,* https://evidencebased.education/lethal-mutations-in-education-and-how-to-prevent-them/.

Kimbell, R., Stables, K., Wheeler, T., Wosniak, A., & Kelly, V. (1991). *The Assessment of Performance in Design and Technology.* London: HMSO.

Lemov, D (2021) *Teach Like a Champion 3.0: 63 Techniques that Put Students on the Path to College.*

McLean, M. (2020) Key pedagogies in design and technology, in Hardy A. (Ed.), *Learning to Teach Design and Technology in the Secondary School.* London: Routledge

Nuffield Design & Technology (2000a) Mechanisms Chooser Chart, https://dandtfordandt.files.wordpress.com/2013/07/cc-mechanisms.pdf.

Nuffield Design & Technology (2000b) Electrical Components Chooser Chart, https://dandtfordandt.files.wordpress.com/2013/07/cc-electric-components.pdf.

Nuffield Design & Technology (2000c) Sensing with Electronics Chooser Chart, https://dandtfordandt.files.wordpress.com/2013/07/cc-electronic-sensing.pdf.

Nuffield Design & Technology (2000d) Structural Elements Chooser Chart, https://dandtfordandt.files.wordpress.com/2013/09/ks4-product-design-cc-structural-elements.pdf.

Nuffield Foundation (2000) KS3 Strategy Resource Tasks from the Nuffield Design & Technology Materials, https://dandtfordandt.wordpress.com/resources/nuffield-ks3-dt-resources/strategy-resource-tasks/.

Papert, S., & Harel, I. (1991). Situating constructionism. In S. Papert, & I. Harel (Eds.), *Constructionism.* New York: Ablex Publishing.

Pitt, J., & Webster, K. (2021) *Education Unbound - How to Create Educational Opportunity in Abundance.* Mold: TerraPreta.

QAA (2014) *Frameworks for Higher Education Qualifications of UK Degree-Awarding Bodies,* https://www.qaa.ac.uk/the-quality-code/qualifications-frameworks.

Rosenshine B (2012) Principles of Instruction: Research-Based Strategies That All Teachers Should Know, *American Educator,* 36(1):12–19, 39 Spr 2012.

Seery, N. (2020) Pedagogy involving social and cognitive interaction between teachers and pupils, in Wiliams, J. and Barlex, D. (Eds.). *Pedagogy for Technology Education in Secondary Schools.* Switzerland: Springer.

Segundo (1973-1974) The phrase *Artisans of a New Humanity* is taken from the title of a series of books by the Uruguayan theologian Juan L Segundo (1973-1974). Segundo was an important figure in Latin American liberation theology.

Sherrington, T. (2020) *A Model for the Learning Process. And Why It Helps to Have One,* https://teacherhead.com/2020/03/10/a-model-for-the-learning-process-and-why-it-helps-to-have-one/.

Stables, K. (2020) Signature Pedagogies for Designing: A Speculative Framework for Supporting Learning and Teaching in Design & Technology. In P. John Williams & David Barlex (Eds.), *Pedagogy for Technology Education in Secondary Schools.* Switzerland: Springer

Steeg, T.J. (2003) The Presentation of Systems Thinking in Support Materials for Secondary Design & Technology pupils: A review, in Norman E. & Spendlove D. (Eds.), *DATA International Research Conference 2003,* DATA, pp. 107–113.

TES (2023) *Daniel Willingham on Memory, Phonics and Metacognition,* https://www.tes.com/magazine/teaching-learning/general/dan-willingham-interview-memory-phonics-metacognition.

Welch, M., & Barlex, D. (2009, July). So We're Going to Have This Huge Spike Here? Pupils' Talk While Designing and Making. In E. W. L. Norman, & D. Spendlove (Eds.), *The Design & Technology Association Education and International Research Conference 2009* (pp. 103–109). Loughborough, UK: Loughborough University.

Welch, M., & Barlex, D. (2010, July). The pattern of a teacher's questions in elementary design and technology. In D. Spendlove & K. Stables (Eds.), *The Design & Technology Association Education and International Research Conference 2009* (pp. 123–127). Keele, UK: Keele University.

Willingham, D. (2021) *Why Don't Students Like School?: A Cognitive Scientist Answers Questions About How the Mind Works and What It Means for the Classroom,* 2nd Edition. San Francisco: Jossey-Bass.

Recommended Reading

Hallström, J., & Williams, P.J. (Eds.) (2023) *Teaching and Learning about Technological Systems, Philosophical, Curriculum and Classroom Perspectives, Contemporary Issues in Technology Education*. Singapore: Springer.

Klapwijk, R. M., Gu, J., Yang, Q., & de Vries, M. J. (Eds.) (2023) *Maker Education Meets Technology Education Reflections on Good Practice*. The Netherlands: Brill.

6 Assessing design & technology

This chapter is in seven parts:

- Purposes of assessment
- The messy nature of progress
- Integration of assessment into curriculum planning and implementation
- Feedback as part of 'in the moment' assessment
- Feedback at 'end of task' assessment
- Identifying impact
- Public examinations.

The chapter closes with a short summary, followed by references and recommended reading.

Purposes of assessment

A key purpose of assessment is to help learners understand where they are in their learning – supporting them to know what they are secure with in terms of their knowledge, understanding, skills, and values and helping them identify areas to develop. Such assessment is focused *on* the learner and is *for* the learner and provides useful information for a variety of stakeholders including teachers, parents/carers, and others such as school leaders, governors, and Ofsted.
   Assessment can:

- Allow learners to reflect on their learning over time and improve their progress
- Be used to find out where learners are before they start something new
- Help teachers reflect on and improve their pedagogy
- Help teachers to develop a better understanding of the learner
- Help to identify learning issues to support the planning of strategic interventions
- Provide a basis for a meaningful dialogue with learners, and other stakeholders about learners' progress.

Formative assessment identifies what a learner needs to do to progress and helps the teacher and learner decide on the next learning steps. This has been called "responsive teaching" (Fletcher-Wood, 2018). **Summative assessment** indicates a learner's level of

DOI: 10.4324/9781003008026-6

achievement at a particular time and may also provide formative information that can be used to inform future teaching and learning.

The messy nature of progress

It is crucial that the nature of any assessment technique is appropriate for both the nature of the learning activity being undertaken and the substance of what is intended to be learned. Because design & technology is a **broad and complex subject** encompassing a wide range of knowledge, understanding skills, and values, it may be taught by at least four different teaching methods as we have noted in chapter 4. Progress in learning for an individual learner, by means of a particular method of teaching, is **likely to be uneven.** Hence in developing making skills, a learner may, for example, excel at using a sewing machine whilst at the same time experience considerable difficult in becoming competent at using a vibro saw. In developing design ability, a learner may tackle one 'designing without making' activity well whilst a later similar activity less well. This often depends on how compelling the context of the activity is to a particular learner. Progress in learning for an individual learner, by means of different methods of teaching, is **likely to be uneven.** A learner may make steady progress in developing making skills but find designing in both design without making and designing and making challenging whilst at the same time excel at considering the consequences of utilising particular technologies or artefacts.

Integration of assessment into curriculum planning and implementation

Implicit in the discussion above is that decisions made in planning your curriculum are accompanied by decisions as to how learners' progress is assessed. A range of approaches to teaching across a term each assessed appropriately will give all learners the opportunity to show what they have learned and demonstrate fully the extent to which their knowledge, understanding, skills, and values have grown and also where there are gaps which may hinder further progress. As discussed in chapter 4, talking with and listening to learners while they are actively engaged in the task at hand is important as it enables teachers to gain insight into the learners' thought processes. Such 'assessment conversations' will only be open and honest if the teacher has established a trusting relationship with the learners so that they are prepared to be open and reveal their thinking in the certain knowledge that the teacher's response will be both respectful and useful. These responses, both 'in the moment' of a conversation in a busy classroom and at the end of a particular task provide the learner with feedback as to their progress but such feed-back has to be constructed wisely if it is to be effective. Paul Black has often made the following perceptive comments (Black & Wiliam, 1998) with regard to the impact different sorts of feedback has on learners.

- Marks alone are counterproductive.
- Marks plus comments aren't much better.

- Written comments can be useful.
- Verbal comments can be very useful and are often more useful than delayed feedback.

It is essential that any comments provoke a useful response from the learner and this may not always be the case. Kluger and DeNisi (1996) have noted that if a learner falls short of a goal, then the teacher wants the learner to increase effort. If a learner exceeds a goal the teacher wants the learner to increase aspiration. But learners do not always respond in this way. Sometimes they reduce aspiration and effort or even ignore the feedback completely. It is important that teachers use their conversations with learners to uncover any difficulties with the learning. In the case of such difficulties, the conversation should focus on helping the learner to make more effort. If the learner has mastered the required learning, then the conversation should focus on helping the learner go further with their learning. This kind of feedback generally does not need recording. The learners themselves may find it helpful to record their response to such conversations, but an all-embracing, onerous system of centralised recording may be counter-productive to the effectiveness of such 'in the moment' feedback.

More formal feedback which is recorded usually takes place at the end of a learning activity. To provide useful feedback to a learner, it is essential that the teacher is clear about the learning intentions of the activity, has made observations and collected other evidence that indicates the extent to which the learner has achieved the required learning and can communicate this quickly to the learner with specific guidance as to how any shortcomings may be overcome. Note that without the initial clarity of learning intentions useful feedback cannot take place.

John Hattie (2012) has identified three levels of feedback:

1 *Feedback at task level*

This focuses on providing feedback with regard to the learning of basic concepts. The learning is not aimed at developing more complex understanding in terms of the relationship between different concepts or extending the concepts. But such learning is very important, as without it deeper learning cannot be achieved.

2 *Feedback at the process/strategy level*

This focuses on the processes underlying the tasks and relating and extending tasks. It helps learners identify relationships between ideas and detect errors for themselves. It leads the learner to different learning strategies.

3 *Feedback at the self-regulation level*

This focuses on the learners' monitoring of their own learning processes. It helps learners to decide what to do next when this isn't immediately apparent.

Hattie is very clear that it is important not to confuse feedback with praise. Empty praise, e.g., 'Oh you are clever to do that', directs attention away from the task and related learning as it invariably contains little task-related information. Of course, learners welcome praise as it provides comfort and support and it may help some learners stay on task. Hattie (2012, p. 136) writes:

> For feedback to be effective in the act of learning, praise dissipates the message. Praise the students and make them feel welcomed to your class and worthwhile as learners, but if you wish to make a major difference to learning leave praise out of feedback about learning.

The following two sections will consider feedback during 'in the moment' assessment and 'end of task' assessment.

Feedback as part of 'in the moment' assessment

Feedback during a task to teach about mechanisms

Here is the situation in the classroom. The teacher has organised a circus of activities through which learners can tackle simple mechanisms calculations, explore the actions of model mechanisms, and build mechanisms to achieve a particular output from a particular input. Each station of the circus concerns a particular group of mechanisms; Station 1 – simple and complex gear trains, Station 2 – simple and complex pulley systems, Station 3 – linked levers, Station 4 – for racks, pinions, and worms.

The teacher has very clear learning intentions; through the circus of activities the learners will:

- be able to recognise and name the components in each group of mechanisms,
- be able to describe how each group of mechanisms can change the speed, force, and nature of movement of the output compared to the input,
- be able to use both qualitative and quantitative thinking, and use this learning in solving simple mechanism design tasks.

This is an ambitious learning agenda, and small groups of learners will probably need to spend at least 20 minutes at each station. The teacher has allowed two double lessons, i.e., a total of two hours for the activity. As homework activity, the teacher has asked the learners to find examples of the mechanisms in the workings of some everyday products.

Task level feedback at Station 1

Consider the learner who is struggling with calculating the number of teeth in the gears in a simple gear train to achieve a particular output. Rather than showing her how to do the calculation, the teacher might enable her to increase her effort by saying, 'You've only identified the number of teeth on the driver. You need to think about the number of teeth on the driven gear'. This feedback comment focuses the learner's thinking so that she is better placed to achieve the learning. If this proves unsuccessful the teacher might suggest particular numbers of teeth for the driven gear and ask her what would happen in such cases. Once the learner is showing signs that that she has 'got it', the teacher can move on. The whole encounter might take no more than 30 seconds.

Consider the learner who appears to have grasped the idea of gear ratios and their relationship with the number of teeth on the driving and driven gears. Here there is an opportunity to increase aspiration. In which case the teacher might say to the learner, 'You've got the gear ratio in this example sorted. What would you need to change if the driver gear had twice as many teeth?' The question will extend the learner's thinking and the answer she gives will indicate whether the learner really has understood the idea. This encounter is likely to take little more than a minute.

Process/strategy level feedback at Station 1

Consider the learner who is struggling with a simple gear ratio calculation. Rather than providing the answer the teacher might enable her to increase her effort by saying to the learner, 'OK, so the task is to calculate the gear ratio that would give you an output speed of 20 rpm but you can't decide how to start. How about thinking about the input speed of the motor? Will the output need to turn faster or slower?' Once the learner has realised that the input speed has to be decreased (say) by the gearing mechanism the task becomes clearer, and she may be able to make progress without further assistance from the teacher.

Consider the learner who has shown that he can devise a compound gear train to decrease output speed, the teacher might enable the learner to increase his aspiration by asking, 'What else could you use to get this change in speed?' and, 'Which would be the easiest mechanism to assemble?'

Note that in all the examples given above the feedback required the learners to share with the teacher the difficulties or successes that they were having in tackling the tasks set and the teacher's response was in the form of questions that provoked further thinking from the learner as opposed to providing an answer. Given that the learning activities at each station are quite explicit, there is little requirement for self-regulation on the part of the learners so feedback at the self-regulation level will not be considered here.

Pause for thought

Appreciating where learners are likely to 'get stuck' in understanding concepts is a first step to being able to identify the sorts of questions a teacher might ask to help a learner overcome difficulty. How often are the teachers in your department able to trial and discuss learning activities in terms of their probable difficulties in understanding? Such discussion will enable the teachers to develop and share a repertoire of useful questions.

Feedback during a task to teach particular making skills

Here is the situation in the workshop. The teacher has set up a lesson in which learners will practice the construction of halving joints and mortise-and-tenon joints in making a simple wooden sculpture inspired by the *Red Blue Chair* of Gerrit Rietveld as shown in Figure 6.1.

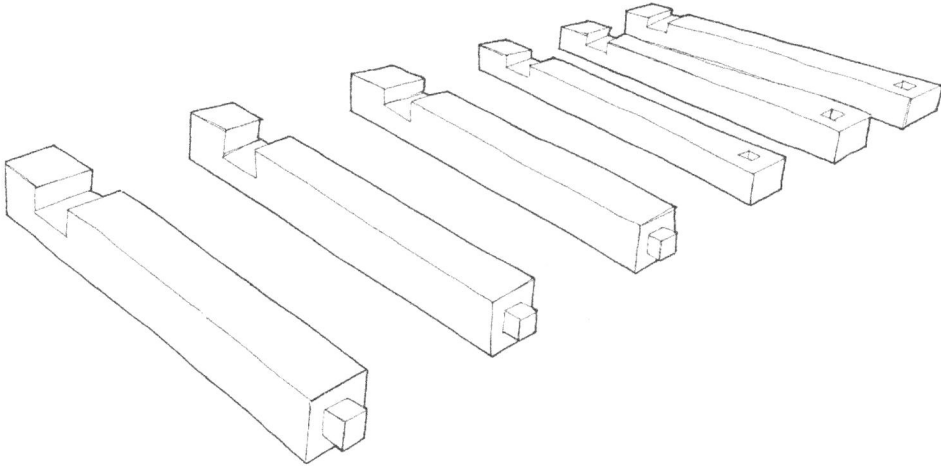

Figure 6.1 An exercise in the construction of halving joints and mortise and tenon joints

Having demonstrated the construction of such joints to the class, each learner then has to produce six parts each with a halving joint; three of these have a tenon, and three a mortise. With this assortment of joints the six pieces can be assembled into the desired sculpture which can then be given an appropriate finish. As the learners are acting under precise instructions to produce six pieces and assemble these into a prescribed structure, there is little need for process/strategy feedback or self-regulation feedback but task level feedback will be very important.

Task level feedback

There are many factors contributing to the accurate and safe means of using tools and even small errors in one or two of these can lead to finished items with significant flaws or faults. So, at every stage of the process there will be the possibility of learners making small errors that have a cumulative effect on the quality of the finished piece. One way of providing task level feedback is for the teacher to ask 'Are you sure ... ?' questions as the learners progress through the instructions. For example:

- Are you sure that you've measured the length of the tenon correctly?
- Are you sure that the tri-square is up tight against the wood?
- Are you sure you're cutting to the waste side of the line?
- Are you sure that you've cut across the grain with the chisel first?

This will give the learners pause to think about what they are doing and make adjustments. Of course, some learners will make mistakes and then the questions become about how to retrieve the situation, e.g., 'Okay, so you've made the mortise too big (or the tenon too small), what can you do about that?' Again, the feedback puts the ball back in the learner's court so that they understand what they have to do to develop their skills, knowledge and the quality of the end product.

Pause for thought

Being aware of the common mistakes that learners might make when carrying out a making sequence for the first time is a first step to being able to identify the sorts of questions a teacher might ask to help a learner develop good practice. How often are the teachers in your department able to discuss making activities in terms of the probable mistakes likely to occur? Such discussion will enable the teachers to develop and share a repertoire of useful questions.

Feedback during a design without make task

Here is the situation in the classroom. The teacher has asked the class to consider how they might use aerogels. Aerogels are synthetic, porous, ultralight materials derived from a gel, in which the liquid component for the gel has been replaced with a gas without significant collapse of the gel structure. The result is a solid with extremely low density and extremely low thermal conductivity. If the learners are to develop an application for an aerogel, it is essential that they appreciate their unique properties, so an understanding of density and thermal conductivity is vital. Questions probing how a group's design proposal capitalises on these properties will be important, e.g., 'What makes the really low density useful here?' or 'What if the thermal conductivity wasn't so low?' This is process/strategy level feedback in that it will help the learners identify relationships between ideas and detect errors for themselves.

Pause for thought

In deciding upon the applications for different materials an understanding of the idea of properties and how properties relate to fitness for purpose is crucial. Some properties are difficult to understand, and talking about the implications of particular properties is important if learners are to develop an insightful understanding. Hence it is important that teachers in a department have the opportunity to unpack the difficulties in understanding that learners might have. How often are you able to spend time on this in your department?

Feedback during a designing and making task

Perhaps the most difficult area of feedback is that given during a designing and making task. If a learner is struggling with what to do next, it is very tempting for the teacher to simply tell her so that she can get on with doing it and the teacher can move on to dealing with the next request for help. In the short term this solves the immediate problem of keeping this and other learners on-task, but in the long term it is a disservice to the learners, as they are not being challenged to make their own decisions. Plus it doesn't prepare them for the GCSE Non-Examined Assessment (see page 227). We know that effective feedback helps learners increase effort or increase aspiration and this is achieved by asking questions to stimulate the learners to think for themselves (Aguiar, Mortimer, & Scott, 2010). Getting learners to think and act for themselves is the challenge in providing 'in the moment' feedback during a designing and making task. Note also that over time, such in the moment feedback is likely to improve confidence in learners and provide insights that empower them to make progress.

Consider a designing and making task in which a learner has to design and make a moving toy that is powered by a small electric motor, taking into account the preferences of the user of the toy such that:

- it moves in a way that will appeal to the user,
- has an appearance which pleases the user, and
- incorporates a range of special effects, that will give the toy more play value for the user.

Task level feedback

Consider the learner who has identified a few of her users likes but is not yet taking into account where the toy might be used. To increase effort the teacher might ask, 'OK so you've found out that your user likes horses and dogs; but what about where she lives and will play with the toy? Does that tell you anything about the sort of toy she'd like?' And to increase aspiration the teacher might ask, 'OK what else is your user interested in that might be useful to know about?'

Process/strategy level feedback

Consider the learner who wants the toy to move in a circle but isn't sure how to achieve this. Rather than simply supply information about how to mount stub axles so that they allow wheels to change direction, to increase effort the teacher might ask, 'Why not look at the way a cars wheel move when a car is turning a corner? What happens to the wheels? How could you make that happen in your toy?'

Consider the learner who has quickly made the decision on how to get the toy to move slowly by opting for an obvious solution. The teacher might increase aspiration by saying to the learner, 'OK, you think the pulley drive will slow it down a bit and you're right. If you wanted to slow it down a lot more, what could you use? Why not check out the mechanisms chooser chart?' (Nuffield D&T, 2000) This comment would move the learner towards considering other possible solutions and choosing which is the best for his situation.

Self-regulation feedback

Here the questions to provide feedback are very open and could be used during any designing and making task. Rather than promoting increased effort or aspiration they are concerned with helping learners check that they are not making costly blunders. They are a way for the teacher to help the learners manage the risks inherent in designing and making. Here are some examples:

- How can you be sure your design will do what it's supposed to?
- How can you be sure you have enough materials?
- How can you be sure you have enough time for the making?
- How can you tell whether the user will like the product?

There will be times, of course, when you may need to simply correct a learner's mistakes in the hope of preventing repetition. But this is probably the least useful form of feedback as unless it is accompanied by a significant conversation such correction often falls on deaf ears especially if it is in the form of marking. 'In the moment' feedback to increase effort and/or aspiration almost always relies on a conversation between the teacher and learner and involves the teacher listening to the learner and then asking questions in response to what the learner has said.

Pause for thought

Being aware of the likely difficulties that learners are likely to face in a designing and making assignment is a first step to being able to provide support by asking questions. The difficulties will range across the entire task; for example: developing initial ideas, ensuring that the design will 'work' technically, appreciating the aesthetic requirements of the user, using appropriate making skills, being able to reflect and identify next steps, and carrying out a final evaluation. As teachers gain experience of dealing with such difficulties, they develop a large repertoire of questions that they can call upon and adapt quite fluently. This is an example of case-based reasoning. How often do teachers in your department have the opportunity to share these personal funds of knowledge?

Implicit within 'in the moment' assessment is the idea that using questions provokes learners to develop their cognitive understanding. Malcolm Welch has researched teachers' use of questions and in this Thought Piece he comments on importance of the use of questions as the basis for teacher – learner conversations.

Classroom conversations - *A Though Piece by Malcolm Welch*

Malcolm Welch is Professor Emeritus at Queen's University, Kingston, Ontario.

Just as in life outside of school, conversations within a classroom serve multiple purposes, including exchanging ideas and thoughts, developing language skills, learning to listen, and promoting self-reflection. These classroom conversations, which play a central role in learning, can comprise two elements: (a) conversation between teacher and pupil(s) or between pupils; and (b) questions asked by the teacher and by pupils.

Robin Alexander (2006) tells us that pupils need to talk, not only to the teacher but also to each other, in order to think and learn. And Ann Kruger (1993) shows that when pupils collaborate to solve a problem and operate at the level of ideas, they advance more in their understanding of the problem than they do when they work alone. Of particular importance is what Douglas Barnes and Frankie Todd (1977) have labelled "exploratory talk", in which pupils engage critically but constructively with one another's ideas. This is particularly true in design & technology. When pupils are engaging in "designerly thinking" (Cross, 1982), classroom discussions enable them to analyse and solve problems, speculate and imagine, explore and evaluate ideas, and share knowledge. Analysis, speculation, imagination, exploration, evaluation, and sharing are essential activities for pupils when designing and making.

Asking questions

In the fourth of ten letters to a young poet, Rainer Maria Rilke (2000) exhorts Franz Kappus to "be patient toward all that is unsolved … and try to love the questions themselves". This is also sound advice for design & technology teachers and pupils, for research has shown that (a) asking questions is a fundamental cognitive mechanism in design thinking (Eris, 2003), and (b) teachers' use of questions to guide pupils' thinking is central to supporting their learning (Aguiar, Mortimer, & Scott, 2010).

Questions asked by a teacher will, like conversation, serve multiple purposes, including eliciting what pupils think, assessing how much they understand of what the teacher is saying, encouraging pupils' elaboration of previous answers and ideas by turning an answer given by a pupil back into a question, a technique called a "reflective toss" (van Zee & Minstrell, 1997). Each of these help pupils construct conceptual knowledge (Chin, 2006). For example, when introducing a new topic, the teacher can check for under-standing by asking preliminary questions connecting the topic to pupils' prior experiences and knowledge about the topic. This strategy combines so called "test" questions, to which the teacher already knows the answer, with "exploratory" questions to which the teacher cannot know the answer. For example, in the introduction to a lesson about ergonomics, the teacher may ask pupils: Which is more comfortable to hold, a hot saucepan with a metal handle or one with a plastic handle? The teacher already knows the answer; hence this is a test question. Next, the teacher can ask: What other objects have you used that are uncomfortable to hold? This is an exploratory question, since there will be multiple answers based on the pupils' experience. These two types of questions scaffold pupils' learning and create a "zone of proximal development" (Vygotsky, 1978).

Questions asked by the teacher can also be designed to allow for factual responses, for imaginative and speculative ones, and for developing pupils' competence in asking meaningful questions themselves (Atkinson & Black, 2007). Interrogative questions that require pupils to explain, justify and evaluate their design ideas, followed by an opportunity to modify or revise them, can lead to improvements to those ideas. According to Marilyn Daudelin, (1996) **what** *questions lead to a description of the challenge and later for the implications of a solution,* **why** *questions are useful during analysis of the problem, and* **how** *questions lead to explanation of the problem.*

Conclusion

Establishing a reflective discourse between teacher and pupils is essential in class-rooms. Teacher questioning is a central component of this discourse and must be woven into everyday instruction. Yet the types of questions teachers ask and the way they ask them will influence the type of cognitive processes that pupils engage in as they grapple with the process of constructing knowledge. And design & technology teachers need to ask of themselves: What types of questions will enable pupils to become better designers and makers?

In the hurly burly of a busy workshop where the time spent making often dominates lessons it is all too easy to forget that success in design &technology requires learners to develop significant conceptual understanding if they are to make sound design decisions. Malcolm's Thought Piece underscores the significance of conversations and within that the role of questioning to help learners develop such understanding.

Feedback as part of 'end of task' assessment

In design & technology learners are learning to carry out a range of activities integral to the subject. Hence in design & technology the learning activities invariably involve some sort of 'doing': making, designing, designing and making, or considering consequences. So, defining the learning intentions is not as simple as defining what needs to be remembered and understood, although acquiring knowledge and developing understanding will be important. Some knowledge acquisition and understanding will need to precede the activity, some will be gained during the activity and the outcomes of the activity, be they an artifact, a design proposal, or a critique, will need to be seen as an embodiment of the learning that has taken place.

To provide useful feedback to a learner, it is essential that the teacher is clear about this range of learning intentions associated with the activity – what is it they are learning 'to do' through the activity and what will the various degrees of success look like. And it is important that there is evidence available from the various stages of the task that can be used to indicate the extent to which the learner has achieved the required learning. And the teacher needs to communicate the implications of this learning to the learner through the end of task feedback and provide specific guidance as to how any shortcomings may be overcome. Without the initial clarity of learning intentions useful feedback cannot take place. Hence in the examples below the learning intentions are identified as a starting point so that feedback can be given accordingly. Although it will often be appropriate to praise a learner for effort, it is important that this does not deflect attention from or undermine the feedback that is focused on success or otherwise in the learning. Praise must be accompanied by feedback that leads to progress.

Feedback at the end of a making without designing task

Making without designing is particularly useful for teaching making skills and it is not difficult to create a set of criteria by which the results of such making might be assessed: the level of precision in producing the parts, the quality of the assembly, and the care taken over finishing for example.

Here is the situation in the classroom. The learners are in Year 7. The teacher has decided that she will teach them a range of making skills through an activity in which the learners make and fly a simple kite from plans that she has provided. She has developed the following criteria for the learning activity:

• *Tools, materials and equipment used*

Scissors, craft knife, safety ruler, iron, sewing machine, junior hacksaw, sawing board, ruler, polyester cotton, hard wood dowel, abrasive paper, thin card, string.

• *Skills developed*

Use of craft knife with safety ruler (to cut card along a marked line to produce template). Use of template (to mark out fabric). Use of iron (to press and crease polyester cotton fabric). Use of scissors (to cut fabric along a marked line and cut string to length). Use of sewing machine (to produce a straight seam to prevent fraying and to join separate pieces of fabric). Use of ruler (to measure out hardwood dowel and string). Use of junior hacksaw and sawing board (to cut hardwood dowel to length). Use of abrasive paper (to smooth dowel ends). Assembly of components into a finished artefact (the assembly of the fabric, dowel and string into a finished kite).

• *Level of execution*

Could be: Low precision, moderate precision, high precision.

• *Quality of assembly could be:*

Weak, fragile. Sound, stays together in normal flight. Very sound, survives crash landing.

• *Kite flies:*

Poorly, with difficulty. Well, after lift-off. Very well with easy lift off.

At the end of the task each learner will have a finished kite which they have flown.

Ideally the teacher will discuss face to face with each learner how well he or she has succeeded in the task in terms of the skills they learned and showed in using the tools, material and equipment with regard to level of execution, soundness of assembly, and the flying performance of the kite, see Table 6.1. The kite the learner has made should be present during the

Table 6.1 Assessment for making and flying a kite

Precision of making the parts	Low precision	Moderate precision	High precision
Quality of assembly	Weak, fragile	Sound, stays together in normal flight	Very sound, survives crash landing
Flying performance	Poorly, with difficulty	Well, after lift-off	Very well with easy lift off

discussion so that the reasons for the comments on execution and soundness can be made clear by referring to the kite. Discussion with the learner to decide where ticks should be placed in the following table is a first step in recording and providing feedback. It should be accompanied by a discussion that identifies changes that would lead to improvement.

At the end of such a discussion each learner will have a clear view of where he or she needs to improve. If this task becomes a topic of conversation with a learner's parents or carers, they know what the learner has to do to improve and can provide support and encouragement.

Feedback at the end of a designing without making task

Designing without making tasks are useful for developing creativity in designing as the learners are unencumbered by the necessity of making their proposed designs and so are able to develop highly original, conceptual design proposals. However, such proposals do have to be realistic and justified from a variety of perspectives.

One way of ensuring such realism is to require learners to take into account four factors:

1 The technology that is available for use. This should be a new and/or emerging technology and be concerned primarily with how the new product or service will work. In this case learners need not be concerned with manufacture.
2 The society in which the technology will be used. This will include the prevailing values of the society, what is thought to be important and worthwhile. This in turn will govern whether a particular application of technology will be welcomed and supported.
3 The needs and wants of the people who might use the product or service. If the product does not meet the needs and wants of a sufficiently large number of people, then it will not be commercially successful.
4 The market that might exist or could be created for the products or services. Ideally, the market should be one with the potential to grow, one that will last, and one that adapts to engage with developments in technology and changes in society.

Clearly, these factors interact with one another and influence the sorts of products and services that can be developed and will be successful. This framework for designing can be represented diagrammatically as a tetrahedron as shown in Figure 6.2. In developing and

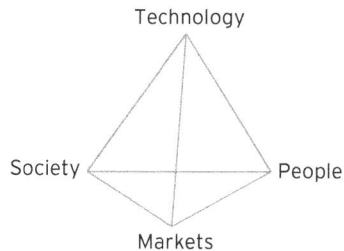

Figure 6.2 A 'tetrahedron' showing four factors to take into account when designing products and services for the future

justifying the design proposal learners have to visit each vertex of the tetrahedron. There need be no prescribed starting point but it is generally simplest to start with the technology and what it can do.

Here is the situation in the classroom. The learners are in Year 8. The teacher wants to develop their designing skills through a designing without making task and thought that any of the following new and emerging technologies involving modern materials might be appropriate: Quantum Tunnelling Composite (QTC), aerogels, and shape memory alloys. The learners were provided with web links to information about each of these materials so that they could find out about their properties as a starting point to considering what they might be used for.

The teacher had in mind the following learning intentions:

- Learn about new technologies
- Learn to develop creative design ideas
- Learn to justify design ideas
- To develop communication and collaboration skills.

To achieve this, the teacher organised the learners to work in mixed ability groups of four and gave them a single lesson to find out about their chosen material and consider possible uses. A further single lesson was allowed for developing justifications, and in a third lesson each group had to present their design ideas to the rest of the class and take feedback from the class. A fourth lesson was devoted to revising the design in the light of the feedback and developing a clear visual that

- Showed the product and services the group had designed

And

- Provided a justification of the proposal from the four perspectives.

The comments on the feasibility feature gives insight into whether the learners have learned about a new technology. The overall design provides insight into the creativity achieved. The comments on acceptability, appropriateness, and marketability provide insight into the extent that the learners have learned to justify their ideas.

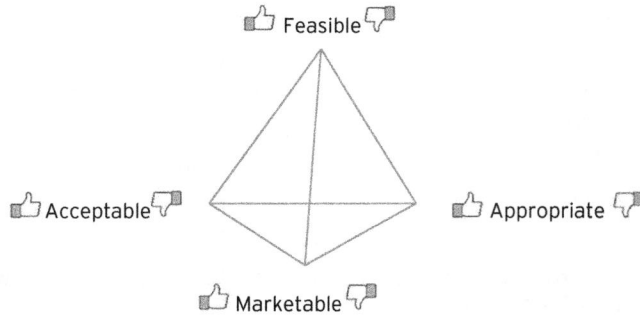

Figure 6.3 A 'thumbs up' / 'thumbs down' visual to support feedback for designing without making

At the end of the task each group will be able to discuss with the teacher their proposal and its justification. It is important that this doesn't get bogged down in too much detail. The visual in Figure 6.3 shows how the justification criteria might be presented to support feedback discussion with each group. The simple 'thumbs up' versus 'thumbs down' provides a focus for discussing the group's justification for their proposal. At the end of such a discussion the learners in each group will have a clear view of where they have been successful and where it is necessary to improve. This can be noted on the learners' assessment records with a brief comment on the way they collaborated and communicated. If this task becomes a topic of conversation with a learner's parents or carers, they know what the learner has to do to improve and can provide support and encouragement. More details concerning designing without making tasks can be found in Barlex (2012). The Young Foresight resources are available on the authors' website.

Feedback at the end of a considering consequences task

Considering consequences activities are likely to cover a wide range of issues such as the possibility of developing a circular economy, the possible impacts of disruptive technologies, the influences of iconic designers. It is important that learners become proficient in using tools that enable them to think about the effects, both good and bad, when technologies are deployed. Identifying winners and losers is a well-established visual technique for achieving this, which learners can be taught to use from the beginning of Key Stage 3. This is described in detail in Teaching Critique in chapter 4.

Here is the situation in the classroom. The learners are in Year 9. The teacher set the scene by providing some examples of the way robots were currently being used in society, e.g., surveillance, environmental monitoring, manufacturing, surgery, and companionship for the elderly. The learners were then organised to work in mixed ability groups of four and given a single lesson to develop their initial winners and losers chart with regard to the use of robots in society. In the next lesson, the teacher split the class into groups of winners and losers. Using the charts from the first lesson the winners argued that it was OK for them to win at the expense of the losers, whilst the losers argued that the winners should make some

Table 6.2 A 'thumbs up' / 'thumbs down' visual to support feedback for considering consequences

In the case of deploying robots in society, Ruth, Surrendra, Bart, and Eve could:		
	👍	👎
Identify winners		
Identify losers		
Argue for the winners		
Argue for the losers		

compensation for the damage they were causing the losers. For the final lesson, the teacher asked the learners to return to their original groups and required them to produce an agreed summary of the costs and benefits of deploying robots in our society. The summaries were shared across the class who then developed an agreed class summary, which was presented to a member of the SLT with a special interest in the design & technology curriculum.

Table 6.2 shows how an assessment of the work of the group might be presented to support feedback discussion with each group. This simple 'thumbs up' versus 'thumbs down' summary which should include brief agreed notes from the teacher provides a focus for discussing the group's justification for their proposal. At the end of such a discussion the learners in each group will have a clear view of where they have been successful and where it is necessary to improve. If this task becomes a topic of conversation with a learner's parents or carers, they know what their child has to do to improve and can provide support and encouragement.

Feedback at the end of a designing and making task

Designing and making tasks lie at the very heart of design & technology. In such tasks learners have to design, make, and evaluate a product that meets the needs and/or wants of an identified user. The teacher usually indicates the type of product to be designed and made for younger learners (Years 7, 8, and 9), but older learners are required to explore a context to identify problems that can be met through designing and making and then develop their own design brief for an as yet unidentified product that will solve one of the problems.

In the case where the teacher has decided upon the type of product to be designed, it is relatively easy to identify preliminary learning that will be useful in the design activity. Such learning might include aspects of:

- technical understanding (to inform how the product might work),
- aesthetics (to inform what the product might look like),
- construction (to inform how the product might be made)
- investigating user requirements (to inform how needs and wants might be identified).

Teachers can use this preliminary learning to ensure that there is progression across a sequence of designing and making tasks, i.e., that learners have to use a greater range and depth of knowledge, understanding, skill, and values in response to the tasks. It will be important for teachers to write criteria describing different levels of achievement in any response to the task. Three different levels for each of designing, making, and evaluating will provide enough discrimination between learner's differing achievements. The following vocabulary can be used to differentiate the response:

• Designing may be Modest, Moderate, or Outstanding;
• Making may be Limited, Adequate, or Excellent
• Evaluation may be Basic, Reasonable, or Insightful.

The teacher has worked with others who will be teaching this task and together they have developed and agreed upon the assessment criteria shown in Table 6.3. They have a shared understanding of how a piece of work would reflect the criteria. Note that each of statements is substantiated by examples of the sort of work that the learner operating at that level of achievement might attain.

A learner's response can be graphically represented as a tripod with learner's performance across the criteria presented by drawing a line between the variously coloured discs as shown in Figure 6.4.

Here is the situation in the classroom. The learners are towards the end of Year 8. The teacher has set the class the task of designing and making a moving toy that is powered by a small electric motor. Learners must take into account the user of the toy and design a toy that:

• moves in a way that will appeal to the user,
• has an appearance which pleases the user,
• can incorporate a range of special effects – light and sound – that will give the toy more play value for the user.

The basis of the toy is a simple motorised frame as shown in Figure 6.5.

In order to provide feedback to a learner at the end of a designing and making task, it is essential to have a record, all on the same sheet, consisting of the following:

• A description of the assignment
• An image of the item the pupil had produced
• The table listing the criteria.

This gives anyone reading the sheet, including learners themselves, all the information needed to think about the learner's achievement in the particular designing and making task. At the bottom of such a record of achievement sheet, there might be a sequence of tripods each with the appropriate lines showing how the learner had performed in previous designing and making tasks, thus giving a record of how the learner was progressing with this aspect of design & technology across five or six designing and making assignments during

Table 6.3 Assessment criteria for a designing and making task

	Modest	Moderate	Outstanding
Designing	Identification of a narrow set of user preferences and the design taking only limited account of these, e.g., simple movement, dull appearance, and limited special effects.	Identification of a wide set of user preferences and the design taking account of these, e.g., intriguing movement, unusual appearance, and some special effects	Identification of a full set of user preferences and the design taking account of these in novel ways, e.g., surprising movement, imaginative appearance, and exciting special effects
	Limited	*Adequate*	*Excellent*
Making	The quality of making is basic and in some cases poorly carried out preventing the toy working properly and detracting from its appearance, e.g., the motor shaft and pulley wheel are poorly aligned, the axles 'bind' and do not run smoothly, the net forming the body shell is crumpled.	The quality of making is sound and enables the toy to work properly and look attractive, e.g., the chassis is 'square' allowing the axles to run smoothly, the net forming body shell has been masked/ sprayed carefully, the switch controlling the motor is well mounted in a sensible place.	The quality of making is high and enables the complex technical workings to function well and the toy to have high visual appeal, e.g., the cam operating three switches in sequence works reliably, the body shell is composed of three separate nets joined 'invisibly'.
	Basic	*Reasonable*	*Insightful*
Evaluating	The evaluation considers a few features and makes only limited comments, e.g., written from the view of the learner designer as opposed to the actual user with no observation of the user playing with the toy.	The evaluation considers most of the relevant features and makes sound comments on each, e.g., takes into account the performance of the toy and the users views.	The evaluation considers all relevant features and makes thorough comments on each, e.g., not only takes into account the performance and users views but also makes suggestions for improvements.

Key Stage 3. It will be important to ensure that learners at least maintain their achievements and do not regress.

It is important to remember that the criteria on which this performance is assessed are task specific, and it will be part of the remit of those teaching at Key Stage 3 to ensure that the tasks become progressively more demanding across time and that this increasing demand is reflected in the criteria they write. This won't be easy but will focus departments' efforts on devising a learning journey that is progressive with regard to designing and making. It is easy

DESIGNING

MAKING

EVALUATING

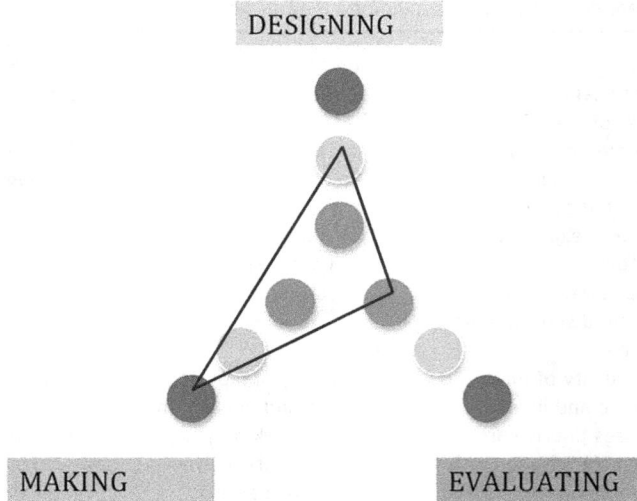

Figure 6.4 A 'traffic lights' assessment tripod

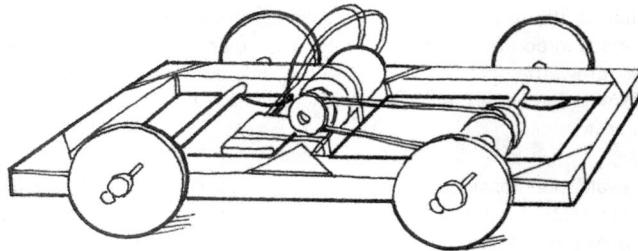

Figure 6.5 A simple motorised frame as the basis for a moving toy

to imagine such progress tracking sheets being the focus of useful discussions taking place with learners. During Key Stage 3 the on-going data provided could be used to help learners discuss with the teachers what they need to do to improve. Towards the end of Key Stage 3 the overview provided should be a great help to parents/carers and learners in thinking about GCSE prospects in design & technology should the learner choose the subject.

Pause for thought

When the teachers in your department are discussing with learners and their parents/carers whether taking design & technology GCSE is a viable option for their child, what criteria do they consider as relevant to the choice? To what extent do all the teachers use the same criteria? How are such criteria determined?

Identifying impact

The Ofsted Inspection Framework (HMSO, 2022) has three features: intention, implementation, and impact, and this section is concerned with impact. As design & technology teachers we must ask to what extent do we and can we know our impact. In exploring this we must be focused on 'what has been learned?' as opposed to 'what has been done?'. One way to find out what has been learned is to use pre- and post-activity questions related to the learning that is expected to take place through an activity, such as a designing and making assignment. This approach may reveal that whilst some learners have made learning gains others, whilst successful in carrying out the activity, have not learned anything new. Yet others might even have regressed. Such information is important if we are to ensure that in design & technology learners make progress in their learning.

A general approach

If learners are to be taught through a designing and making task, it is usually necessary to provide some preliminary learning that will be useful in tackling the task. Such learning often comes in the form of short learning activities sometimes described as Resource Tasks or Focused Practical Tasks. This was discussed in chapter 3. In terms of knowing the impact of the teaching of the preliminary learning and the designing and making task, there are two features to consider: the learning that takes place in the preliminary learning and the extent to which that learning is used in the designing and making task. To understand what learning has taken place through the preliminary learning, it is necessary to assess the amounts of knowledge, understanding, and skills the learners have *before* they tackle this learning. This may be achieved through a written test, Test 1, in which learners are required to indicate their previous experience, if any, with particular making skills, or designing particular sorts of artefacts, alongside the knowledge and understanding of relevant areas of technical understanding. It is important that the learners realise that this test is aimed at informing the teacher about what they have done in the past and already know so that the teacher can ensure everyone in the class gets some new learning out of the designing and making task.

The learners then carry out the preliminary learning followed by the designing and making task, after which they are given another written test, Test 2, made up of identical or equivalent questions to those used for Test 1.

The difference between learners' results for Test 2 and Test 1 will give an indication of the learning that has taken place. Inspection of the way they tackled the designing and making task and the artefact they produced will give some insight into the extent to which they have used their preliminary learning. This will give the teacher an appreciation of the impact they have had on the learning and enable improvements to be made the next time the task is taught. Figure 6.6 summarises this process.

A specific example

Let us consider the specific example of a designing and making task that requires each learner to design and make an illuminated mask suitable for use in a school play in which there are scenes of darkness.

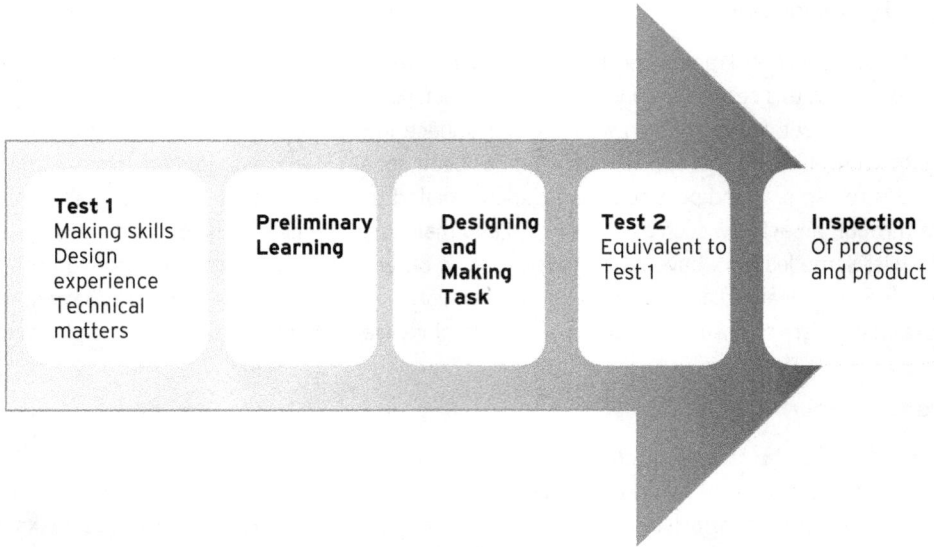

Figure 6.6 A general approach to identifying impact

To be successful in this task learners will need to have:
Technical knowledge and understanding about simple electrical lighting circuits, including:

- basic switching to control the lighting circuits
- how to construct such circuits.

Making knowledge and skills to construct mask forms including:

- selecting materials (such as card, plastic, textiles, or a combination of these)
- applying decoration to the surface of these materials
- accommodating the lighting circuits into the mask
- holding the masks in place.

Possible test items

Some of these items should audit learners' previous making experience. For example:

- Have you ever made anything from card? If so, please describe it using a sketch and notes.
- Have you ever made anything from plastic? If so, please describe it using a sketch and notes.
- Have you ever made anything from textiles? If so, please describe it using a sketch and notes.
- Have you ever applied surface decoration to textiles? If so, please describe it using a sketch and notes.
- Have you ever soldered electrical circuits? If so, please describe what you did using a sketch and notes.

Simply sorting these into a set of yes/no piles will give a clear indication of the learners' previous making experience. As learners move through the school, teachers will be aware of their learning experiences hence this approach will be useful for learners who are 'late arrivals'.

Some of the items should audit learners' previous designing experience. For example:

- Have you ever designed anything that includes electrical circuits? If so, please give a list of the things you have designed.
- Have you ever designed anything based on card, plastic or textiles? If so, please give a list of the things you have designed.
- For each item you have designed, indicate how difficult you found this: It was easy / I had some problems / It was hard

Sorting these into sets of the kinds of items that learners have previously designed will give an overview of the designing experience of members of the class.

Some of the items should test learners' knowledge and understanding of simple electrical circuits. For example:

- Provide some photographs of electrical circuits involving simple lighting and equivalent circuit diagrams and ask for the circuit diagrams to be matched to the photographs
- Provide some circuit diagrams including switches and ask learners to predict what will happen when particular switches are operated.

Based on the responses from the test, the teacher will be able to provide a suite of preliminary learning tasks providing learning that is likely to be useful for tackling the designing and making task, and indicate which of these that particular learners should do according to the information from the test. Some learners might need to do most of the preliminary learning tasks whilst others might need to do only a few. For those who need to do only a few, it is possible to provide extension tasks that take their knowledge, understanding and skill further with the expectation that this learning will play out in the sophistication of the mask they eventually design and make.

Ideally, we would want all learners to do better in Test 2 than in Test 1; in devising the preliminary task suite to ensure new learning relevant to the designing and making task the teacher has tried to achieve this. However, this may not be the case for all learners, and it is important to investigate the causes. Some learners may have simply 'stood still' with no new learning demonstrated, using what they already knew to perform competently in designing and making their light-up mask. For such learners, it will be important to find ways of increasing their aspiration so that they are not satisfied with 'coasting'. Some learners may appear to have 'gone backwards' in that they performed less well in Test 2 than in Test 1. It will be important to look closely at the mask they have produced as this might indicate that significant new learning was used in producing the item and this has not been reflected in the Test 2 score. However, if the mask produced was of little merit, then there is the need to have serious conversations with such learners about how they can improve their progress.

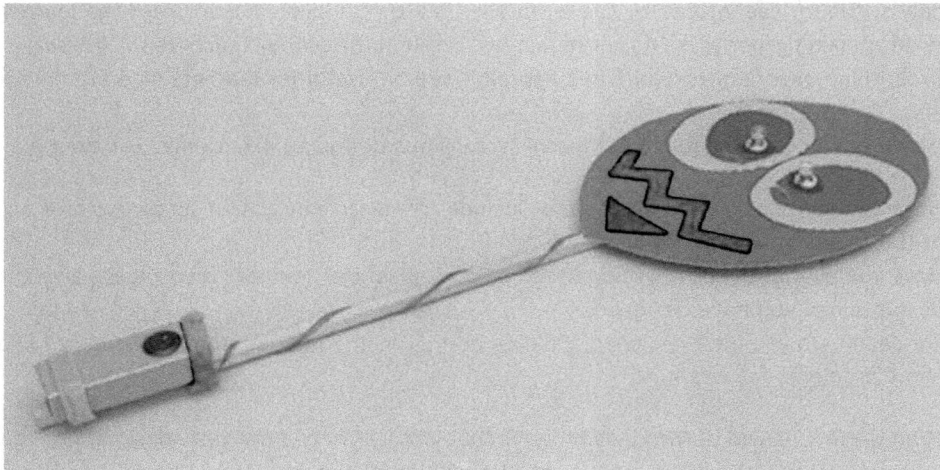

Figure 6.7 A relatively simple response to the task

For those learners who have shown increased learning that was applied in designing and making their masks there is cause for acknowledgement and congratulation with the expectation that such progress will be maintained in the next designing and making task.

Two possible outcomes

The light-up mask shown in Figure 6.7 is a relatively simple response to the task with the following features:

• The mask is made from card
• The mask is 2D
• The mask does not attach to the head but is held up by a stick
• The circuit is a simple series circuit involving light bulbs
• There is a simple on off switch allowing the eyes to 'blink'
• The switch is incorporated into a battery housing which is attached to the stick.

If this mask has been made by a learner with little previous experience of working with card or knowledge of electrical circuits, then it is a great achievement. On the other hand, if the learner has had a lot of experience in working with card and significant knowledge of electrical circuits then although an adequate solution to the task it is not a particularly great achievement; the learner has been coasting.

The light up-mask shown in Figure 6.8 is a more complex response to the task with the following features:

• The mask is made from card
• The mask is 3D

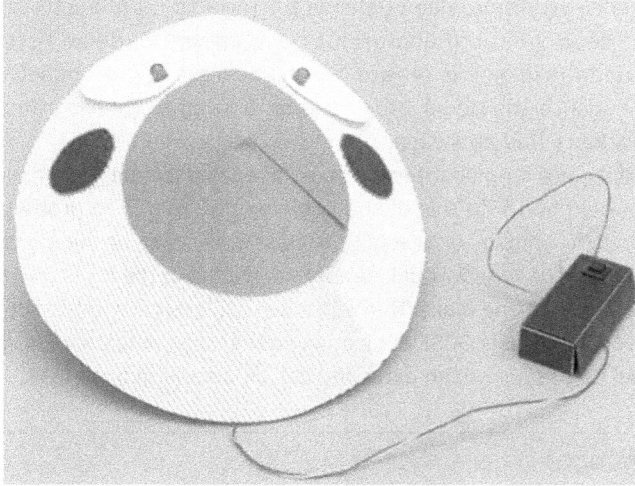

Figure 6.8 A more complex response to the task

- The mask is worn on the head
- The circuit is a parallel circuit involving LEDs
- The switch controlling the LEDs is a double pole double throw switch with a neutral position which allows each eye to wink but does not allow blinking
- The switch is incorporated into a battery housing which is held by the operator.

The designing and making of this mask clearly requires greater knowledge, understanding and skill than that required for the mask shown in Figure 6.7. The difference in the test scores for a learner producing such a response will give an indication of the extent to which new learning has informed the response.

In conclusion

What are we to make of this approach to *knowing thy impact*? Is it possible to use this across a sequence of designing and making assignments so that the teacher can ensure there is new learning taking place for all learners and that this informs the quality of the designing and making taking place? This would certainly require a design & technology department to commit to using previous learning tasks in conjunction with designing and making tasks. Providing an appropriate bank of designing and making tasks and related previous learning tasks is a major undertaking although a wide range of examples of such tasks were produced by the Nuffield Design & Technology Project for both KS3 and KS4 and these are available as free downloads at https://dandtfordandt.wordpress.com as Capability Tasks and Resource Tasks. Writing the test items for Tests 1 and 2 is also a major exercise and as yet we are not aware of banks of such tests on which teachers might draw. However, close scrutiny of the learning requirements for each of the designing and making tasks in the sequence would provide guidance for the writing of such tests. So, whilst we acknowledge that developing the approach to assessment outlined here is a major and time-consuming undertaking, the reward will be to reveal the impact of the teaching taking place and enhance the rigour of the design & technology programme of study of a department that adopts this approach.

Rather than setting pre- and post-tests as part of each designing and making task, a more limited approach would be to do this at the beginning of Year 7 to probe previous primary school learning and the impact of teaching a class their first designing and making task. Repeating this at the end of Year 9 would identify the impact of the KS3 curriculum with regard to learners' ability to design and make. This will be particularly relevant for those learners who opt for design & technology as a GCSE subject given that the contextual challenge required as a Non-Examination Assessment is an extended designing and making task.

Pause for thought

Given that assessing impact is part of the Education Inspection Framework it is worth a department considering how they might explore the impact of their teaching. This will entail developing a clear and shared understanding of what it means to get better at design & technology over time and how this is embedded in the KS3 and KS4 schemes of work.

Public examinations

The results of public examinations provide a snapshot of the level of achievement by a candidate at a particular time. In schools the results of GCSE examinations are used by SLT to look at the performance of learners in particular subjects across time and also to compare differences in performance between different subjects. This data may of course be used as a means of discerning the effectiveness of subject departments and individual teachers within a department. Such scrutiny can be the basis for providing support and guidance and identifying professional development requirements. The government uses the results to compare the performance of different schools by means of Attainment 8 and Progress 8. The situation is complicated by the government's introduction of the English Baccalaureate (the EBacc) a school performance measure based on a school's results in English language and literature, Mathematics, the sciences, geography, or history, and a language. The nature of the Progress 8 and Attainment 8 measures are described in in detail on the government website (https://assets.publishing.service.gov.uk/government/uploads/system/uploads/attachment_data/file/561021/Progress_8_and_Attainment_8_how_measures_are_calculated.pdf).

The government argues that it privileges the EBacc subjects because these are gatekeeper subjects in that success in these subjects opens doors to many courses in further and higher education. They also argue that the choice of a further three subjects ensures a broad and balanced education up to the age of 16 years. So, in theory design & technology should be able to take its place as one of these other three subjects. The devil, as always is in the detail. Those learners who opt for triple science, for example, may find that they have only one further subject available which may well limit the numbers of such learners opting for design & technology. Those learners who find academic subjects overly demanding might opt for a single, general science course, and they will find they have a full range of choice in the remaining three which may, in some schools lead to an uptake of design & technology by learners who will find the assessment demands of both the written paper and the extended project (the contextual challenge) overly demanding. This may lead to poor examination performance to the detriment of the subject in the other performance measures. Suffice it to say here that the best way to deal with these difficulties is to provide an excellent, engaging, and challenging KS3 design & technology course such that your learners find the thought of taking GCSE design & technology irresistible and if the option arrangements for KS4 make it difficult if not impossible for them to study design & technology their parents beat a path to the head teacher's door demanding a change in the arrangements! Note also that GCSE grades used by learners in identifying strengths and weaknesses before choosing subjects for further study are also used by employers and HE providers in considering whether to accept learners' applications.

Design & technology GCSE

Ofqual (2016) laid down the assessment framework for design & technology in terms of four assessment objectives. Their weighting across the two assessment items – a non-examined assessment (NEA) and a written paper are summarized in Table 6.4. This summary was supplemented by unpacking the precise meanings of the terms used in objective statements as shown in Tables 6.5 a), b), c), and d).

This framework with its clarifications of interpretations and definitions plus the resultant specifications made much greater demand on learners and teachers than previous design & technology GCSEs. There were, and still are, two main areas of concern – the NEA and the written paper. These are now discussed in detail.

Table 6.4 Distribution of marks according to assessment objectives (AO) and assessment items in GCSE D&T

	Objective	Weighting	NEA	Written Paper
AO1	Identify, investigate and outline design possibilities to address needs and wants	10%	10%	0%
AO2	Design and make prototypes that are fit for purpose	30%	30%	0%
AO3	Analyse and evaluate:	20%	10%	10%
	Design decisions and outcomes including prototypes made by themselves and others			
	Wider issues in design and technology			
AO4	Demonstrate and apply knowledge and understanding of:	40%	0%	40%
	Technical principles			
	Designing and making principles			
Totals		100%	50%	50%

Table 6.5 a

AO1: Identify, investigate, and outline design possibilities to address needs and wants			10%
Strands	Elements	Coverage	Interpretation
n/a	1a – Identify and investigate design possibilities to address needs and wants. 1b – outline design possibilities to address needs and wants.	Full coverage in every task that addresses it. A reasonable balance between elements 1a and 1b.	Identify means looking at areas and opportunities in which designs can take place. Investigate means pursuing ideas and gathering information relating to a context. Identify and investigate are interdependent. The processes work together and take place in no particular order. Outline means to produce a design brief and specification to inform AO2.

Table 6.5 b

AO2: Design and make prototypes that are fit for purpose			30%
Strands	Elements	Coverage	Interpretation and definitions
n/a	This assessment objective is a single element.	Full coverage in every task that addresses it.	Design means the generation and development of ideas that can be presented to a third party, and can be evaluated and tested. However, the actual analysis and evaluation forms part of AO3. Prototype means an appropriate working solution to a need or want that is sufficiently developed to be tested and evaluated (for example, full sized products, scaled working models, or functioning systems). In the context of a prototype, fit for purpose means (in addition to being a working solution) addressing the needs/wants of the intended user. Making skills can be assessed through the designing and making of the prototype(s), as well as the nature and quality of the final prototype.

Table 6.5 c

AO3: Analyse and evaluate -
- *design decisions and outcomes, including for prototypes made by themselves and others*
- *wider issues in design & technology*

20%

Strands	Elements	Coverage	Interpretation and definitions
1 - Analyse and evaluate design decisions and outcomes, including for prototypes made by themselves and others.	1a - Analyse design decisions and outcomes, including for prototypes made by themselves and others. 1b - Evaluate design decisions and outcomes, including for prototypes made by themselves and others.	Full coverage in each set of assessments (but not in every assessment). A reasonable balance between the strands within this assessment objective, and between the elements within each strand.	In the context of this assessment objective: Analyse means deconstructing information and/or issues to find connections and provide logical chain(s) of reasoning. Evaluate means appraising and/or making judgements with respect to information and/or issues. Analysis and evaluation should draw on underpinning knowledge and understanding.
2 - Analyse and evaluate wider issues in design & technology.	2a - Analyse wider issues in design & technology. 2b - Evaluate wider issues in design & technology.		Each set of assessments need not cover both design decisions and outcomes in the context of both prototypes made by the Learner and prototypes made by others. But there should be a reasonable balance between each of:: Design decisions and outcomes. Prototypes made by the Learner, prototypes made by others, and other contexts within design & technology.

Table 6.5 d

AO4: Demonstrate and apply knowledge and understanding of:
- Technical principles
- Designing and making principles

40%

Strands	Elements	Coverage	Interpretation and definitions
1 – Demonstrate and apply knowledge and understanding of technical principles.	1a – Demonstrate knowledge of technical principles. 1b – Demonstrate understanding of technical principles. 1c – Apply knowledge and understanding of technical principles.	Full coverage in each set of assessments (but not in every assessment). No more than 10% of total marks should reward demonstrating knowledge in isolation.	Both technical principles and designing and making principles are aspects of subject content. Awarding organisations should explain their approach to targeting them in their assessment strategies. The emphasis in this assessment objective should be on the demonstration and application of knowledge and understanding of technical principles.
2 – Demonstrate and apply knowledge and understanding of designing and making principles.	2a – Demonstrate knowledge of designing and making principles. 2b – Demonstrate understanding of designing and making principles. 2c – Apply knowledge and understanding of designing and making principles.	A reasonable balance between the elements in each strand.	

The NEA

In previous design & technology GCSE's, it was permissible for a learner to decide on what she was going to design and make, whom it was for and where it would be used. These three features are clearly related and inform one another but usually the learner decided first on the 'something', then on the 'somebody' and then the 'situation', e.g., a small storage unit, for my younger brother to go in his bedroom. This has been called the 'triple S' approach to designing and making.

Now the position has been reversed. The learner has to explore the situation, the context, first to identify problems being experienced by people in that context, then choose one of these problems that she can solve by designing and making an artifact of some kind and then identify what sort of artifact this will be. Hence the learner is starting in a position of considerable uncertainty and, as she moves through the challenge, becoming more and more confident as she resolves the issues facing her and can begin to make definitive design decisions. Different Awarding Organisations will have their own particular requirements as to the detail of how the contextual challenge should be tackled to meet their assessment requirements, but we think the following three phase model provides a useful overview in general agreement with most Awarding Organisation's requirements.

In Phase 1 ...

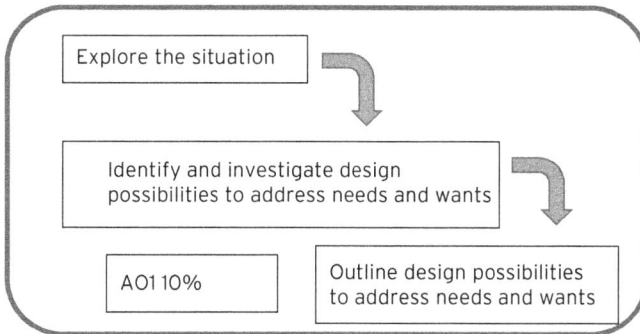

In this phase learners face considerable uncertainty. Just what will they find in the context that helps identify needs and wants? What sort of needs and wants will there be? And there is no guarantee that the needs and wants they identify can be resolved with the sort of designing and making they feel comfortable with. And what if they decide on something and it doesn't pan out and they have to begin again? The learners have to decide on the sort of item that can meet the needs and wants of the people in the context. They are on the cusp of making a conceptual design decision that will underpin all the other design decisions they make as they move from this concept (an idea in the mind) to the item(s) they actually produce (a physical artifact). Understandably they will be concerned that they might make a decision that proves unsound. So, this can be a butterfly in the tummy situation. Hence it is important that they have been in similar situations in their design & technology curriculum before. They have to record their thinking as it happens to provide assessment evidence for AO1 and as this activity is part of a public examination the teacher can provide only minimal guidance.

In Phase 2 ....

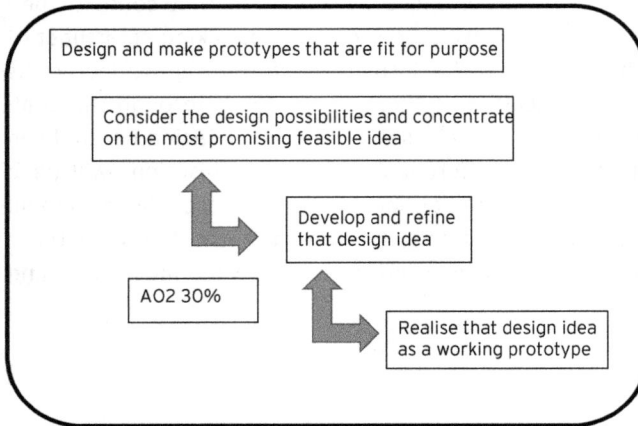

In this phase the learners are moving onto less shaky ground. In Phase 1 they have outlined design possibilities that have potential and now they have to decide on the most promising or feasible idea. With this in mind they will start to start develop the details of that design – how it might work, what it will look like, how it might be made, the materials and components required, and how all this will appeal to all those who have some sort of stake in the final outcome. If this proves difficult it may be that they will need to revisit their work in Phase 1 to develop further design possibilities, hence the double headed arrow but it is important that they move back into Phase 2 activities as quickly as possible. Almost inevitably they will need to produce a range of different types of models to resolve these issues before they are in a position to draw up the detailed plans required for manufacture and then to actually make their design. It is worth noting that as the making takes place, issues will emerge that require the design to be further refined, hence the double headed arrow linking these activities. Learners have to keep a real time record of this process to provide assessment evidence for AO2. Again, the teacher may provide only minimal guidance, and there is the temptation for the learners to 'over egg' the pudding in producing their evidence. Our view is that 'less is more' and an Occam's razor approach should be adopted. Only do and record that which helps with making the design decisions. Do not spend time on unnecessary embellishment.

In Phase 3

The elements of AO3 that are relevant here are as follows:

- Analyse design decisions and outcomes, including for prototypes made by themselves and others
- Evaluate design decisions and outcomes, including for prototypes made by themselves and others.

The interpretation and definition details provided by Ofqual indicate that the analysis of the design decisions made should inform the evaluation.

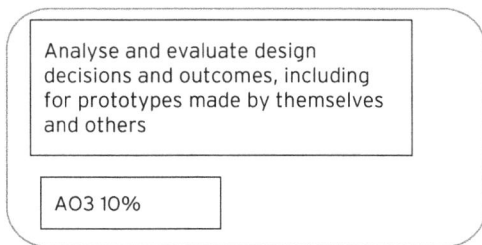

Analyse and evaluate design decisions and outcomes, including for prototypes made by themselves and others

AO3 10%

In this phase there is little if any uncertainty. The design idea has been transformed into physical reality, prototypes, that can be seen, held, touched, and used. In meeting the requirements for analysis and evaluation the following set of questions shown in Panel 6.1 provides a useful starting point

In the case of 'Did it do what it was supposed to do?' utilisation of the performance specification may be seen as analysis and the comparison with each item therein as evaluation. In the case of 'Was it well made?' the 'looking' to identify aspects of making may be seen as analysis and making a judgment as to their quality as evaluation. In the case of 'Will it last?' the learner has to deliberately put the prototype under various sorts of stress – dropping, pulling,

Panel 6.1

- Did it do what it was supposed to do?
  - Find out by comparing the way the product functions with each item in the performance specification
- Was it well made?
  - Look and see
- Will it last?
  - Treat it roughly and see
- Was it easy to use?
  - Take a user trip or observe a user trip
- Did it delight the user
  - Talk to the user
- And of course record your findings

pushing, banging – and this may be seen as analysis. Observing the way the prototype responds and commenting on this will constitute evaluation. In the case of 'Was it easy to use?' there is the opportunity for learners to involve others in the exercise as well as themselves. They can use the prototype, ask others to use it, watch them and ask questions. These others might be potential users or clients. Recording the responses may be seen as analysis and then judging the extent to which these constitute ease of use is evaluation. In the case of 'Did it delight the user?' developing questions for the user to answer and recording the answers may be seen as analysis whilst interpreting these in the light of how delightful the item was to use is evaluation.

The Awarding Organisations give details of the contexts in the year prior to which the learner wishes to be awarded the qualification and the candidates work on this challenge for the rest of that academic year and the following academic year in order to submit their portfolio, sometimes in electronic format for internal, standardized, moderated marking by a deadline date, usually during the month of May. Candidates will have some 40 hours overall in which to complete the contextual challenge and are advised not to spend overly large amounts of time on their portfolio. It is worth noting that any practical work produced outside the classroom does not count towards the assessment although portfolio work can as long as it can be authenticated by the teacher. The Awarding Organisations provide grade related criteria statements for each of the Assessment Objectives which teachers are required to use when marking learners' work. Examination Centres are required to send a selection of portfolios to the Awarding Organisation to ensure comparability between Centres and the maintenance of standards year on year.

It is here that we think it is useful to turn to the work of Richard Kimbell who has pioneered the use of Adaptive Comparative Judgement as a valid and reliable means of assessment which provides an alternative to the conventional approaches to assessment involving teachers and examiners judging the quality of learners work by reference to lists of criteria or other 'outcome' statements as described above. Here is his Thought Piece on the topic.

All assessment judgements are comparative – *A Thought Piece by Richard Kimbell*

Richard Kimbell is Emeritus Professor, Goldsmiths University of London.

Imagine for a moment that you are holding an apple. How heavy do you think it is? Is it 15 gms or maybe 18 or 22? Ask this question of a group of friends and they will all give you a different answer. And most of them will be wrong. It is interesting that whilst we know exactly what the apple is, and we know exactly what a gram is, we are astonishingly unable to judge how many grams it weighs. And the error is typically huge; you can expect answers ranging from 5–50.

Imagine now that you are holding two apples – one in each hand. I know it's no good asking you how much they weigh, because you will get that wrong. So I'll ask a different question. Which is heavier? As you consider that question, with your hands (like the scales of justice) 'weighing' the two apples, you will decide with ease which is heavier. And if you ask the same group of friends what they think, they will all give the same answer, and they will all be correct.

The explanation of this phenomenon is pretty obvious. In the single apple case, the numbers are arbitrary and meaningless, and the only way you can get a purchase on the problem is by trying to imagine a weight that you know (e.g., a bag of sugar is 1 kg). To make sense of meaningless numbers you have to invent a comparator. But in the two-apple case, they are their own direct comparators, so the judgement is simple and the result is reliable.

Imagine finally that you are in charge of assessment policy for the whole nation. Which principle of assessment shall we use? We could use a system of meaningless numbers, within which a piece of work is assessed and given a score by every teacher, and most are wrong, and inter-marker reliability is shockingly bad, and no-one trusts the result. Or we could use a system of direct comparative judgement within which every teacher makes correct judgements (because the comparators make it so simple), and inter-marker reliability is therefore astonishingly high. Which of these options shall we choose? You guessed it. We'll use numbers. Because we always have. And because exam boards love them.

The first tragedy of this choice is that the approach requires a piece of real performance to be split into hundreds of little bits of performance (ideas / research / making, etc.) and each is assigned a meaningless number. Teachers then waste hours and hours of their lives poring over lengthy assessment sheets. When considering a single quality, 'Shall I give this piece 5/20 or maybe its 6/20 or 7/20'. You desperately search for a comparator, 'I gave Sean 6/20 and I know this is better so it must be 8/20 or maybe even 10/20'. We make judgements by comparison even when we think we are using numbers. And exam boards compound the nonsense that they have created by providing endless words trying (and failing) to describe the quality in question. Quality cannot be described in words. It can only be judged by comparison (see Polanyi M. [1958] Personal Knowledge, Routledge).

But the real tragedy is that a properly workable system of direct comparative judgement was developed a decade ago as 'project e-scape' at Goldsmiths University of London in association with the Qualifications and Curriculum Authority. It has been proved to work in schools and could be used for GCSE assessments. But instead – like so many great ideas developed in Britain – it is finding more receptive ears overseas.

For teachers interested in reading about how it works, and trying it for yourself, see: https://rmresults.com/digital-assessment-solutions/rmcompare.

What are we to make of Richard's Thought Piece? We can see how a department might use the comparative pairs approach at, say towards the end of Year 9, to assess a significant designing and making task, the results to be used to inform discussion with parents and students about whether taking GCSE D&T in Year 10 and Year 11 is a sensible choice. Imagine the option choice conversation with a student and parent going something like this:

PARENT: *'I can see that our Shanaz is in the middle and if she stays there her grade probably won't be that good.'*
SHANAZ: *'But I really do enjoy it, Dad.'*
PARENT: *'I know, Shani, and it's important you study subjects you enjoy. My question is, "What does Shani have to do, and how can we help her do it, to move her position in the rank order from around the middle to being in the top 10%?"'*
And the teacher says, *'I think that the assessment data collected at the "end of task assessments" over Key Stage 3 might come into play there.'*

Pause for thought

As usual Richard has presented a provocative and challenging view on assessment. To what extent do you think it would be useful to adopt this approach, for example, in assessing a significant designing and making task carried out by learners towards the end of Year 9, to inform their suitability for studying design & technology in Key Stage 4?

However the assessment of NEA changes in the future, it seems unlikely that their intrinsic nature of being an extended task in response to candidate identified needs and wants will be compromised and it is therefore essential that the KS3 curriculum includes designing and making tasks that prepare students for such an endeavour.

The written paper

Previous GCSE design & technology specifications were 'media' specific in that candidates could specialise in one of textiles, graphics, food, resistant materials, electronics, or systems and control. The introduction of new specifications removed food as a material area for design & technology and required that all candidates should have a broad knowledge across the range of media (core knowledge) plus at least one chosen specialist media in which they should have deeper knowledge (specialist knowledge). The written examination would assess the candidate's core knowledge as well as their chosen specialist knowledge. This presented two problems. Firstly, the total amount of content to be assessed had increased and secondly the teachers with a specialist knowledge in a particular area might find teaching core content outside this specialist knowledge challenging. The wider range of content can to some extent be addressed by the content of the KS3 curriculum which should teach learners a significant amount of the core content such that the majority of this is covered BEFORE learners begin the GCSE examination course. This is common practice in the science curriculum, and we cannot see why this should not be the case for the design & technology curriculum. Of course, it will be necessary to revisit some of the material taught at KS3, but this should not require large amounts of teaching time. The second problem may to some extent be tackled by a circus approach in which appropriately qualified teachers teach particular items of core content on a rotational basis. This has the disadvantage of disrupting the contact between learners and teachers and in many small departments is not a possibility. The preferred approach in our opinion is that teachers take part in the necessary in-service training to be able to teach across the core content. In departments with several members of staff with differing specialities, this may be achieved on a self-help basis, but in small departments this will require input for outside specialists. And in both situations, it is important that the department makes the case for this in service training with SLT so that the necessary resources of time and funding are made available.

Candidates will need to answer different type of questions in the written paper. It is important, therefore, that they have significant experience of answering such questions well before they sit the written paper. One way of providing such experience is through homework activities which not only give practice at answering different types of question but explicitly teach about the nature of particular types of question and strategies for answering them. This is particularly important for those questions that require extended written answers and cover more than one item in the specification – synoptic questions. Panel 6.2 presents a summary of some of the different sorts of question that candidates might face in the written paper.

Panel 6.2 Possible written paper question types

The written paper may require candidates:

- To remember names of, for example, materials, types of materials, properties of materials, uses of materials, tools and their uses, components, types of components, and their behaviour. In some cases such questions may be presented as multiple-choice questions in which the candidate is given a choice of possible answers from which to choose the correct one.
- To identify a true statement from a selection of statements
- To provide descriptions of processes
- To provide justifications and/or explanations for technical, aesthetic, and manufacturing decisions
- To use their knowledge and understanding of design movements and designers to comment on and discuss products of various kinds
- To answer synoptic questions, discussing a particular issue from several points of view using examples and content from different parts of the specification. This might involve using knowledge and understanding from science to consider issues such as pollution, global warming, and resource depletion
- To complete partly finished scale drawings
- To interpret graphical information given in the form of, for example, pi charts, bar charts, or line graphs
- To calculate costs from given information
- To convert from imperial to metric units
- To use information in diagrams and tables to calculate features such as percentages, length, area, volume, angle, and mass
- To use information in diagrams and tables to calculate component values and behaviour in mechanical, electrical, and electronic systems.

Individually none of the features in Panel 6.2 is particularly difficult but taken together they represent a demanding examination of candidates' knowledge, understanding, skills, and values. Hence it is important that from the beginning of Key Stage 3 learners are introduced to the various type of question and become familiar with how to answer them. A department will need to ensure that the question types used match the types of question used in their specification. A drip feed approach from Year 7 will introduce learners, their parents and SLT to the requirements of the GCSE Assessment as well as provide useful preparation for the GCSE examination in Year 11 for those learners who opt for the subject at Key Stage 4.

Pause for thought

Does your department find itself in a position where, to comply with the school homework policy, it finds itself setting homework exercises that are not that beneficial to learners. Could setting past GCSE examination questions that relate to the knowledge and understanding being taught as homework for Key Stage 3 be a way out of this quandary?

At this stage in our discussion of design & technology GCSE, we thought it important to get the views on what we have written so far from someone working for an Awarding Organisation. So, it is to a Thought Piece by Louise Attwood, Head of Curriculum – Design & Technology at AQA, we now turn.

Valid assessment: grades and marks – *A Thought Piece by Louise Attwood*

Louise Attwood is the Head of Curriculum – Design & Technology for the Awarding Organisation AQA.

Introduction

Design & Technology in schools is a complex web of knowledge and skills requiring complex assessment techniques in order to ensure students gain the grades they deserve. Aside from the obvious assessment of in-depth knowledge, skills such as how well a student can analyse and evaluate information, whether they can respond to a client's needs and wants, and their ability to communicate solutions to problems through practical demonstration, all play a vital role in the breadth of picture necessary to assess competency across the subject. The process of assessment therefore is multifaceted, with no simplistic one-dimensional answer and a need for various stages to ensure consistency across students and from year to year. In this piece, I look at how grades are awarded, debunk myths about the simplicity of the marking process, and share good practice for high-level marking accuracy in the classroom.

Ensuring year-on-year comparability

Every year at AQA, we work through over 60% of all GCSE Design and Technology examination papers and NEA portfolios. Teachers play a crucial role in this process, assessing their students NEA portfolios against the published assessment criteria. Many also work as moderators and examiners for AQA, playing a valuable role in the quality assurance of marking and improving their own practice to develop solid marking judgements for their own students. Once NEA portfolios and exam papers are marked and quality assured, they go through a process called awarding. Here, we decide on where the grade boundaries for each individual qualification should sit in that particular year. These boundaries are set using both statistics and an assessment of candidates' performance by a group of lead examiners. The statistical data we use draws on information about that cohort of students, including their previous performance in SATs (when we set grade boundaries for GCSE), and GCSEs (when we set grade boundaries for A Level).

Students' prior attainment analysis is one way in which we ensure standards remain comparable year on year. Specifically, we compare each year's cohort's performance profile (how good on average their SATs or GCSEs were) to a reference cohort performance profile and use statistics to ensure that grade boundaries account for any differences. In other words, when a given cohort is 'stronger' or 'weaker' than that of the reference year, we know to expect a higher or lower number of high grades, and boundaries are adjusted accordingly.

Importantly, however, grade boundaries are never fixed and purposefully so, as they must have the flexibility to change each year to account for small inevitable variations in paper difficulty. Their positions can therefore be refined later in the process when expert judges review the completed scripts. It is important that we ensure fairness for students regardless of the year they complete their GCSE or A Level. Inevitably, exams can sometimes be slightly more or less difficult year on year, and performance in both the exam and NEA can vary for other factors outside of the ability level of students.

This is particularly obvious after the reform of a qualification and in the first year of entry. In this year, teachers don't have the same experience of teaching the course, they may not have as many past papers or resources available as they may gather in future years. Students are less clear of the expectations as they don't have previous cohorts' work to look at, only examples generated by exam boards or publishers, etc., and in the last round of reform, there was a purposeful decision by the DfE to increase the demand of qualifications. For that year, in most subjects you will have seen a slight lowering in the grade boundaries compared to the following years.

The use of data is a really important part of the awarding process, but we don't rely solely on the numbers, we involve the lead design & technology associates in a process of quality assurance. These highly qualified professionals go through individual examination papers and NEA portfolios to determine how many marks 'represent' a given attainment standard (e.g., a GCSE grade 4 or 7). They consider the difficulty of that year's paper or task, and set the grade boundary (3/4 or 6/7) at that mark. Awarding panels answer a very specific and technical, but crucial, question: how many marks are needed before we have enough evidence of a candidate's performance to claim with confidence that they have attained a certain grade? In other words: how good a candidate's work has to be (as summarised by number of marks) before we can say it is 'worth' a 4 rather than a 3? Inevitably discussions take place as to which students work is of a higher quality than another and judgements are made at, above, and below each grade boundary mark. This way we can see if there are examples of students' work that don't match the initial statistically recommended boundary and we can adjust the grade boundary to suit.

While teachers are giving students a mark rather than a grade; the process of coming to a judgement about the placement of each piece of work is similar, and we encourage teachers to have these discussions when assessing their own students.

Assessing NEA portfolios

When assessing your NEA portfolios, a number of factors are important, but the assessment criteria form the basis of this judgement. In Design & Technology NEA, we are not dealing with a one-dimensional assessment such as the relative height of students for example. Rather the quality of a student response is a multidimensional construct, and therefore the scaffolding that assessment criteria provide is necessary to ensure we are all assessing the same set of skills. What is important is that the judgement is not simply 'which one do I feel is better' as clearly 'better' means different things to different people, but which ones fulfil this specific assessment criteria best.

Read the assessment criteria carefully and consider the band that a student best fits into for each aspect of the portfolio. Remember that you are looking for evidence of each of the assessment criteria throughout the whole portfolio rather than in a distinct section. Investigation, for example, happens throughout the project, and you can award marks for examples of this wherever they occur in the design process.

Use the example portfolios available to you. These could be your previous students' work as long as your marks were upheld when moderated. More likely they will be examples marked by the lead examiner such as the marked examples/answers and commentaries on centre services and those in our 'Teacher Online Standardisation' tool. These are your benchmark and should allow for comparisons to be made between prior student performance and that of your own pupils.

Using both the assessment criteria and a comparison between benchmarked work and your students', it is possible to establish a rank order of achievement within an assessment band.

This may help you make decisions about the marks you give to students for that aspect of their portfolio.

In conclusion

When I was teaching, I would use rank ordering to help me to make judgements about where practical work sits in the assessment criteria. Practical work is the obvious choice for this type of assessment aid because of its visual nature. By considering each of the assessment bands carefully, and then moving prototypes around the room to create a rank order, I could make judgements about the success of each student against set criteria. Maybe you are clear on what band the students work sits but want to use rank ordering to add to your judgement of which marks to award within that band of assessment criteria.

In both classroom-based assessment and awarding, marks, and/or statistical data are important in anchoring assessment and providing benchmarks. But the human ability to make judgements is a part of what we have always done in design & technology.

Comparisons to other students' work are made and rank ordering may be used to help teachers to differentiate between evidence, but it is crucial that we do so within the parameters of the assessment criteria. This ensures that we are anchored to a standard and not to the subjective criteria of 'which NEA is better'. This way we only assess what we have told students we are assessing, we ensure transparency in terms of what is being assessed, keeping the goal posts clear for students to see, our marking is accurate, and it properly reflects the achievements of each individual.

Panel 6.3 provides links to several useful documents should you wish to read further about this important topic.

What are we to make of Louise's Thought Piece? Firstly, her piece reinforces our view that GCSE assessment of a subject inherently as complex as design & technology will be a demanding activity. Secondly that teachers are an essential and integral part of the process, and that without their involvement it would be impossible to produce valid and reliable assessment. Thirdly the interaction between teacher professional judgement and statistical data is an important feature of the overall activity; both are necessary and if assessment relied on just one of these components it would be less dependable.

Panel 6.3 Further readings about assessment

Rank-order approaches to assessing the quality of extended responses (aea-europe.net)
This leaflet is a guide to AQA's normal procedures for setting standards in all its qualifications.
Maintaining Standards (publishing.service.gov.uk)
Comparable outcomes and new A levels - The Ofqual blog
Comparative Judgement: The pros and cons | AQi powered by AQA

Summary

This chapter has considered the purpose and benefits of assessment mainly with regard to learners but also noting its usefulness for other stakeholders. The main emphasis has been on formative assessment with a strong focus on the important place of classroom talk including a Thought Piece by Malcolm Welch concerning the significance of questioning. There has been some consideration of summative assessment with Thought Pieces from Richard Kimble and Louise Attwood. The necessarily messy nature of progress was acknowledged. The importance of integrating assessment into curriculum planning has been emphasised and the nature and pitfalls of feedback explored. The majority of the chapter has focused on two types of feedback. Firstly 'in the moment' feedback and providing examples of this during a variety of learning activities concentrating particularly on the use of questions asked by the teacher for this to be achieved. The aim of such feedback in whatever learning task is being tackled is to either increase the effort being applied by the learner or to increase the learner's aspiration. Secondly 'end of task' assessment in which the learning achieved is scrutinised with the learner against the learning intentions of the task. The crucial importance of having detailed learning intentions was emphasised and examples of such intentions for a range of learning activities were described. Approaches to enable rapid feedback were detailed. How teachers might be able to find out the impact of their teaching of learners in a designing and making task was discussed in some detail and the use of test items involving auditing their previous design & technology experience as well as their knowledge, understanding and skills, before and after the designing and making task were considered. The additional demands, on both teachers and learners, of the new design & technology GCSE assessment introduced in 2016 were discussed in some detail and possible ways to address these demands identified. Key features of these solutions were the quality of the Key Stage 3 curriculum in being devised to prepare students for a Key Stage 4 GCSE course and the availability of appropriate professional development for teachers.

References

Aguiar, O. G., Mortimer, E. F., & Scott, P. (2010) Learning from and responding to students' questions: The authoritative and dialogic tension. *Journal of Research in Science Teaching, 47*(2), 174-193.

Alexander, R. J. (2006) *Towards dialogic teaching: Rethinking classroom talk (3rd ed.)*. Cambridge, UK: Dialogos.

Atkinson, S., & Black, P. (2007) Useful assessment for design &technology: Formative assessment, learning & teaching. In D. Barlex (Ed.) *Design & technology for the next generation* (pp. 199-215). Whitchurch, UK: Cliffe & Company.

Barlex (2012) The Young Foresight Project A UK Initiative in design creativity involving mentors from industry In B France and V Compton (Eds.), *Bringing Communities Together: Connecting learners with scientists or technologists*. Rotterdam: Sense

Barnes, D., & Todd, F. (1977) *Communication and learning in small groups*. London: Routledge & Kegan Paul.

Black, P., & Wiliam, D. (1998) *Inside the Black Box: Raising Standards Through Classroom Assessment*. London: NFER-Nelson.

Chin, C. (2006) Classroom interaction in science: Teacher questioning and feedback to students' responses. *International Journal of Science Education, 28*(11), 1315-1346.

Cross, N. (1982) *Designerly ways of knowing. Design studies, 3*(4), 221-227.

Daudelin, M. W. (1996) Learning from experience through reflection. *Organizational Dynamics*, *24*(3), 36–48.

Eris, O. (2003, August) *Asking generative design questions: A fundamental cognitive mechanism in design thinking*. Paper presented at the International Conference on Engineering Design ICED 03, Stockholm.

Hattie, J. (2012) *Visible Learning for Teachers*. Oxford: Routledge.

HMSO (2022) https://www.gov.uk/government/publications/school-inspection-handbook-eif/school-inspection-handbook)

Kimbell, R. A. (2017) Making Assessment Judgements: Policy, Practice and Research, in M.J. de Vries (Ed.), *Handbook of Technology Education*, Springer International Handbooks of Education, DOI 10.1007/978-3-319-38889-2_52-1.

Kluger & DeNisi (1996) The Effects of Feedback Interventions on Performance: A Historical Review, a Meta-Analysis, and a Preliminary Feedback Intervention Theory, *Psychological Bulletin*, *II9*(2), 254–284.

Kruger, A. C. (1993) Peer collaboration: Conflict, cooperation, or both? *Social Development*, *2*(3), 165–182.

Ofqual (2016) GCSE Subject Level Guidance for Design and Technology, https://assets.publishing.service.gov.uk/government/uploads/system/uploads/attachment_data/file/503497/gcse-subject-level-guidance-for-design-and-technology.pdf.

Polanyi, M. (1958) *Personal Knowledge*. Routledge.

Rilke, R. M. (2000) *Letters to a Young Poet (J. Burnham, Trans.)*. Novato, CA: New World Library.

van Zee, E., & Minstrell, J. (1997) Using questioning to guide student thinking, *The Journal of the Learning Sciences*, 6(2), 227–269.

Vygotsky, L. S. (1978). *Mind in society: The development of higher psychological processes*. Cambridge, MA: Harvard University Press

Williams P. J., & Kimbell, R. A. (Eds.) (2012) Special Issue of 'e-scape', *International Journal of Technology and Design Education*, 22(2 May). ISSN: 0957-7572 (Print) 1573-1804 (Online).

Recommended Reading

Barlex, D., Moreland, J., & Jones, A. (2008) *Design and Technology Inside the Black Box: Assessment for Learning in the Design and Technology Classroom*. London, England: GL Assessment.

Fletcher-Wood, H. (2018) *Responsive Teaching Cognitive Science and Formative Assessment in Practice*. Oxon: Routledge.

Wiliam, D. (2018) *Embedded Formative Assessment*. Bloomington, IN: Solution Tree Press.

7 Supporting design & technology

This final chapter deals with a range of features that can play a useful part in providing support for design & technology. These are:

- Liaison with primary schools
- Enrichment & enhancement activities
- STEM and STEAM
- Research
- Continuing professional development
- Maker education
- Interested parties including:
  - Learners
  - Parent/Carers
  - SLT
  - School governors
  - Awarding organisations
  - Local community
  - Local industry and employers
  - Local MP
  - Pearsons, the educational publisher
- Vision and mission statements for design & technology.

Each will be considered in turn and links made to the recommendations made in the Design & Technology Associations Reimagining D&T Report (Design & Technology Associations, 2023).

Liaison with primary schools

Clare Benson (2021) writes informatively about the liaison between primary and secondary schools and identifies different activities that successfully support this. These include undertaking an audit of design & technology in the primary school to include planning, activities, and resources so that secondary colleagues are familiar with learners' experiences and teaching design and make activities that move between the primary and secondary schools as this introduces learners to the school they might well be attending and may provide the

DOI: 10.4324/9781003008026-7

opportunity to use materials and equipment not available in the primary school. Although Clare is positive about the benefits of such liaison, she acknowledges that it is not easy and that there are challenges which include developing a shared understanding of the nature of design & technology, identifying primary and secondary members of staff to be responsible for the liaison, and forging a positive and effective relationship between them. Despite these difficulties we believe that such liaison is worthwhile and beneficial as the following examples show.

The first example concerns the way one school in the southwest of England organised a transition experience for Year 6 learners. It began when one of the teachers attended an in-service activity based on the Nuffield Primary Design & Technology unit *'Will your creature be fierce or friendly?'* (Barlex, 2001). In this activity individual learners design and make some small animal statues using triangular pieces of card as a precursor to working in groups in which they design and make a much larger statue of a creature that will welcome visitors to the classroom during the day or act as a guardian 'after school' and deter intruders. It has to be large enough to create an immediate impression, stable so that it doesn't fall over, stiff so that it keeps its shape, strong so that it doesn't break easily, durable so that it lasts a long time, made from readily available and inexpensive materials, and impressive through quality of construction and decoration. As a result, the primary school linked with its partner secondary school for a transition experience in three stages. In Stage 1 the head of design & technology from the secondary school visited the primary school to support the Year 6 learners in designing and making the small creature statues. In Stage 2 the Year 6 learners visited the secondary school with their class teacher who worked with the secondary head of design & technology to design and make the large creature statues. This visit took place over three consecutive days. The resulting creatures were taken back to the primary school. In Stage 3 working with their class teacher the Year 6 learners organised an assembly to share with Year 5 what they had done at the secondary school. The assembly was impressive. Each large creature was carried into a drum roll and a musical accompaniment and placed centre stage. Then members of the class read out examples of stories and poems they had written about their creatures. They even recited extracts from encyclopaedia entries they had written describing the creatures' life cycles.

The second example also involves a suggested transition experience (Barlex, 2019) and is related to the STEM agenda. A key feature of this transition experience is 'a visit' in which the primary school children visit their intended secondary school with examples of STEM work. Clearly such visits will require some orchestration to be successful. Prior to the visit, it will be important for the primary school to discuss with the secondary school the nature of the work that the children will be bringing on the visit. The work could be discussed well in advance so that the secondary school might, if it is appropriate, make some suggestions. Whether this can take place or not, it is important that the secondary schools know about the work the children have undertaken. Meeting the children with their work will give the secondary school teachers real insight into the achievements of the primary children and reveal the extent to which the STEM subjects have been able to collaborate in the primary school. And the secondary school teachers will be able to organise the visit so that they provide experiences and activities that consolidate and extend the learning that has taken place as well as introducing the children to some of the teachers and the facilities in the mathematics, science, and design & technology departments. Such transition experiences will benefit the three key stakeholders. The secondary school teachers will understand the learning that has taken place in the primary school and be in a stronger position to build on this. The primary school teacher will see where their teaching leads and be able to tailor their teaching to support this. The children will see that their work is valued by both the primary school and the secondary school, and realise that their learning will have continuity.

Three possibilities of work are suggested. The first started with mathematics. Taking the study of 'properties of shape' as the starting point, children will use their knowledge and understanding of polygons to design and make creatures living on the imaginary world *Geomiter* where creatures are constructed from geometric shapes. They will also think about their possible life cycles and habitats. This work will be followed by a transition experience in which children take some of the creatures with details of their possible life cycles and habitats with them when they visit the secondary school towards the end of primary school. These learning outcomes will form the starting point of the transition experience. The secondary school teachers can talk with children about what they have done and work with them on how they can extend this learning. Children will be able to use their knowledge and understanding of the nature and classification of living things, habitats, and life cycles to write encyclopaedia entries describing life on planet *Geomiter*.

The second possibility started with science. Taking 'exploring and explaining forces' as a starting point, children will investigate the performance of simple parachutes and use the results to inform designing and making simple parachute toys for particular users. The parachute canopies will be made from single sheets of tissue paper cut, folded, and joined to produce a variety of 3D forms from nets, including cones. Children will be able to investigate the effect of form and the number of attachments on the speed of falling and the stability of the chute. The toys might be simple 'throw as high as you can and enjoy the descent' or a chute for a small toy figure, e.g., a LEGO person. Larger toy figures might require several chutes that would complicate the design as it would be important for the multiple chutes not to interfere with one another. These learning outcomes will form the starting point of the transition experience. The secondary school teachers can talk with children about what they have done and work with them on how they can extend this learning.

The third possibility started with design & technology. Taking the designing and making of a lighting device as a starting point the children needed to use their understanding of simple circuits with switches, bulbs, and reflective materials (from science) to produce a useful, controllable lighting circuit, and nets to provide an enclosure (from mathematics). The task is to design and make a light that is suitable for use in a particular situation. The children will take the lighting devices plus their circuit diagrams with them when they visit the secondary school during Year 6. These learning outcomes will form the starting point of the transition experience. The secondary school teachers can talk with children about what they have done and work with them on how they can extend this learning.

The third example concerns the way three primary schools worked with their partner secondary school to build CADCAM into the primary school's design & technology curriculum (Barlex & Miles-Pearson, 2008, 2009). Together they identified three Nuffield Primary design & technology units of work that could be modernised to incorporate CADCAM. These were:

What should be stuck to your fridge? In this unit pupils are required to design and make a fridge magnet that is made of layers and is part of a set that will appeal to young children. This unit was taught to Year 2 pupils.

How will you store your favourite things? In this unit pupils are required to design and make a container to act as a treasure chest for favourite small items. This unit was taught to Year 4 pupils.

How fast should your buggy be? In this unit pupils are required to design and make a controllable, battery-powered toy vehicle for an identified user. This unit was taught to Year 5 pupils.

The teachers decided to use Techsoft 2D software in combination with the Craft ROBO cutter plotter. Over two months three secondary school teachers worked with three partner primary schools to provide in service training for the primary teachers and to develop some learners as peer mentor experts. Each secondary school teacher, accompanied by the primary teacher taught a unit of work that incorporated CADCAM to a small number of primary learners so that they could become experts and provide advice and guidance to their peers when the unit was taught to their class. Later in the year the entire class from each school visited the secondary school with their class teacher and together with the secondary school teacher and the help of the pupil experts tackled the modernized primary solutions unit. The following comments indicated how effective this liaison had been.

- A deputy head from one of the primary schools commented on the extent to which the primary secondary partnership respected the primary perspective and provided useful professional development for the primary teachers and appropriate curriculum development for the primary schools.
- The secondary teachers recounted how impressed they had been by the autonomy and capability of primary learners. They were enthusiastic about the potential for learners on transfer at the end of Key Stage 2 being able to use the software and hardware in the secondary school without much in the way of additional teaching. They talked of needing to revise the Year 7 curriculum in design & technology in the light of these developments and their new understanding of the abilities of primary learners.
- Of the learners who acted as mentors all enjoyed being trained as an expert with reasons including 'feeling good to help other people', 'learning new skills', and 'enjoyment of using computers'. All agreed that they were able to help other learners, would recommend it to others and would like to be trained as an expert in future projects because 'you get to learn more and feel special'.
- The learners who were mentored indicated that they enjoyed being taught by an expert learner and that the experts had explained things well.

> ### Pause for thought
>
> The examples described above clearly involve a lot of hard work over some considerable time but it is clear that if such liaison activities can be undertaken then there are benefits for primary teachers, secondary teachers, and learners. To what extent do you think that your department would be able to develop such liaison activities.

D&T Association Reimagining D&T Report connection

The report emphasises the need for curriculum development for both Primary and Key Stage 3 design & technology both with a focus on sustainability and net zero. For primary teachers it proposes a ring-fenced training budget. Using this budget to develop transition activities like those described above but concentrating on climate change issues would provide development across the Key Stage 2 and Key Stage 3 divide and enable development of the Key Stage 3 curriculum to build on the learning taking place in primary schools.

Enrichment & enhancement activities

Enhancement and enrichment activities sometimes take the form of science, technology, engineering, and mathematics (STEM) career events in which there are all sorts of science and technology stands that learners can visit and find out about different technical professions along with career entry requirements and pathways. The Big Bang Fair (see https://www. thebigbang.org.uk) is one such event, takes place over three days and gives learners the opportunities to meet with professional scientists, engineers, and designers. The Big Bang organisation also provides the resources, tools, and guidance for schools to run their own Big Bang in house. British Science Week (see https://www.britishscienceweek.org) operates over ten days and provides a wide range of activity packs and 30 plus stories celebrating diverse peoples and careers in science and engineering. The careers education dimension of enhancement and enrichment activities is also supported by the STEM Ambassador scheme (see https://www.stem.org.uk/stem-ambassadors). STEM Ambassadors are volunteers from a wide range of STEM related jobs and disciplines across the UK. They offer their time and enthusiasm to help bring STEM subjects to life and demonstrate the value of them in life and careers. Their services are free of charge. They bring a wealth of experience from their varied STEM roles and diverse backgrounds, working for over 7,000 different employers. More than half (59%) are under 35 years of age, 43% are female, and 13% are from minoritized backgrounds. The organisers argue that there are significant benefits for employers, as well as teachers and learners, in that being a STEM ambassador increases staff engagement and boosts their confidence, communication and presentation skills. Volunteering increases Ambassadors' job satisfaction and knowledge, as well as opportunities to develop their own professional network within and beyond their own organisation or sector. Young people experiencing any of the above activities will almost certainly enjoy themselves and become better informed about career opportunities although whether these impact on their actual career pathways has proved difficult to quantify (Banks & Barlex, 2021).

An alternative to the above careers-oriented activities is the CREST Awards scheme (see https://www.crestawards.org/). This requires young people at school to undertake projects of their own choice in the STEM subjects and, depending on the demand of the project, learners can achieve bronze, silver, or gold awards. Bronze Awards are typically completed by 11–14-year-olds. Over the course of 10 hours, teams of learners design their own investigation and record their findings, giving them a taste of what it is like to be a scientist or engineer in the real-world. The Bronze level works well in a STEM club setting or as something that is completed across a term, although there is no deadline for completion. The projects are assessed by the teacher against the CREST Bronze award criteria which are available online. Upon completion, teachers upload a sample of their learners' work on to the CREST online platform for moderation purposes. Learner's personalized CREST certificates are sent to the schools within four weeks of the project's submission. The Silver and Gold levels are designed to stretch learners. They are long-term, in-depth projects that are run by the learners themselves. Learners choose the topic and type of project they want to run from four options: a practical investigation, a design and make project, a research project, or a communication project. Silver projects are typically completed by learners aged 14+ years and Gold by learners aged 16+. At this level, learners are encouraged to collaborate with a CREST mentor – an academic or person from industry with expertise in their project's theme. All Silver and Gold level projects are assessed externally via the online platform by assessors who are experts across various STEM areas and have received assessment training. The costs for entering for a CREST award in England are modest; Bronze award £5.00 per learner, Silver award £10.00 per learner, and Gold award £20.00 per learner. Importantly UCAS (the organisation responsible for managing applications to higher education courses in the UK) have endorsed CREST Awards for inclusion in young people's personal statements in their application for admission into university.

And it is possible for schools to run their own enhancement and enrichment activities as after school or lunch time clubs fuelled by the enthusiasm and interests of teachers and learners. Such clubs would benefit from involvement with the local Maker Movement as discussed elsewhere in this chapter. Such local enhancement and enrichment initiatives might well develop highly engaging activities that could migrate into the mainstream provision. One way of looking at these activities could be to see them as a means of curriculum development in which activities could be devised and piloted with learners before transfer into timetabled lessons. A particular feature of some enhancement and enrichment activities which makes them attractive is the extent to which they allow those taking part to choose what they do. This can create problems when a syllabus requires certain features to be taught and learners choose to do things that do not meet these requirements. However, it should be possible to run a mixed economy and provide significant choice at times and limited choice at others. Migration into the mainstream would in no way detract from the work of those currently engaged in supporting enhancement and enrichment. On the contrary, it could be argued that it would see their contribution to the curriculum having a more pervasive effect, concentrating on developing a curriculum with both appeal and intellectual coherence for all learners, as opposed to a minority. Indeed, a useful intention for some enhancement and enrichment programmes would be to develop activities that could migrate into the mainstream and the evaluation criteria for such activities would be the extent to which this occurred.

Pause for thought

Can you and colleagues see a role for enhancement and enrichment activities in your department? What are the opportunities that these might provide and what might prevent these from being realised?

D&T Association Reimagining D&T Report connection

The report emphasises the need for curriculum development at Key Stage 3 and to achieve this it will be important to test out a wide range of possible developments. The use of enhancement and enrichment activities as a preliminary exploration of possible activities some of which can then migrate into the mainstream curriculum for further piloting provides an effective and economic way of conducting a wide range of possible developments suitable for the contexts in which they are to operate.

STEM and STEAM

We noted in chapter 2 that any form of curriculum collaboration between science, mathematics, and design & technology should respect the legitimate differences between the subjects as well as capitalising on areas of common interest and that in collaborating through STEM the integrity of the collaborating subjects is maintained. This integrity may be compromised by the different status of the contributing subjects. This disparity is captured by the following graphic which compares the relative significance of the subjects in school and in the world outside school:

S~TE~**M**
In school

~s~**TE**~M~
In the world outside school

Whilst this may be seen as an oversimplification of the world outside school, it reflects to a very large extent the situation in school where design & technology is often seen as the 'poor relation' with regard to science and mathematics. Also, in chapter 2 we noted that the utility-purpose model proposed by Janet Ainley and colleagues (2006) goes a long way to redressing this balance. Jim Al-Khalili makes a strong case for greater collaboration between science, mathematics, and design & technology:

> The idea that studying STEM subjects is ... to prepare the next generation of technologists and engineers – is way off the mark ... pupils do not appreciate the interconnectedness of what they are learning or how these subjects overlap in the real world, which is becoming increasingly broad and interdisciplinary. ... In addition, STEM

teaching must encompass softer skills, often acquired in group-based work, such as communication skills or an appreciation of the values and ethics of the application of new scientific knowledge in technology and an appreciation of the role of scientific evidence. … Young people may have grown up in a world of instant access, echo chambers and polarizing ideologies, but that doesn't make them any better at understanding what and whom to trust. Teaching pupils the necessary skills to cope with the modern world will involve an integration of STEM into all areas of their education.

Jim Al-Khalilli in Banks and Barlex (2021, p. vii, viii)

Given the status of the T and E outside school, one way to redress the balance of the in-school experience is to consider T and E from the world outside school as a possible focus for STEM activities. Here is an example. In India farmers are using small drones to substantially improve the way they farm (Chummar & Saraskanth, 2023). The short video (2 minutes 36 seconds) describes how farming in India is suffering due to a lack of farm labourers and that the use of drones enables a single farmer, without labourers to plant seeds, spray pesticide, and water crops single-handed. The video also shows how one innovative farmer is thinking of setting up a drone hiring business to make this facility available to other farmers who can't afford the capital investment to buy their own drones.

Starting with this as a case study, it is possible to identify where science, mathematics, and design & technology have each played their part in this tale of agricultural improvement. One way to do this would be to ask pupils to write a narrative that identifies the key points of farming improvement whilst watching the video (it might be necessary to show it two or three times for them to get all the points) and then require them to annotate where science, mathematics, and design & technology were playing key parts in this narrative. As a practical follow-up, learners could be tasked with producing simplified drones that carry out similar tasks. Ed Charlwood (2023) has developed a wide range of 'free to download drone education' resources. Of course, drones are a mixed blessing. In addition to supporting agriculture, the same technology is also being used in warfare to deliver bombs and there is the added complication that whilst the drones in the video were under human control with the farmer flying them by means of a joystick controller, there is the very real possibility that drones used for warfare might oversee a battlefield and be given autonomy with regard to where and when they delivered their explosives. So, it is easy in this example for learners to have to move on to consider the ethical issues involved in deploying technology. An important requirement of STEM education made by Jim Al-Khalili above.

What about STEAM?

Several educators propose that the appeal of the STEM subjects could be enhanced if aspects of art could be included such that STEM becomes STEAM. In the US as long as ten years ago, Harvey White, a highly successful businessman in wireless communications, argued that the Arts should be an essential feature of education for economic prosperity as it embraces a creativity component (Banks & Barlex, 2014) and more recently both Israel and Taiwan have introduced STEAM activities into their curricula (Banks & Barlex, 2021). In devising STEAM learning activities, it will be important that they are true to the intrinsic nature of art as well as the intrinsic nature of the other contributing subjects. One defining feature of art which distinguishes it from design & technology is that the artist is *not* trying to meet the needs or wants of those who might interact with the art. The artist is trying to elicit a response of some sort, often emotional but maybe political or social. To some extent the artist is indifferent to whether the viewer likes or dislikes the piece but is concerned that the viewer is engaged and responds.

Here is an example of a STEAM activity first reported by one of the authors in 2009 (Barlex & Welch, 2009). Twelve learners aged 12–13 years worked in pairs over three full days in response to the following design brief: *Design and make a large statue of a creature that can be friendly (and welcome visitors to a classroom during the day) or fierce (and deter intruders to a classroom after dark).* The response of one pair of learners, shown in Panel 7.1,

Panel 7.1 The outcome of a 3-day immersive STEAM activity

Preliminary sketches of the intended creature

Card model of the intended creature

The completed creature; some 3 metres long and definitely fierce

captures the essence of a STEAM activity. All other learners had produced creatures based on four legged dinosaurs, but this group decide on a 'sea snake' type creature that would lie comatose on the classroom floor until it became dark and then would awaken and be ready to attack any intruders who had broken into the school. It is difficult to look at the creature without feeling an emotional response – fear, discomfort, fascination – which indicates that to some extent an art dimension to the outcome. The outcome is creative according to the Robinson (1999) criteria for creativity in that the learners had pursued a purpose, developed an outcome of value and originality, and used their imagination. This chimes with the US contention that including art in STEAM will enable more creative responses than STEM alone. The work could be extended using contributions from the conventional STEM subjects in that the creature itself could be enhanced with the addition of 'eyes' that could be made to glow and the production of hissing sounds. This physical outcome could be the starting point for digital outcomes such as animations featuring the activities of the creature in protecting the school which would enhance the art dimension.

Throughout her career Dawne Irving-Bell has shown an interest in both design & technology education and STEM learning so it is to her Thought Piece we now turn.

Support for curriculum collaboration – *A Thought Piece by Dawne Irving-Bell*

Dawne Irving-Bell, PhD, is a professor at BPP University.

Chapter 2 highlighted the challenges of curriculum collaboration between science, mathematics, design & technology, and engineering. Such collaboration is important because STEM education is vital for economic growth, but there is a disparity in the status of the contributing subjects within the STEM acronym. With, as the authors imply, technology and engineering often being seen as the 'poor relation' particularly when compared to science and mathematics within the context of compulsory schooling.

Effective collaboration between each of the individual STEM disciplines, is essential to maximize the potential benefits of STEM education. Benefits that include increased creativity and innovation. A good STEM curriculum should respect the differences between each subject, while capitalizing on common interests. Adopting this approach, while working collaboratively, the integrity of each subject is maintained. Where possible during collaborations efforts should be made and opportunities taken to raise the status of design, technology, and engineering.

Moving the debate forward, the authors turn their attention to the benefits to learner's not only of a good STEM education but illuminate the enhanced benefits that can be achieved when STEM collaborates with the creative arts to make 'STEAM'. Integrating knowledge and skills from art can help foster creativity and innovation. Helping to encourage learners to think 'outside the box' and to approach problems from a different perspective. Boosting ingenuity and problem-solving abilities, and as illustrated by the authors example, can lead ultimately to ingenious and imaginative solutions to real-world problems. In addition to holding the potential to enhance the creative component of STEM learning, STEAM has the potential to make each of the individual STEM subject disciplines more appealing to learners.

Through authentic collaboration between each of the STEM disciplines and Art, teachers have the capacity to maximise STEM education. The chapter presents one way this could be achieved. Another approach could be to engage learners in a 'design fiction' based activity.

Under the further reading section, I have included a reference to work that explains what design fiction is, and how it can be used in practice, but in a nutshell, it tasks learners to design products for the future, using technologies not yet invented. Encouraged to develop concepts without the constraints of function, ideas flow freely, leading to some amazing innovations!

Another approach could be to explore the notion of 'technological determinism'. The authors raise this concept when they encourage you to consider the ways humans use drones. Encouraging debate is a brilliant way for learners to consider the implications that STEM and STEAM innovations may have on society. Put simply, technological determinism asserts that technological innovations drive social change, and shapes our culture and values. Hard technological determinism contends that once unleashed, people are powerless to halt the march of technological advances. Again, I have included a reference to further information (*The Bloomsbury Handbook of Technology Education*) where you can gain more insights into how you could include this concept into your teaching.

Irrespective of the approach you adopt, there can be no doubt that when educators from different disciplines work together, they can create powerful learning experiences where leaners develop vital skills, knowledge, and understanding. Working together, STEM and STEAM teachers and educators can help ensure that everyone can develop critical-thinking skills and technical knowhow necessary not only for their future careers but understanding the value of technology within society. My suggestions for reflective questions and useful further reading are shown in Panel 7.2.

What are we to make of Dawne's Thought Piece. First, we are pleased that she endorses 'design fiction' as this is very similar to the design without make activity that we have identified as an important way of teaching design & technology. Second, we welcome her identification of technological determinism as an important issue to discuss with learners. This was discussed in chapter 2 in the section about the Philosophy of Technology. What

Panel 7.2 Reflective questions and useful further reading from Dawne Irving-Bell

---

Reflective questions

- Within your working and learning environment who are your contacts? and what action could you take in order to move forward to forge strong working relationships with your STEM and STEAM colleagues?
- Is there potential to work with colleagues in neighbouring schools, colleges, and institutions?
- Thinking beyond your immediate context, are there any local or national groups or organisations you could reach out to?

Useful further reading

Design fiction: Irving-Bell, D., McLain, M., & Wooff, D. (2022) Shaping Things: Design Fiction as a Catalyst for Design in Design and Technology Education. *Australasian Journal of Technology Education*, 7. https://doi.org/10.15663/ajte.v7i.74.

Irving-Bell, D. (2023) Technology, Education and Society. In Gill et al. (eds.), *The Bloomsbury Handbook of Technology Education*, Bloomsbury Publishing. ISBN 9781350238411, https://www.bloomsbury.com/in/bloomsbury-handbook-of-technology-education-9781350238428/.

Memorial University's Design Students 'Interview the Expert' series, https://www.youtube.com/watch?v=kgC9n17fbg0.

---

comes across so strongly is Dawne's 'joie de vivre' with regard to curriculum collaboration whether in STEM, STEAM, or as yet undeveloped activities. Her enthusiasm is inspirational.

D&T Association Reimagining D&T Report connection

Collaboration between the STEM subjects provides an important path for the Key Stage 3 curriculum development that the report emphasises. The utility-purpose model outline above enables such collaboration to the benefit of all the subjects involved without the risk of loss of subject identity.

Research

Research can inform various aspects of our subject. We noted in chapter 4 that how the intellectual resources needed for the subject are supported by publications that are research based (see for example Panel 4.1). Chapter 4 also notes that some research enables us to contemplate the subject's current position through identifying significant trends in important features affecting the subject. This is the case in the Education Policy Institute's recent report (EPI, 2022). Other research focuses on relationships with other subjects in the curriculum often in the context of STEM/STEAM initiatives or on interesting developments in informal education such as the Maker Movement both of which are discussed in this chapter. The current interest in pupil voice discussed in the *Learners* section of *Interested parties* in this chapter provides a useful opportunity for research into learners' views on our subject. In this section we want to focus on research that might inform the way young people learn in design & technology. Here we think it is useful to look at the way research has informed the way young people learn in science lessons. This has its origins in the seminal work of Rosalind Driver (1983) which led her to formulate the idea of alternative frameworks. Through her research she showed that young people's cognitive development may be more like a series of paradigm shifts with new ideas about a phenomenon replacing older ones. She argued that children's learning was dependent upon their existing ideas about phenomena, ideas that they had developed through their everyday experience of the world around them. These ideas 'make sense' to the learner, are deeply embedded and resistant to change. The problem for science teachers is that many scientific concepts are counter intuitive, at first sight they don't make sense! If young people are going to develop a new and genuine scientific understanding of a phenomenon, then they must abandon their current understanding in favour of the new one. This requires learners to reconstruct their understanding if they are to overcome their misconceptions. Driver was very clear that any such misconceptions, or as she called them alternative frameworks, should be treated with respect as teachers helped learners construct new understandings. Her work led to a radical change in the way science was taught with a move away from rote learning of scientific facts towards helping learners to develop concepts that enabled them to make sense of the world around them and were in harmony with current scientific understanding. This leads us to ask do young people harbour misconceptions about design & technology; if so, what are they and how might the way we teach help them to develop a more robust understanding? Before we do this, it is important to acknowledge that the purposes of science education and design & technology education are different. Science educations is primarily concerned with enabling young people to make sense of the natural phenomena in the world around them using scientific knowledge and understanding. It is also concerned with enabling young people to critique the way this knowledge is used in society. Design & technology is concerned with enabling young people to be capable in the sense of being able to intervene in the made world and also critiquing the interventions made by professional designers, technologists, and engineers. Given this difference in purpose it is likely that misconceptions in a particular area of understanding relevant to both science and design & technology might be different from one another.

The Big Ideas of design & technology have been discussed at length in this book. These concern materials, manufacture, functionality, design, and critique all in the context of being useful for intervention. Each of these can be broken down into sub-categories and it would be an interesting and useful research exercise to find out if young peoples' understandings of these sub-categories were conceptually sound or based on misconceptions. This might be investigated by asking learners questions about these sub-categories to elicit their understandings. Such questioning might reveal, for example, whether they appreciate the difference between stiffness and strength. An alternative approach might be to scrutinise the design decisions they make. These will be informed by their knowledge and understanding. For example, what do learners need to know and understand about electric circuits if they are designing something that needs to work electrically? It would be a useful and interesting research exercise to find out about their understanding. The work of Rosalind Driver revealed that young learners had many alternative frameworks for the way electricity flowed in a circuit and some of these would definitely hinder the design and construction of a working circuit to be used in, for example, a simple lighting device. Anyone who has taught learners to design and make simple circuits will know that in many cases the first attempt at construction doesn't work and that a queue of learners seeking help quickly forms. It is

What to do if the circuit doesn't work

Use this checklist before you ask your teacher.

Must have got something wrong ... where's that diagram?

Check carefully against your circuit diagram.

Maybe the battery isn't connected properly?

Check to be sure.

Might be a dud battery ...

Test it with a light bulb that your know works.

1 of 2

Perhaps it's the solder?

Check for any 'dry' solder joints.

Could be a loose connection somewhere ...

Look carefully to check.

Must be something else not working?

Remove components one at a time and test them in a circuit that does work.

Figure 7.1 Assistance with fault finding

imperative to keep this queue short and it is tempting to trouble shoot for the learners. This solves the problem of the queue but doesn't help learners use their knowledge and understanding of electricity to fault find for themselves. Hence the advice shown in Figure 7.1. Does such advice really work? Does the learners' understanding of electricity help them use the advice? How is such advice best mediated to learners? Does it work better if learners use it collaboratively?

Given that making sound design decisions depends on knowing specific and relevant knowledge the Nuffield D&T Project developed the idea of chooser charts (Nuffield Foundation, 2000). These summarise potentially useful knowledge in a way that enables learners literally to 'choose' from a range of possible design options. These are discussed in more detail in chapter 5. Suffice here to say that investigating the way learners use chooser charts in making design decisions might reveal misconceptions. Both Hilda and Torben have been told by teachers that chooser charts enable young people to make design decisions, but as far as we know, no formal research has yet been carried out to explore whether this is in fact the case. The chooser chart shown in Figure 7.2 a) and b) provides information about simple electrical components. Does this chart help learners design, say, simple lighting circuits? Does the use of the chart reveal conceptual misunderstandings? Might such findings be useful to the learners' science teachers?

There are of course design and make activities in which learners make decisions without recourse to chooser charts. One such task, developed by Jon Parker in 1998, involved designing and making a desktop storage system. He was keen to move away from the hackneyed 'desk tidy' task and wanted to ensure that learners used their understanding of forces, such as compression and tension, to produce different effects, and to take account of these in designing their products (Barlex & Parker, 1998). He was also keen for learners to explore the use of thin flexible plywood in their designing and take into account its intrinsic properties and working characteristics. He piloted the task as an in-service activity with participants required to design and make a desk top storage system that will hold and display at least five compact

What the components might need to do	Options	Symbols	Points to check
To provide a power supply	batteries: • zinc carbon for low current, Infrequent use • zinc chloride for medium current, regular use • alkaline for high current, heavy use		Make sure voltage of battery is suitable for components in the circuit.
To make light			
To give a signal	a light-emitting diode a flashing light-emitting diode		Use protecting resistor. Must be correct way round. Does not need protecting resistor. Must be correct way round.
To provide illumination	a light bulb		Must match power source.
To give rotary movement	an electric motor		Must match power source. May need 'gearing'.
To make sound	a bell a buzzer		Must match power source. Buzzer must be correct way round.

Figure 7.2 a: Electric Components Chooser Chart

discs and be suitable for sale in IKEA so the design would need to reflect the 'house style' of this retail organisation. Clearly such a task is now outmoded in that most learners now access music via streaming. Nevertheless, the resultant artefacts revealed elegant use of thin flexible plywood and Jon encouraged some understanding of forces in structures by using simplified annotated diagrams as shown in Panel 7.3. A question we must ask is to what extent is it worth learners being taught about forces in structures so that they might use this explicitly in their designing? Or will some hands-on exploration of the properties of flexible plywood give sufficient intuitive understanding as to make the formal teaching unnecessary?

There are of course many other areas of research involving the investigation of learner misconceptions that are worth pursuing; learners understanding of designing and their appreciation of various value positions are just two. What is clear is that design & technology education needs to be research informed as is the case in the teaching of other school subjects.

What the components might need to do	Options	Symbols	Points to check
To control current size			
By setting at a fixed value	a fixed resistor 		Value provides the required current
To switch			
To hold something on or off	a push-to-make switch		Two connections to the switch.
	a push-to-break switch		
	a reed switch		
	a tilt switch		
To set something on or off	a single-pole, single-throw switch • push switch • slide switch • toggle switch • rocker switch • bimetallic switch 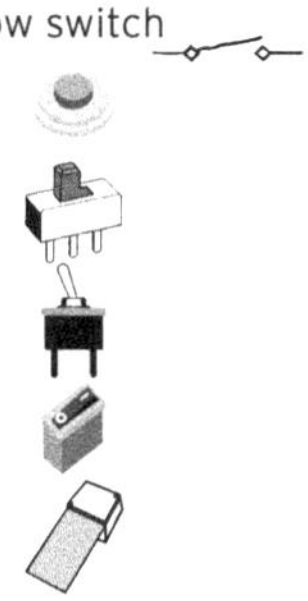		Two connections to the switch. Which type will be most suitable for the user?
To turn something on and something else off	a single-pole, double-throw change-over switch • micro switch • slide switch • toggle switch • rocker switch 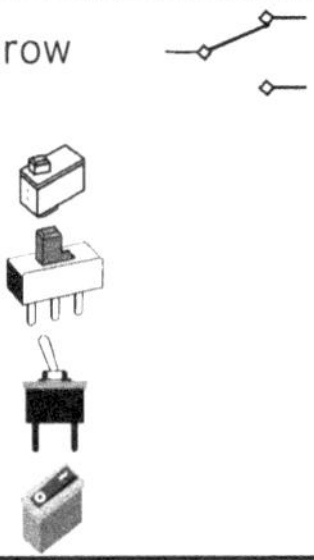		Three connections to the switch. Which type will be most suitable for the user?
To reverse direction	a single-pole, double-throw change-over switch • slide switch • toggle switch • rocker switch 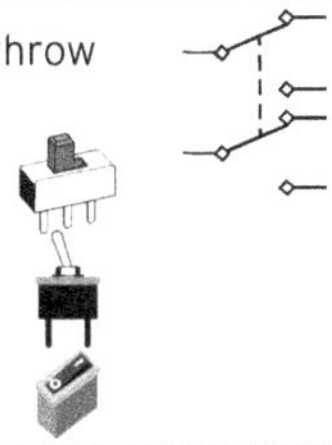		Four connections to the switch. Which type will be most suitable for the user?

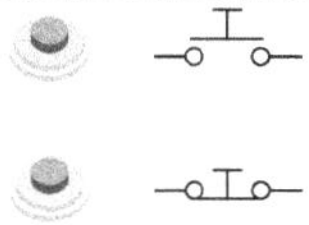

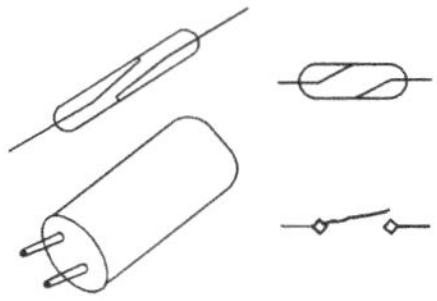

Figure 7.2 b: Electric Components Chooser Chart

Panel 7.3 A structures approach to designing desktop storage

A tower construction involving three different pieces of flexible plywood slotted together

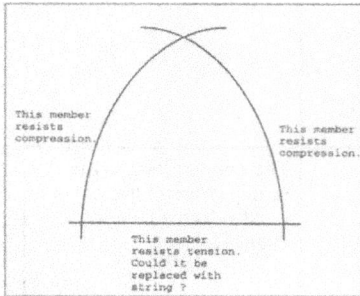

This member resists compression

This member resists compression.

This member resists tension. Could it be replaced with string ?

This simplified diagram engages with the forces in the structure

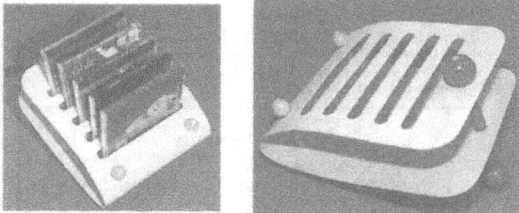

A solution that uses just a single piece of flexible plywood

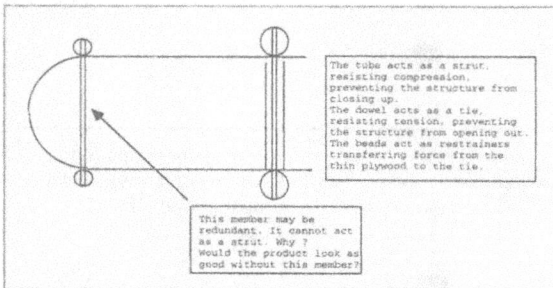

The tube acts as a strut, resisting compression, preventing the structure from closing up.
The dowel acts as a tie, resisting tension, preventing the structure from opening out.
The beads act as restrainers transferring force from the thin plywood to the tie.

This member may be redundant. It cannot act as a strut. Why ?
Would the product look as good without this member?

This simplified diagram engages with the forces in the structure

> **Pause for thought**
>
> Collaboration between teachers in school and academics in higher education is a possible means of developing a rigorous approach to classroom-based research that is formulated by teachers with a view to informing practice. Such research may take place as part of master's courses in education, but it is also possible for researchers in higher education to apply for grants to support collaborative research with schools.

D&T Association Reimagining D&T Report connection

The report is, quite rightly, insistent on the need for more research into the teaching, learning and assessment of design & technology to inform practice in schools. There is no shortage of topics to explore as indicated above. It is the authors' hope that the Association will develop a taxonomy of research possibilities along with guidance for grant applications that those working in schools, and HE can use to get funding to carry out research and so contribute to a coherent on-going research agenda firmly based in classroom reality.

Continuing professional development

In chapter 4 we used the DEPTH model of three related areas of teachers' professional knowledge; subject knowledge, pedagogic knowledge, and school knowledge (related to the way subject knowledge is specific to schools) as elements of the intellectual resources that teachers need to acquire and maintain. There is little point in acquiring new subject knowledge that you can't teach and little point in learning about effective ways of teaching if you can't deploy them in your own school. Good professional development will need to take all these elements into account. The research carried out by the Teacher Development Trust (2015) has identified ten key features that need to be considered in developing robust and effective professional development. Each will be considered in turn.

1 Duration and rhythm

To be effective in producing profound, lasting change, professional development interventions have to be prolonged, at least two terms, more usually a year or longer. Professional development activities must create a rhythm of follow-up, consolidation, and support activities in order to impact on practice.

2 Designing for participants' needs

Buy-in is achieved through creating an overt relevance of the content to participants' day-to-day experience with, and aspiration for their students. Opportunities for individual teachers both to reveal and discuss their beliefs and engage in peer learning and support are important.

3 Creating a shared sense of purpose

Achieving a shared sense of purpose during professional development is an important factor for success.

4 Alignment

It is important to create opportunities for teacher learning that are consistent with the principles of student learning being promoted.

5 Content

Key building blocks are:
- Subject knowledge
- Subject specific pedagogy
- Clarity around learner progression, starting points, and next steps
- Content and activities dedicated to helping teachers understand how pupils learn Programmes should put forward
- Alternative pedagogies for pupils with different needs
- A focus on formative assessment to allow teachers to see the impact of their learning and work on their pupils. Input should allow for the consideration of participants' existing theories, beliefs, and practice, and for opportunities to challenge these in a non-threatening way.

6 Activities

Successful CPD included explicit discussions about how to translate CPD content to the classroom; participants engaged in analysis of and reflection around the underpinning rationale, evidence and relevant assessment data which was important in bringing about and embedding changes in practice.

7 Providers

External facilitation is a common factor in successful CPD, sometimes working in tandem with internal specialists. Facilitators of the most successful programmes act as coaches and/or mentors to participants.

8 Support from specialists

Successful facilitators employed activities that aim to:
- Introduce new knowledge and skills to participants
- Help participants access the theory and evidence underlying the relevant pedagogy, subject knowledge, and strategies
- Help participants believe better outcomes are possible, particularly where achievement has been depressed over time

- Make the link between professional learning and pupil learning explicit through discussion of pupil progression and analysis of assessment data
- Take account of different teachers' starting points and – from the strongest review – the emotional content of the learning.

9 Effective collaboration

What makes collaboration effective is still contested. Peer support in which all participants have an opportunity to try out and refine new approaches was a common feature in effective professional development. But while collaboration is necessary it alone is not sufficient.

10 Leadership

Four key roles for school leaders in effective professional development:
- **Developing vision** – including helping teachers believe alternative outcomes are possible and creating coherence so teachers understand the relevance of CPD to wider priorities.
- **Managing and organising** – including establishing priorities, resolving competing demands, sourcing appropriate expertise, and ensuring appropriate opportunities to learn are in place.
- **Leading professional learning** – including promoting a challenging learning culture, knowing what content and activities are likely to be of benefit, and promoting 'evidence-informed, self- regulated learning'.
- **Developing the learning of others** – including encouraging teachers to lead a particular aspect of pedagogy or of the curriculum.

Pause for thought

Developing a professional development programme that incorporates all the above features is a significant undertaking and one that should be seen as a strategic activity as discussed in chapter 4. Ensuring that this strategy is in place and implemented is a crucial element for the support of the subject in your school and a necessary investment if it is to thrive.

D&T Association Reimagining D&T Report connection

The centrality of teachers in the process of curriculum reform and development is widely acknowledged as indicated:

"Educational change depends on what teachers do and think – it's as simple and complex as that." – *Fullan & Stiegelbauer, 1991, p. 117*
"It must be recognised that teachers are the sole and essential means to educational improvement. If they do not share the aims, and do not want to do what needs to be done, it cannot happen effectively." – *Black* in *Dillon & Maguire, 1997, p. 60*

Hence the involvement of teachers has been a key feature in developing the Reimagining report. The guidance from the Teacher Development Trust outlined above provides a template for the Association in creating a long-term strategy for the professional development of design & technology teachers.

Maker education

Makers are people who like to make stuff, often, but not always, using high technology tools (microcontrollers, laser cutters, 3D printers, for example) and in some cases designing and making such tools themselves. Making, as practised by makers takes in a broad swathe of interests that include crafting, heavy engineering, electronics, embedded control, programming, robotics, and biotech among many other things. There is a strong bias among makers towards open-source tools, both hardware and software and a belief that the products you make (as well as those that you use) should be covered by 'open' licences, such as those from Creative Commons (https://creativecommons.org) and the Open Source Initiative (http://opensource.org), thus allowing them to be developed and modified (hacked) by others. Makers operate in makerspaces. These are physical locations where people gather to co-create, share resources and knowledge, work on projects, network, and build. They help intermediate and advanced users develop their skills and creativity. Typically, makerspaces contain a mix of conventional hand and light machine tools and digital tools such a laser cutters and 3D printers with the necessary computers and design software. Most have dedicated technicians to maintain this equipment and help people using the space. These facilities enable people to repair broken items (some makerspaces run sessions dedicated to this; a typical session might be entitled Mend It Mondays) and also to get inside and understand electronic hardware. Users of a makerspace can also pursue their own design and make projects often incorporating microcontrollers. The users of makerspaces help one another with their projects and the overall ethos is one of mutual support with people giving and taking advice freely. The government argues that their activity promotes development of high-end technology skills needed for prosperity and social mobility and is part of its Digital Strategy (DDCMS, 2022). Many maker spaces are located in libraries, and in 2019 the government listed 24 library-based maker spaces across England (DCMS, 2019). Some are known as Fab Labs (short for fabrication laboratories, a term coined by Neil Gershenfeld (2005) who developed the idea at MIT during the early 2000s.

Given their facilities and ethos, makerspaces would seem an ideal partner for school design & technology departments. In any partnership it is important that there are benefits to all the partners and that the commitment and activities required of partners are realistic and not over-burdensome. Hence while the knowledge and skill embedded in a maker community may well be extremely useful to a teacher and her learners we must ask:

1 What are the mechanisms by which such knowledge can be made available to the teacher and learners?
2 How can this knowledge and skill be incorporated into the school curriculum?
3 What benefits are there to the maker community in providing this knowledge and skill?

It is not difficult to see how a design & technology teacher who lacked expertise in the use of 3D printing or laser cutting could visit the maker space and acquire such expertise. There are staff at the space who are tasked with providing such expertise. This could lead to equipment in the school being better used or the school purchasing such equipment for the first time. It would also be possible for the teacher to bring a small group of learners to the space to develop similar knowledge and skills and then organize design & technology lessons in which these learners acted as 'in-class experts' to support the learning of other learners. Such activities have the potential to bridge the gap between the informal maker space and the more formal school space without compromising the integrity of either. The benefit for the schools in this arrangement is that the maker spaces can provide dedicated, bespoke CPD for design & technology teachers who are faced with developing their curriculum in response to the modernization of the subject. The benefit for the maker space is that the learners will (it is hoped) begin to attend the makerspace independently as a leisure time activity and become part of the maker community of practice centred on the makerspace. It is also possible to imagine a reversal of this situation in which schools' design & technology departments act as maker spaces for the community using the expertise of teachers and technicians plus the equipment in the department. However, given the emphasis on achieving good and improving examination results and the requirement to modernize the design & technology curriculum, this may not be seen as feasible or desirable by most schools.

Makerspaces are relatively new initiatives in England and if school design & technology departments are to develop partnerships with them it is important to consider the extent to which the existence of makerspaces will be sustainable. For our purposes sustainability might mean that the initiative becomes embedded in practice and widespread such that it is seen as the norm and no longer an initiative. Beaumont (2023) has suggested that the following features should be considered in this regard.

- Continued perception of worth by key stakeholders

Stakeholders who are involved in formulating national or regional education policy may, for various reasons, decide that such initiatives are no longer worthwhile. If that happens the initiatives will inevitably flounder. Ensuring that this does not happen requires effective political lobbying by those who are convinced of the worth of the initiatives. Stakeholders who are involved in implementation, i.e., the teachers and mentors, are crucial to sustainability. If, for any reason, they decide that the initiatives no longer have worth then sustainability will be compromised.

- Continued funding

This is essential to ensure appropriate hardware and software is available not only to enable the continuation of pilot initiatives but for roll out across the educational system.

- Professional development for those responsible for implementation

It is essential to ensure that all the teachers involved are inducted into the culture of the maker movement, experience hands-on makerspace activities and have the opportunity to refresh and enhance this knowledge and skill at regular intervals. This has implications for both initial teacher education and continuing professional development.

D&T Association Reimagining D&T Report connection

The maker movement is making its presence felt in many communities with the appearance of maker spaces. These are not evenly distributed across the country and vary greatly in size and facilities but if there is one in your locality it is well worth making contact. In terms of the professional development that the Association is promoting through the Reimaging report such contact may well provide useful opportunities as indicated above. It may be that the Association can build links with the Maker Movement into its long-term professional development strategy.

Interested parties

The section will deal with a range of interested parties who are important in establishing and maintaining the status of design & technology as a subject of worth for all learners until the age of 16 years.

Learners

It is learners who have first-hand experience of the design & technology curriculum, and it is essential that those involved in formulating this curriculum give learners the opportunity to present their views on this experience and to take these views into account in developing the curriculum further. This is sometimes called 'listening to pupil voice'. One way to 'listen' is through questionnaires. Schools give out such questionnaires online when they are being inspected to enable learners to say what they think about their school. The questions probe the issues listed in Panel 7.4.

The questions in Panel 7.4 are aimed at revealing what the learners think about their school experience in general. They do not probe, nor are they meant to probe, learners' views on a particular subject. However, it is possible for departments to devise questionnaires that ask learners what they think about the way they have been taught and what they have learned in a particular topic or module of work. Completing such an 'end of topic' questionnaire could become standard practice for a department and provide useful feedback. Using Survey Monkey or Google Forms software would enable the results to be analysed and displayed graphically. It is also possible to conduct pupil voice interviews in which a teacher selects a group of learners and asks them questions about their learning experience in the school. Interviews can be used to monitor learner's opinions, thoughts, and understanding in a subject or area of learning. It is important that the interview is conducted in a relaxed atmosphere so that learners feel able to voice their opinions freely and that they understand

Panel 7.4 Issues probed by the pupil questionnaire used during inspection

---

Whether the learners enjoy school
Whether teachers help then do their best
Whether the work is challenging
Whether they enjoy learning
Whether they are listened to in lessons
Whether there is an adult they can confide in
Whether the behaviour of other pupils is good, in their lessons and around the school
Whether bullying is a problem
Whether they feel safe at school
Whether they are encouraged to look after their physical, emotional and mental health
Whether they take part in school activities outside lessons
Whether they are encouraged to be independent and take on responsibilities
Whether they are encourages to respect people from other backgrounds and treat everyone equally
Whether they have enough information to 'take next steps'
Whether they would recommend the school to a friend moving into the area.

---

it is their views that are important and there are no right or wrong answers. It is also important that the interviews are semi-structured in that there is a set of questions which the learners can answer, the order in which the learners are asked to respond changes so that everyone gets a chance to 'go first' and no one interviewee dominates. The interviewer can record the interview by taking notes or making an audio recording that can be transcribed in a way that does not identify the individual learners. It is worth having a very open question at the end inviting the learners to talk about anything that they think important but haven't had the chance to say anything about so far. Conducting such interviews could become standard practice, but it is worth noting that analysing the results is more time consuming than with the online questionnaire.

The combination of the online questionnaire and pupil voice interviews will give a department a very rich set of data through which members of staff can scrutinise their current curriculum offerings with a view to making significant improvements. It is very important that the changes made to the curriculum in light of learners' comments are communicated to the learners so that they can see that it isn't a waste of time and that their comments are taken seriously. A sample of possible questions that could be used in either online questionnaires or pupil voice interviews is shown in Panel 7.5.

Pause for thought

Use the questions in Panel 7.5 and others you devise yourself to develop an online questionnaire and a pupil voice interview for a topic your department is thinking of revising so that you can get learners' input into its next iteration.

Panel 7.5 Possible questions for pupil voice

If you were the teacher, what would you do differently?
What did you find easy?
What do you think you learned?
Were you proud of what you made? Why?
What did you find difficult?
What did you find boring?
What did you find interesting?
Were you able to help someone who was stuck? If so, in what way?
Did somebody help you when you were stuck? If so in what way?
What, if anything, took too long to do?
What did you think of your final design idea?
Were you able to get the tools and equipment you needed when you needed them? If not, why not?
Were you able to get the materials you needed when you needed them? If not, why not?
What would be your top tip for the next class to do this topic?

Parent/Carers

Many parents and carers are unsure as to the nature of design & technology and its educational benefits. Hence it is difficult for them to be supportive of the subject or discuss the pros and cons of the subject with their children at the end of Key Stage 3 when option choices are being made. So, it is important that department produces information about the subject and its curriculum in an easily digestible form. SLT often request such information as a preparation for option choice evenings but in our opinion, this is too late in the day. Our view is that parents/carers of learners in Years 7 and 8 should receive information about the subject so that they are in a strong position to understand and respond positively to the information sent out to inform option choices taking place Year 9. A short termly newsletter targeted at particular year groups is one possible way to achieve this. Such a newsletter should highlight the work carried out in that term with appropriate visuals and explanatory captions, give a clear indication of what has been learned as well as what has been done and take no more than a few seconds to read. And it is worth including a suggestion as to what the reader might ask their son or daughter about their design & technology lessons. In one of these newsletters, it is worth pointing up design & technology related career opportunities. The desktop publishing software now available makes it a simple matter to produce such a newsletter as a side of A4 and distribute to parents as a PDF via email.

It is also worth reinforcing the way learners work is assessed as this is likely to be different from the way other subjects are assessed. So before subject evenings and when reports are sent home it is worth providing a summary of the assessment methods your department uses. Possible approaches to assessment were fully described and discussed in chapter 6. Again, an information sheet of a single side of A4 as a PDF will suffice.

> **Pause for thought**
>
> Might it be worth making particular members of staff responsible for communicating with parents about the design & technology that is taking place in each Year group?

SLT

Mary Myatt and John Tomsett (2021) have written an extremely useful book entitled somewhat enigmatically *Huh*, after the Egyptian deity of everlasting things associated with fertility, creation, and regeneration. Its subtitle *Curriculum Conversations between Subject and Senior Leaders* gives clue to its intention. They see ongoing conversations between SLT and subject leaders as the basis for developing better understanding. To frame these conversations, they suggest five questions that senior leader line managers might ask subjects leaders. For design & technology these are:

1 What is design & technology? Why is it on the curriculum?
2 What are the key concepts of big ideas in design & technology?
3 What does a high-quality lesson look like in design & technology at Key Stage 3.
4 Talk me through how design & technology learning is structured and sequenced over Key Stage 3?
5 Can you show me examples of an expected year of learning evidence for Year 7?

As the answers become a conversation, there are opportunities to illustrate them in vivo by inviting members of SLT into the department to see subject learning taking place. This can be done formally through agreed walkthroughs but also more spontaneously by inviting them to see a lesson that is going really well. Often, they will be too busy to attend but occasionally they will have the time. These occasions will enable learners and their teacher to feel proud of their learning in design & technology. Of course, there will be tough conversations about funding for staffing and resources, but these are likely to be much more successful if SLT have a clear understanding of the subject and have seen just how joyful the learning can be.

> **Pause for thought**
>
> It might be worth devoting a department meeting to developing answers to the five questions from SLT suggested in *Huh*.

School governors

Subject leaders are often required to make presentations at governors' meetings, and these provide opportunities for any subject to establish its unique contribution to the curriculum and its worth. Any such presentation about design & technology should meet the following criteria:

- Short – no more than 15 minutes
- Be visually appealing involving a minimum of words on any slides and using illustrations which prompt an engaging commentary
- Have a commentary which is amusing and entertaining as well as informative
- Shares key elements of the Vision and Mission statements
- Feature the staff, (including TAs and technicians) and their areas of expertise emphasising the team approach
- Feature illustrations of learners working in the department
- Include examples of learners' work showing how they become more sophisticated across time
- Identifies strategic development plans
- Offer the opportunity to ask questions

Pause for thought

The TED Talk by Sunni Brown (https://www.ted.com/talks/sunni_brown_doodlers_ unite?language=en) is an interesting example of a short talk (only 5 minutes) to slides with few words and no bullet points. As a model for presenting about something which has a tarnished reputation it might provide a good model for presenting about design & technology. We guess that Sunni practised her commentary over the slides many times to achieve her impressive eloquence.

Awarding organisations

Awarding Organisations (AOs) have played a large part in the development of our subject. Although the different specifications they develop must all meet the Ofsted criteria for content and assessment of our subject there are differences between them in terms the details of their assessment procedures and the nature and range of the questions they require candidates to answer in timed written examinations. It is a matter of your professional judgement as to which specifications you choose in the light of the curriculum you develop at Key Stage 3 which forms a springboard for teaching towards the GCSE at KS4 and the way your learners respond. Some schools have a policy of adopting a single AO for all their public examinations. If you are in this position and find that, for sound reasons, the design & technology specifications they offer do not meet your needs then it will be necessary to make a strong and robust argument for design & technology to be an exception.

D&T Association Reimagining D&T Report connection

The report specifically recommends that AOs introduce a student investigation (worth 25% of GCSE marks) "to be chosen from a range of contexts and allowing young people to deep dive into a field of particular interest to them, for example, an investigation into the practicalities of growing a circular economy when taking into account consideration of capitalist demands for fast fashion". Assessment for this unit could be split between a written submission to a deadline produced under teacher supervision and a video recorded presentation to an unfamiliar audience on their chosen topic. There is no doubt that this will be challenging for young people, but the learning that can take place and the potential to develop human skills such as self-management, working with people, problem solving, new knowledge/skill acquisition, and flexibility is considerable.

Local community

Giving learning in design & technology status in your local community is important as it creates a context in which there is agreement that the subject has worth. One way to do this is to organise activities that enhance the visibility of learners' design & technology activity. One of the authors, Hilda, worked with a school that did this by suspending the Year 10 timetable for three days and involved every learner, working in groups of four, in working with a local charity to produce materials that advertised the charity at key locations in the community. This involved, as you might imagine, a great deal of preparation before the event in communicating with the charities, identifying those who wished to take part, and putting them in touch with the learners who would work with them. The three days were structured as follows. On the first day a there was an introductory keynote from an established graphic designer on approaches to working with clients to produce graphic media, followed by each charity group finding out about the work of the charity, developing ideas for how to advertise the charity in the locality. On the second day there were face to face sessions between the groups and charity representatives in which the charity identified which ideas they wanted to be taken forward. By the end of the second day the ideas had been developed into working prototypes. On the third day the working protypes were put on display in an exhibition at the school which was attended by representatives of all the charities involved and important members of the local community. The local press was invited and the whole exercise, including interviews with learners, was reported in the local paper. Many of the charities took the ideas of the working prototypes and included them in their promotional materials. The three-day event involved groups of learners operating autonomously in deciding what to do and when in meeting the various deadlines over the three days. Many learners found this challenging. The whole endeavour was supported by members of staff who provided advice and guidance throughout the three days and acted as a safety net for those learners who were struggling. It was without doubt a massive amount of work and could not have taken place without the full support of the SLT. In fact, the whole idea was the brainchild of the deputy head. Such an activity will not be possible for every school but there are elements within the activity that could become more modest activities and achievable in a variety of situations.

Pause for thought

What might your department do that raises the visibility of design & technology in the local community. Are there any elements in the activity described above that you could use as a starting point?

D&T Association Reimagining D&T Report connection

One of the main action points of the report is that as a community of practice we should demonstrate and show the worth of design & technology. The example of raising community awareness of the subject described above provides a very concrete example of just this.

Local industry and employers

Often this is seen as those working in industry visiting schools to provide information about particular careers or role models for young people in order to attract them into STEM occupations. This is useful although research by Clare Gartland (2014) has indicated that this might not always be as effective as it might be due to young people sometimes being suspicious of the 'marketing approach' and possibly feeling alienated because they are seen as lacking appropriate ambition. One other extremely effective way of working with local industry is to involve them in designing without making activities. This was initiated by Young Foresight and introduced the idea of employees from local industry acting as critical friends, called mentors, to groups of learners as they attempted to de- sign, but *not* make, products and services for the future. (This activity is discussed at length in chapter 4.)

The evaluation by Patricia Murphy of the Open University (Barlex, 2012) identified several features required for success. Panel 7.6 describes a number of mechanisms that resulted in partnership between mentors and teachers being effective. Panel 7.7 identifies the shared values, behaviours and concepts necessary to maintain an effective teacher-mentor re- lationship. Panel 7.8 describes the practical details that are necessary for success. It is worth noting that many of the mentors found the process useful for their own professional de- velopment. As one mentor commented:

Panel 7.6 Mechanisms that resulted in partnership between mentors and teachers being effective

---

- Teachers and mentors are encouraged to exchange their views and interests in the designing without making activity in order to develop a shared perspective.
- Teachers and mentors identify their expert strengths in relation to the activity to inform their plans.
- Teachers and mentors discuss, negotiate, and plan in advance the implementation to maximize learning.
- The partnership is maintained through a process of collaborative reviewing and planning.
- The requirements for expert input from mentors should be flagged in the session plans.
- Teachers and mentors identify essential inputs, and whose responsibility it will be to implement them.
- Practices and tools introduced from industry by mentors will need to be modified by teachers for use with young learners.
- In the classroom mentors are identified as particular experts whose role it is to teach when that expertise is called upon.
- Teachers have the responsibility to make explicit the expert partnership in the classroom and to maintain it.

Panel 7.7 The shared values, behaviours, and concepts necessary to maintain an effective teacher-mentor relationship

---

- Recognise that creativity is a human attribute that can be fostered and developed.
- Be genuinely interested in learners' ideas and their potential to make a difference.
- Understand how to value individual contributions and constructively challenge learners' thinking.
- Recognise the significance of dialogue in learning and how to engage in this.
- Recognise the value of collaboration and teamwork.
- Have a broad and authentic conception of design that is related to production and retail.
- Have an understanding of how design ideas are generated, and the tools needed to support this.
- Model aspects of design activity and solutions so that pupils can access them and make decisions about their significance and value to their own design problems.
- Recognise when learners need access to additional information or examples of design practices.

Panel 7.8 Practical details that are necessary for success

- Introduction to the school
  - It is often helpful to mentors if they can visit their schools informally before the project starts. This enables them to introduce themselves to other teachers in the department so that they will be recognised and greeted. The teacher can also introduce them to members of the senior management team, which is a useful way of reminding them that the school is taking part in Young Foresight and emphasising the business-education links that are such an important part of the Project. The informal visit also allows mentors to explore journey times and best routes.
- Modes of address
  - Discuss with mentors how they would like to be addressed by learners. Some mentors are often quite happy to be called by their first name. Others prefer a more formal approach. It is important that the chosen mode of address sits comfortably with school policy and that learners are able to use it without embarrassment.
- Dress codes
  - If the school has a very formal approach to dress, for example, if male teachers always wear a suit plus a shirt with collar and tie, it is important that mentors dress in line with this.
- Boundaries
  - The teacher needs to explain to mentors that permissions are something that only he/she can give however reasonable the request seems. It is a simple matter for mentors to say, 'That's something you need to ask your teacher', with regard to, for example, leaving the room to visit the library or answer a call of nature.
- Introduction to the learners
  - The teacher will need to introduce the mentor(s) to the class and explain why they are there. The mentors should say a little bit about themselves: who they are, whom they work for and what they do, for example. This introduction can be used to establish appropriate modes of address.
- Visiting the company
  - Some mentors arrange for the teacher to visit their place of work and spend time shadowing them and seeing at first-hand the industrial context of the mentor's work. Teachers who have experienced this always comment on how useful it has been.

I would encourage colleagues to get involved, as it's a great opportunity for personal development. Giving a presentation to management is nothing compared to standing in front of twenty-odd year 9's! Moderating meetings should be simple now too.

(Barlex, 2012, p. 121)

Another significant benefit for the design & technology department in addition to enhanced learning is that the mentor learns about the work of department and the worth of the subject. This can enable you to obtain the voice of local industry to support the presence of the subject in the curriculum.

Pause for thought

Involving local industry and employers to provide mentors in a bespoke scheme embedded within the design & technology curriculum will undoubtedly require considerable effort both in setting up and maintaining the endeavour. How might this be managed such that it does not become overburdensome and ensures that the benefits outweigh the costs?

D&T Association Reimagining D&T Report connection

The report describes the work of the association in identifying businesses willing to support design & technology in the school curriculum. The title of this initiative is Blueprint 1000®. If you develop links with local businesses as described above, then it is a small step for those businesses to become involved in the Association's Blueprint 1000® initiative.

Local MP

There are occasions when our subject is discussed in parliament, and these certainly provide an opportunity for departments to contact their local MP and comment on the debate. Such an occasion was the publishing by the House of Lords Communications and Digital Committee *At Risk Our Creative Future* in January 2023 (Parliament Publications, 2023) which mentioned specifically, and bemoaned, the drop in GCSE design & technology entries over the past 10 years. Having used such opportunities to put design & technology on your MPs radar, then a next step might be to invite him or her to see some of the course work that is being submitted for GCSE or GCE and meet the young people responsible. This provides an important opportunity to inform your MP about the benefits of the subject beyond those of economic utility.

Pause for thought

Informing your MP about the work in the department should probably be part of a wider initiative to involve him or her in the work of the school so it is important to discuss any such invitations with SLT

The Pearson Initiative

It is clear that in recent times design & technology has been struggling to maintain its presence in the secondary school curriculum. This is exemplified by the number of young people studying GCSE design & technology falling by 50% from 2009 to 2020. Pearson that operates the EdExcel GCSE Design & Technology specification, viewed this situation with some alarm and have been working with the Department for Education to develop an alternative specification. At the time of writing it is called, 'Responsible Design & Innovation' and full detail may be found at https://www.pearson.com/uk/news-and-policy/news/2023/05/driving-forward-the-future-of-design-education-.html. Hilda has submitted a full critique to Pearson and is involved in discussions of further development. At the moment her position is that the current proposal over emphasises design at the expense of technology and this needs to be addressed. This could be achieved a) by considering the nature of technology and the way it works (to mirror the 'how science works' aspects of many science curricula), and b) by considering the role of disruptive technologies in the ways they might be used to tackle the problems currently facing society and the planet. It is worth considering the thinking of Shannon Vallor, a philosopher of technology, who has identified 12 technology virtues which could mitigate to a large extent the negative impacts of the way technologies have been used in the recent past (Vallor, 2028). These virtues are honesty, self-control, humility, justice, courage, empathy, care, civility, flexibility, perspective, magnanimity, and wisdom. In critiquing the way technologies have been deployed in the past and may be in the future, it might be useful if learners were asked to consider the extent to which such deployments reflected these 12 virtues.

Pause for thought

To what extent do you and your colleagues agree with Hilda that technology and technologies have been underrepresented in design & technology compared to design? If you agree how do you think this disparity might be addressed in any future development of the subject.

Vision and mission statements for design & technology

Vision and mission statements for design & technology are important for the following reasons:

- In the process of developing such statements members of a department can share their beliefs about the subject, develop a common understanding of its worth, and debate how best it might be taught.
- The vision statement provides guidance as to the long-term goals of a department and as such can be used to make strategic decisions.
- The mission statement provides tactical guidance as to how a department might move forward in achieving its vision.

A **Vision Statement** will have the following characteristics:

- It will be concise and clear
- It will be inspiring

- It will be future oriented, describing where the subject is going rather than the current state of affairs
- It will offer a long-term perspective and be stable, i.e., unlikely to change frequently
- It will be challenging, not something that can be easily met or discarded
- It will be general enough to provide strategic direction.

After some dwell time the authors arrived at the following:

> *We humans have the unique ability to use our hands and minds in unison to envisage and create an ever more complex made world. Learning design & technology introduces young people to this field of human endeavour and empowers them to become people who see the world as a place of opportunity where they and others can, through their own thoughts and actions build a future worth wanting.*

Pause for thought

Does the statement meet the requirements for a Vision Statement as listed above? Is it, for example, inspiring, sufficiently challenging? How would you want to change it for your school?

A **Mission Statement** for design & technology will have the following characteristics:

- It will be concise
- It will identify its unique contribution to the curriculum
- It will describe what the department does
- It will describe how the department does this
- It will identify the stakeholders the department is supporting.

The following mission statement is derived from the work of one of the authors (Barlex, 2014).

> *We believe that the unique contribution of design and technology education to the education of young people is to develop both technological capability and technological perspective. We define technological capability as designer maker capability, capturing the essence of technological activity which is intervention in the made and natural worlds. We define technological perspective as insight into 'how technology works' which informs a constructively critical view of technology, avoids alienation from our technologically based society and enables consideration of how technology might be used to provide products and systems that help create the sort of society in which young people wish to live. We intend to achieve these qualities in young people through a range of research informed teaching methods. Young people and their aspirations are central to our mission hence we will engage fully with their parents and carers, the school SLT and Governors and the wider community in pursuing our mission.*

Pause for thought

Does the statement meet the requirements for mission statement as listed above? Does it, for example, identify its unique contribution to the curriculum and the stakeholders the department is supporting? How would you want to change it for your school?

D&T Association Reimagining D&T Report connection

Embedded in the report are key elements of vision and mission statements. Reading the report as a whole will enable you and members of your department to develop and refine the vision and mission statements for your school such that there is synergy between your efforts to explain and promote our subject and the national effort being made by the Design & Technology Association.

Summary

This chapter considered a range of features that have the potential to support design & technology. Working with primary schools benefits both parties. Enrichment and enhancement activities have the potential for curriculum development. With the caveat of respecting subject integrity STEM and STEAM can be advantageous to those collaborating. Making the comparison with the research of Rosalind Driver into science learning that radically changed the way school science was taught, the importance of research into the teaching, learning, and assessing of design & technology is endorsed. Continuing professional development is essential for all design & technology teacher but needs to be based on sound approaches as defined by the Teacher Development Trust. Links between schools and local maker spaces has the potential for mutual benefit and may support both curriculum and professional development. Responding to the concerns of a wide range of interested parties is beneficial to both the subject and those showing interest. The Pearson initiative provides the opportunity to rethink and refine the nature of the subject. Developing vision and mission statements enables colleagues to explore and influence the future of the subject in the context of their own situation. Throughout the chapter links were made to the recommendations in the Design & Technology Association's Reimagining D&T Report (Design & Technology Associations, 2023).

References

Ainley, J., Pratt, D., & Hansen, A. (2006) Connecting engagement and focus in pedagogic task design, *British Educational Research Journal*, 32(1): 23-38.

Banks, F., & Barlex, D. (2014) *Teaching STEM in the Secondary School*, Oxford: Routledge.

Banks, F., & Barlex, D. (2021) *Teaching STEM in the Secondary School*, Oxford: Routledge.

Barlex, D. (2001) Should your creature be fierce or friendly? A Nuffield Primary Solutions unit. London: Nuffield Foundation, https://dandtfordandt.files.wordpress.com/2013/01/creaturesy61.pdf.

Barlex, D. (2012) The Young Foresight Project A UK Initiative in design creativity involving mentors from industry, in B. France and V. Compton (Editors), *Bringing Communities Together: Connecting Learners with Scientists or Technologists*, Brill.

Barlex, D. (2014) Developing a technology curriculum, in Williams, J., Jones, A., & Bunting, C. (Eds.), *The Future of Technology Education*, The Netherlands: Springer.

Barlex, D. (2019) Preparing for transition to secondary STEM in Helen Caldwell and Sue Pope (Eds.), *STEM in the Primary Curriculum*, London, Sage.

Barlex, D., & Miles-Pearson, S. (2008) *Introducing CAD/CAM into Primary Schools Part 1 of a case study – Developing the Curriculum* Paper presented at the Design & Technology Association Research Conference, Loughborough, July 2008.

Barlex, D., & Miles-Pearson, S. (2009) *Assessing the impact of peer – peer mentoring on primary pupil's engagement with CADCAM,* Paper presented at the 7th International Primary Design and Technology Conference, Birmingham, UK, June 2009.

Barlex, D., & Welch, M. (2009) *Revelations of Designerly Activity During an Immersion Experience,* Paper presented at the 7th International Primary Design and Technology Conference, Birmingham, UK.

Beaumont, HR. (2023) Sustainability of the case study Maker Education Initiatives, in de Vries et al. (eds.), *Maker Education and Technology Education: Reflections on Good Practices, Brill Sense.*

Benson. C. (2021) Design and Technology in the Primary School, in Alison Hardy (Ed.) *Learning to Teach Design and Technology in the Secondar School*, Oxon: Routledge.

Black, P. (1997) in Dillon, J., & and Maguire, M. (Eds.), *Becoming a teacher: Issues in secondary teaching*, Buckingham, UK: Open University Press.

Bronowski, J. (1973) *The Ascent of Man*, London, BBC.

Charlwood, E. (2023) Ed has provided a miscellaneous collection of slides he use for a unit on drones / flight / quadcopters with Year 12s, at https://drive.google.com/file/d/1HNMhscNxFJwW93guAQOoqM7Hlp7aPOdE/view.

Chummar, J. A., & Saraskanth, T. K. (15 January 2023) How drones could be the future of Indian farming, https://www.bbc.co.uk/news/av/world-asia-india-64248510.

Driver, R. (1983) *The Pupil as Scientist*, Buckingham: The Open University.

Education Policy Institute (2022) *A spotlight on Design and Technology study in England*, London: Education Policy Institute, https://epi.org.uk/wp-content/uploads/2022/03/Spotlight-on-DT-report_EPI-March-2022.pdf.

Fullan, M. G., & Stiegelbauer, S. (1991) *The New Meaning of Educational Change*, London: Cassell.

Gartland, C. (2014) *STEM Ambassadors and Social Justice in HE*, London: Trentham Books.

Gershenfeld, N. (2005) *Fab: The Coming Revolution on Your Desktop – From Personal Computers to Personal Fabrication*, New York: Basic Books.

Myatt, M., & Tomsett, J. (2021) *Huh Curriculum Conversations between Subject and Senior Leaders*, Woodbridge: John Catt.

Nuffield Foundation (2000) Chooser Charts, https://dandtfordandt.wordpress.com/resources/nuffield-ks3-dt-resources/chooser-charts/.

Parliament Publications (2023) At Risk Our Creative Future, https://publications.parliament.uk/pa/ld5803/ldselect/ldcomm/125/125.pdf.

Robinson, K. (1999). *All Our Futures: Creativity, Culture & Education*, London: Department for Education and Employment.

Teacher Development Trust (2015) *Developing Great Teaching Lessons from the International Reviews into Effective Professional Development*, London: Teacher Development Trust.

Vallor, S. (2018) *Technology and the Virtues: A Philosophical Guide to a Future Worth Wanting*, Oxford: Oxford University Press.

Recommended reading

Banks, F., & Barlex, D. (2021) *Teaching STEM in the Secondary School*, Oxford: Routledge.

Barlex, D., & Steeg, T. (2017) The maker movement and schools, in R. Luckin (Ed.), *Enhancing Learning and Teaching with Technology*, London: Institute of Education Press.

Barlex, D., & Williams, P. John, (Eds.) *Pedagogy for Technology Education in Secondary School*. Switzerland: Springer.

Caldwell, H., & Pope, S. (Eds.) (2019) *STEM in the Primary Curriculum*, London: Sage.

Gill, D., Irving-Bell, D., McLain, M., & Wooff, D. (Eds.) (2023) *The Bloomsbury Handbook of Technology Education*, London: Bloomsbury Publishing.

van Dijk, G., Elwin Savelsbergh, E., & and van der Meij, A. (2020) Maker Education: Opportunities and Threats for Engineering and Technology education, in Barlex, D., & Williams P. J., (Eds.), *Pedagogy for Technology Education in Secondary School*, Switzerland: Springer.

Index

Note: *Italic* page numbers refer to *figure* and **Bold** page numbers reference to **tables**.

For Product Safety Concerns and Information please contact our EU
representative GPSR@taylorandfrancis.com
Taylor & Francis Verlag GmbH, Kaufingerstraße 24, 80331 München, Germany